URBAN POLICY IN **THE TIME OF OBAMA**

GLOBALIZATION AND COMMUNITY

Susan E. Clarke, Series Editor
Dennis R. Judd, Founding Editor

(continued on page 347)

URBAN POLICY IN **THE TIME** OF OBAMA

James DeFilippis, Editor

Afterword by Cedric Johnson

GLOBALIZATION AND COMMUNITY, VOLUME 26

UNIVERSITY OF MINNESOTA PRESS
Minneapolis • London

Published by the University of Minnesota Press
111 Third Avenue South, Suite 290
Minneapolis, MN 55401-2520
http://www.upress.umn.edu

Printed in the United States of America on acid-free paper

The University of Minnesota is an equal-opportunity educator and employer.

22   21   20   19   18   17   16   10   9   8   7   6   5   4   3   2   1

Library of Congress Cataloging-in-Publication Data
Names: DeFilippis, James, editor.
Title: Urban policy in the time of Obama / James DeFilippis, editor ; afterword
    by Cedric Johnson.
Description: Minneapolis : University of Minnesota Press, [2016] | Series: Globalization
    and community ; volume 26 | Includes bibliographical references and index.
Identifiers: LCCN 2016014549 | ISBN 978-0-8166-9656-7 (hc) |
    ISBN 978-0-8166-9659-8 (pb)
Subjects: LCSH: Urban polic—United States. | City planning—United States. |
Community development, Urban—United States. | Sociology, Urban—United States. |
    United States—Social policy.
Classification: LCC HT123 .U74657 2016 | DDC 307.760973—dc23
LC record available at https://lccn.loc.gov/2016014549

CONTENTS

ACKNOWLEDGMENTS

Books are almost always products of more than just the person whose name is on the cover. Nothing I have ever written has been the product solely of my own intellectual work, independent of outside influences, and this book is no exception. I have never found a Walden Pond, am not looking for one, and seriously doubt that being isolated and staring at a small body of water would bring me any insight into humanity. Instead, as befitting a book about the urban, this work has been a collective endeavor among many people. It began as a set of sessions at the Urban Affairs Association (UAA) meetings in San Francisco in the spring of 2013. Those sessions were co-organized by me and Amy Khare, and we conceived of the idea of this book collaboratively. In many ways, this book is as much a product of her work as it is mine, and I am very grateful to her for her insights, ideas, and support during this project. Many of the papers presented in those sessions were first published in a special section of the *Journal of Urban Affairs*, and some of those articles were the seeds of the chapters in this book.

The authors in this book have been, without exception, great collaborators. They all devoted a great deal of time and effort to their chapters, submitted them punctually, and required little editorial work from me. I cannot imagine a better group of people with whom to embark on a book like this. The editor at the University of Minnesota Press, Pieter Martin, has been an enthusiastic supporter of this project since I first pitched the idea to him. Similarly, Susan Clarke, the series editor for the Globalization and Community series and someone I have long respected as an intellectual, has been invaluable to the project. Her insights and observations have pushed the project forward in productive directions. She and Pieter have been an excellent editorial team.

My intellectual home for several years has been the Bloustein School of Planning and Public Policy at Rutgers, and it has been great. I consider myself really lucky to work with such a collegial and professional group. In particular, Bob Lake and Kathe Newman are people I know I can lean on, learn from, and trust, and I respect them immensely. It is also because of them that I get to work with a wonderful group of graduate students, who consistently amaze me with their abilities, their enthusiasm, and the quality of their work. If Bloustein is my professional home, then the UAA is my professional community, and it is fitting that this book emerged from a set of sessions at the UAA conference. I am proud to be part of such a great group of engaged scholars, and the association has been incredibly supportive of me and my work over the years.

Finally, every book I have worked on has placed a set of demands on my family. Time working always means time not spent with Allison Lucas and our wonderful daughters, Alexa and Marley. But this book, in particular, placed extra demands on Allison and the family, and I am so glad to have such a strong, supportive, and understanding group of women in my life.

ABBREVIATIONS

ABLE   Adolescent Behavioral Learning Experience
ACA   Affordable Care Act
ACS   American Community Survey
AHAR   Annual Homeless Assessment Report
ARRA   American Recovery and Reinvestment Act
BNCP   Building Neighborhood Capacity Program
CAAs   community action agencies
CAP   Community Action Program
CBAs   community benefits agreements
CCI   critical community improvement
CCIs   comprehensive community initiatives
CDBG   Community Development Block Grant
CDCs   community-development corporations
CDFI   Community Development Financial Institutions
CFPB   Consumer Financial Protection Bureau
CNI   Choice Neighborhoods Initiative
CNYCN   Center for New York City Neighborhoods
COGs   councils of government
CORE   Caucus of Rank and File Educators
CRA   Community Reinvestment Act
DACA   Deferred Action for Childhood Arrivals
DAPA   Deferred Action for Parental Accountability
DCP   Developing Communities Project
DOE   Department of Education
DREAM   Development, Relief, and Education for Alien Minors Act
DSRIP   Delivery System Reform Incentive Payment Program
EFCA   Employee Free Choice Act
ESEA   Elementary and Secondary Education Act
EZ/EC   Empowerment Zone/Enterprise Community
FHA   Federal Housing Administration
FHEO   Fair Housing and Equal Opportunity
FHLB   Federal Home Loan Bank

FNMA /   Federal National Mortgage Association
Fannie Mae
FTA   Federal Transit Administration
GIIN   Global Impact Investing Network
GIS   geographic information system
GSEs   government-sponsored enterprises
HAMP   Home Affordable Modification Program
HARP   Home Affordable Refinancing Program
HCF   Housing Certificate Fund
HCV   Housing Choice Voucher
HERA   Housing and Economic Recovery Act
HMDA   Home Mortgage Disclosure Act
HOLC   Home Owners' Loan Corporation
HUD   U.S. Department of Housing and Urban Development
HUD-VASH   HUD-VA supportive housing
ICE   Immigration and Customs Enforcement
ISTEA   Intermodal Surface Transportation Efficiency Act
JD NEG   Jobs-Driven National Emergency Grant
LAI   Location Affordability Index
LIHTCs   low-income housing tax credits
LISC   Local Initiatives Support Corporation
MAHRA   Multifamily Assisted Housing Reform and Affordability Act
MALDEF   Mexican American Legal Defense Fund
MBS   mortgage-backed securities
MDHA   Metropolitan Development Housing Agency
MFY   Mobilization for Youth
MHA   Making Home Affordable
MPOs   metropolitan planning organizations
NCFHEO   National Commission on Fair Housing and Equal Opportunity
NCLB   No Child Left Behind
NCSL   National Conference of State Legislatures
NHS   Neighborhood Housing Services
NHTF   National Housing Trust Fund
NLRA   National Labor Relations Act
NLRB   National Labor Relations Board
NRI   Neighborhood Revitalization Initiative
NSP   Neighborhood Stabilization Program
NWRO   National Welfare Rights Organization
OEO   Office of Economic Opportunity
OFC   Opportunity Funding Corporation
OFHLEO   Office of Fair Lending and Equal Opportunity
OFN   Opportunity Finance Network

OMB	Office of Management and Budget
PATCO	Professional Air Traffic Controllers Organization
PETRA	Preservation, Enhancement and Transition of Rental Assistance
PFS	Pay for Success
PHA	public housing authority
PhRMA	Pharmaceutical Research and Manufacturers of America
PRE	Promoting Regional Equity
QHWRA	Quality Housing and Work Responsibility Act
RAD	Rental Assistance Demonstration
RAP	Rental Assistance Payment
Rent Supp	Rent Supplement
RTTT	Race to the Top
S&Ls	savings and loan associations
SC2	Strong Cities, Strong Communities
SCHIP	State Children's Health Insurance Program
SCI	Sustainable Communities Initiative
SCI-RPG	Sustainable Communities Initiative-Regional Planning Grant
SIBs	Social Impact Bonds
SIF	Social Innovation Financing
STEM	science, technology, engineering, and mathematics
TARP	Troubled Assets Relief Program
TOD	transit-oriented development
UAA	Urban Affairs Association
UDAG	urban development action grant
UIG	Urban Investment Group
VA	Department of Veterans Affairs

INTRODUCTION

JAMES DEFILIPPIS

Why This Book, Why Now, and Why Obama?

The past eight years should have been a remarkable time for American urban policy. The need for a strong urban policy has been abundantly clear. The country was devastated by a housing—and housing finance—crisis that wrought extensive damage to both already struggling old urban centers (such as Newark, Detroit, Cleveland, and Baltimore) and Sunbelt boomtowns (such as Las Vegas, San Diego, and Miami). The slow-motion human tragedy of urban unemployment and underemployment has still not been fundamentally addressed, let alone rectified. The criminalization of black men in America has ruined (and ended) the lives of countless people and has led to significant political protest and unrest in our urban areas. Urban school districts struggle to educate America's children, and the vital infrastructure that enables our metropolitan areas, and the people within them, to prosper has continued to decay. The patterns of racial segregation and its sibling of disinvestment in black neighborhoods continue to shape American urban areas (although disinvestment had its equally destructive mirror image of reinvestment in the form of predatory lending from the late 1990s to 2006). The inequality between different sections of urban areas remains a defining feature of American urbanization processes, with economic segregation becoming an increasingly prominent issue (Dreier, Mollenkopf, and Swanstrom 2014). Millions of immigrants, the vast majority of whom are in our metropolitan areas, are unable to live full lives because of a dysfunctional immigration policy regime. Major American cities continue to lose people and energy, and we have even seen the once great city of Detroit go bankrupt. Detroit might be the most high profile case, but other local governments have also struggled with the worst fiscal problems they have had since the "fiscal crisis" of the mid-1970s.

The "urban crisis" is therefore not over; it is not now, and certainly was not when President Nixon said it was in 1973. In many ways, the larger trajectory of American urbanization has continued unabated since then. The issues mentioned above are not at all new, and have been evident for decades now. But *the urban* has also become a much larger, more complex, and ambiguous category in the more than

1

forty years since Nixon's famous proclamation. The transformation of urban areas from manufacturing centers built for a national economy to postindustrial, service-dominated nodes in a globalized economy has built a new set of apparatuses and processes onto the remaining institutions, organizations, people, and geography. And the old urban-suburban dichotomy has been swept away by the transformation of suburbia into a demonstrably heterogeneous realm, which both belies any attempts to easily categorize it and has many of the problems that used to be associated solely with inner cities. Conversely, many inner cities have been transformed by processes of gentrification (itself closely connected to deindustrialization) into bastions of wealth and opulence in which even middle class people struggle to afford housing.

Added to this context is the biography of the president. Obama is a political and intellectual product of Honolulu, Los Angeles, New York, Boston, and, most importantly, Chicago, where he famously worked as a community organizer. As an organizer, he worked for, and eventually became the executive director of the Developing Communities Project (DCP), in Chicago's South Side. As such, he is the first "urban" president the country has had for many decades; probably the most urban president since Teddy Roosevelt more than one hundred years ago. Here is a president who understands and speaks thoughtfully and cogently about urban issues. He can do so because he has lived a quintessentially urban life. And as product of different cultures he is, in many ways, the embodiment of cosmopolitan urbanism.

Finally, President Obama's elections in 2008 and 2012 were driven by an incredible mobilizing campaign. The get-out-the-vote work that the campaigns conducted was incredibly effective and disproportionately concentrated in America's cities. It was a mobilization effort that was a remarkable marriage of traditional community organizing tactics with twenty-first-century big data analyses, and it helped bring out large majorities in cities, which more than compensated for the president's electoral weaknesses in rural areas. He was, in short, elected by an energized and urban electorate. Thus the context of the president's inauguration in 2009, his own biography, and the constituencies that twice elected him would suggest a period of significant, and very public, discussions and policies about urban issues.

To a limited extent, this has been in the case. In February 2009, shortly after taking office, the Obama administration created the first-ever White House Office of Urban Affairs to "take a coordinated and comprehensive approach to developing and implementing an effective strategy concerning urban America."[1] Also, several urban policies have been launched, including, but not limited to Strong Cities, Strong Communities (SC2); The Partnership for Sustainable Communities; Promise Neighborhoods; Choice Neighborhoods; and Immigration Action Roundtables.

And yet, despite these initiatives, there is remarkably little substantive discussion of urban issues in American policy circles or, more generally, its public sphere.

This lack of discussion is mirrored and magnified by the fact that these initiatives are all fairly small, modestly funded, and low profile. They are, for the most part, a set of pilot projects, not large-scale endeavors meant to fundamentally impact life in American urban areas or shape the trajectories of American urbanization processes. This is mirrored by the fact that the U.S. Department of Housing and Urban Development (HUD) remains a very-low-profile, cabinet-level department. Most people—even those concerned with politics and public policy—would struggle to name the secretaries of HUD in the Obama administration. Urban policy, it seems, has remained on the back benches of American public life and policy-making, despite a context and a president that would suggest a resurgence of it. It unfortunately seems likely to remain there.

In this brief introductory chapter I do not analyze the Obama administration's policies; I leave that to the chapters that follow, which go into great depth about those policies and what can be learned from them. Instead, I simply frame the discussion with a set of brief comments on the larger urban policy arc in which the Obama administration sits, and how we can understand those policies. Thus, the stories of urban policy we are telling here are not just about the outgoing administration, but also about urban policy in the twenty-first century more generally. This book is therefore simultaneously backward- and forward-looking. To be sure, the book's immediate concern is the Obama administration and assessing what has been accomplished. But the bigger focus is on how to properly interpret this policy regime, and how to build toward a more equitable and just policy regime for American urban areas and the people who live and work in them.

On Places, Policies, and the Urban

Most public policies in the United States are not, in theory, specifically spatial, place-based, or urban in nature. This has long been the case for federal policy. When Franklin Delano Roosevelt was constructing the basic framework and policies of the American welfare state, and when that welfare state was expanded and solidified under Lyndon Johnson, poverty, unemployment, and health were primarily considered individual-level issues. These issues would therefore be addressed by policies that used the individual (or, in some cases, the family or household) as the basis for public sector interventions. Places, communities, cities, urban areas, and regions usually did not enter the conversation, let alone become the unit of analysis and social intervention. This is not to say that we have not sporadically and episodically embarked on place-based policies and initiatives. We have, but those initiatives have historically been "swimming against the tide," to use Alice O'Connor's evocatively accurate description of a dominant policy framework that is first and foremost about people as individuals, regardless of space and place (O'Connor 1999). This has continued in current policy-making. For example, while the Affordable Care Act (ACA), probably the most significant domestic policy achievement of the Obama administration, has real implications for urban areas and includes some moneys for place-based work,[2] *the urban* has never been considered central, given the ACA's role in reshaping health insurance markets. In short, the ACA is a significant social policy achievement that acts through individuals operating in the market. In this way, and in so many more, the administration has followed the path of those who trod it before them.

And yet, policies regarding education, immigration, labor, capital markets, health care, and many others are "urban" in the sense of having significant impacts on urban areas, urbanization processes, and, of course, urban residents. Some of them are urban precisely because of how disproportionately these nominally placeless policies impact urban areas, while others are urban simply because the vast majority of the American people (more than 80 percent) live in metropolitan areas. The ACA, for instance, by expanding coverage to millions of formerly uninsured people, is having significant impacts on urban areas. And it could be argued that perhaps the most socially transformative *urban* policies of the Great Society period were the Civil Rights Act of 1964 and the Hart-Cellar Act of 1965 (which enabled the large influx of transnational migrants into the United States in the last fifty years).

Thus, on some level, all public policies are urban because we are an urbanized country. It has been a long time since we were the country of Jefferson or even de Tocqueville. This was already evident by the late 1960s, when Daniel Patrick Moynihan bluntly stated "the federal establishment must develop a much heightened sensitivity to its 'hidden' urban policies. There is hardly a department or agency of the national government whose programs do not in some way have important consequences for the life of cities, and those who live in them" (Moynihan 1969, 11). This is therefore not a particularly novel observation, but if it was true in Moynihan's time, it is far truer today. Almost half a century has passed since Moynihan made that observation, and yet the heightened sensitivity he called for is still lacking in American policies and in the American public realm. Our nominally placeless policies are usually very much urban policies, we just do not have the language or framework to recognize them as such. And this "urbanization of public policy" is only likely to continue as *the urban* continues to encompass more of the country and, for that matter, the globe.

This all raises the question of "what do we mean when we talk about *the urban* in urban policy?" And it is fair to observe that once something becomes everything, it becomes nothing; that is, it loses all analytical utility. Therefore it makes sense to explain how I understand *the urban*. There has been much written on the subject (see, for instance, Castells 1979; Harvey 1985; Brenner 2013), but while this is not the place for a lengthy treatment of this issue a few clarifications are needed. First, at a descriptive level, and following the classic framing of the Chicago School of Urban Sociology (see, in particular, Wirth 1938), *the urban* can be characterized by its density, diversity, and size. Urban areas are large and crowded, and contain a myriad of different kinds of people and activities. Second, and more analytically, the urban is the ever-changing result of large-scale processes that lead to the agglomeration of people and economic activities in geographic space. That is, we have urban areas because a host of political and economic forces—primarily economic—make concentrations of people and economic activities logical and efficient. Third, and at the level of causal forces, urban areas are thus a product (and, in turn, a producer) of large-scale flows of labor and capital. The geographical patterning of those flows is what drives the creation, growth, decline, and, in some cases, abandonment of urban areas. And that geographical patterning of flows is also what differentiates neighborhoods or communities within particular urban areas.

Finally, there is the question of the city-suburban political divide. By convention, when Americans refer to *the urban* they understand it to mean inner cities. But that is not necessarily the case, and that is not how the term is used in this book. Being urban is not a function of the political jurisdiction in which a place is located (that is, either central city or suburb). Political jurisdictions invariably matter, in terms of how people's daily lives are lived (and the values, priorities, and competence [or lack thereof] of local governments are incredibly important), but they do not alter the characterization of a place as urban or not. And this book does not subscribe to a simplistic, urban-inner-city framework.

Thus, in this book, urban policies are policies that impact people in large, dense, and diverse places. Policies may do so by actively trying to shape the lives of people concentrated in those places (as, for example, education, labor, and health care policies do), or by actively trying to shape the characteristics of the places themselves (as community development policies do). They may also be urban policies in that they shape the rules, logics, or patterns of the larger flows that produce urbanization (as, for example, immigration and housing finance policies do). Urban policies, therefore, may act on the city as an object, or may act on urbanization as a set of processes.

A Brief Introduction to Obama's Urban Policy Regime

With that background, we can turn to urban policies in the time of Obama. I should say at the outset that the Obama administration began in the midst of the worst economic crisis since the 1930s, and with two ongoing, protracted wars. Resolving those very significant problems was always going to dominate the thinking of the administration. Formulating an active and aggressive urban policy regime was certainly likely to be less immediately important, regardless of the demonstrable need for one. The administration was also faced with Republican opposition that not only sought to defeat any and all things it proposed, but that also understood—completely accurately—that its core constituency was both not living in urban areas and not particularly interested in policies designed to address urban issues. And yet, it is hard to fully (or even mostly) explain the timidity of the administration's policies solely in terms of the recession, the wars, and the Republican opposition. This is simply because the policies, in both their content and size, so closely follow those laid out by the Clinton administration and have been advocated for by center-left think tanks and policy shops since the 1990s.

Despite the rhetoric of "hope and change" that animated the 2008 campaign, Obama's urban policies have been characterized by a striking degree of path dependence. Some of this path dependence is a function of institutional momentum, and many of the entities (public or private, for-profit or not-for-profit) tasked with making and implementing public policies have been in place for decades now. Obama was coming onto a ball field with the players already present and in their established positions. The other reason for the path dependence is that the ideas on urban policy continue to come from the same places and people as they have for more than twenty years.

Together, this has meant that Obama's urban policy regime has been defined by its rootedness in the center-left of American politics in the United States. It is a product of a set of ideas that have been dominant among center-left policy and planning circles since the early 1990s. This is evident in a whole host of policy arenas, some of which are complementary and some of which are contradictory. For instance, the administration has embraced regionalism, regional planning, and metropolitan-scale solutions to urban problems,[3] all products of neoliberal consensus in American policy circles. Accordingly, it has pushed through a set of initiatives that support regional planning efforts. Closely related to this is the fact that the administration has pursued policies that attempt to deconcentrate poor people—believing, again with the liberal consensus, that the concentration of poor people is itself a problem in the production and reproduction of poverty. Thus it has not only adopted a version of the Clinton administration's HOPE VI housing policies, but has expanded it in several key ways.[4] Essentially, using the regional scale to solve urban problems and using deconcentration to tackle poverty are siblings in liberal political consensus.[5]

There is also a strong belief in the centrality of partnering with not-for-profit and, in some cases, for-profit corporations in the creation and implementation of urban policies. The "community," in the form of the organizations within American communities, plays a central role in the thinking and policies of the Obama administration. We see this in a whole set of policy initiatives, such as Promise Neighborhoods and Strong Cities, Strong Communities (SC2). We could attribute this to Obama's time as an organizer in Chicago, but it is too central a component of neoliberal thought for that to be convincing. Hillary Clinton may not have won the 2008 election, but her phrase "it takes a village" has been an important part of Obama's governing. Herein lies a contradictory element of the administration's thinking. On the one hand, communities of poor people of color are *the problem* and need to be broken up (via the poverty deconcentration of Choice Neighborhoods or through increased enforcement of fair housing laws); on the other hand, communities are *the solution* and need to be relied upon in remedying urban social problems. This contradiction is not a product of the Obama administration per se, but rather a product of the liberal policy frameworks of the last twenty years. The Obama administration did not create the contradiction, only made it evident through policies that embodied it.

Finally, through the American Recovery and Reinvestment Act of 2009 the administration has also, as part of what Hilary Silver, in her chapter, calls "stealth urban policy," funded a whole set of human capital and R&D investments, thus embracing the creative class that has been so fashionable in liberal policy circles the last fifteen years. The "creative class," an urbane, intellectual form of the private sector, is expected to transform cities and the lives of those within them. But the creative class is really just one expression of the profound influence of market-centered thinking in the current urban policy regime. As the chapters from Lake, Lipman, Khare, Newman, and others make clear, the market, and in particular finance capital, is assumed to be a central component of any and all solutions to urban problems. And the embrace of the market alongside the community, which have been the twin pillars of neoliberal thought since President Clinton, is abundantly clear.[6]

In short, this is a broadly and unambiguously neoliberal agenda, which follows the paths worn by Obama's predecessors. And despite the rhetoric about how divided and contentious Washington is, this is very much a bipartisan consensus, even if the two parties differ in some of the particulars. While "neoliberalism" is a contested and often sloppily used term, I understand it in ways well-articulated by David Harvey's definition:

> Neoliberalism is in the first instance a theory of political economic practices that proposes that human well-being can best be advanced by liberating individual entrepreneurial freedoms and skills within an institutional framework characterized by strong private property rights, free markets and free trade. The role of the state is to create and preserve an institutional framework appropriate to such practices. (Harvey 2005, 2)

Of course, the issues of neoliberalism and urbanization are surely more complex than that, and have accordingly garnered a significant amount of academic attention (see, for instance, Hackworth 2007; or Brenner and Theodore 2003), but for our purposes this general definition will suffice.

If the content of these urban policies reflect the theoretical understanding and agendas of the neoliberalized center-left in the United States, so too do the size and scope of the policies. That is, the solutions are small and incremental. This is a direct product of the neoliberal turn in the Democratic Party in the past quarter century. In short, if the market is always going to be the central organizing principle of society, then public policies are always going to be small. The biggest questions are essentially off the table—assumed away—and the policy agenda becomes one of tinkering around the edges. Ambitious policies are pursued only if they are going to enable new or renewed forms of capital accumulation. We can, and do, use the state to create new markets for capital, but we do not pursue policies that might constrain the capacity of capital to find ways to reproduce itself.

The small size of all these policies is also a product of the politics of neoliberalism. That is, the solutions are small because there is no mobilized constituency behind them. People do not rally or march or organize in any clear way to support Transit Oriented Development, regional planning, poverty deconcentration (if anything, it is the contrary in that case!), or any of the other fashionable ideas in neoliberal urban policy circles. Perhaps it is because I work in a school of urban planning and public policy, but the smallness of the urban interventions in our time consistently remind me of the old mantra from Daniel Burnham, the master planner in Chicago more than a hundred years ago, that we should "make no little plans. They have no magic to stir men's blood." There has been nothing in the Obama administration's urban policies that stirs anyone's blood.

The Organization of This Book and Its Readings

After this introductory chapter, the book is divided into four sections. The first section lays out the context for urban policy in the Obama administration. This context is the history of urban policy in the United States; the transformation of the state and the nature of *the urban* in the contemporary political economy; and the significance of race—both in that Obama is black and in that American cities have long been disproportionately populated by people of color.

The second section is on nominally aspatial policies such as labor, immigration, and education that have particular significance or impact in urban areas, and/or that shape urbanization processes in particularly important ways. As I already indicated, most public policies are not, in theory, specifically spatial or urban in nature. And yet, policies regarding education, immigration, labor, and many others are "urban" in the sense of having significant impact on urban areas and urbanization processes. Related to that is the question of why we are so reluctant to name and understand urban policies as such.

The third section of the book focuses on policies—both new and old but continuing—that are explicitly urban or spatial in their character. The country has a long, if episodic, history of place-based policies, and such policies have always been significantly under-resourced and marginal to the larger American political economy. Several of these are discussed here, including community development, public housing, and fair housing. This section also discusses several initiatives and policies from the Obama administration that have foregrounded urban places as important realms that shape the lives and life courses of those within them, including Choice Neighborhoods, the Partnership for Sustainable Communities, and the Neighborhood Stabilization Program.

The last section of the book looks forward and asks what a progressive urban policy regime might look like, and how we might get it. It includes two chapters.

The first, by Lorraine C. Minnite and Frances Fox Piven, is about the possibility and necessity of urban social movements to realize social change. The second is my concluding chapter, which discusses the importance of urban policy, why such policies continue to disappoint, and why we need a better urban policy regime in the United States. Finally, there is a brief afterword by Cedric Johnson on the issues raised by the events of 2014 and 2015 in urban areas from Ferguson to Baltimore and what they say about *the urban* and urban policy of our time.

I should also note a couple of things about the scope of this book and its contributors. First, this book is about urban policy at the national level. It is not about all of the other arenas in which urban policy is made. Local governing regimes—be they durable regimes or short-lived mayoral administrations—certainly play an active role in shaping urban policy for people in the municipalities they govern. So too do the myriad of nongovernmental actors who play such a central role in the implementing of social welfare policy in urban areas in this country. And while some of the chapters deal directly with this issue (Todd Swanstrom's in particular), most limit their analyses to federal policy-making. So it is not exhaustive, nor could any one volume covering such a vast terrain expect to be.

Finally, I should say a bit about the contributors to this volume. All of the contributions to this book were solicited, and all are original essays. A handful of them appeared, in very truncated and reduced forms, in a special section of the *Journal of Urban Affairs* that I edited in 2015. But the chapters here are very significant expansions of those essays. I asked for contributions from people whom I knew to be experts in the particular fields they are writing about; I did not want to write this book on my own and produce poorer versions of what others, more knowledgeable than myself about particular policy arenas, could write. The issues covered, though, invariably reflect my own biases and perspectives, and several other policy arenas (welfare, criminal justice, and the environment being the three most obvious to me) could have been included and would have contributed greatly to the book. What we have, however, is a fairly broad and comprehensive set of chapters that cover an array of different policy arenas and how they are playing out in, and shaping, America's urban areas.

Notes

1. Executive Order, Establishment of the White House Office of Urban Affairs, February 19, 2009.
2. See Thompson's chapter in this volume.
3. See the chapter by Karen Chapple in this volume.
4. See the chapters by Janet Smith and Amy Khare in this volume.
5. For a critique of these twin pillars of liberal urban thought, see Imbroscio (2010).
6. Years ago, I referred to this marriage between the community and market as "neoliberal communitarianism," a framing I have not yet seen a reason to revise (DeFilippis 2004).

References

Brenner, Neil, ed. 2013. *Implosions/Explosions: Towards a Study of Planetary Urbanism*. Berlin: Jovis.

Brenner, Neil, and Nik Theodore, eds., 2003. *Spaces of Neoliberalism: Urban Restructuring in North America and Western Europe*. Malden, Mass.: Wiley-Blackwell.

Castells, Manuel. 1979. *The Urban Question: A Marxist Approach*. Cambridge, Mass.: MIT Press.

DeFilippis, James. 2004. *Unmaking Goliath: Community Control in the Face of Global Capital*. New York: Routledge.

Dreier, Peter, John Mollenkopf, and Todd Swanstrom. 2014. *Place Matters: Metropolitics for the Twenty-First Century*. 3rd ed., rev. Lawrence: University of Kansas Press.

Hackworth, Jason. 2007. *The Neoliberal City: Governance, Ideology, and Development in American Urbanism*. Ithaca, N.Y.: Cornell University Press.

Harvey, David. 2005. *A Brief History of Neoliberalism*. New York: Oxford University Press.

———. 1985. *The Urban Experience*. Baltimore, Md.: Johns Hopkins University Press.

Imbroscio, David. 2010. *Urban America Reconsidered: Alternatives for Governance and Policy*. Ithaca, N.Y.: Cornell University Press.

Moynihan, Daniel. 1969. "Toward a National Urban Policy." In *The Engineer and the City*, edited by the National Academy of Engineering, 9–19. Washington, D.C.: National Academies Press.

O'Connor, Alice. 1999. "Swimming against the Tide: A Brief History of Federal Policy in Poor Communities." In *Urban Problems and Community Development*, edited by Ronald Ferguson and William Dickens, 77–109. Washington, D.C.: Brookings Institution.

Wirth, Louis. 1938. "Urbanism as a Way of Life." *American Journal of Sociology* 44 (1): 1–24.

1

NATIONAL URBAN POLICY IN THE AGE OF OBAMA

HILARY SILVER

Barack Obama should have been America's first urban president. As a candidate and then president-elect, he gave every indication that he would be. But he entered office during the worst downturn since the Great Depression and soon confronted a hostile Republican congressional opposition prepared to go to the mattresses to prevent new spending. If Obama had any big plans for new urban initiatives, they were quickly diminished. Yet he did have a beneficial impact on American cities, as I will show, primarily as a by-product of nonurban federal programs, stimulus expenditures, and organizational efficiencies that required no new dedicated allocations. In his second term, after a wave of racial disturbances, he also benefited from a fortuitous Supreme Court decision on fair housing. Whether Obama's accomplishments add up to a national urban policy, therefore, is a matter of how one conceives of such a policy.

A look back at the history of national urban policy in the United States reveals at least such two conceptions. First, one can discern a series of federal policies between 1929 and 1968 that stimulated the economy and ultimately rebuilt American cities in a modernist vein. Early in the 1930s, faced with the Great Crash in finance, presidents Hoover and Roosevelt restructured federal regulation of the banking and housing markets. These institutional innovations ushered in three decades of Keynesian intervention that increased demand, helped organize labor, and reduced unemployment through public works, infrastructure, and public housing construction. As the postwar suburban boom took off, the "federal bulldozer" cleared away "slums," built interstate highways, and introduced master planning for downtowns. The process was racially biased, of course. In response to civil rights protests, large-scale demolition of minority neighborhoods ceased, and the War on Poverty infused these places with federal funds. Federal spending expanded local government services, and the Community Action Program under the Office of Economic Opportunity provided African Americans with public or nonprofit sector jobs, and cemented this "urban" constituency in the Democratic Party. The expansionary, interventionist period of national urban policy culminated in 1965 with the establishment of the Department of Housing and Urban Development.

The ensuing urban disorders, however, marked a watershed in the activist type of national urban policy. Just as African Americans were turning votes into mayoralties, President Richard M. Nixon initiated a decade-long period of national urban policy *sensu stricto*. What passed for "national urban policy" in this second sense was the consolidation of many discrete programs and interagency cooperation in governing them. Nixon initiated what would become a long-term shift from Keynesian to neoliberal macroeconomics, from public works to private partnerships, and from federal to state and local-level program priorities. Although Democratic president Jimmy Carter took up the theme of national urban policy once again, his successor, Ronald Reagan, largely gutted federal aid to the cities, recruiting the private sector and lower-level governments to the role. Federal urban policy shrunk to subsidizing neighborhoods with tax reductions in a limited number of cities: enterprise, empowerment, and under Obama, promise zones. Budgetary starvation eroded the few public programs that remained, with little change during the Bush I, Clinton, and Bush II administrations.

The Obama administration pursued a national urban policy in both senses. First, the Great Recession afforded an opportunity to conduct a neo-Keynesian urban policy by stealth. Stimulus funds went directly to "shovel ready" infrastructure projects and to keeping government employees on the job, with disproportionate urban impact. However, the scale of federal intervention in distressed neighborhoods—Choice Neighborhoods—was anemic compared to the postwar effort. In addition, the president and Congress reformed the financial system, especially for housing, through new institutions and regulations. The American Recovery and Reinvestment Act (ARRA) included a foreclosure-prevention program, Making Home Affordable (MHA), which had two components, the Home Affordable Modification Program (HAMP) and the Home Affordable Refinancing Program (HARP). Obama also capitalized the National Housing Trust Fund for the first time, and signed the Dodd-Frank Wall Street Reform and Consumer Protection Act, establishing the Consumer Financial Protection Bureau (CFPB) and creating a mechanism to close failing banks without future taxpayer-funded bailouts and to break up banks that are "too big to fail." Second, like the Nixon and Carter administrations and unlike his immediate predecessors, Obama adopted a national urban policy in the formal sense, innovating in governance. Early in his first term, he created a White House Office of Urban Affairs to reassess existing, explicitly urban programs with evidence on their performance, to coordinate them across agencies, or to consolidate them to realize efficiencies. Some programs were repackaged to receive additional funding or to attract private resources, but few new signature urban programs emerged. President Obama was more successful at shaping the governance aspects of national urban policy than at producing results on the ground. The scale of and resources for Obama's urban, housing, and other place-based programs were modest, and the results disappointing. The minor impact is a result not only of the recession, but also of the sequester and other Republican budget shenanigans designed to undermine the Democrats politically.

If President Obama has one potential legacy in urban policy, it may be "ending" homelessness. Federal homelessness policy dates from the 1987 McKinney-Vento Act. Because it was enacted after the heyday of national urban policy, urban scholars often neglect to discuss federal homelessness policy in favor of more long-standing programs. At the turn of the twenty-first century, advocates began pressing for an end to homelessness and for a change from the linear continuum of care to a "Housing First" model. In 2003, the administration of President George W. Bush adopted a plan to end chronic homelessness, including funds for 150,000 additional permanent supportive housing units for disabled adults.[1] Hundreds of American cities organized local service providers and advocates, both secular and church-based, for local campaigns to end chronic homelessness in ten years. But this effort gained traction, expanded to veterans, and changed course under the Obama administration. Unlike most urban line items, the federal government did increase spending for Housing First approaches to homelessness and extended the goal to end homelessness among the "deserving poor" of homeless veterans and families. As the deadlines now approach, President Obama could claim credit for this mostly urban accomplishment. It is still too early to assess his record on fair housing, which was another area in which executive powers enabled him to act without congressional approval.

Two Eras of National Urban Policy

Keynesian Era Urban Policy

Federal intervention in the cities began in earnest after the Great Crash of 1929. Overwhelmed by foreclosures and bank runs, unemployment and poverty, state and local governments turned to Washington. The first phase of national urban policy helped to stimulate the economy while rebuilding American cities. President Obama would adopt this approach too, but on a much more modest scale.

The first phase of federal engagement in cities entailed the regulation and restructuring of the housing finance system to encourage housing construction. Initially President Herbert Hoover did what he could to resurrect the financial system through the Federal Home Loan Bank Act of 1932, providing savings and loan associations with capital to make mortgage loans and extending the terms and maximum loan-to-value of home loans. But it took President Franklin Delano Roosevelt to address the hemorrhaging foreclosure rate, further liberalize mortgage terms, and restructure the edifice regulating and insuring banking and housing markets. With half of all home mortgages in default by 1933, he established the Home Owners' Loan Corporation (HOLC), which bought and refinanced over a million mortgages with long-term federal bonds (Jackson 1985, 193–96). HOLC institutionalized long-term, fixed-rate, low down-payment, self-amortizing home loans, bringing homeownership within reach of middle-class Americans. This was followed by the National Housing Act of 1934, which established the Federal Housing Administration (FHA). The FHA offered federal mortgage insurance, protecting lenders in case borrowers defaulted on their loans and freeing up bank funds to build homes and to reduce interest rates. Although FHA underwriting conditions included the racial and ethnic composition of the house's neighborhood, producing "redlining" that benefited the suburbs, the institution nonetheless provided a serious stimulus to demand that revived the construction industry for decades to come. Lastly, in 1938, the Federal National Mortgage Association (FNMA, later known as "Fannie Mae") was established as a private subsidiary of the Reconstruction Finance Corporation to issue bonds paid off with borrowers' mortgage payments. With these funds, FNMA purchased FHA-insured mortgages to encourage more such loans.[2] This Depression-era history is worth recalling in light of Obama's housing finance reforms during the Great Recession.

The FHA tied housing construction to job creation, a Keynesian principle that would continue in the U.S. Housing Act of 1937, establishing the federal public housing program for low-income households. Reflecting political compromises at the time, the 1937 Housing Act had multiple goals. It aimed to not only house the poor but also employ the submerged middle class. Indeed, if there is a single statement of national urban policy in the Keynesian era, it is found in the "Declaration of Policy" in Section 1 of the U.S. Housing Act of 1937:

> It is hereby declared to be the policy of the United States to promote the general welfare of the Nation by employing its funds and credit, as provided in this Act, to assist the several States and their political subdivisions to alleviate present and recurring unemployment and to remedy the unsafe and insanitary housing conditions and the acute shortage of decent, safe, and sanitary dwelling for families of low income, in rural or urban communities, that are injurious to the health, safety, and morals of the citizens of the Nation. (United States Housing Act of 1937, Pub. L. No. 75–412, 50 Stat. 888, 891)

Should there be any doubt that urban policy had a Keynesian dimension, it is worth noting that in 1950, President Harry Truman reduced the numbers of new public and FHA housing units out of concern that the Korean War might compete for materials and together would increase inflation (Davies 1966). Unfortunately, this cutback created a precedent for subsequently funding a low number of units in the Eisenhower years. It took a decade to produce the authorized number of public housing units. But bricks and mortar meant jobs. After the war, the thrust of FHA- and VA-insured homeownership pushed the domestic economy full steam ahead. Suburbanization, fueled by cheap mortgages and new highways, set off a virtuous circle of mass production and mass consumption for a glorious thirty years (Harvey 1973).[3]

The Keynesian interventionist period of national urban policy culminated in 1965 with President Lyndon B. Johnson's establishment of a full-fledged Department of Housing and Urban Development. In elevating the House and Home Financing Agency (HHFA) to the cabinet level under an African American secretary, Robert Weaver, who had previously served as President John F. Kennedy's director of HHFA, Johnson reiterated the same policy found in the preamble to the 1949 Housing Act. The Housing Act of 1965 authorized 600,000 units of new, leased, rehabilitated, or purchased public housing. The scale of construction was unprecedented.

In response to the backlash against urban renewal of the cities and the urban disorders of the 1960s, President Johnson passed the "Model Cities" program (Demonstration Cities and Metropolitan Development Act of 1966). To accomplish the comprehensive, coordinated revitalization of the economies of distressed neighborhoods, the program introduced master planning. Like the inner-cities Community Action Program under President Kennedy, it called for "maximum feasible participation" of citizens, especially African Americans newly empowered under the 1965 Voting Rights Act. The program quickly fell victim to politics. The number of sites rapidly proliferated to win votes in Congress. The original legislation had dedicated $2.3 billion for just six "Demonstration Cities" in each region, but every legislator wanted one in his or her district. Soon the number burgeoned to seventy-five planning grants, with implementation grants to follow. Then, a total of 225 Model Cities were designated, spreading funds too thinly to make a real dent in urban problems (Hetzel 1994). HUD also found it difficult to win "buy-in" from other federal agencies or lower levels of government, even as the urban riots increased the urgency for results.

The year 1968 marked a watershed in interventionist national urban policy. That year, the report of President Johnson's National Advisory Commission on Civil Disorders, also known as the Kerner Commission, argued the country was "moving toward two societies, one black, one white—separate and unequal." It linked the devastating riots that consumed Detroit and Newark in 1967 to residential segregation sustained and aggravated by federal policies that concentrated poor black citizens in ghettos. As part of the remedy, the commission called on the government to outlaw housing discrimination in both the sale and rental markets and to "reorient" federal policy so that housing for low- and moderate-income families would be built in integrated, mixed-income neighborhoods, where residents would have better access to jobs and decent schools. Soon after the King assassination, Congress passed the Fair Housing Act, which banned housing discrimination and required states and local governments that receive federal housing money to try to overcome historic patterns of segregation and to "affirmatively further" federal fair housing goals. Yet the act proved hard to enforce.

All told, ample funding for urban renewal during the 1960s injected a sizable stimulus into the economy. Kennedy's 1961 housing bill authorized another $2 billion in federal capital grants, and Johnson dedicated over $5 billion to the cities, including $600 million for the Model Cities program. Thus, total federal urban renewal funding from 1949 to 1968 exceeded $10 billion for 1,946 urban renewal projects in 912 communities (National Commission on Urban Problems 1968; von Hoffman 2000). Domestic expenditures of this magnitude coupled with defense spending on the Vietnam War together contributed to inflation in the 1970s.

Yet, a backlash against urban interventionism was already apparent. Minority leaders castigated urban renewal as "Negro removal," while conservatives called for "law and order" after the riots. Critics on the left and right pointed to the deficiencies of high-rise public housing, culminating in the mid-1970s demolition of the recently built Pruitt-Igoe project in Saint Louis. Private alternatives, like Sections 235 and 236 of the 1968 Housing Act subsidizing homeownership and private rental housing would both fall to scandals in the 1970s. The defeat of LBJ and the election of Richard M. Nixon brought the Great Society and urban Keynesianism to a screeching halt.

Consolidation-Era National Urban Policies

When policy experts refer to "national urban policy," they usually mean not the New Deal or urban renewal, but the comprehensive federal intervention in cities of the 1970s. Both Nixon and Carter explicitly proposed holistic "national urban policies," which were not fully implemented. The hallmarks of these policies were less the actual programs and their quantitative costs or outputs, but rather their governance arrangements and institutional reforms. These included four principles: interagency collaboration, program consolidation, federalism, and public–private partnership. The Obama White House Office of Urban Affairs would similarly adopt such principles.

Soon after his election, President Nixon courted Professor Daniel Patrick Moynihan to join the "liberal bloc" of his domestic policy team and largely gave him carte blanche to choose his cabinet post. Upon learning that Transportation was already taken, Moynihan said, "I'd like to have the urban equivalent of Henry Kissinger's job on the National Security Council. A National Urban Council or whatever the name will be" (Hess 2015, 11). He got his wish. Three days after his inauguration in January of 1969, Nixon issued Executive Order no. 11452, creating the Council for Urban Affairs, which was charged with "the formulation and implementation of a national urban policy" (49). Moynihan pointed out, "the United States does not now have an urban policy. The idea that there might be such a policy is new" (49).

After the riots, Moynihan felt there was an "emerging sense that some coherent national approach needs to be made to the problems to be encountered in cities." Unfortunately, Moynihan reflected, "too many programs have produced too few results."

> The federal establishment must develop a much heightened sensitivity to its "hidden" urban policies. There is hardly a department or agency of the national government whose programs do not in some way have important consequences for the life of cities, and those who live in them. (Moynihan 1970, 6–8)[4]

Reflecting the interdepartmental nature of urban problems, the National Urban Council would coordinate eight cabinet departments and agencies working on committees of cabinet officers. The National Urban Council also served to consolidate the myriad urban programs that had proliferated by the 1960s.[5] In fact, Nixon wanted to combine or eliminate five years of "government programs for the unemployed, programs for the cities, programs for the poor" that he considered failures. But for "prudential" reasons at a time of racial instability, he decided to do this gradually. For example, he reorganized the components of OEO and Johnson's Great Society—the Community Action Program, Head Start, VISTA, Job Corps, Legal Services.

Model Cities too was slowly squeezed budgetarily out of existence so as not to provoke its many constituencies. Edward Banfield chaired a 1969 taskforce recommending the combination of Model Cities and other federal programs into general-purpose revenue sharing (Hess 2015, 145). In 1973, President Nixon imposed a moratorium on all federal housing programs and the next year enacted his own bill (signed into law by Gerald Ford after Nixon resigned due to the Watergate scandal). Reiterating the same goals as the Housing Act of 1949—the elimination of slums and blight and conditions that threatened the public health, safety, and welfare—the Housing and Community Development Act of 1974 would consolidate Model Cities, urban renewal, open space, water and sewer grants, public facility loans, and historic preservation into the more flexible Community Development Block Grant program. CDBG shifted policy emphasis from new construction toward rehabilitation of housing. The program did not have to be focused on one neighborhood and had a broader constituency, providing support for newer, smaller cities in the South and West.

Model Cities nonetheless bequeathed a number of lessons to future programs aimed at comprehensive neighborhood revitalization. For example, to broaden political support (or spread "pork" in return for votes), President Bill Clinton would amply fund six Empowerment Zones as well as ninety-five small "Enterprise Communities." Later, we will see, Obama's Choice Neighborhoods program offered many planning grants and fewer implementation grants.

Johnson's Housing and Urban Development Act of 1968 had set the ambitious goal of building 26 million new dwelling units, including 6 million for low- and moderate-income households, over the next ten years. Construction on this scale offered the Nixon administration the opportunity to desegregate American housing. Former Michigan governor George Romney, Nixon's HUD secretary, intended to use the 1968 act to eliminate the "high income white noose" of the suburbs around heavily African American inner cities, an act "essential if we are going to keep our nation from being torn apart" (Hannah-Jones 2012). In 1969, there were discussions within HUD about how to use the threat of withdrawing federal housing subsidies to integrate any suburbs trying to block the construction of affordable housing. Romney launched an "Open Communities" program that would reject applications for sewer and highway projects from segregating cities and states. HUD even terminated grants to the Boston, Baltimore, and Toledo metro areas after they rejected low-income housing slated for white neighborhoods, and thereby won concessions. But Nixon soon reined in Romney who had been withholding HUD funds to integrate Warren, Michigan.

To stop the Open Communities program, Nixon ostracized Romney and ordered HUD to stop all efforts to pressure cities and states to foster integrated housing. The president later wrote, "I am convinced that while legal segregation is totally wrong, that forced integration of housing or education is just as wrong." The 1974 Housing and Community Development Act would require localities accepting federal block grants to comply with the Civil Rights Act of 1964, which banned racial discrimination, but not to follow the 1968 Fair Housing Act's mandate to "affirmatively further" inclusionary housing. Romney resigned in November 1972. Over the next four decades, Democratic and Republican presidents would not leverage HUD funding to promote integration. The Obama administration—prodded by private lawsuits—would later withhold money from Joliet, Illinois, and Westchester, New York, for not meeting civil rights obligations, but took years to issue fair housing regulations for municipal obligations.

Nixon also reoriented housing subsidies, shifting attention from aid to places and toward aiding needy people and bringing the private sector further into subsidized housing. On the one hand, recognizing the fiscal problems of public housing authorities with declining rent receipts, the 1974 law loosened income caps on tenants and required all households to pay some rent. On the other hand, Section 8 of the 1974 law created portable rent subsidies that low-income households could redeem in privately constructed, rehabilitated, or maintained buildings and take with them if they moved. Today, Section 8 and its successor, Housing Choice Vouchers, are the main source of subsidized low-income housing, slightly exceeding the dwindling number of public housing units.

Another legacy of Nixon's urban policy was general revenue sharing and block grants. Nixon's "New Federalism" returned non-earmarked federal dollars to states and localities, giving lower-level governments more discretion over spending. It also consolidated many programs into four categorical block grants for training, education, law enforcement, and community development (CDBGs). Politically speaking, the approach furthered the Republican "Southern strategy" by redistributing some federal resources away from older, larger cities toward Republican constituencies in the growing suburbs and the Sunbelt. Nixon's policies of decentralization, private sector involvement, and preference for assisting needy people over aid to places presaged the neoliberal urban policies of Ronald Reagan.

After Gerald Ford's short term in the mid-1970s, President Jimmy Carter readopted the idea of an explicit national urban policy. Shortly after taking office, Carter formed the cabinet-level Urban and Regional Policy Group headed by HUD secretary Patricia Harris, and later established the Interagency Coordinating Council with the assistant secretaries from all federal agencies to coordinate execution of urban policy. Carter issued executive orders to conduct community impact analyses of all federal programs and, in place of politically distributed pork, to target federal spending and procurement on "distressed" cities and neighborhoods. He not only expanded the Economic Development Administration's urban grants and reauthorized CDBGs, but unlike the Model Cities program, instituted urban development action grants (UDAG). The UDAG program awarded $4.6 billion to assist about 3,000 economic development projects in more than 1,200 cities during its twelve years of operation (1978–1989). It reoriented local economic development policy from one based on grants, tax abatements, and infrastructure improvements to a more entrepreneurial approach that recaptured public funds (Rich 1992). Carter also proposed legislation for, among other things, a national development bank to guarantee investments in distressed areas, but it was not established, partly because HUD, the EPA, and the Treasury fought over which department would run it, partly because of Sunbelt/Snowbelt disputes over allocations. Carter's proposal for a public works program, like Obama's to come, also failed to be approved.

All told, Carter's proposed urban policy package would have cost $8.3 billion, of which $7.2 billion was for jobs and investment in distressed inner cities (Kingsley and Fortuny 2010). It mixed assistance to distressed places with training and other assistance to people in distress. However, distracted by inflation, fiscal crises, and political woes, Carter abandoned the urban policy just as it was getting off the ground. In fact, his own President's Commission on a National Agenda for the Eighties issued a 1980 report that called for federal aid to go to people rather than places. "The urban consequences of essentially nonurban policies will continue to outweigh those of narrow and explicitly urban policies," said the report. "Localities have proved to be very difficult to shore up or 'revitalize,' despite all our place-oriented redevelopment programs" (President's Commission 1980, 68–69).[6] No wonder the history of national urban policy has been called "a narrative of failure" (M. Katz 2009).

The Neoliberal Retrenchment Era

The election of Ronald Reagan spelled the end of national urban policy ambitions. The president ushered in an era in which HUD became a backwater of the federal government, or worse, a feeding trough for Republican political cronies (Welfeld 1992).[7] Between 1980 and 1990, federal urban expenditures fell 46 percent, or some $26 billion in constant 1990 dollars (Caraley 1992). State aid did not replace them. Reagan's "new federalism" ended general revenue sharing. On average, federal aid covered 22 percent of large cities' expenditures in 1980, but only 6 percent in 1989 (Caraley 1992). From a peak of 17 percent in 1978, the federal share of total municipal expenditures gradually fell to 5 percent in the twenty-first century, with state contributions through the years remaining a constant 20 percent (Barnes 2005, 582).

Both Reagan and George H. W. Bush began their first terms with recessions, but rather than stimulate the domestic economy, they cut back on federal expenditures and cut taxes in line with supply-side economics. Without countercyclical spending through grants to city and state governments, and saddled with unfunded mandates, many cities experienced their worst fiscal and service crises since the Great Depression of the 1930s (Caraley 1992). Of all the domestic programs Reagan cut back, housing and community-development programs were the hardest hit. Reagan also shifted the remaining funding from aid to places toward aid to people who live in them (Reischauer 1990; Peterson and Lewis 1986).

Compassionate conservatism under Jack Kemp and George H. W. Bush did little to increase the federal role in urban policy after Reagan left office. The Republicans preferred to support nonprofit, voluntary, and charitable social efforts, as illustrated by homelessness policy and the switch to low-income housing tax credits to stimulate private and nonprofit construction. Public housing was residualized, the stock deteriorated by defunding of capital and operating budgets. Private subsidized housing saw use restrictions expire. Instead, the number of voucher subsidies for private rental housing increased.

Over time, what passed for urban policy narrowed in focus. From Model Cities, which touched a large number of distressed places, urban policy telescoped its investments, directing tax breaks and federal aid to a small number of neighborhoods of "concentrated poverty." The Republicans' "Enterprise Zones" targeted specific places for a reduction or elimination of taxes and regulations in the expectation that firms would open in response to such incentives. Instead, many companies simply moved from elsewhere in the city, creating no new jobs. A "third way" politician triangulating the ideological center, Clinton combined features of enterprise zones and Model Cities. Enacted in 1993, Empowerment Zones—which were expensive and few in number (six)—were accompanied by many more "Enterprise Communities" offering both new spending and tax incentives to poor neighborhoods across forty-one states and the District of Columbia.[8] The program mandated involvement of the private sector as well as the community in strategic planning for how to use these coordinated targeted resources to transform local economies and communities.

The cumulative impact of these changes was to disempower cities politically and to starve housing and urban programs fiscally. In 2005, William Barnes of the National League of Cities concluded, "The era of federal urban policy is, like, way over. . . . Under Democratic and Republican leaders alike, urban policy has receded into a Washington backwater, and is unlikely to reemerge as a priority any time soon."

Obama's Urban Policy

The election of Barack Obama as the first president of the United States with a mixed-race background and experience in community organizing raised expectations for greater federal attention to the nation's cities. His memoir, *Dreams from My Father*, recounts how, at the age of twenty-three, he worked for a coalition of churches in Roseland on Chicago's deindustrializing far South Side (Obama 2004). From 1985 to May 1988, he was director of the Developing Communities Project, organizing black working-class residents to win improved playgrounds, afterschool programs, housing, youth mentoring, parenting, job training, and other neighborhood services to fight joblessness. During that time, he organized a tenants' rights organization in the troubled Altgeld Gardens low-rise public housing project nearby. During those Chicago years, he advocated for comprehensive change in high-poverty neighborhoods. In 2007 and during his 2008 presidential campaign, then-Illinois Senator Obama called for replicating Geoffrey Canada's Harlem Children's Zone, a public–private partnership providing a full network of neighborhood services from "cradle to college," reminiscent of the Developing Communities Project. Accordingly, in the 2008 presidential election, he won the votes of city residents by a twenty-eight-point margin.

Barack Obama experienced the rough-and-tumble world of Chicago politics after graduating from Harvard Law School. Barack and Michelle Obama cemented their friendship to Valerie Jarrett, who had worked for mayors Washington and Daley and had recruited Michelle to the Mayor's Office and then to Chicago's Department of Planning and Development. Jarrett connected the Obamas to the city's elite, worked hard on their election campaigns, and became a loyal confidante. Similarly, Obama's inner circle included chief campaign advisor and strategist David Axelrod, who helped reelect Harold Washington, the first black mayor of Chicago, and successfully ran mayoralty races in a half dozen other cities. Axelrod was known for his experience in shaping urban coalitions of blacks, Hispanics, and white liberals like the coalition that made Obama "the first urban president in more than a century" (Gergen 2015, BR12). After Obama's election in 2008, Axelrod and Jarrett were appointed White House senior advisors. Axelrod left the White House and returned to Chicago in early 2011, as did former chief of staff, now Chicago mayor Rahm Emanuel in 2010. Jarrett remained as assistant to the president for Intergovernmental Affairs and Public Engagement, managing among other agencies the White House Office of Urban Affairs, created by President Obama in his first month in office.

Obama's background, associates, and early presidential actions led many to the reasonable expectation that the newly elected chief executive would adopt a comprehensive national urban policy, moving the federal government back into an active role in American cities. As his newly appointed Housing and Urban Development secretary Shaun Donovan reported in 2009, the president "talked about community organizing, working in public housing where there were no jobs around. He talked about what he saw in Harlem when he was a student at Columbia University. It is a very personal issue for him that comes from his own experience" (Fletcher 2009, A08).

Yet President Obama seemed to abandon his affinity for community organizing and tackling poverty at the grassroots soon after he entered the White House. With two wars, the economic crisis, and health care reform to contend with, most other domestic policies disappeared from the front burner. Instead of a major federal initiative to help cities with large black populations, the White House continued the tradition of supporting private efforts. For example, Obama advocated for My Brother's Keeper, a nonprofit program for mentorship, grants, and other services for black youth funded by African American celebrities, corporations, and foundations already active in urban social initiatives.

Indeed, trying to build consensus around the center, Obama rarely talked about poverty, race, or urban problems (Herbert 2012). He took pains to avoid singling out the "special" concerns of African Americans or targeting aid on cities per se. Rather, the administration adopted the Brookings Institution's emphasis on large "metropolitan areas" encompassing some four-fifths of the American population rather than "cities." Given that the Republicans gained control of Congress in 2010 and then refused to compromise with the president, Obama's rhetoric aimed to unite, not divide Americans, to good electoral effect in 2012. When questioned about Obama's avoidance of urban issues, Valerie Jarrett explained that he preferred to speak about "paths of opportunity for everyone. We try to talk about this in a way where everyone understands why it is in their self-interest." The president would propose broad programs like the Affordable Care Act or Race to the Top that raised the standard of living of all Americans, an approach that Jarrett described as "inclusive" (Tough 2012; Dreier 2014). Thus, even the experts can be excused for missing the July 13, 2009, speech that Obama gave on urban affairs, since press coverage of it was minimal.[9]

After his reelection, there was a *volte-face*, and President Obama began hesitantly to speak about race. In early 2013, he talked passionately about opportunity and race with a group of teenage boys in Chicago, and a few months later, imagined that a killed black Florida teenager, Trayvon Martin, "could have been me 35 years ago." After another meeting with young black youth, he reflected, "I grew up without a dad. I grew up lost sometimes and adrift, not having a sense of a clear path. The only difference between me and a lot of other young men in this neighborhood and all across the country is that I grew up in an environment that was a little more forgiving" (Baker 2015, A1). Yet the anger and rioting in cities after a series of racial incidents with police propelled Obama to speak out in 2015: "In addressing the issues in Baltimore or Ferguson or New York . . . if we're just looking at policing, we're looking at it too narrowly. If we ask the police to simply contain and control problems that we ourselves have been unwilling to invest and solve, that's not fair to the communities, it's not fair to the police" (A1). He added that, if society "writes off" some people, "that's not the kind of country I want to live in; that's not what America is about" (A1). Again, his language sought to unify and balance. Yet with rising racial violence and polls showing greater polarization around race, it may be that race relations is another urban-related area in which the high expectations for President Obama fell short.

After more than seven years in office, can one properly speak of an Obama administration national urban policy? I would contend that there is an Obama urban policy of sorts with three main prongs reminiscent of earlier administrations. First, like presidents in the consolidation era, Obama instituted some important governance reforms to break down agency silos, to leverage limited discretionary funds, and to address urban problems transversally. His urban policy was interdepartmental, multijurisdictional, comprehensive, inclusive, and evidence-based. The White House Office of Urban Affairs, the Domestic Policy Council generally, and the resurrected Interagency Council on Homelessness are cases in point. Second, the Great Recession was not only a constraint, but also an opportunity to help cities. As in the Great Depression, Obama restructured the U.S. housing finance architecture, rescuing homes from foreclosure, infusing the economy with new capital for mortgages, and passing new regulations for lenders and consumers. He also used stimulus funds in a manner that favored urban infrastructure, services, and municipal employees. Third, in the long line of his predecessors, Obama tweaked some existing place-based housing and urban programs into signature initiatives: Promise Zones, modeled on Empowerment Zones, and Choice Neighborhoods, a new-and-improved version of HOPE VI, a program established in 1993 under Clinton. However, for want of a dedicated funding stream, federal urban policy consisted of small-scale reformed versions of the few programs that had survived years of attrition.

Governance

Public administration practices have changed considerably in recent years, partly under fiscal pressures, partly reflecting a shift to evidence-based policy assessment. Trends in governing urban policy include program consolidation or silo busting; interagency coordination aimed at greater efficiency and resource sharing; rescaling or decentralizing to lower levels of government; and especially prominent in the neoliberal era, private sector involvement.[10] Faced with congressional opposition to new spending programs, Obama's urban policy came to employ new principles of governance. It is interagency, multijurisdictional, comprehensive, inclusive, and evidence-based.

From the start, interagency cooperation was central to Obama's urban policy strategy. Like Nixon's Council for Urban Affairs and Carter's Urban and Regional Policy Group, the White House Office of Urban Affairs was created in 2009 to coordinate seventeen agencies and engage cities and metropolitan areas. Early on, the

Office of Urban Affairs conducted a comprehensive review and evaluation of federal "place-based" programs, the first of its kind in thirty years. In an August 11, 2009, White House memo for the 2011 budget, the Office of Urban Affairs said it aimed to "increase the impact of government dollars by leveraging place-conscious planning and place-based programming" and called for modernizing and "investing in what works by evaluating existing place-based policies and identifying potential reforms and areas for interagency coordination." The office articulated national goals for cities and metropolitan areas—competitiveness, sustainability, and inclusion—and then developed policies that advance those goals and measures progress.

In September 2010, the White House launched the Neighborhood Revitalization Initiative (NRI) whose July 2011 report called for integrating Promise Neighborhoods, Choice Neighborhoods, and other "centerpiece place-based programs in distressed neighborhoods" (Byrne Criminal Justice Innovation; Building Neighborhood Capacity Program; Health Center Program). The NRI's approach to federal engagement was designed to be interdisciplinary, place-based, locally led, data- and results-driven, and flexible. Procedures were central to its work. The NRI called for resident engagement; strategic and accountable public–private partnerships; evidence of results and data to monitor progress; building organizational capacity; and aligning resources to a unified goal, including the "braiding" of federal funds into local resources. Resources were concentrated on a few areas, perhaps because "the interconnected challenges in high-poverty neighborhoods require interconnected solutions." As of 2012, only Baltimore, Boston, Camden, Newark, San Francisco, and Washington, D.C., had received both Promise Neighborhoods and Choice Neighborhoods funds.

Former Bronx Borough president Adolfo Carrión Jr. was the first director of the Office of Urban Affairs, but he left in 2010. Reflecting on the lack of accomplishments of the office, Carrión rationalized that "the focus at the time was to rescue the American economy from the precipice of a second Great Depression and health care" (Schlanger 2013). His successor, Racquel Russell, deputy assistant to the president for Urban Affairs and Economic Mobility, is similarly lackluster. The Office of Urban Affairs quietly merged with the economic mobility team under the Domestic Policy Council and reports to both Cecilia Muñoz and Valerie Jarrett. Today, the office has fallen into obscurity. Key urban leaders have had no contact with it. Richard Florida said it has "little to show for its efforts," and Bruce Katz judges that "it failed miserably" (Holeywell 2013). "The Office of Urban Affairs," said Patrick Sharkey, is an "example of a grand idea that was implemented in a half-hearted way, and then lost its momentum over time" (Schlanger 2013).

Much urban "place-based" policy was made in the Domestic Policy Council and the White House Office of Management and Budget (OMB). Like Moynihan's Council for Urban Affairs, the Domestic Policy Council is comprised of numerous policy teams and offices that implement domestic policy priorities, including the

"Urban Affairs and Economic Mobility" team that works for "Sparking Community Revitalization." The four programs listed under this rubric are Promise Zones, Bringing Healthy Food to Communities, Creating Sustainable Communities, and Ending Homelessness. Creating Sustainable Communities, for example, is a partnership among the Department of Housing and Urban Development (HUD), the Environmental Protection Agency, and the Department of Transportation. The inclusive interagency collaboration of the White House Domestic Policy Council, White House Office of Urban Affairs, HUD, and the departments of Education, Justice, Health and Human Services, and Treasury was supposed to develop and execute the Obama administration's place-based strategy "to transform neighborhoods of concentrated poverty into neighborhoods of opportunity." In mid-2014, the president reshuffled his cabinet and moved Shaun Donovan, HUD secretary since the outset of the Obama administration, to head up the OMB. His replacement at HUD, Julián Castro, was a three-time mayor of San Antonio, as was Henry Cisneros, Clinton's HUD secretary.

Restructuring Housing Finance

As in the Great Depression, the Great Recession forced leaders to restructure the institutions regulating private housing finance. The 2007 crisis led to 7 million foreclosures and rocked New Deal institutions as stable and successful as the FHA and some Federal Home Loan Banks. Like the 1930s' establishment of the HOLC, the Bush administration aimed to help financial institutions lower monthly mortgage payments, keep people in their homes, and jumpstart the economy. However, the scale of the crisis dwarfed the sums allocated for these objectives.

Under George W. Bush, Congress passed the $700 billion Troubled Assets Relief Program (TARP) to rescue the nation's largest financial institutions, and put Fannie Mae and Freddie Mac, the government-sponsored enterprises (GSEs) that dominate the secondary mortgage market, into federal conservatorship. Bush did little for "Main Street" until July 2008, when Congress passed the Housing and Economic Recovery Act (HERA). In addition to an ultimately unsuccessful FHA program to refinance subprime adjustable-rate mortgages into fixed-rate ones, Congress enacted the First Time Homebuyers Tax Credit to stimulate sagging house sales, a program Obama would extend in 2009.

HERA established the Neighborhood Stabilization Program (NSP). The NSP transferred a meager $4 billion to states and localities for the acquisition and disposition of foreclosed houses. There was fear that vacant homes would lead to squatting or crime and harm neighboring property values (Schwartz 2015, 2012; Immergluck 2011). In 2009 and 2010, President Obama allocated additional TARP funds to NSP2 and NSP3 that nonprofits and community-development corporations could also use to redevelop vacant homes. "There has rarely been a less loved or more necessary emergency program than TARP," Obama (2009) said, but "as galling as the assistance to banks may have been, it indisputably helped prevent a collapse of the entire financial system." In fact, after the Treasury Department released projections that taxpayers would get back most of the $700 billion budgeted for TARP, Obama (2009) said the resulting savings could lower the deficit and "shift funds that would have gone to help the banks on Wall Street to help create jobs on Main Street."

Reforming housing finance, managing foreclosed properties, and stimulating the economy went hand in hand. In February 2009, weeks after assuming office, President Obama persuaded Congress to pass the American Recovery and Reinvestment Act and to launch a foreclosure prevention program, Making Home Affordable (MHA). MHA was funded with $50 billion from TARP and had two parts: (1) the Home Affordable Modification Program (HAMP), lowering the high subprime debt-service costs of homeowners at risk of foreclosure, and (2) the Home Affordable Refinancing Program (HARP), helping eligible homeowners refinance their mortgages through Fannie Mae and Freddie Mac. According to the March 2013 Housing Scorecard released by HUD and the Treasury, over 1.5 million homeowners were assisted through Making Home Affordable, including 1.1 million permanent reductions in payments or principal through HAMP. Nearly 3 million mortgages were refinanced under HARP. And FHA offered more than 1.7 million loss-mitigation and early-delinquency interventions.

Nevertheless, the administration had expected to assist as many as 8 million homeowners. Many in arrears did not qualify for the program, and most loan modifications were only temporary, postponing default. The program was also voluntary. HAMP incentives to lenders to modify monthly payments of "underwater" borrowers—up to one-third of the 52 million households with mortgages, Moody's reported, owing more than their house is worth—were insufficient compared to their fees on delinquencies or the value of foreclosure. As the recession wore on, the causes of foreclosures shifted from high-cost loans to the terms of adjustable rate mortgages, both prime and subprime, and toward defaults due to unemployment. The Obama administration repeatedly reformed the foreclosure prevention programs to overcome weaknesses and expand eligibility for assistance (Immergluck 2013). HERA also created the Federal Housing Finance Agency that, in 2009, placed Fannie Mae and Freddie Mac into conservatorships. After wading into high-risk Alt-A mortgage-backed securities, Fannie Mae (reconstituted as a private corporation in 1968) and Freddie Mac (founded as a private corporation in 1970), came close to collapse. Because private lending had dried up, the federal government provided these institutions with $187 billion in public capital to acquire mortgages under strict regulations. By 2015, the GSEs and FHA were financing virtually the entire mortgage market (Schwartz 2015).

Since 2011, the Obama administration has called for winding down the GSEs and limiting the government role in the secondary mortgage market to regulating and insuring these securities. Republicans favor recapitalizing and privatizing Fannie. While politicians argue, Fannie Mae and Freddie Mac have remained wards of the state. Since they began earning profits in 2012, the GSEs have returned to the Treasury more than $50 billion over the amount they drew down in the bailout, prompting some shareholders to sue (Morgenson 2016). At the end of 2014, the Mortgage Finance Reform Working Group of the bipartisan Housing Commission were discussing how to reduce Fannie and Freddie's share of the mortgage market and to prevent public assumption of private sector risk. As of mid-2016, no one had decided what to do with the housing finance system.

In the Housing and Economic Recovery Act of 2008, Congress established the National Housing Trust Fund to be funded by a percentage of the profits from Fannie Mae and Freddie Mac. HERA had provided for the GSEs to set aside funds for this purpose, but FHFA temporarily suspended the rule until after the recovery. The Obama administration tried to allocate $1 billion to the National Housing Trust Fund, but after the nationalization of the GSEs, Congress refused to provide any new source of funding. Instead of waiting for Congress, the Obama administration tried to increase funds for affordable rental housing from other governmental sources for loans already guaranteed through FHA's risk-sharing program. By 2012, the GSEs were in the black, profits driven largely by one-time, tax-related adjustments and legal settlements and shrinking loan portfolios. They paid taxpayers back more in dividends than they were loaned, monies now available for the National Housing Trust Fund. At the very end of 2014, the FHFA directed Fannie Mae and Freddie Mac to allocate between $250 million and $350 million to the National Housing Trust Fund for distribution to the states to house very low-income renters. The disbursements would be the first new money in decades to produce low-income rental housing in the United States. The National Alliance to End Homelessness reports that the National Housing Trust Fund will receive $136 million in 2017, or $46 million less than the $182 million the administration predicts will be available to allocate to states for the first time in summer 2016.

Recognizing that the foreclosure crisis was precipitated by inadequate federal oversight of subprime loans, President Obama proposed in June 2009 a new agency to protect consumers from unfair, deceptive, and abusive financial practices. In July 2010, Congress passed and President Obama signed the Dodd-Frank Wall Street Reform and Consumer Protection Act. The act created the Consumer Financial Protection Bureau (CFPB), which consolidated most federal consumer financial protection authority in one place. Housed within the Federal Reserve System, CFPB supervises banks, credit unions, payday lenders, and other financial companies, and enforces federal consumer financial laws. Lenders must now ensure that borrowers can repay their loans and must retain a stake in the mortgages they sell to the secondary market to discourage passing the risk of default to investors. Built mainly on bills Congress drafted before the crisis, Dodd-Frank was actually a modest set of regulatory reforms compared to calls for breaking up and limiting the size of American banks so they would never again be "too big to fail."

Nevertheless, Republicans opposed the law and, since gaining control of Congress in the fall 2010 elections, tried to repeal arcane measures, worked to loosen regulations, pushed for delays, threatened legal challenges, and filed lawsuits.[11] As soon as the Republicans took control of both houses of Congress in January 2015, they set about dismantling Dodd-Frank one provision at a time. Democrats in Congress fought back, but "systematically important" banks continue to chafe under the regulations, transparency requirements, and federal powers to take control of them in a future crisis (Krugman 2015).

The Stealth in the Stimulus

During the Great Depression, it will be recalled, FDR reformed the mortgage market before increasing public expenditures and launching the public works projects of the New Deal. Similarly, building on Bush II measures, President Obama first worked on stabilizing the financial system that brought about the crisis and, in 2009, succeeded in getting the stimulus bill through Congress. A copious definition of national urban policy encompasses expansionary spending programs like those of the Keynesian era. Just as President Roosevelt "primed the pump" in the 1930s, President Obama's expansionary fiscal response to the Great Recession preserved urban jobs, and invested in the built environment to sustain urban growth over the long term. Since most government spending in the United States takes place through states and localities, direct investments in place-based assets that drive economic prosperity disproportionately benefit cities (B. Katz 2010). Thus, implicit in Obama's budget priorities, including for programs with goals that are not explicitly oriented to places *per se*, was a "stealth urban policy."

Immediately upon assuming office, President Obama persuaded Congress to pass an economic stimulus bill offering $788 billion in new spending and tax breaks, including $13 billion for housing-related purposes.[12] Many of the largest and most important investments of the stimulus went to institutions and organizations that were essential to cities. The American Recovery and Reinvestment Act of February 2009 provided funds to states and localities for construction and investments in education, Medicaid, and transportation projects. ARRA included the issuing of Build America Bonds, generally high-quality infrastructure bonds with above-average yields. Traditional tax-exempt bonds indirectly provide for lower borrowing costs for state and local governments through a federal tax exemption to investors for the interest income received on the bonds. In contrast, Build America Bonds are taxable bonds issued by state and local governments for which the federal government makes direct payments to state and local governmental issuers (called "refundable tax credits") to subsidize a portion of their borrowing costs in an amount equal to 35 percent of the coupon interest on the bonds. It is difficult to estimate ARRA's net impact because no one knows what the economy would have done in the absence of the law. Most of the stimulus impact on output and employment was felt in 2010, but even in 2013, ARRA was still officially funding about

76,000 jobs. While the stimulus somewhat helped improve U.S. infrastructure, the president himself conceded that he lacked the political capital to increase the magnitude of the stimulus. Despite the need for greater pump-priming, congressional Republicans insisted on layoffs. "This is the first recovery where you actually saw the government work force decline, and that created this massive fiscal drag throughout the recovery," the president argued. "Progressives don't fully appreciate the degree to which the 2011 budget deal not only averted a potential default but actually limited the potential damage of a newly emboldened Congress in imposing austerity on a still-fragile recovery," Obama said (Sorkin 2016).

Some administration policies worked at cross-purposes to the stimulus. Dodd-Frank and Federal Reserve banking regulations may have made capital scarcer and more expensive. Even the president's signature bill, the Affordable Care Act, may have dampened economic growth, since it slowed the rise of medical costs in a sector that comprises almost one-fifth of the American economy. The administration gave Obamacare priority in Congress at the expense of more stimulative infrastructure programs.

There has not been a new issue of Build America Bonds since the securities' federal subsidy expired in 2010. Although it was once a bipartisan issue, the president subsequently had difficulty finding resources for infrastructure. Obama's 2011 and 2013 proposals for an infrastructure bank to leverage private investment with public money went nowhere with congressional Republicans who labeled the president "Santa Claus." Republicans and Democrats could not agree on the Highway Trust Fund, gas tax, and other capital spending. Indeed, net federal nondefense investment had been falling from its peak in the late 1960s (at $45 billion in today's dollars). The 2009 stimulus brought it back up to $28 billion in 2010, but since then it plummeted further to $10.3 billion in 2013, the lowest level since 1958. In contrast, net nondefense investment by states and cities soared since the mid-1980s until 2010, after the housing boom collapsed (Wessel 2015). In 2013, Obama again picked up the theme of infrastructure in his State of the Union address. To rebuild the nation's "raggedy" roads, bridges, schools, and other infrastructure, he proposed more stimulus grants, tax breaks, and loans to attract private investment, both American and foreign. He also suggested new "America Fast Forward Bonds" to enable state and local governments to borrow money for construction projects, to no avail (Baker and Schwartz 2013). In hindsight, the president mused, "our failure in 2012, 2013, and 2014 to initiate a massive infrastructure project—it was the perfect time to do it; low interest rates, construction industry is still on its heels, massive need—the fact that we failed to do that, for example, cost us time. It meant that there were folks who we could have helped and put back to work and entire communities that could have prospered that ended up taking a lot longer to recovery" (Sorkin 2016).

Of course, cities also benefited indirectly from social programs and income transfers. People-based policies also help places, although the poor do not only live in cities nowadays. A central tenet of Keynesian stimulus spending is that in an economic crisis, you try to get as much money as quickly as possible into the hands of people who will spend it right away, and the less money people have, the more likely they are to spend every dollar they receive from the government. Thus, ARRA supported Americans in need through extended Unemployment Insurance, SNAP, and tax relief such as the new Making Work Pay tax credit. The total amount in the stimulus package targeted specifically at low-income Americans in 2009 topped $80 billion. The multiplier effects were huge, but their role in helping cities went largely unperceived as such. Thus, it may be that "urban revitalization is a happy accident of federal legislation with other goals" (M. Katz 2009, 19). However, that happy accident was soured by the 2013 sequester, automatic budget cuts that removed billions of dollars of stimulus from the economy and slashed programs for the poor.

Although ARRA funds soon ran out, the president's economic record seems remarkable when one considers what could have happened without a stimulus. Since Obama took office, the deficit declined by $1 trillion or roughly three-quarters, all the bank bailout funds were recouped, GM and AIG are still operating, 14.4 million new jobs were added, unemployment—which peaked at 10 percent the year Obama took office—fell to 5 percent, the stock market rose from the 6,000s to the 16,000s, and economic growth exceeded that of other advanced countries (Sorkin 2016).

Obama's Urban Programs

While federal housing programs saw a significant budgetary increase in the first year of the Obama administration, due mostly to the stimulus bill, federal spending for most affordable housing categories has been flat or reduced in the years since. Transportation expenditures rose from $70 billion to nearly $100 billion after Obama took office, but HUD's outlays fell overall from $60 billion to barely $36 billion in 2015, or 1.7 percent to 0.9 percent of total outlays (OMB 2016, 85).[13] Funds earmarked specifically for HUD were internally transferred across programs, phasing out HOPE VI, for example, for Choice Neighborhoods (see Table 4.1). As the National Low Income Housing Coalition reported, one of the only areas not to be cut was the budget for homeless assistance grants. Judged in historical perspective, therefore, Obama's explicitly urban programs were modest and reached only a small number of the cities and neighborhoods in need.

Private involvement in public housing can be traced back to the 1960s' leased housing and Sections 235 and 236, accelerated in the 1980s, and culminated under Obama in the Rental Assistance Demonstration (RAD). Given the many years of underfunded capital budgets, even the best managed public housing is in need of physical repairs (Finkel et al. 2010). Table 1.1 shows authorizations fell from $2,500 million in 2010 to $1,970 million in 2016. Since large infusions of capital funds were not forthcoming from Washington, local housing authorities have considered

TABLE I.I. BUDGET AUTHORIZATIONS FOR SELECTED HUD PROGRAMS UNDER OBAMA (IN $ MILLIONS)

	FY 2010 Enacted	FY 2011 Enacted	FY 2012 Enacted	FY 2013 Enacted	FY 2014 Enacted	FY 2015 Enacted	2016 President's Request with Sequestration	Cut
Tenant-Based Rental Assistance	18,184	18,371	18,914	17,964	19,177	19,304	21,123	—
Project-Based Rental Assistance	8,552	9,257	9,340	8,851	9,917	9,730	10,760	—
Public Housing Capital Fund	2,500	2,040	1,875	1,777	1,875	1,875	1,970	v
Public Housing Operating Fund	4,775	4,617	3,962	4,054	4,400	4,440	4,600	v
HOPE VI	135	100	—	—	—	0	0	
Choice Neighborhoods Initiative	65	65	120	114	90	80	250	v vs HOPE
Community Development Fund	4,450	3,501	3,308	3,135	3,100	3,066	2,880	v
Veterans Affairs Supportive Housing	75	50	75	75	75	75	MERGED	
Homeless Assistance Grants	1,865	1,901	1,901	1,933	2,105	2,135	2,480	—

Source: National Low Income Housing Coalition, February 2015

raising funds by selling some of their land to private developers or by selling the buildings themselves and giving the residents housing voucher subsidies instead. RAD allows public housing authorities to convert their current assistance to long-term Section 8 contracts or "project-based vouchers." These contracts leverage additional debt that can be used to address critical capital needs. As of 2014, sixty-eight public housing authorities received an initial RAD commitment from HUD.

As late as 2010, it looked as though President Obama had launched an innovative national urban policy (Peirce 2010). The budget called for additional housing vouchers, full funding of public housing, as well as the Housing Trust Fund, new rounds of the Neighborhood Stabilization Program, and Build America infrastructure bonds. Early in his administration, the president also proposed several signature programs for neighborhoods, each based in a particular department but, as mentioned, cooperating transversally with other ones. For example, Sustainable Communities, an interagency partnership of HUD, DOT, and EPA, provides grants as incentives for interjurisdictional cooperation on metropolitan transportation, housing, and land use projects like transit-oriented development, light rail, and smart growth initiatives. Obama's proposed Promise Neighborhoods go beyond the schools, offering early-childhood, afterschool, and parental education in distressed neighborhoods. Other cooperative ventures among federal agencies included the Healthy Food Initiative, Promise Zones, and most notably, the Choice Neighborhoods Initiative.

Choice Neighborhoods

A centerpiece of Obama's housing policy is the Choice Neighborhoods Initiative (CNI). It addresses three dimensions at once: housing, people, and neighborhood. Choice Neighborhoods is a central part of the White House Neighborhood Revitalization Initiative, an interagency partnership between HUD and the departments of Education, Health and Human Services, Justice, and Treasury, dedicated to locally driven transformations of distressed neighborhoods. As part of the White House's recognition that "interconnected challenges in high-poverty neighborhoods require interconnected solutions" (https://www.whitehouse.gov/administration /eop/oua/initiatives/neighborhood-revitalization), CNI offers "a comprehensive approach to community development centered on housing transformation" whose goal is "to transform neighborhoods of poverty into viable mixed-income neighborhoods with access to economic opportunities" (Urban Institute 2013, 1–5). The intention is to use the revitalization of severely distressed public and assisted housing to leverage comprehensive neighborhood investments ranging from early childhood education to employment, safety, and public transportation.

In many respects, CNI is a rebranded, new and improved version of its predecessor, the Clinton-era HOPE VI program. HOPE VI grew out of the National Commission on Severely Distressed Public Housing, created by Congress in 1989. It was established in 1992 for the rehabilitation and replacement of about 86,000 severely distressed public housing units by 2000. By 2007, it had demolished more than 78,000 distressed public housing units, with another 10,000 units readied for redevelopment. Grantees could also spend up to 15 percent of HOPE VI funding for community and supportive services. In place of public housing, HOPE VI constructed hundreds of mixed-income housing projects in the attempt to deconcentrate neighborhood poverty. In fact, HOPE VI demolished more low-income units than the total number of mixed-income units built.

Both HOPE VI and CNI share the goal of deconcentrating poverty, but CNI made some changes in response to recent critical evaluations of the earlier policy. Unfortunately, in the earlier mobility program, most relocated public housing tenants ended up living in very poor, sometimes high-crime neighborhoods (Buron, Hayes, and Hailey 2013), and not all those who wished to return to their old neighborhoods qualified for the new mixed-income housing.[14] When Obama spoke about creating "neighborhoods of choice," he meant that after revitalization, *nonpoor* households would voluntarily choose to live in previously poor neighborhoods. Less attention was devoted to the choices of relocated residents. They are supposed to receive case management and wraparound services to help them move to better housing in substantially safer neighborhoods.

CNI differs from HOPE VI in several ways. First, the revitalization may extend beyond the perimeter of public housing developments to encompass their surrounding neighborhood, to improve all residents' health, safety, employment, and education. It extends residents' access to services, effective schools and educational programs, public assets, public transportation, and jobs. Second, it supports the replacement or rehabilitation of both distressed public housing and other types of HUD-subsidized rental housing with energy-efficient, mixed-income housing that would remain physically and financially viable and affordable for at least twenty years. "Mixed-income" means a combination of extremely low-income, low-income, and, as appropriate, moderate-income housing. To entice private capital investment, mixed financing techniques may also yield housing with various income limits, including no income restrictions. Third, unlike HOPE VI or much earlier urban renewal programs, CNI requires one-to-one replacement of demolished subsidized units, although it permits replacing up to half the units with vouchers in metropolitan areas with soft rental housing markets. Fourth, public housing authorities need no longer be the lead agencies for neighborhood transformation.

Congress has never legally authorized Choice Neighborhoods, which exists as a HUD demonstration project by virtue of annual appropriations since FY 2010. Each year notices of funds availability are issued and applications evaluated. As in Model Cities and EZs, more cities—forty-seven between 2010 and 2012—received small planning grants, while nine were awarded more lucrative implementation grants (twelve as of 2016). HUD maintains that the $200 million in grants are leveraging over $1 billion in local and regional dollars.[15]

An Urban Institute/MDRC (2015) interim report on five initial recipients of these grants found much unevenness in outcomes. For example, while all the sites rely on federal low-income housing tax credits (LIHTCs), the Boston project has no unrestricted housing units, while the others are mixed-income. Similarly, the lead agencies in Boston and Chicago are not public housing authorities so they cannot issue vouchers and have no experience with services for people. None of the projects devote attention to improving the lives of those who move away permanently. Citizen engagement in planning varies across the sites. As for neighborhood improvements, Choice Neighborhoods will have a modest impact, only complementing or filling gaps in larger recent, committed, and expected public and private investments. The first CNI awards went to places where significant efforts already were under way (Urban Institute 2013). This may accelerate apparent gains, but the sequester budget cuts meant that implementation grants for other cities were delayed. After increasing from $80 million in FY 2015 to $125 million in FY 2016, Obama has requested a considerable expansion of the program to $200 million in FY 2017.

A review of the 176 applications for planning grants under Choice Neighborhoods in the first three rounds also found that the targeted neighborhoods with concentrated poverty were also racially and ethnically segregated and suffered from other difficulties like low education, low labor force participation, and high unemployment (Gebhardt 2014). Thus, like HOPE VI, CNI is likely to have racially differential impacts and may lead to gentrification. However, enforcement of "affirmatively furthering" fair housing may allow existing minority residents to choose to stay, not only to move on as their neighborhoods become "choice" for higher-income whites.

Promise Communities

In a 2007 speech, Senator Obama painted urban poverty as "a disease that infects an entire community. . . . We can't just treat those symptoms in isolation. We have to heal that entire community" (Obama 2007). Like William Julius Wilson (Wilson 2010), he was much taken by the apparent success of Geoffrey Canada's Harlem Children's Zone to overcome the effects of spatially concentrated poverty. In a ninety-seven-block area, HCZ combines some two dozen structural and cultural programs and innovative charter schools. Assessments using random assignment techniques provided convincing evidence that intensive schooling—long school years and school days, after-school and weekend tutoring—can radically improve English and math test scores, helping inner-city students of color surpass their peers in other public schools and close the gap with whites. In a 2008 campaign speech, candidate Obama promised to replicate the Harlem Children's Zone in twenty cities.

The Department of Education took the lead on Promise Communities, and accepted over three hundred applications in the summer of 2010. Promise Communities takes aim at concentrated poverty with holistic urban policies addressing two fronts, structural and cultural. It involves multiple agencies providing a full network of services to an entire low-income neighborhood "from birth to college." Yet some argue that Promise Communities does not actually replicate the Harlem Children's Zone, and so, equal success should therefore not be expected. Not only did HCZ have an annual $80 million budget, compared to just over $200 million for twenty Promise Neighborhoods, but much of its budget came from private sources.[16] The federal government provides half of the funding for Promise Communities, with the rest coming from philanthropy and businesses at a cost of a few billion per year.

PROMISE ZONES

Turning to local economic development in his 2013 State of the Union Address, President Obama announced the Promise Zones Initiative as part of his plan to help the American middle class. It creates partnerships between local communities, faith-based and nonprofit organizations, and businesses to create jobs, increase economic security, expand educational opportunities, open up access to quality, affordable housing, and improve public safety. Again, it calls for the pursuit of multiple goals. In August 2014, the president named the first five Promise Zones of the twenty planned over the following three years. They will have zone designations for ten years.

Like Obama's other signature programs, the Promise Zones Initiative builds on earlier programs, continuing the neoliberal approach. The administration admits that Promise Zones are modeled on Clinton-era Empowerment Zones, offering tax credits to promote job creation, with interagency coordinated efforts addressing social problems, such as high crime and poor education in the designated neighborhoods. Perhaps realistically, Obama did not propose any new direct spending on Promise Zones, whereas Empowerment Zones provided up to $100 million per EZ as well as smaller grants to the many Enterprise Communities. While Republicans have favored enterprise zones in the past, Congress has not yet approved the tax incentives.

Ending Homelessness

Homelessness became an issue in the United States just as national urban policy went into eclipse. In 1981, President Ronald Reagan cut domestic spending, which instigated a recession and raised unemployment. Veterans returning from Vietnam, many with substance abuse problems, received little assistance upon reentry. Soon, people living on the streets became visible. In the nation's capital, activist Mitch Snyder set up a "Reaganville" or tent city deliberately echoing the Hoovervilles of the Great Depression and shamed the president into a federal commitment to the city's shelter. Snyder and other activists drew public attention to the growing problem of homelessness, resulting in the 1987 McKinney Act, the first federal homeless assistance.[17]

Although the George W. Bush administration set a goal in 2002 to end chronic homelessness in ten years, the Obama administration shepherded that objective into law. The Homeless Emergency Assistance and Rapid Transition to Housing Act of 2009 was a clear turning point, reauthorizing and amending the McKinney-Vento Act and creating a federal-level program with measurable, time-delimited goals. The HEARTH Act aims to ensure that no family is homeless for more than thirty days, and to prevent those at imminent risk of homelessness from losing shelter. HEARTH broadened the definition of homelessness to include those at risk of homelessness (e.g., doubled up) and consolidated into one Continuum of Care program the Supportive Housing Program, rental subsidies for permanent supportive housing, and Moderate Rehabilitation/SRO long-term rental subsidies. In addition, the 2009 Helping Families Save Their Homes Act contained preventative provisions to protect renters who face eviction when their landlords go into foreclosure. After 2012, the budget for homelessness, three-fourths of which is urban, also increased (Table 1.1). Under President Obama, Homeless Assistance Grants through HUD rose from $1,865 million to $2,250 million, with even more requested for FY 2017.

In keeping with his transversal, evidence-based governance approach, Obama resurrected the Interagency Council on Homelessness. Initially established in 1987, the Interagency Council fell dormant in 1996 until it was revitalized in 2002 in commemoration of the fifteenth anniversary of the signing of the McKinney-Vento Homeless Assistance Act. The council coordinates and combines services of nineteen federal agencies and monitors the results of federal funding to local service providers. Local "Continuums of Care" (CoCs) distribute Homeless Assistance Grants to fund transitional and permanent housing as well as services for homeless individuals. They also collect information on clients. Local Homeless Management Information Systems, established by Congress in 2001, collect data for HUD, which compiles it into the Annual Homeless Assessment Report (AHAR) to Congress, the first of which was issued in 2005. The AHAR estimates the number of individuals who are homeless within a given year. Local CoCs also conduct point-in-time counts of homeless individuals on one day in January at least every two years. Today, the vast majority of CoCs participate in the Homeless Management Information System. The administration charged the Interagency Council on Homelessness with executing *Opening Doors,* the first national strategic plan to end homelessness. *Opening Doors* called for ending chronic and veteran homelessness by 2015, mainly with supportive housing, and homelessness among families, youth, and children by 2020.[18] It signaled the federal government's commitment to make homelessness a priority for all federal agencies and to partner with states, localities, private organizations, and other stakeholders to use strategies proven to be effective. For example, HUD partnered with the Department of Veterans Affairs (VA) to establish joint goals and monitor progress in the fight to end veterans' homelessness, notably by combining housing and supportive services. In FY 2015, HUD received $75 million for approximately 10,000 new joint HUD-VA supportive housing (HUD-VASH) vouchers targeted toward chronically homeless veterans. Since 2010, veterans' homelessness has declined 36 percent, although family homelessness has remained high, given the high cost of housing. According to the AHAR, approximately 1.42 million people used a shelter during the course of the 2013 year, which is a 10.5 percent decline from 2007. However, the average length of stay in a shelter program increased slightly. From 2009 to 2015, overall homelessness in the U.S. decreased from 630,227 to 564,708 at one point in time, for a decline of 10 percent (National Alliance to End Homelessness 2016). At this rate of change, the administration is actually moving closer to its goals. Indeed, the nonprofit Common Ground asserts that eight cities are already on a path to essentially ending homelessness in their metropolises in the not too distant future. Although veterans' homelessness has declined, the ambitious 2015 goals were not met, and target dates were pushed back to 2020.

Obama also changed the approach to ending homelessness. Before 2000, most experts thought that people experiencing chronic homelessness had to go through a linear process or continuum of care, addressing personal and health problems while living in transitional housing before they were "ready" for a permanent home. The Clinton administration's HUD secretary Andrew Cuomo launched the "continuum of care" to institutionalize these pathways through shelter plus care. Yet evidence from controlled experiments in New York and Philadelphia found instead that chronically homeless individuals do better coping with substance abuse or health issues if they were provided with "housing first." Hundreds of cities have now adopted the Housing First approach, persuaded by research that it in fact saves taxpayer dollars that would otherwise go to hospitals, prisons, and other costs. They have also developed local plans to end homelessness within the parameters of *Opening Doors*. Key to Housing First is the provision of more rent subsidies for those at risk of homelessness. The National Housing Trust Fund allocations may help supply these rental subsidies. The Obama administration continues to propose increases in expenditures to end homelessness and implement the HEARTH Act. The president's FY 2017 budget proposed $2.664 billion for HUD's McKinney-Vento Homeless Assistance Grants, a $414 million or 18 percent increase. Although it slightly reduced capital funds for public housing and community development funds, the administration advocated for a ten-year $11 billion program of housing vouchers ($8.8 billion) and short-term rapid re-housing assistance ($2.2 billion) to enable 550,000 families to escape homelessness. In addition, Obama proposed discretionary spending, which requires congressional appropriations, for 10,000 new housing vouchers for homeless families with children and increases permanent supportive housing for the chronically homeless by 25,500 units (Stewart 2016). In total, the HUD budget for existing programs would increase by $1.8 billion over FY 2016 (National Alliance to End Homelessness 2016). Since sequestration has ended, these proposed priorities have a better chance of being funded than they had earlier in Obama's second term.

Late Developments

Frustrated by Republican recalcitrance in both houses of Congress, President Obama focused on policies and regulations he could order with executive powers instead of requiring legislation. Fair housing is an example. John Trasviña, a civil rights lawyer and head of the Mexican American Legal Defense Fund, whom Secretary Donovan had appointed to lead HUD's fair housing office, began rewriting federal rules to enforce racial desegregation. It took close to six years, but in 2015, the Obama administration released the new rules. Pointing to academic evidence on neighborhood effects on opportunities, HUD Secretary Julián Castro remarked that, "a ZIP code should never prevent any person from reaching their aspirations" (Davis and Appelbaum 2015, A1).

The moment was right. The president was under pressure to act after serious racial clashes over police mistreatment of African Americans in Ferguson, New York, and Baltimore. He was buoyed by the stunning Supreme Court decision in *Texas Department of Housing and Community Affairs v. The Inclusive Communities Project*.[19] Whereas earlier interpretations of the Fair Housing Act forbade housing discrimination, they did not mandate proactive steps to promote integration. The court expanded the interpretation of the 1968 Fair Housing Act to include the mandate to "affirmatively further" racial integration and provided new legal means to enforce the act with penalties. HUD was now justified in requiring localities to report how they used federal housing funds to reduce racial disparities. While localities can refuse federal funding to avoid these requirements, most cannot afford to do so and thus are expected to comply. This change may have a long-term impact on segregation in the United States, but any credit must be shared with the Supreme Court.

Conclusion

President Obama came to office amid high hopes that American cities and urban minorities would once again receive the attention they enjoyed from the 1950s to 1970s. Despite some repurposed programs and administrative innovations, most observers have been disappointed.[20] Stymied by fiscal constraints due to the economic downturn and Republican intransigence, the administration had few resources with which to help the cities. Nevertheless, it made do with less, issuing executive orders and finding efficiencies through interagency collaboration. The president can point to three areas of accomplishment in national urban policy.

First are the administration's reforms of urban governance. Like the Nixon and Carter consolidation approach to national urban policy, the Obama White House began with an interagency review of programs that work. Then, the Domestic Policy Council of the White House set about coordinating efforts transversally, breaking down the "silos" of federal departments and agencies and ostensibly leveraging resources and economizing. Evidence of program performance was required in return for federal funds. Governance innovations broadened the scope of what now passes in Washington as "urban" policy, encompassing environmental, transportation, education, justice, and other fragmented program jurisdictions under the broader rubric of aid to cities and metropolitan areas. The administration also devised new ways to engage the private sector in urban policy.

Second, much as FDR responded to the Great Depression, Obama used housing finance reform and the Recovery Act to help cities. There was urban stealth in the federal stimulus. Just because spending is not earmarked as urban does not preclude it having a disproportionate impact on cities or metropolitan areas. ARRA funds, extended unemployment benefits, and intergovernmental transfers were of particular benefit to economically hard-hit cities, many with a backlog of infrastructural repairs ready for implementation. Federal interventions in the financial sector also helped cities reeling under the weight of foreclosures and lost property tax revenues. Obama programs to assist underwater homeowners simultaneously helped municipalities, keeping potentially foreclosed houses on the property tax rolls. Similarly, the federal takeover and recovery of the GSEs capitalized the National Housing Trust Fund for the first time. However, Obama's programs for neighborhood revitalization through the Choice Neighborhoods Initiative and other efforts at community development were modest at best.

Finally, despite the hardships imposed by the Great Recession, the Obama administration made some serious progress in reducing homelessness. Funding for housing special populations increased, and the president also tried to multiply the available low-income housing vouchers. In 2014 and 2015, as economic growth and job creation picked up, the president finally engaged with the urban issues of race, policing, and segregation. There is some reason to hope that Obama's last year in office will fulfill his original promise.

Notes

1. "Chronic homelessness" refers to having a disability and being continuously homeless for one year or more or experiencing four or more episodes of homelessness in the last three years.

2. Fannie Mae and the other GSEs underwent many reforms from the late 1960s to the early 1980s in response to inflation and rising interest rates. In the 2000s, they ventured into risky investments like Alt-A mortgages lacking full documentation of borrowers' incomes and with higher loan-to-value or debt-to-income ratios. For a timeline of changes to the GSEs, see *A Brief History of the Housing Government-Sponsored Enterprises* (Federal Housing Finance Agency 2011).

3. That the postwar stimulus created secure jobs with sufficiently high wages to furnish and equip new homes should not imply that homeownership was a good deal for the workers who bought homes. See Jackson (1985) and Edel, Sclar, and Luria (1984).

4. Moynihan's involvement in urban policy and revenue sharing was more successful than his effort at consolidated welfare reform, The Family Assistance Plan, which Congress rejected. Moynihan finally left Washington in 1970 after his "benign neglect" gaffe: "We may need a period in which Negro progress continues and racial rhetoric fades."

5. Nominally chaired by the president, who actually attended the professor's meetings, the council included the vice president and secretaries of Agriculture, Commerce, Labor, Health, Education and Welfare (HEW), HUD, and Transportation, with the later addition of Interior and Office of Economic Opportunity (OEO).

6. The commission was chaired by William J. McGill (Kingsley and Fortuny 2010).

7. Indeed, since the Clinton years, Republicans have periodically attempted to close down HUD entirely.

8. Hetzel (1994, 63) recalls that as a candidate, Clinton promised an "Enterprise Zone" (EZ) program, the exact term used by conservative HUD Secretary Jack Kemp, who unsuccessfully tried to enact a supply-side, deregulated, tax-free zone program with that name during the Bush I administration. Some 600 state-authorized EZs were created before legislation during the Clinton administration authorized six "Empowerment Zones" and ninety-five "Enterprise Communities." Clinton not only offered tax breaks for businesses to locate in these poor areas but also subsidies, tax-exempt bonds, and social services for the neighborhoods. Strategically, like Reagan, Clinton cleverly passed changes in urban policies through the budget reconciliation process, a single vote permanently authorizing programs like low-income housing tax credits that had previously required annual reauthorizations. As Clinton took office, grants to cities and the poor were used to pump-prime the economy and reward the cities, a major constituency instrumental in electing him. Like Obama's ARRA, a central element of his proposed "stimulus package" also called for substantial infusions of funds for immediately implementable projects in the Community Development Block Grant (CDBG) program that would have helped jump start a stalled economy, but that proposal was shot down in Congress.

9. After the Baltimore riots, Obama's urban policies were at last scrutinized in the press. The *Washington Post* concluded that "the report card is mixed." Even a staunch supporter like Brookings Institution pundit Bruce Katz conceded, "The Obama policies or initiatives labeled urban policy tend to be coordinating efforts" (Mufson and Eilperin 2015).

10. The public administration literature classifies national urban policy components along at least three continua: people versus place, economic versus social, and publicly led versus privately led (Holland 2015).

11. The rules changes included delaying for two years a Dodd-Frank rule to sell off bundled debt, known as collateralized loan obligations; exempting some private equity firms from registering with the Securities and Exchange Commission; allowing some small, publicly traded companies to omit historical financial data from their financial filings; and loosening regulations on derivatives. One of Congress's last acts of 2014 was to repeal a Dodd-Frank swaps push-out requirement to segregate into subsidiaries any derivatives whose deposits are uninsured by the government. According to the Office of the Comptroller of Currency, five huge firms conduct 95 percent of derivatives trading. In early 2015, Republicans passed two measures to weaken regulations intended to help lessen the risk of another financial crisis. The bill failed to get the two-thirds majority needed to pass under fast-track House rules (Weisman and Lipton 2015). Nevertheless, in January and July 2015, the president vowed to veto any bill that weakens the Consumer Financial Protection Bureau or rolls back Dodd-Frank. Republicans have persisted, trying to attach a reform of the so-called one-size-fits-all method of regulating major banks to broader spending bills that could force a government shutdown if Mr. Obama vetoed it. By early 2016, House Financial Services Committee Chairman Jeb Hensarling claimed to have successfully tweaked six minor changes to Dodd-Frank through small bills that could survive a veto. In April 2016, at the height of the presidential campaign, Dodd-Frank again came under attack. A federal judge had overturned a major decision from Mr. Obama's Financial Stability Oversight Council about MetLife. Also, a federal appeals court panel was questioning the constitutionality of Mr. Obama's Consumer Financial Protection Bureau because, despite Federal Reserve funding, it is publicly (i.e., congressionally) unaccountable. Regulators believe many American

banks are still too big and too complicated to fail, and sunset plans submitted by the giant financial institutions are not deemed credible (Freeman 2016).

12. The original estimated cost of the Recovery Act was $788 billion, with $499 billion allocated for outlays such as entitlements, contracts, grants, and loans, and $288 billion for tax benefits. Politically, Obama was barely able to get that $788 billion on a straight party-line vote, a sum too modest for the task of stimulating growth. In 2011, the estimated cost of the Recovery Act was increased to $840 billion based on scoring changes made by the Congressional Budget Office. The CBO estimates that the total impact on the budget deficit from 2009–2019 will be $830 billion, half of which occurred in fiscal year 2010 and 95 percent of which was completed by the end of 2013 (Congressional Budget Office 2014). Yet, the federal deficit shrank over time. When the extension of tax breaks is added to the classic stimulus measures, the original figure doubles, for a total of $1.4 trillion (Sorkin 2016).

13. In February 2016, the White House released its FY 2017 budget request for HUD, the largest amount this administration had ever requested for the agency and $4 billion or 8.7 percent above HUD's enacted FY 2015 level. This figure aims to reverse the earlier cuts caused by sequestration, as spending caps were already set in negotiations to end the mechanism. Nevertheless, with a Republican Congress, it is unclear how much will be authorized.

14. The shortcomings of HOPE VI for relocated tenants were reinforced by the results of the Moving to Opportunity demonstration. Long-term (ten- to fifteen-year) effects of moving from high-poverty to low-poverty neighborhoods significantly improved mental health and subjective well-being, as movers on average perceived their new neighborhood to be safer. But moving to these neighborhoods did not significantly affect economic self-sufficiency (e.g., employment and welfare receipt). Also, MTO movers had difficulty finding an apartment and staying in nonpoor neighborhoods (three-fifths move to highly segregated black neighborhoods, and after seven years, most live in above average poverty rate neighborhoods). Furthermore, they move no closer to areas of employment growth (Ludwig et al. 2012).

15. As HOPE VI was phased out in FY 2011, its $100 million budget was combined with the $65 million CNI budget for a total of only $120 million in FY 2012. The president's budget proposal for 2013 called for more than tripling the funds for Choice Neighborhoods Initiative to improve distressed HUD-assisted housing in very poor communities, but it was only funded at $114 million, which fell to $90 million in FY 2014. Obama repeatedly asked for more resources, but Congress cut them back. The administration requested a $170 million expansion of Choice Neighborhoods to $250 million for FY 2017. The twelve current implementation grantees are Boston, Chicago, Cincinnati, Columbus, New Orleans, Norwalk, Philadelphia, Pittsburgh, San Antonio, San Francisco, Seattle, and Tampa.

16. For criticisms, see Schlanger (2013) and the Grassroots Education Movement film *The Inconvenient Truth behind Waiting for Superman* (2011).

17. The 1987 Homeless Act was renamed the McKinney Homeless Assistance Act after the death of Stewart B. McKinney, the chief Republican sponsor of the act, and then retitled the McKinney-Vento Homeless Assistance Act when Representative Bruce Vento died, after having been the strongest supporter of the act once it became law. The Homeless Act established the Interagency Council on Homelessness to coordinate and streamline the federal response to homelessness across agencies and between the government and the private sector, insofar as assistance to the homeless was until then largely charitable.

18. Chronic homelessness fell from nearly 156,000 in 2006 to 111,000 in 2009, after the Bush administration added 42,000 permanent supportive housing slots. In deference to the Bush effort, *Opening Doors* proposed "finish[ing] the job of ending chronic homelessness in five years."

19. The case concerned how Texas allocated low-income housing tax credits without regard to the effect on segregation (Semuels 2015).

20. Poll data show that, initially, scholars and the public alike expected Obama to be a great president and praised him prematurely, but over time, though personally regarding him

highly, scholars view his skills and performance as mediocre to poor (Rottinghaus and Vaughn 2015).

References

Baker, Peter. 2015. "Obama Finds a Bolder Voice on Race Issues." *New York Times,* May 4.

Baker, Peter, and John Schwartz. 2013. "Obama Pushes Plan to Build Roads and Bridges." *New York Times,* March 29, A1. http://www.nytimes.com/2015/05/05/us/politics/obama-my -brothers-keeper-alliance-minorities.html?_r=0.

Barnes, William. 2005. "Beyond Federal Urban Policy," *Urban Affairs Review* 40 (5): 575–89.

Buron, Larry, Christopher Hayes, and Chantal Hailey. 2013. "An Improved Living Environment, But . . ." *Urban Institute.* Brief no. 3. http://www.urban.org/sites/default/files/alfresco/publi cation-pdfs/412762-An-Improved-Living-Environment-But-.PDF.

Caraley, Demetrios. 1992. "Washington Abandons the Cities." *Political Science Quarterly* 107 (1): 1–30.

Congressional Budget Office. 2014. *Estimated Impact of the American Recovery and Reinvestment Act on Employment and Economic Output in 2013.* https://www.cbo.gov/publication/45122.

Davies, Richard. 1966. *Housing Reform during the Truman Administration.* Columbia: University of Missouri Press.

Davis, Julie Hirschfeld, and Binyamin Appelbaum. 2015. "Obama Unveils Stricter Rules against Segregation in Housing." *New York Times,* July 9, A1. http://www.nytimes.com/2015/07/09/us /hud-issuing-new-rules-to-fight-segregation.html.

Dreier, Peter. 2014. "Organizer in Chief?" *Huffington Post,* December 9. Updated February 8, 2015. http://www.huffingtonpost.com/peter-dreier/organizer-in-chief_b_6293598.html.

Edel, Matthew, Elliott Sclar, and Daniel Luria. 1984. *Shaky Palaces: Homeownership and Social Mobility in Boston's Suburbanization.* New York: Columbia University Press.

Federal Housing Finance Agency. 2011. *A Brief History of the Housing Government-Sponsored Enter- prises.* Washington, D.C.: Office of the Inspector General. http://fhfaoig.gov/Content /Files/History%20of%20the%20Government%20Sponsored%20Enterprises.pdf.

Finkel, Meryl, Ken Lam, Christopher Blaine, R. J. de la Cruz, Donna DeMarco, Melissa Van- dawalker, Michelle Woodford, Craig Torres, and David Kaiser. 2010. *Capital Needs in the Public Housing Program.* Revised final report for the U.S. Department of Housing and Urban Development. Bethesda, Md.: Abt Associates. http://portal.hud.gov/hudportal/documents /huddoc?id=PH_Capital_Needs.pdf.

Fletcher, Michael A. 2009. "Obama Sets Sights on Urban Renewal." *Washington Post,* October 7, A08.

Freeman, James. 2016. "Dodd-Frank in Retreat." *Wall Street Journal,* April 13. http://www.wsj .com/articles/dodd-frank-in-retreat-1460588528.

Gebhardt, Matthew. 2014. "Race, Segregation, and Choice: Race and Ethnicity in Choice Neigh- borhoods Initiative Applicant Neighborhoods, 2010–2012." *Cityscape* 16 (3): 93–115.

Gergen, David. 2015. "The O Team." *New York Times Sunday Book Review,* February 12, p. BR12.

Grassroots Education Movement. 2011. *The Inconvenient Truth behind Waiting for Superman.* Documentary, 1:08:52. http://gemnyc.org/our-film/. Available on YouTube at https://www .youtube.com/watch?v=yLmXV4-CBOQ.

Hannah-Jones, Nikole. 2012. "Living Apart: How the Government Betrayed a Landmark Civil Rights Law." *ProPublica,* October 29. Updated July 8, 2015. http://www.propublica.org/article /living-apart-how-the-government-betrayed-a-landmark-civil-rights-law.

Harvey, David. 1973. *Social Justice and the City.* Baltimore: Johns Hopkins University Press.

Herbert, Bob. 2012. "Obama, Romney Both Shy Away from the Plight of Poor Kids." *New York Times,* May 21.

Hess, Stephen. 2015. *The Professor and the President: Daniel Patrick Moynihan in the Nixon White House.* Washington: Brookings Institution Press.

Hetzel, Otto J. 1994. "Some Historical Lessons for Implementing the Clinton Administration's Empowerment Zones and Enterprise Communities Program: Experiences from the Model Cities Program." *The Urban Lawyer* 26 (1): 63–81.

Holeywell, Ryan. 2013. "Whatever Happened to the Office of Urban Affairs?" *Governing*, March 29. http://www.governing.com/blogs/fedwatch/gov-federal-office-of-urban-affairs-still-exist.html.

Holland, Brian. 2015. "Typologies of National Urban Policy: A Theoretical Analysis." *Cities* 48: 125–29.

Immergluck, Dan. 2011. *Foreclosed: High-Risk Lending, Deregulation, and the Undermining of America's Mortgage Market*. Philadelphia: Temple University Press.

———. 2013. "Too Little, Too Late, and Too Timid: The Federal Response to the Foreclosure Crisis at the Five-Year Mark." *Housing Policy Debate* 23 (1): 199–232.

Jackson, Kenneth. 1985. *Crabgrass Frontier: The Suburbanization of America*. New York: Oxford University Press.

Katz, Bruce. 2010. "Obama's Metro Presidency." *City & Community* 9 (1): 23–31.

Katz, Michael. 2009. "Narratives of Failure? Historical Interpretations of Federal Urban Policy." *City & Community* 9 (1): 13–22.

Kingsley, G. Thomas, and Karina Fortuny. 2010. *Urban Policy in the Carter Administration*. Washington: Urban Institute, May 18. http://www.urban.org/research/publication/urban-policy-carter-administration.

Krugman, Paul. 2015. "Wall Street Vampires." *New York Times*, May 11.

Ludwig, Jens, Greg J. Duncan, Lisa A. Genntian, Lawrence F. Katz, Ronald C. Kessler, Jeffrey R. Kling, and Lisa Sanbonmatsu. 2012. "Neighborhood Effects on the Long-Term Well-Being of Low-Income Adults." *Science* 337 (6101): 1505–10.

Morgenson, Gretchen. 2016. "Documents Undercut U.S. Case for Taking Mortgage Giant Fannie Mae's Profits." *New York Times*, April 12.

Moynihan, Daniel Patrick, ed. *Toward a National Urban Policy*. New York: Basic, 1970.

Mufson, Steven, and Juliet Eilperin. 2015. "Baltimore Riots Put Obama Strategy for U.S. Cities under Closer Scrutiny." *Washington Post,* May 4. https://www.washingtonpost.com/business/economy/baltimore-riots-put-obama-strategy-for-american-cities-under-closer-scrutiny/2015/05/04/e2542dba-f253-11e4-b2f3-af5479e6bbdd_story.html.

National Alliance to End Homelessness. 2016. *FY 2017 Budget Proposal Rundown.* http://www.endhomelessness.org/page//files/FY%202017%20Budget%20Rundown_2.11_final_3.pdf.

National Commission on Urban Problems. 1968. *Building the American City: Report of the National Commission on Urban Problems to the Congress and to the President of the United States.* Washington, D.C.: U.S. Government Printing Office.

National Low Income Housing Coalition. 2016. *FY17 Budget Chart for Selected Department of Housing and Urban Development Programs.* Washington, D.C.: NLIHC, April 22. http://nlihc.org/sites/default/files/NLIHC_HUD-USDA_Budget-Chart.pdf.

Obama, Barack. 2004. *Dreams from My Father: A Story of Race and Inheritance.* New York: Three Rivers Press/Random House.

———. 2007. "Changing the Odds for Urban America." Remarks in Washington, D.C., July 18. *American Presidency Project.* http://www.presidency.ucsb.edu/ws/?pid=77007.

———. 2009. "Remarks by the President on Job Creation and Economic Growth." Washington, D.C.: The White House, December 8. https://www.whitehouse.gov/the-press-office/remarks-president-job-creation-and-economic-growth.

OMB (Office of Management and Budget). 2016. *Fiscal Year 2017: Historical Tables. Budget of the U.S. Government.* https://www.whitehouse.gov/sites/default/files/omb/budget/fy2017/assets/hist.pdf.

Peirce, Neal. 2010. "The Obama Administration's Innovative Policy for Nation's Urban Areas." *Seattle Times,* February 15.

Peterson, George and Carol Lewis, eds. 1986. *Reagan and the Cities.* Washington D.C.: Urban Institute.

President's Commission for a National Agenda for the Eighties, The. 1980. *A National Agenda for the Eighties.* Washington, D.C.: U.S. Government Printing Office.

Reischauer, Robert. 1990. "The Rise and Fall of National Urban Policy." In *The Future of National Urban Policy,* ed. Marshall Kaplan and Franklin James, 225–34. Durham, N.C.: Duke University Press.

Rich, Michael J. 1992. "UDAG, Economic Development, and the Death and Life of American Cities." *Economic Development Quarterly* 6 (2): 150–72.

Rottinghaus, Brandon, and Justin S. Vaughn. 2015. "Measuring Obama against the Great Presidents." *Brookings Brief,* February 13. Updated April 2, 2015. http://www.brookings.edu/blogs/fixgov/posts/2015/02/13-obama-measuring-presidential-greatness-vaughn-rottinghaus?utm_campaign=Brookings+Brief&utm_source=hs_email&utm_medium=email&utm_content=16059786&_hsenc=p2ANqtz—7jC6Og17m15ii6mvCUIpaer5rJTvze_YyiLCTEKcBNFWjXGLGolMueI8-R-_vxxci3EGPMwaMsoLBK7e95GaZZIAlIw&_hsmi=16059786.

Schlanger, Danielle. 2013. "Obama's Urban Affairs Office Brings Hope but Not Much Change." *Huffington Post,* July 26. http://www.huffingtonpost.com/2013/07/26/white-house-office-of-urban-affairs_n_3654660.html.

Schwartz, Alex. 2012. "US Housing Policy in the Age of Obama: From Crisis to Stasis." *International Journal of Housing Policy* 12 (2): 227–40.

———. 2015. *Housing Policy in the United States.* 3rd ed. New York: Routledge.

Semuels, Alana. 2015. "Supreme Court vs. Neighborhood Segregation." *The Atlantic,* June 25.

Sorkin, Andrew Ross. 2016. "President Obama Weighs His Economic Legacy." *New York Times,* April 28. Also published as "The Obama Recovery." *New York Times Sunday Magazine,* May 1, MM54.

Stewart, Nikita. 2016. "Obama Will Seek $11 Billion for Homeless Families." *New York Times,* February 8, A11. http://www.nytimes.com/2016/02/09/nyregion/obama-to-propose-11-billion-to-combat-family-homelessness.html?action=click&contentCollection=U.S.&module=RelatedCoverage&region=EndOfArticle&pgtype=article.

Tough, Paul. 2012. "What Does Obama Really Believe In?" *New York Times,* August 15.

Urban Institute. 2013. *Developing Choice Neighborhoods: An Early Look at Implementation in Five Sites.* Washington D.C.: HUD. https://www.huduser.gov/publications/pdf/choice_neighborhoods_interim_rpt.pdf.

Urban Institute and MDRC. 2015. *Choice Neighborhoods: Baseline Conditions and Early Progress.* Washington D.C.: HUD.

Von Hoffman, Alexander. 2000. "A Study in Contradictions: The Origins and Legacy of the Housing Act of 1949." *Housing Policy Debate* 11 (2): 299–326.

Weisman, Jonathan, and Eric Lipton. 2015. "In New Congress, Wall St. Pushes to Undermine Dodd-Frank Reform." *New York Times,* January 13.

Welfeld, Irving. 1992. *HUD Scandals: Howling Headlines and Silent Fiascos.* New Brunswick, N.J.: Transaction Publishers.

Wessel, David. 2015. "Spending on Our Crumbling Infrastructure." *Wall Street Journal,* March 10.

Wilson, William Julius. 2010. "The Obama Administration's Proposals to Address Urban Poverty," *City & Community* 9 (1): 41–49.

2

THE SUBORDINATION OF URBAN POLICY
IN THE TIME OF FINANCIALIZATION

ROBERT W. LAKE

Midway through the Obama administration's first term, on October 21, 2011, the White House Office of Social Innovation and Civic Participation and the Nonprofit Finance Fund convened a meeting, with support from the Rockefeller Foundation, attended by ninety-six representatives from government, nonprofits, philanthropic foundations, and academia (Nonprofit Finance Fund 2012). The convening aimed to generate interest and expand participation in "Pay for Success: Investing in What Works," described in the White House blog as "A New Results-Oriented Federal Commitment for Underserved Americans" (Munoz and Gordon 2012). Meeting participants heard presentations explaining and illustrating the use of Pay for Success (PFS) contracts, also referred to as Social Innovation Financing (SIF), Social Impact Bonds (SIBs), and "impact-first investing," as a policy and funding mechanism for addressing urban social problems. As the Nonprofit Finance Fund reported in its summary of the meeting, "at a time when citizens and governments are being asked to do more with less, innovators around the world are seeking cost-effective solutions that can deliver better outcomes for their communities [and] Pay for Success has emerged as one such strategy" (2012).

The agenda for the day-long White House meeting included presentations from a coalition of voices informing the Obama administration's approach to urban and social policy delivery. These included speakers from the Office of Management and Budget and the White House Domestic Policy Council; leading philanthropic organizations, including the Rockefeller Foundation, Bloomberg Philanthropies, and the Pershing Square Foundation; nonprofit community-development financial institutions, including Third Sector Capital, Social Finance U.S., and the Nonprofit Finance Fund; social policy consultancies and think tanks, including the Center for American Progress, MDRC, the Coalition for Evidence-Based Policy, and the Urban Institute; and academics from Harvard, Johns Hopkins, and the University of Maryland. This alignment of government, nonprofits, foundations, think tanks, and academics both reflected and contributed to an explosion of interest in the Pay for Success formula in the relatively short period since issuance of the first Social

Impact Bond in 2010. According to Judith Rodin, president of the Rockefeller Foundation and a strong proponent, "Social Impact Bonds have the potential to substantially transform the social sector, support poor and vulnerable communities, and create new financial flows for human service delivery" (Social Finance, Inc. 2012, 2). The Federal Reserve Bank of San Francisco devoted a 2013 issue of its *Community Development Investment Review* to twenty-two mostly celebratory articles discussing "Pay for Success financing," asserting in the editor's introduction that "Pay for Success has the potential to improve the social sector's effectiveness by rewarding programs that work, encouraging innovation, validating progress, and attracting private capital to the anti-poverty cause" (Galloway 2013, 3). Within the private sector, the international consulting firm McKinsey and Company reported that "SIBs are another example of how incentives and investment can be recalibrated to stimulate social change" (McKinsey and Company 2012, 4). The Urban Investment Group (UIG) at Goldman Sachs established a Social Impact Fund to "provide investors with an opportunity to deploy capital to address a range of pressing social challenges in the US, while also seeking a risk-adjusted financial return" (Goldman Sachs 2015). In the words of Goldman's CEO Lloyd Blankfein, "anytime you can get natural forces to do what you want to have done, that's perfect" (DePillis 2013).

As revealed by this alignment of interests, the Pay for Success model of urban social policy delivery has attracted a substantial and powerful following in the brief span of years coinciding with the Obama presidency. According to the White House Office of Social Innovation and Civic Partnership, "The Obama administration is fostering a PFS market using all the tools at our disposal. . . . These strategically designed programs are meant to encourage both smarter government and the development of a robust capital market for PFS" (Greenblatt and Donovan 2013, 19). The White House partnered with the Nonprofit Finance Fund and the Arnold Foundation in 2014 and early 2015 to follow up the 2011 national convening with "Pay for Success Regional Summits" in Bridgeport, Connecticut, Chicago, and Salt Lake City to "help communities catalyze future PFS projects" (Nonprofit Finance Fund 2014). The president's annual budget proposals sought congressional authorization for PFS funding beginning in FY 2012 with a $100 million allocation for exploratory programs in the departments of Education, Justice, and Labor. This amount expanded to a requested $300 million in FY 2014, to be administered by the Treasury Department for "Strategies to accelerate the testing and adoption of Pay for Success (PFS) financing models," and to over $900 million in FY 2016 (Cohen 2015a; *Federal Register* 2013; Greenblatt and Donovan 2013). Thirty-five state and local governments had adopted or were considering Social Impact Bond programs, feasibility studies or enabling legislation by early 2016 (Nonprofit Finance Fund 2016). A bipartisan group of congressional cosponsors introduced H.R. 4885, the Social Impact Bond Act, in June 2014, described in a press release as "legislation utilizing social impact bonds (SIBs) in order to improve social and public health outcomes, save taxpayer resources, and unleash non-governmental investment capital to help at-risk Americans" (Young and Delaney 2014).

This scale of interest and activity being directed at PFS and SIBs under the Obama administration raises several questions. What is the logic underlying the Pay for Success approach and how is it unrolling in practice? Does the accelerating adoption of PFS and SIBs represent an innovative departure in the design and delivery of urban social programs, as is frequently asserted by proponents, or is it a continuation of longstanding practices? What explains the rapid emergence and diffusion of PFS at this particular historical moment? To what extent does the proliferation of PFS and SIBs reflect the subordination of urban and social policy to the financialization of the economy framing the Obama presidency and with what short- and long-term consequences for the future?

The Logic and Practice of Pay for Success Social Innovation Financing

Although the White House blog's description of Pay for Success claims that "the concept is simple" (Munoz and Gordon 2012), implementation of PFS requires the coordinated efforts of several types of actors (Barclay and Symons 2013; Kohli et al. 2012; Liebman 2011; McKinsey and Company 2012; Nonprofit Finance Fund n.d.; Roman et al. 2014). Private investors supply capital funding by purchasing Social Impact Bonds or Pay for Success contracts issued by a government entity, a private syndicator such as Goldman's Social Impact Fund, or a nonprofit intermediary or bundler such as Social Finance, Inc. (2012). Revenues received from the sale of SIBs are deployed to pay a nonprofit social service provider to deliver a preventative treatment or curative intervention to a target population whose suboptimal behavior (e.g., criminal recidivism, joblessness, homelessness) is defined as constituting a problem that otherwise would require a costly government program to address. An independent evaluator or assessor is engaged to determine whether the program intervention produces the level of quantifiably measured performance outcomes (e.g., a 10 percent reduction in recidivism as compared to a control group not receiving the treatment) contractually specified in the SIB. If the targeted program outcome is achieved, the government entity pays the investors a return on capital, financing the repayment through savings realized from the reduced need for government intervention to address the problem. As summarized in an Urban Institute report, "Pay for Success (PFS) financing directs private capital to social programs, with the opportunity for a return on investment if the programs achieve performance targets" (Roman et al. 2014, 2). Or as stated somewhat differently by the *National Journal*, "upfront investments in evidence-based interventions for at-risk individuals can save lots of money down the line, and . . . there is no reason why a for-profit company shouldn't cash in on those savings" (Johnson 2015). SIB proponents often refer to the potential for double- or triple-bottom-line benefits as a compelling reason for expanding PFS programs: "The power of SIBs lies in their ability to align all stakeholders' interests around achieving common objectives. . . .

Stakeholders in SIBs—nonprofits, investors, government, and communities—would all benefit from successful SIB programs" (Social Finance, Inc. 2012, 11).

The first Social Impact Bond was launched in the United Kingdom in September 2010 to fund a program aimed at reducing recidivism among male adults released after short-term (less than a year) incarceration in Peterborough Prison, a privately managed facility located near Cambridge, about seventy-five miles north of London, that was experiencing a reconviction and reincarceration rate above 60 percent (Social Finance, Inc. 2012; Social Finance, Ltd. 2011). Social Finance, Ltd., a nonprofit financial syndicator and intermediary established in 2007 with funding from the Rockefeller Foundation, raised £5 million (US $8 million) through the sale of SIBs to seventeen investors, primarily private philanthropic foundations willing to absorb the risk of investing in this still-novel arrangement. As originator of the SIB, Social Finance, Ltd. used the funds to contract with a cluster of non-profit providers to administer a variety of mentoring, advising, and behavioral counseling services (the "One*Service") to 3,000 prisoners before and following release "to facilitate successful reentry into the community" (Social Finance, Ltd. 2012, 9). The UK Ministry of Justice and the Big Lottery Fund, as signatories to the SIB, agreed to repay the investors' principal plus a rate of return of up to 13 percent if an "independent assessor" contracted by Social Finance, Ltd. ascertained that reconvictions fell by at least 10 percent in the first year and by 7.5 percent or more over an eight-year period, as compared to a control group of offenders released from similar prisons elsewhere in the UK who were not recipients of the One*Service counseling and behavioral interventions funded by the SIB (Roman et al. 2014, 5).

The first program financed through a Social Impact Bond in the United States was initiated by the Urban Investment Group at Goldman Sachs in New York City in August 2012, less than a year after the White House introduced the PFS model to the U.S. urban policy community. The Goldman SIB, closely modeled on the Peterborough Prison project in the UK, raised $9.6 million to reduce the rate of reincarceration among sixteen- to eighteen-year-old adolescent inmates in New York City's Rikers Island prison (Olson and Phillips 2013; New York City 2012a,b; Rudd et al. 2013). MDRC, a private nonprofit policy research organization serving as intermediary for the SIB, used the capital provided by Goldman Sachs to contract with two nonprofit service providers to administer the Adolescent Behavioral Learning Experience (ABLE) program, described in a New York City fact sheet as "an evidence-based intervention that focuses on improving personal responsibility and decision-making" (New York City 2012b). As described by MDRC:

> ABLE aims to equip adolescents . . . incarcerated in the New York City jail system with the social and emotional skills to help them make better life choices when they leave jail, yielding financial savings to city government by reducing readmissions to Rikers Island. During their time on Rikers

adolescents participate in Moral Reconation Therapy, a cognitive behavioral program designed to help offenders reevaluate their choices and enhance their decision-making abilities. (Rudd et al. 2013, iii)

MDRC also retained the Vera Institute of Justice as independent evaluator to assess whether ABLE succeeds in reducing the recidivism rate among participants by 10 percent or more at twelve- and twenty-four-month postrelease intervals. If Vera determines that the 10 percent target is exceeded, the city's Department of Correction will repay Goldman's investors their $9.6 million principal plus "success payments" equivalent to a rate of return between 5 percent and 22 percent, depending on the amount of reduction in reincarceration achieved (Olson and Phillips 2013, 98). Or as explained by the *National Journal*, "last fall, Mayor Michael Bloomberg inked an unusual contract with Goldman Sachs. The bank would put up a $9.6 million 'investment' to teach 10,000 young offenders moral reasoning before August 2015. If these teens stay out of jail, the city saves money and Goldman Sachs will make a 22 percent profit. If not, the government pays Goldman nothing" (Quinton 2013). The provision that investors will not be repaid if the targeted reduction is not achieved, however, while consistent with the Pay for Success formula, was offset in the Goldman SIB by a $7.2 million grant from Bloomberg Philanthropies to MDRC to be used to repay investors regardless of the program's outcomes.

Goldman quickly expanded its investment in PFS by originating three new SIBs within little more than a year: for an antirecidivism program in Massachusetts in January 2013; a program for pre-kindergarten education in Salt Lake City in August 2013; and a second early-education program in Chicago in October 2014. New York State launched the first state-sponsored SIB in December 2013, aimed at reducing criminal recidivism through employment training and job placement, and Cuyahoga County, Ohio, announced the first county-level SIB in January 2015 for services to homeless mothers with children in the foster-care system. Programs to promote and adopt the use of SIBs were being considered or had been launched in California, Colorado, Connecticut, Illinois, Massachusetts, Michigan, New Jersey, New York, Ohio, Oklahoma, Oregon, Pennsylvania, South Carolina, Texas, Utah, Washington, and sixteen other states, and the District of Columbia by early 2016 (Nonprofit Finance Fund 2016). The California legislature debated a bill (SB-9) in December 2012 to establish an Office of Social Innovation and Entrepreneurship designed "to facilitate the use of social impact bonds (SIBs)" and considered new legislation (AB1837) in 2014 for a Social Innovation Financing Program for antirecidivism projects in three California counties (http://leginfo.legislature.ca.gov/).[1] The federal Corporation for National and Community Service has provided annual rounds of competitive grants through its Social Innovation Fund, beginning in FY 2014, for technical assistance to improve the capacity of local governments and service providers to develop and implement PFS projects (Corporation for National and Community Service 2014a).

The national media have taken note of the emergence and spread of PFS and SIBs. According to *The Atlantic,* "suddenly, everybody seems to be looking for 'impact' investments that promise measureable social and environmental benefits along with financial returns" (Bank 2012). *Forbes* magazine described SIBs as an opening "to rethink the role of the capital markets in enabling social progress, and to explore the opportunity and the need to connect investment capital and the non-profit sector" (Kanani 2012). Reporting on "The Promise of Social Impact Bonds," the *New York Times* called SIBs "a new idea that in a very short time has caught the attention of governments around the world" by offering "a more intelligent approach to social programs" (Rosenberg 2012; Preston 2012). *The Economist* (2013) hailed SIBs as "a new way of financing public services" and "a big financial experiment" that "promises returns to private investors if social objectives are met." Specialized and professional media have also widely commented on—and thus contributed to—the proliferation of SIBs. The *Chronicle of Philanthropy* reported that "With a Few Pay for Success Plans Under Way, the Idea Is Gaining Currency and Criticism" (Wallace 2014) and the *Nonprofit Quarterly* affirmed that "Wall Street Finds Social Impact Bonds to Be Attractive Investment Options" (Cohen 2015b). *The Bond Buyer* has closely followed the spread of SIBs (Burton 2012) even while noting that "Social-impact bonds . . . are not traditional financial instruments and the use of the term 'bond' is somewhat inaccurate" (Jensen 2013). Writing in *The Chronicle of Higher Education,* researchers from the American Enterprise Institute opined that "it's time to experiment with a new way of leveraging private capital to finance postsecondary education and training—the social-impact bond" (Kelly and McShane 2013).

The academic community has not been slow to join the movement toward SIBs and PFS. Harvard's Kennedy School of Government established a Social Impact Bond Technical Assistance Lab with initial funding from the Rockefeller Foundation and a grant from the Social Innovation Fund provided by the Corporation for National and Community Service. Harvard's SIB Lab "provides pro bono technical assistance to state and local governments implementing pay-for-success contracts using social impact bonds" (Harvard Kennedy School of Government n.d.) and has prepared a *Guide for State and Local Governments* offering detailed instructions for issuing SIBs for social programs (Liebman and Sellman 2013). (SIB Lab director Jeffrey Liebman previously served as chief economist at the federal Office of Management and Budget during the first two years of the Obama administration.) In January 2013, the University of Chicago received a $5 million gift to endow the Social Enterprise Initiative (SEI) within the Booth School of Business "to support initiatives that simultaneously promote entrepreneurial innovation and social benefit . . . in the impact economy" (University of Chicago 2013; http://research .chicagobooth.edu/sei/). That same month, the University of Utah announced receipt of a $13 million donation to the Eccles School of Business to establish the James Lee Sorenson Center for Global Impact Investing (http://www.sgiicenter .com/about/), "to provide students with . . . interaction with industry leaders in the impact investing space." The Policy Innovation Lab within the Sorenson Center received a $3.5 million grant from the federal Corporation for National and Community Service in 2014 to "provide capacity-building funds and high-level technical assistance to governments to explore the feasibility of implementing PFS projects in their jurisdictions" (Corporation for National and Community Service 2014b). Stanford University's *Social Innovation Review* advocated the expansion of SIBs in two articles written by Tracy Palandjian (2013, 2014), the founder and CEO of Social Finance, which describes itself as "a vertically integrated Social Impact Bond intermediary dedicated to launching high-quality Social Impact Bonds in the U.S." (Social Finance, Inc. 2012).

The Financialization of Urban Policy

Financing public purposes with private capital obtained through the sale of bonds has a long history. European monarchs sold bonds to finance territorial wars beginning in the sixteenth century. In the United States, the Pacific Railroad Act of 1862 authorized the federal government to issue thirty-year bonds to help finance the construction of the first transcontinental railroad. Baptist (2014) documents the intricate bond-financing mechanisms that provided the investment capital needed to expand the slave economy (using the bodies of slaves as collateral) throughout the South before the Civil War. In the aftermath of World War II, housing advocate Catherine Bauer recounted the private real estate industry's opposition to expanding the federal public housing program despite postwar shortages, yet pointed to "the spectacle of Wall Street backing public housing because the investment houses find local authority bonds profitable" (Bauer 1946, 68). The Opportunity Funding Corporation (OFC) established by the federal Office of Economic Opportunity (OEO) during the War on Poverty in the early 1970s issued "opportunity bonds" to generate private capital for economic development projects in minority urban communities (Doctors and Lockwood 1971). Four decades later, in 2010, the U.S. Treasury Department announced a Community Development Financial Institutions (CDFI) Bond Guarantee Program to support $325 million in bonds for local community and economic development purposes (Affordable Housing Finance Staff 2014). State and municipal governments and quasi-public authorities across the United States issue general obligation bonds, revenue anticipation bonds, tax anticipation bonds, industrial revenue bonds, and similar instruments to raise revenues for public purposes as a matter of course (Peck and Whiteside 2016).

References to the innovative character of SIBs and PFS may appear misplaced in face of this long historical precedent. As a new form of an enduring practice, by this account, SIBs provide a mechanism to access the private capital needed to bring social programs "to scale" in an era of diminished public resources (Leventhal 2013, 529). Yet while the consistency of the "bond" terminology presents SIBs as a familiar and thus easily understood and accepted financial form, SIBs are not bonds in the traditional meaning of debt instruments and are more properly understood as performance contracts, that is, promises to repay the investor if a stipulated service target or cost savings is attained. More important than the technical distinction, however, and despite the terminological familiarity, the financial logic underlying SIBs produces a radical realignment of ends and means in the structure and implementation of urban social policy. In all of the historical examples above, bond funding provided a means for attaining substantive public goals ranging from territorial wars and plantation agriculture to infrastructure development, public housing, community economic development, and municipal services. With the advent and proliferation of SIBs, a financial return on the funding mechanism is the goal for which substantive programmatic outcomes provide the means. While, previously, attainment of substantive program goals required a means to fund them, now PFS and SIBs name a funding source in search of substantive applications. Adoption of the "bond" nomenclature provides the appearance of continuity with earlier practice but it is precisely that apparent normalcy that allows SIBs to achieve a fundamental reversal of ends and means in the practice of urban social policy without attracting notice or concern.

The reorientation of ends and means within the logic of SIBs both reflects and advances the financialization of urban social policy within the larger transformation of the U.S. economy that has coincided with the Obama presidency. At the level of the economy as a whole, "financialization" refers to the process through which the financial sector commands an increasing share of the economy (Krippner 2005, 2011), ultimately leading to the organization of the economy and society according to the logic and rationality of finance—the "penetration of finance into the fabric of daily life" (Moreno 2014, 244; see also Arrighi 2010; French, Leyshon, and Wainwright 2011; Warner and Clifton 2014). Financialization as a process represents the continuation of what Polanyi described as "the great transformation" accomplished through the intrusion of the market economy into all aspects of social relations, from the market serving as a useful attribute of society to "the running of society as an adjunct to the market" (Polanyi [1944] 2001, 60).

At the level of urban policy, financialization constitutes the most recent phase in the long-term and continuing evolution of urban governance. Observers of the fiscal crisis of the 1980s noted the transformation of urban governance from a managerial logic of project design and program implementation to an entrepreneurial logic of financial deal-making in support of substantive policy goals, a shift necessitated by the massive reduction in public spending ushered in by the neoliberal governance regimes of Reagan and Thatcher (Clarke and Gaile 1989; Fainstein 1991; Harvey 1989; Lake 1993; Leitner 1990). Municipal governance in the pre-1980 managerial city, a legacy of progressive-era political reform, concerned the efficient delivery of municipal services according to principles of scientific management financed through local tax revenues in service of the public interest. The resurgence of global economic competitiveness in the 1970s and 1980s, however, accompanied by the cascading effects of global oil shocks, national economic stagflation, and urban deindustrialization and disinvestment generated strident demands for tax reduction at all levels that forced a retreat from Keynesian monetary and fiscal policies. Taxation, in the process, was rhetorically, politically, and materially redefined from a desirable means to support mass production through social consumption to an anticompetitive and unsustainable cost of production (Jessop 2002). This economic transformation culminated in the antitax pledge disseminated by the conservative political operative Grover Norquist in 1986 and since signed by nearly 2,300 elected officials at all levels of government (Americans for Tax Reform 2013).

The confluence of rapid private disinvestment and the abrupt curtailment of tax-funded public spending, symbolized in the infamous *New York Daily News* (1975) headline "Ford to City: Drop Dead," raised the recurrent and widespread specter of fiscal crises and municipal defaults (Alcaly and Mermelstein 1988; O'Connor 1973). Municipal governance, in response, became entrepreneurial, enacting a "paradigmatic shift" (Clarke and Gaile 1989, 574) from the efficient design of municipal service delivery to the structuring of increasingly complex public–private financing arrangements that enabled and therefore dictated the substantive possibilities for, and effects of, urban programs. A 1986 HUD handbook celebrated "the recent surge of entrepreneurialism throughout the nation . . . lighting the path of America's urban progress and destiny. . . . The name of the urban game today is turning city functions into money-makers," which "requires a creative entrepreneurial mind and solid business sense." City government officials were urged to adopt business-like practices, to partner with business, and "to approach their work as if they were private entrepreneurs" (Duckworth, Simmons, and McNulty 1986, 3–6, 25). The new economic environment of the 1980s and its attendant downward pressure on federal spending required a radical transformation in the practice of urban governance:

> Public entrepreneurs must retool. Grantsmanship skills are no longer salient; even to continue with public entrepreneurial strategies will require a new knowledge base and financing skills more relevant to private capital markets. In particular, learning to make connections with private placement capital markets, to compete on the taxable bond market, and to link with global capital markets are fast becoming essential new local policy skills. (Clarke and Gaile 1989, 591)

The result of this reorientation and retooling was the emergence and refinement of a new set of programmatic approaches and attendant financing mechanisms in the form of tax-increment financing, special district tax schemes, and other revenue-sharing arrangements under the general heading of public–private partnerships for urban and community development.

If the transformation from urban managerialism to entrepreneurial deal-making marked a significant turning point in urban governance in the Reagan era, the shift from entrepreneurialism to financialization during the Obama presidency marks the next generation in the continuing evolution of the underlying logic governing the aims, design, and effects of urban public policy. While the entrepreneurial turn in the 1980s reoriented urban governance toward an encounter with finance, now financialization refers to the ascendance of finance to a dominant position driving urban governance in the twenty-first century. Within the realm of urban policy, financialization refers to the reimagining, repurposing, redesign, and implementation of urban governance as a practice directed by the logic of the financing instrument rather than a practice driven by the social and economic needs of urban residents (Lake 2015). Under financialization, the calculus of profitability of the investment vehicle becomes the medium—the language, the conceptual frame, the underlying logic, and the discursive field—within and through which urban governance is practiced and urban policy is formulated and enacted. In this context, PFS and SIBs represent the most recent manifestation of financialization as the process through which financial rationality becomes entrenched as the governing logic of urban public policy.

SIBs and the Subordination of Urban Policy

Because PFS and SIBs name a funding mechanism rather than a substantive focus, they select policy objectives and program designs congruent with the underlying logic of the financial instrument rather than in furtherance of a social purpose. Programs that do not correspond to this logic are unlikely to be financed in a context of declining public funds for social programs. Program selectivity occurs at the level of substantive focus, delineating the locus and nature of the problem to be addressed and aligning the corresponding policy response with the problem as defined (Cohen 2014; McHugh et al. 2013).

According to the Nonprofit Finance Fund, "PFS/SIBs work best in funding preventative or early intervention programs" (Nonprofit Finance Fund 2015). In every program implemented to date, SIBs fund a social service provider to deliver a preventative intervention intended to reduce the incidence of problematic behavior. The most commonly targeted behaviors—criminal recidivism, homelessness, poor health care practices, insufficient educational preparation, and poor parenting—are viewed as amenable to correction through counseling, therapy, education, training, or other techniques of behavioral modification. SIBs fund service providers to work with clients to correct their dysfunctional behaviors.

The Peterborough Prison SIB, for example, targeted the high rate of reoffending among male prisoners released after serving less-than-one-year sentences. An interim report reviewing the program's first year found that "68% have a substance misuse (addiction) need" and "66% have an Attitudes, Thinking and Behaviour (ATB) need (e.g., anger management, communications difficulties)" (Helbitz et al. 2011, 16–18). The $8 million raised through the sale of SIBs funded a network of twelve partner organizations engaged in a variety of behavioral interventions designed to help released offenders make better life decisions and thereby reduce the rate of repeat offending and reincarceration. Service providers sought to "instill the aspiration that everyone can change" and delivered therapeutic treatments aimed to "reduce anti-social behavior," "help . . . service users . . . to identify and achieve their goals," and help "offenders live a stable, healthy, law-abiding life" (Helbitz et al. 2011, 31–34). In the same vein, the $9.6 million SIB-funded ABLE program to reduce recidivism among juvenile offenders at Rikers Island prison in New York City delivered Moral Reconation Therapy (MRT), described as a cognitive behavioral intervention designed to promote "the process of relearning how to think and act as a responsible person" (Osborne Association 2012). A description of MRT on a U.S. Department of Health and Human Services Web site explains that:

> Moral Reconation Therapy (MRT) is a systematic treatment strategy that seeks to decrease recidivism among juvenile and adult criminal offenders by increasing moral reasoning. Its cognitive-behavioral approach combines elements . . . to . . . progressively address ego, social, moral, and positive behavioral growth . . . focusing on seven basic treatment issues: confrontation of beliefs, attitudes, and behaviors; assessment of current relationships; reinforcement of positive behavior and habits; positive identity formation; enhancement of self-concept; decrease in hedonism and development of frustration tolerance; and development of higher stages of moral reasoning. (U.S. Department of Health and Human Services n.d.)

Such cognitive interventions aim to reduce behaviors that otherwise produce repeated criminal offenses and high recidivism rates. The criminal offenses producing recidivism in Peterborough, according to the independent evaluator's program assessment, are breach of court order, drug possession, burglary, drunk driving, weapons possession, and breach of a suspended sentence (Jolliffe and Hedderman 2014, 14–15). An illustration is provided in the case of Bryan reported in the program's first-year review:

> He has a court order which prevents him drinking in public. If he opens a can of beer this means he can be arrested. This happens often because he is a homeless alcoholic. He's not a quiet drunk. On a good day he sings loudly and will become overfamiliar with passers-by, on a bad day he will be insulting. Working together under the One*Service umbrella, (service providers) can achieve a sustainable, long-term outcome which enables Bryan to make choices about how he lives in the future. We are working with him to consider the social aspects of his previous lifestyle so relationships can be managed in ways that do not cause a nuisance to others. (Helbitz et al. 2011, 24)

In this example and others, the focus of SIBs on funding preventative interventions situates the problem of criminal recidivism in the dysfunctional behavioral choices and deficient moral reasoning of reoffenders. The governing policy logic conflates the undeniable need for improved mental health services, ironically exacerbated by previous reductions in tax-supported public spending, with a generalized characterization of the problem as situated in dysfunctional individual behaviors that can be corrected with the expenditure of capital raised through the sale of SIBs. Because the locus of the problem is in individual behavior, the solution lies in interventions aimed at altering behaviors through attainment of "higher stages of moral reasoning" leading to a "decrease in hedonism" and the ability to "make better life choices." Alternative understandings of the problem that, for example, would reduce the recidivism rate by removing nuisance behaviors from the criminal justice system—in Bryan's case, treating alcoholism as a medical problem rather than a criminal recidivism problem—are not encompassed within the logic of the funding mechanism and are disregarded. The focus on individual behaviors, furthermore, leaves structural barriers and institutional impediments intact, requiring individuals to improve their "frustration tolerance" rather than addressing the structural inequities or institutional practices that frustrate individual advancement and deepen social inequality. Such deep-seated societal reform is not only unattainable through SIBs funding but is likely to be actively resisted as destabilizing of the structural privileges that establish a financier class able to realize the profit to be made by investing in SIBs. A description of the ABLE program at Rikers Island traces the link between behavioral remediation and investors' profits: "By providing cognitive behavioral services at Rikers, ABLE aims to equip these teenagers with the social and emotional skills to help make better life choices when they leave jail, hopefully leading, in turn, to improved life outcomes, a reduction in the recidivism rate, financial savings to government, and eventually returns to private investors" (Berlin 2014).

Subsumed within the transformational process of financialization, PFS/SIBs are an investment vehicle rather than a social policy instrument and, consequently, "tend to focus on proving the efficacy (and profitability) of the financing mechanism and less on the social policies to be demonstrated and disseminated" (Cohen 2015a). The monetization of policy goals, as suggested earlier, transforms substantive social outcomes from the status of ends in themselves to a means for reducing government spending and producing a financial return for investors. According to Tracy Palandjian, CEO of Social Finance, Inc., "the financial engine for SIBs is 'monetizing future government saving,' which isn't a standard and well-understood investable asset" (Kanani 2012).

By transforming policy objectives into monetary terms, SIBs are more properly understood as an element of fiscal and tax policy than of social policy (McHugh et al. 2013; Warner 2015). The opportunity to access private capital is particularly salient in the long-term context of declining public resources and ideological barriers to taxation as a revenue source for public programs (Roman et al. 2014). In this context, SIBs represent a new asset class that provides access to previously untapped resources of private capital:

> By monetizing social outcomes, Social Impact Bonds create an asset that investors can invest in, expanding the pot of money available beyond philanthropy and government grants to true investment capital. . . . There are some $200 trillion of financial assets; creating a pipeline from social outcomes to these $200 trillion forms a pathway to a new world. (Leventhal 2013, 529; see also Cohen and Sahlman 2013)

The logic of Pay for Success justifies SIBs as a cost-saving strategy when preventative interventions reduce the need for government-funded programs that are widely characterized as "remedial, ineffective and expensive" (Godeke and Resner 2014, i). The savings achieved by reducing or even eliminating the need for public programs are used to compensate investors:

> PFS investors can play a critical role by providing the risk capital to scale preventative programs in exchange for a return on their investment. This risk and return tradeoff will only be achieved with interventions in which there are sufficient savings to compensate the investors as well as provide cost savings to the taxpayers. (Godeke and Resner 2014, 9)

The announcement of H.R. 4885, the Social Impact Bond Act, introduced in Congress in June 2014, references "saving government money" and "saving taxpayer dollars" at least thirteen times in a one-page press release (Young and Delaney 2014). The proposed legislation, according to its sponsors, will "save government money," "realize government savings," "save hardworking taxpayers money," "prevent government waste," "ensure more effective use of tax-payer dollars," and "incentivize the realization of savings across multiple layers of government." A Princeton University report unequivocally states that "the purpose of the SIB model is to generate cost-savings for a government" and that "the biggest motivator for governments to implement SIBs is the potential for cost-savings" (Princeton University Woodrow Wilson School 2014, 8–10). Following the logic of monetization to its conclusion, the cost savings achieved through program interventions are used by government to repay investors and the ability to do so is the primary criterion defining success. The inability of a program to achieve its contractual target (e.g., a 10 percent first-year reduction in recidivism) is not interpreted as a substantive policy failure but as creating an unacceptable investment risk that threatens continued access to private capital (Barby and Gan 2015).

The interrelated policy goals of public cost-saving and investor return are congruent with the long-run transformations affecting the economies of the U.S. and

UK in the first decades of the twenty-first century. While SIBs are often described as benefiting the double-bottom-line of both governments and investors, the logics of monetization and financialization provide a double benefit to private capital: a direct benefit in the form of return on investment and the indirect benefit realized through the reduced tax burden attained through lower government spending.

The Obama Administration in the Age of Financialization

That the financialization of urban policy emerged at this particular historical moment suggests that the Obama administration is an observer rather than the initiator of the transformational processes currently under way. The 2011 White House convening advocating the Pay for Success model for urban social programs was less the bold policy innovation claimed by its proponents than a recognition of and capitulation to an increasingly financialized political economy. The path from a market economy to entrepreneurial governance to the hegemonic dominance of financial rationality can be traced over decades if not centuries, both reflecting and enacting the onward march of neoliberalization within the urban process (Peck 2010; Polanyi [1944] 2001). Rather than inaugurating a new policy model, the Obama administration's enthusiastic embrace of PFS and SIBs reflects an inevitable path-dependency in which urban social policy aligns with the prevailing trend.

Replacing conventional ideas of governing in and through the state, the financialization of urban policy advances the ideology and practice of networked governance involving the finely calibrated interaction of multiple actors spanning the public, private, and nonprofit sectors. The ascendancy of networked governance proceeds through the continuous and highly contested negotiation of the elusive boundaries between the market, state, and civil society (Jessop 2002; Lake 1997, 2002). Networked governance under financialization appears both operationally—in the design and implementation of specific policy instruments such as SIBs—and, at the broadest level, in the enactment of institutional arrangements and ideological formations.

Operationally, implementation of a social impact bond generates private capital to fund a nonprofit service provider to produce savings that the state uses to repay the private investor. The model's success depends equally on each actor fulfilling its role and the practice of governance is dispersed among the interdependent participants, with as yet unaddressed implications for democratic accountability. More broadly, institutionalizing a financialized governing rationality for urban social policy requires the complexly orchestrated interactions of multiple participants pursuing mutually supportive institutional and ideological agendas. The growth and expansion of the financial industry does not fuel the financialization process in the abstract but requires the continuous invention of new products and markets. Social Impact Bonds constitute a robust growth sector within the burgeoning global market for impact investing and social entrepreneurship, with the financial industry aggressively marketing the idea that investors can accomplish a social purpose while obtaining a robust return on their investment (Cohen and Bannick 2014). The Global Impact Investing Network (GIIN), for example, a collaborative with more than 225 banking, foundation, and investment industry members, seeks to "accelerate the development of a coherent impact investing industry" as part of the global marketing of the ideology and practice of social impact investing and social entrepreneurialism (Global Impact Investing Network n.d.).

Markets, however, do not create themselves, and expanding the financialization of social policy requires active facilitation and intervention by the state, articulated through monetary and fiscal reform, processes of regulation and deregulation, discursive statements, ideological formulations, and White House convenings (Krippner 2011; Lake 2002). As Polanyi ([1944] 2001) famously observed, "laissez-faire was planned" and markets cannot operate without the constitutive enactments of the state. The massive reduction in federal spending on social programs initiated by the Reagan presidency in the 1980s and echoed in the 2013 budget sequestration attendant on the recent economic crisis were not the least of the state's actions mediating and facilitating the growth of private funding for urban social policy.

Finally, the mobilization of private capital for social entrepreneurialism required an investment target in the form of an increasingly professionalized and corporatized nonprofit sector able to deliver social services at a scale sufficient to satisfy the burgeoning demand created by the new investment vehicles (Newman and Lake 2006). The Urban Investment Group at Goldman Sachs, for example, has capitalized approximately $5 billion in "impact investing initiatives" since its inauguration in 2001 (Goldman Sachs 2016), requiring the nonprofit sector, in turn, to "scale up" its service-delivery capacity to keep pace. The accelerated development of social metrics and calculative methods of policy evaluation, such as the Robin Hood Foundation's "relentless monetization" of program outcomes used to "assign a dollar figure to the amount of philanthropic good that a grant does per dollar of costs" (Robin Hood n.d.), has rationalized and solidified the relationship between financial investors and nonprofit recipients, with significant if as yet insufficiently documented effects on the composition and practices of the nonprofit sector.

Once achieved through the confluence of interests enacting the financialization of the economy, the dominance of finance in the sphere of social policy appears irreversible. The resulting reversal of ends and means mobilizes social policy on behalf of profitable investment outcomes and financialization is the process through which seeing like a state means enacting policy as a financial transaction. Most disadvantaged in the resulting policy practice are the client recipients of the behavioral interventions provided through the policy mechanism, whose behavioral failures are targeted as the problem to be rectified while the underlying structural and institutional determinants of life chances in a financialized society remain intact.

Note

1. For full text and current status, see leginfo.legislature.ca.gov/faces/billNavClient.xhtml?bill
   _id=201320140ab1837 and leginfo.legislature.ca.gov/faces/billNavClinet.xhtml?bill_id
   =201320140sb9.

References

Affordable Housing Finance Staff. 2014. "New CDFI Bond Program Funds Housing." *Affordable Housing Finance*, August 21. http://www.housingfinance.com/finance/new-cdfi-bond-program-funds-housing_0.

Alcaly, Roger E., and David Mermelstein. 1988. *The Fiscal Crisis of American Cities: Essays on the Political Economy of Urban America with Special Reference to New York*. New York: Random House.

Americans for Tax Reform. 2013. "Taxpayer Protection Pledge Database." http://www.atr.org/pledge-database.

Arrighi, Giovanni. 2010. *The Long Twentieth Century: Money, Power and the Origin of Our Times*. London: Verso.

Bank, David. 2012. "How Financial Innovation Can Save the World." *The Atlantic*, May 31. http://www.theatlantic.com/business/archive/2012/05/how-financial-innovation-can-save-the-world/257920.

Baptist, Edward E. 2014. *The Half Has Never Been Told: Slavery and the Making of American Capitalism*. New York: Basic Books.

Barby, Clara, and Joanne Gan. 2015. *Shifting the Lens: A De-Risking Toolkit for Impact Investment*. London: Bridges Ventures. http://www.trilincglobal.com/wp-content/uploads/2014/01/BV_BoA_de-risking_report_FINAL-2.pdf.

Barclay, Lisa, and Tom Symons. 2013. *A Technical Guide to Social Impact Bond Development*. London: Social Finance, Ltd.

Bauer, Catherine. 1946. "Is Urban Redevelopment Possible Under Existing Legislation?" *Planning 1946. Proceedings of the Annual Meeting, American Society of Planning Officials*, 62–70.

Berlin, Gordon. 2014. "Turning the 'Pay for Success' Promise into Performance." New York: MDRC. http://www.mdrc.org/publication/turning-pay-success-promise-performance.

Burton, Paul. 2012. "'Social Impact Bonds' Generate Buzz in New York, Massachusetts." *The Bond Buyer*, September 7. http://www.bondbuyer.com/issues/121_174/new-york-and-massachusetts-are-exploring-social-impact-bonds-1043748-1.html.

Butler, David, Dan Bloom, and Timothy Rudd. 2013. "Using Social Impact Bonds to Spur Innovation, Knowledge Building, and Accountability." *Community Development Investment Review* 9: 57–62.

Clarke, Susan E., and Gary L. Gaile. 1989. "Moving Toward Entrepreneurial Economic Development Policies: Opportunities and Barriers." *Policy Studies Journal* 17 (3): 574–98.

Cohen, Rick. 2014. "Social Impact Bonds: Phantom of the Nonprofit Sector." *Nonprofit Quarterly*, July 26.

———. 2015a. "The 2016 Federal Budget: What Nonprofits Should Know." *Nonprofit Quarterly*, February 5.

———. 2015b. "Wall Street Finds Social Impact Bonds to Be Attractive Investment Options." *Nonprofit Quarterly*, January 26.

Cohen, Ronald, and Matt Bannick. 2014. "Is Social Impact Investing the Next Venture Capital?" *Forbes*, September 20. http://www.forbes.com/sites/realspin/2014/09/20/is-social-impact-investing-the-next-venture-capital/.

Cohen, Ronald, and William A. Sahlman. 2013. "Social Impact Investing Will Be the New Venture Capital." *HBR Blog Network*. http://blogs.hbr.org/cs/2013/01/social_impact_investing_will_b.html.

Corporation for National and Community Service. 2014a. "Federal Program Marks Fifth Anniversary; Announces $51.8 Million in Investments to Grow Community Solutions That Work." http://www.nationalservice.gov/newsroom/press-releases/2014/federal-program-marks-fifth-anniversary-announces-518-million.

———. 2014b. Sorensen Impact Center at the University of Utah's David Eccles School of Business. Grantee Information. http://www.nationalservice.gov/programs/social-innovation-fund/pay-for-success/university-utah-policy-innovation-lab.

DePillis, Lydia. 2013. "Goldman Sachs Thinks it Can Make Money by Being a Do-Gooder." *Washington Post,* November 5.

Doctors, Samuel I., and Sharon Lockwood. 1971. "Opportunity Funding Corporation: An Analysis." *Law and Contemporary Problems* 36: 227–37.

Duckworth, Robert, John Simmons, and Robert McNulty. 1986. *The Entrepreneurial American City.* Washington, D.C.: U.S. Department of Housing and Urban Development and Partners for Livable Places.

Economist. 2013. "Social-Impact Bonds: Commerce and Conscience," February 23. http://www.economist.com/news/finance-and-economics/21572231-new-way-financing-public-services-gains-momentum-commerce-and-conscience.

Fainstein, Susan. 1991. "Promoting Economic Development: Urban Planning in the United States and Great Britain." *Journal of the American Planning Association* 57 (1): 22–33.

Federal Register. 2013. "Strategies to Accelerate the Testing and Adoption of Pay for Success (PFS) Financing Models." Department of the Treasury, Office of Domestic Finance. 78 (191) (October 2) 60998–61000.

French, Shaun, Andrew Leyshon, and Thomas Wainwright. 2011. "Financializing Space, Spacing Financialization." *Progress in Human Geography* 35 (6): 798–819.

Galloway, Ian. 2013. "Forward: Pay for Success Financing." *Community Development Investment Review* 9: 2–3.

Global Impact Investing Network. n.d. "About GIIN." https://thegiin.org/about/.

Godeke, Steven, and Lyel Resner. 2014. *Building a Healthy and Sustainable Social Impact Bond Market: The Investor Landscape.* New York: Godeke Consulting and the Rockefeller Foundation.

Goldman Sachs. 2015. "GS Social Impact Fund." http://www.goldmansachs.com/what-we-do/investing-and-lending/impact-investing/social-impact-bonds/gs-social-impact-fund-fact-sheet.pdf.

———. 2016. "Impact Investing." Goldmansachs.com. Accessed April 14, 2016. www.goldmansachs.com/what-we-do/investing-and-lending/impact-investing.

Greenblatt, Jonathan, and Annie Donovan. 2013. "The Promise of Pay for Success." *Community Development Investment Review* 9: 19–22.

Harvard Kennedy School of Government. n.d. Government Performance Lab, Social Impact Bond Lab. govlab.hks.harvard.edu/social-impact-bond-lab.

Harvey, David. 1989. "From Managerialism to Entrepreneurialism: The Transformation of Urban Governance in Late Capitalism." *Geografiska Annaler* 71 (1): 3–17.

Helbitz, Alisa, Janette Powell, Emily Bolton, Suzanne Ashman, and Sarah Henderson. 2011. *Social Impact Bonds. The One*Service. One Year On. Reducing Reoffending Among Short-Sentenced Male Offenders from Peterborough Prison.* London: Social Finance, Ltd.

Jensen, Randall. 2013. "'Social Impact Bond' Buzz Heads West." *The Bond Buyer,* January 10.

Jessop, Bob. 2002. *The Future of the Capitalist State.* New York: Wiley.

Johnson, Fawn. 2015. "Goldman Sachs Invests in Government and Expects to Be Paid Back." *National Journal,* January 19.

Jolliffe, Darrick, and Carol Hedderman. 2014. "Peterborough Social Impact Bond: Final Report on Cohort 1 Analysis." Prepared for Ministry of Justice, August 7. London: QinetiQ.

Kanani, Rahim. 2012. "Rethinking the Role of Capital Markets in Enabling Social Progress," *Forbes,* April 19. http://www.forbes.com/sites/rahimkanani/2012/04/19/the-role-of-capital-markets-in-enabling-social-progress/.

Kelly, Andrew, and Michael McShane. 2013. "Private Money, Public Good." American Enterprise Institute, February 18. www.aei.org/publication/private-money-public-good.

Kohli, Jitinder, Douglas Beharov, and Kristina Costa. 2012. "Inside a Social Impact Bond Agreement: Exploring the Contract Challenges of a New Social Finance Mechanism." Center for American Progress.

Krippner, Greta R. 2005. "The Financialization of the American Economy." *Socio-Economic Review* 3 (2): 173–208.

——. 2011. *Capitalizing on Crisis.* Cambridge, Mass.: Harvard University Press.

Lake, Robert W. 1993. "Planning and Applied Geography: Positivism, Ethics, and Geographic Information Systems." *Progress in Human Geography* 17 (3): 404–13.

——. 1997. "State Restructuring, Political Opportunism, and Capital Mobility." In *State Devolution in America: Implications for a Diverse Society,* ed. Lynn A. Staeheli, Janet E. Kodras, and Colin R. Flint, 3–20. Urban Affairs Annual Reviews 48. Newbury Park, Calif.: Sage.

——. 2002. "Bring Back Big Government." *International Journal of Urban and Regional Research* 26 (4): 815–22.

——. 2015. "The Financialization of Urban Policy in the Age of Obama." *Journal of Urban Affairs* 37 (1): 75–78.

Leitner, Helga. 1990. "Cities in Pursuit of Economic Growth: The Local State as Entrepreneur." *Political Geography Quarterly* 9 (2): 146–70.

Leventhal, Rebecca. 2013. "Effecting Progress: Using Social Impact Bonds to Finance Social Services." *NYU Journal of Law and Business* 9: 511–34.

Liebman, Jeffrey. 2011. *Social Impact Bonds: A Promising new Financing Model to Accelerate Social Innovation and Improve Government Performance.* Washington, DC: Center for American Progress.

Liebman, Jeffrey, and Alina Sellman. 2013. *Social Impact Bonds: A Guide for State and Local Governments.* Cambridge, Mass: Harvard Kennedy School Social Impact Bond Technical Assistance Lab. http://www.payforsuccess.org/sites/default/files/social-impact-bonds-a-guide-for-state-and-local-governments1.pdf.

McHugh, Neil, Stephen Sinclair, Michael Roy, Leslie Huckfield, and Cam Donaldson. 2013. "Social Impact Bonds: A Wolf in Sheep's Clothing?" *Journal of Poverty and Social Justice* 21 (3): 247–57.

McKinsey and Company. 2012. *From Potential to Action: Bringing Social Impact Bonds to the U.S.* New York: McKinsey and Company.

Moreno, Louis. 2014. "The Urban Process under Financialised Capitalism." *City* 18 (3): 244–68.

Munoz, Cecilia, and Robert Gordon. 2012. "Pay for Success: A New Results-oriented Federal Commitment for Underserved Americans." *White House Blog,* January 24. Accessed March 28, 2013. http://www.whitehouse.gov/blog/2012/01/24/pay-success-new-results-oriented-federal-commitment-underserved-americans.

Newman, Kathe, and Robert W. Lake. 2006. "Democracy, Bureaucracy and Difference in U.S. Community Development Politics since 1968." *Progress in Human Geography* 30 (1): 44–61.

New York City. 2012a. "Mayor Bloomberg, Deputy Mayor Gibbs and Corrections Commissioner Schriro Announce Nation's First Social Impact Bond Program." City of New York, Office of the Mayor, August 2.

——. 2012b. "Fact Sheet: The NYC ABLE Project for Incarcerated Youth. America's First Social Impact Bond." City of New York, Office of the Mayor, August 2.

New York Daily News. 1975. http://www.nydailynews.com/new-york/president-ford-announces-won-bailout-nyc-1975-article-1.2405985.

Nonprofit Finance Fund. 2012. "Pay for Success: Investing in What Works." Accessed March 28, 2013. http://payforsuccess.org/sites/default/files/pay_for_success_report_2012.pdf.

——. 2014. "Regional Summits." Pay for Success. http://payforsuccesssummit.org/index.html.

——. 2015. "Frequently Asked Questions: Pay for Success/Social Impact Bonds." http://www.nonprofitfinancefund.org/sites/default/files/pfs_faq.pdf.

————. 2016. "Pay for Success U.S. Activity." Pay for Success Learning Hub. Accessed May 10, 2016. http://payforsucess.org/pay-success-deals-united-states.

————. n.d. "PFS 101." Pay for Success Learning Hub. Accessed January 20, 2014. http://payfor success.org/learn-out-loud/pfs-101.

O'Connor, James. 1973. *The Fiscal Crisis of the State.* New York: St. Martin's Press.

Olson, John, and Andrea Phillips. 2013. "Rikers Island: The First Social Impact Bond in the United States." *Community Development Investment Review* 9: 97–101. http://www.frbsf.org/commu nity-development/files/rikers-island-first-social-impact-bond-united-states.pdf.

Osborne Association. 2012. Moral Reconation Therapy. www.osborneNY.org/programSubPage .cfm?subPageID=44.

Palandjian, Tracy. 2013. "The Social Impact Bond Market: Three Scenarios for the Future." *Stanford Social Innovation Review,* December 19.

————. 2014. "Foundations for Social Impact Bonds." *Stanford Social Innovation Review,* March 19.

Peck, Jamie. 2010. *Constructions of Neoliberal Reason.* New York: Oxford University Press.

Peck, Jamie, and Heather Whiteside. 2016. "Financializing Detroit." *Economic Geography* DOI.10 .1080/00130095.2015.1116369.

Polanyi, Karl. (1944) 2001. *The Great Transformation: The Political and Economic Origins of Our Time.* Boston: Beacon Press. Citations refer to the 2001 edition.

Preston, Caroline. 2012. "Getting Back More Than a Warm Feeling." *New York Times,* November 8.

Princeton University Woodrow Wilson School. 2014. *Social Impact Bonds: A New Tool for Social Financing.* http://wws.princeton.edu/sites/default/files/content/Social%20Impact%20Bo nds%202014%20Final%20Report.pdf.

Quinton, Sophie. 2013. "How Goldman Sachs Can Help Save the Safety Net." *National Journal,* May 9.

Robin Hood. n.d. "Metrics." Robinhood.org. Accessed on April 14, 2016. https://www.robinhood .org/metrics.

Roman, John, Kelly Walsh, Samuel Bieler, and Samuel A. Taxy. 2014. *Five Steps to Pay for Success: Implementing Pay for Success Projects in the Juvenile and Criminal Justice Systems.* Washington, D.C.: The Urban Institute.

Rosenberg, Tina. 2012. "The Promise of Social Impact Bonds," *New York Times,* June 20.

Rudd, Timothy, Elisa Nicoletti, Kristen Misner, and Janae Bonsu. 2013. *Financing Promising Evidence-Based Programs: Early Lessons from the New York City Social Impact Bond.* New York: MDRC.

Social Finance, Inc. 2012. "A New Tool for Scaling Impact: How Social Impact Bonds Can Mobilize Private Capital to Advance Social Good." White paper. Boston: Social Finance, Inc. http://www.payforsuccess.org/sites/default/files/small.socialfinancewpsinglefinal.pdf.

Social Finance, Ltd. 2011. *Social Impact Bonds: The One Service, One Year On; Reducing Reoffending Among Short Sentenced Male Offenders from Peterborough Prison.* London: Social Finance, Ltd. Accessed May 10, 2016. http://www.socialfinance.org.uk/wp-content/uploads/2014/07 /SF_PETERBOROUGH_ONE-_YEAR_ON.pdf.

University of Chicago. 2013. "John Edwardson Gives $5 Million to University of Chicago Booth School of Business." *UChicago News,* January 29. Accessed February 12, 2013. http://news .uchicago.edu/article/2013/01/29/john-edwardson-gives-5-million-university-chicago -booth-school-business.

U.S. Department of Health and Human Services. n.d. "Moral Reconation Therapy." Substance Abuse and Mental Health Services Administration, SAMSA's National Register of Evidence-Based Programs and Practices. legacy.nreppadmin.net/viewIntervention.aspx?id=34.

Wallace, N. 2014. "With a Few Pay for Success Plans Under Way, the Idea Is Gaining Currency and Criticism," *Chronicle of Philanthropy,* July 13.

Warner, Mildred. 2015. "Profiting From Public Value? The Case of Social Impact Bonds." In *Creating Public Value in Practice: Advancing the Common Good in a Multi-Sector, Shared-Power,*

No-One-Wholly-in-Charge World, ed. John Bryson, Barbara C. Crosby, and Laura Bloomberg, 143–46. Public Administration and Public Policy. New York: CRC Press.

Warner, Mildred, and Judith Clifton. 2014. "Marketization, Public Services and the City: The Potential for Polanyian Counter Movements." *Cambridge Journal of Regions, Economy and Society* 7: 45–61.

Young, Todd, and John Delaney. 2014. "Reps. Young and Delaney Introduce Social Impact Bond Act." Press release issued June 18, 2014. http://toddyoung.house.gov/press-releases/reps -young-and-delaney-introduce-social-impact-bond-act/.

3

OBAMA, RACE, AND URBAN POLICY
_____

PRESTON H. SMITH II

Obama, Race, and the Post-Racial Debate

The 2008 election of Barack Obama touched off a furious debate over the state of race relations in the United States. The pronouncements in the media and in political circles that the United States had entered a "post-racial era" with the election of the nation's first African American president has elicited a swift and strong response from scholars who have taken pains to demonstrate that racial inequality still persists. While these scholars agree that the United States is far from being post-racial, they disagree over the role Obama has played in aiding and abetting this perception through his discourse and policies (Metzler 2010; Dawson 2012; Harris 2012, 2009; Smith and King 2014). One group of scholars argues that Obama's race-neutral discourse and policies have restricted his ability to respond effectively to the particular concerns of black citizens. These scholars claim Obama entered into a Faustian bargain with whites, receiving their vote in exchange for avoiding discussions about race (Metzler 2010; Harris 2009). A different set of scholars argue that Obama appeals to both race-conscious and color-blind policy alliances by addressing racial disparity indirectly through his inclusive rhetoric and universal policies (Smith and King 2014). According to their view, the lack of prominence of race in Obama's discourse and policy agenda should not be interpreted as a lack of commitment to advancing the interests of African Americans (Fraser 2009; Powell 2009; Wilson 2009).

Because there is considerable overlap between racial and urban policy in the United States, this post-racial debate might be expected to provide a framework for analyzing Obama's urban policies. The problem with this debate, however, is that each side is mainly focused on race, either its absence or presence. The preoccupation with the post-racial debate means that Obama's underclass discourse and the neoliberal urban policies it informs are mistakenly understood in an exclusively racial context, which inexorably calls for a racial policy solution to African Americans' urban problems. Compounding this misunderstanding is the interpretation of Obama's class-inflected discourse as a black "politics of respectability" which elides the material stakes involved and minimizes the range of choices available to black policy elites in urban governance.

While it is important to criticize the assumption of color-blind ideology that racial inequality does not exist, and to acknowledge that race-targeted policies would provide some needed aid for black urban citizens, it is unlikely that racial policies could successfully challenge the neoliberal policy logic adopted by Obama that rules out broad social redistribution to combat economic inequality. Scholars who advocate for race-targeted policies are mistakenly assuming that neoliberal policy is consistent only with a color-blind approach to racial inequality (Mele 2013). However, they fail to realize that policies aimed at correcting racial disparities can also fit within a neoliberal ideological orbit (Reed and Chowkwanyun 2012). I would argue that by examining Obama's discourse through a historical materialist lens, we can gain a clearer picture of the political economic logic informing Obama's urban policy. Despite Obama's calls for smarter government intervention, his commitment to market-based policies reflects his underlying political commitments to a neoliberal urban policy agenda and the class-inflected priorities that agenda entails. Unfortunately, the post-racial debate only distracts us from the need to ascertain the ways in which Obama's urban policies reflect a class-inflected politics that continues to hurt poor blacks and other low-income citizens.

Obama, Race, and Underclass Discourse

Scholars who are critical of Obama and his refusal to craft and implement race-targeted policies lament that the primary way in which Obama attempts to connect with his African American constituents is through his message of personal responsibility (Harris 2012; Sinclair-Chapman and Price 2008). For instance, Obama writes that government can help poor blacks, but "a transformation in attitudes has to begin in the home, and in neighborhoods, and in places of worship" (2006, 245). In a call that foreshadows his Choice Neighborhoods and Promise Neighborhoods initiatives, he insists that "community-based institutions, particularly the historically black church, have to help families reinvigorate in young people a reverence for educational achievement, encourage healthier lifestyles, and reenergize traditional social norms surrounding the joys and obligations of fatherhood" (2006, 245).[1] He claims that, privately, African Americans are disturbed by the "eroding work ethic, inadequate parenting, and declining sexual mores" in the community (2006, 248). It is these deficiencies that Obama refers to as "our own complicity in our condition" (2009, 46).

Political scientist Fred Harris argues that Obama's fixation on the personal responsibility discourse means Obama practices a "politics of respectability." This politics has a long history among black elites going back to black Baptist women, Booker T. Washington, and the "talented tenth" argument that dominated black political discourse at the turn of the twentieth century. In particular, this black political tradition endorses "hard work, conservatism and moral uprightness" as keys to racial equality (Sinclair-Chapman and Price 2008, 739). The politics of respectability focuses on correcting the behavior and habits of working-class blacks in order for all blacks to gain acceptance by white America (Harris 2012). Obama concurs that blacks' common racial identity "makes all of us only as free, only as respected, as the least of us" (2006, 255). However, he adds that the link between affluent and poor blacks is not simply bound by white racial stereotypes, but by blacks' understanding that poor blacks' "self-destructive behavior" is not "innate," but a result of "culture shaped by circumstance" (255). Presumably, if "America" can change the circumstance, "individual attitudes among the poor will change in kind" (255). This environmental logic follows a somewhat different causality than that embodied in his discussion of the need for a "transformation in attitudes" to accompany or even precede policy change. Rather than the ambiguous "America," Obama's hope and change message implies that as president he would begin to change those circumstances. The question is whether his signature urban policies such as the Choice Neighborhoods and the Promise Neighborhoods, in combination with his other policy priorities, will really change those circumstances.

Harris has argued that since black leaders are now partners in the U.S. political regime, "the politics of respectability" has moved from the black community into mainstream American politics (2012). For instance, black elites' public endorsement of draconian policies aimed at low-income blacks legitimizes these "racist practices and policies" (104). Harris points out that after first securing the loyalty of black voters after his Iowa primary victory in 2008, Obama shifted his rhetoric in order to allay white voters' fears that racial minorities would be favored by his administration (Harris 2009, 2012). African Americans, after consuming a steady diet of personal responsibility discourse since the 1980s from both conservatives and liberals, are divided over whether individual behavior or social forces are to blame for the challenges facing black communities (Harris 2009; P. Smith 1999; Reed 1999). Ironically, Harris concludes perceptively, personal responsibility was "a familiar discourse that reinforced the candidate's connections with black voters under the guise of tough love" (2012, 104).

In this discourse, the demonization of poor blacks mostly focuses on their individual failings rather than on structural barriers to their progress. It ends up being, to Harris' disappointment, a "social policy solution" for dealing with the extreme poverty of working-class blacks and its consequences (2012). He argues that although the politics of respectability predates neoliberalism, it is quite consistent with the individual, market-based logic of the latter (Harris 2012; Dawson 2012). Thus the assumption that economic self-sufficiency is possible without altering patterns of public policy, Harris explains, is legitimized by this black-elite respectability discourse, making it politically easier to withhold substantial government support from the poor (Harris 2012). He adds that low-income blacks are told that unless they exhibit greater personal responsibility they do not deserve public benefits (Harris 2012). Harris concludes that middle-class blacks support these efforts because they "believe that black poor people need to be policed by black elites and by the state" (2012, 135). The close collaboration of middle- and upper-class blacks with the state is an indication of how black politics has changed in the post-segregation era.

When it comes to relating to black voters Obama borrowed from Clinton's play-book by presenting a folksy familiarity while avoiding substantive racial policies (Harris 2009; Fraser 2009). Of course, Obama adds the powerful symbol of *actually* being the nation's first black president, rather than a white president anointed by a few notable black literary and political elites. In general, Obama has embraced the centrist policy model inaugurated by Bill Clinton and the Democratic Leadership Council (Sinclair-Chapman and Price 2008). Not only did Clinton avoid substantive race-conscious policies, he also instituted punitive social policies such as the crime bill, welfare reform, and the demolition of public housing (Fraser 2009; Reed 2014; Klinkner 1999). In fact, consistent with the underclass policy discourse of the 1990s, Clinton stressed "personal responsibility" to working-class blacks while his policies sought to punish and contain them (Wacquant 2008; Harris 2009; Reed 2014). Obama (2006) has endorsed Clinton's welfare reform, which ended entitlement to income support for those who could not find living-wage work. He has continued the same broad policy trends of economic deregulation and commodification of public goods, which continue to produce a low-wage service economy and a punitive state (Wacquant 2008). Although Obama has instituted enough economic and social reforms to stem the worst excesses of the Clinton and Bush years, his policies do not significantly depart from the underlying market logic of a neoliberal political economy, and thus he provides legitimacy for its systemic exploitation and political marginalization of working-class blacks and other low-income citizens.

The extent and depth of Obama's commitment and that of other black elites to a neoliberal urban policy cannot be adequately captured by the post-racial debate. Harris' otherwise perceptive discussion of the politics of respectability is hampered by the absence of class in his analysis (2012).[2] He notes that, historically, class status in the black community was determined by public behavior rather than by occupation, income, or wealth. This was due to the truncated nature of the pre-1960 black class structure. While material benefits were never absent from this conception of class, the explosive growth of the black middle class since the 1960s and 1970s exacerbated intraracial stratification. Since increased income and profits were now more possible they became more prominent factors in determining the political commitments of black elites than is acknowledged by Harris (Katz, Stern, and Fader 2005). In fact, although Harris (2012) admits that black elites practice a "politics of respectability" and want the state to police poor blacks, he does not tell us *why* they endorse such practices, or what they gain by doing so.

Harris' "politics of respectability" trope limits his ability to ascertain what might motivate the public attacks leveled by the black gentry on their less fortunate brethren. The deployment of a personal responsibility discourse is one way by which this stratum of society is able to deny poor blacks' attachment to place in former public housing sites prime for redevelopment and gentrification since the "transformation of public housing" with HOPE VI. This underclass discourse thus becomes a key tool in the arsenal of black elites in their revanchist battle with black working classes over urban territory (Boyd 2008; Hyra 2008). Harris's (2012) insistence on using a racial idiom to explain the class power of Obama and black elites reveals his commitment to the fiction of a historic black political tradition that assumes common racial interests. This is encapsulated in his lament of the "decline of black politics" threatened by race-neutral black politicians (see also Dawson 2012). Because Harris never articulates the material stakes in Obama's urban policies and instead employs an exclusively racial analytical framework, the desire to gain the acceptance of white voters becomes the only possible explanation for Obama's politics of respectability discourse. In order to more precisely explain the investment of President Obama and black elites in a neoliberal political economy, these race-first scholars must come to terms with the fact that these elites' own social priorities resemble those of other nonblack members of their class. It is not that Obama and his ilk do not want to help working-class and poor blacks with their policies, it is just that less fortunate folks have to wait until bankers, real estate developers, and high tech firms have their interests secured first. Obama's commitment to a class-inflected politics is made clear by his signature urban policy: the Choice Neighborhoods Initiative.

Choice Neighborhoods, Privatization, and Social Control

Obama's underclass discourse is consistent with the rationale that has informed housing policy since the Clinton administration in the early 1990s. The signature housing program of the Clinton and Bush II years, HOPE VI, was created to fight "concentrated poverty" in public housing (Samara, Sinha, and Brady 2013; Greenbaum et al. 2008). The main idea underlying this concept, and the mixed-income housing policy it informs, is that having too many poor people in public housing multiplies and compounds social problems like crime, drug abuse, teenage pregnancy, and single parenthood (Goetz 2013b; DeFilippis and Fraser 2010; Greenbaum et al. 2008). As James DeFilippis and Jim Fraser put it succinctly, "mixed-income housing policies are largely based on the (hegemonic) mantra that low-income people themselves are the problem, and that a benevolent gentry need to colonize their home space in order to create the conditions necessary to help the poor 'bootstrap' themselves into a better socioeconomic position" (2010, 136).

Under HOPE VI, the goal of deconcentrating poverty was achieved by tearing down public housing and dispersing its inhabitants onto the private rental market. Deconcentrating poverty meant deconcentrating poor people. The Department of Housing and Urban Development (HUD) has eliminated public housing units not only through HOPE VI, but also by selling units to for-profit and nonprofit developers through a demolition process detailed in the original legislation. More public housing units have been eliminated outside of the HOPE VI program than were demolished by that program (Goetz 2013a; DeFilippis and Fraser 2010). By 2012, HUD had demolished more than 250,000 units combined. In all, it has approved demolition for nearly 20 percent of the public housing stock (Goetz 2013a).

Obama has sought to build upon the legacy of HOPE VI with his Choice Neighborhoods Initiative (CNI) (Donovan 2009; Wilson 2010). In a speech in 2009, Obama stated,

> Instead of isolated and monolithic public housing projects that too often trap residents in a cycle of poverty and isolate them further, we want to invest in proven strategies that actually transform communities and enhance opportunity for residents and businesses alike. (2009b)

Although, like its predecessor, CNI embraces the idea of concentrated poverty as the main problem plaguing the urban poor, it takes a more comprehensive approach than HOPE VI toward deconcentrating poverty (see chapter 10 in this volume). While HOPE VI was concerned with "transforming" public housing, CNI aims to redevelop whole neighborhoods by demolishing or rehabilitating public and off-site assisted housing. Instead of mixed-income developments replacing public housing, CNI combines mixed-income with mixed-tenure housing, with a mix of ownership and rental units supplanting most of the public housing units in the targeted neighborhood. Unlike HOPE VI, CNI is a joint agency effort led by the White House Office of Urban Affairs, the departments of Housing and Urban Development, Education, Labor, Justice, Transportation, and Health and Human Services, and the Environmental Protection Agency to coordinate social services, education reform, and job training for neighborhood residents (see chapters 5 and 10 in this volume).

Economic Self-Sufficiency and Social Mixing

CNI is a market-based approach to housing and antipoverty policies, and as such, is consistent with the neoliberal turn in urban policy of the past forty years (Goetz and Chapple 2010; Goetz 2013b; Joseph, Chaskin, and Webber 2007; Hackworth 2007). Its goal of dissolving concentrated poverty is premised on a spatial conception of poverty that does not address its structural causes, and thus continues the misguided focus on public housing residents' social and human capital deficiencies (Khare chapter; O'Connor 2001; Goetz and Chapple 2010; Gans 2010; Steinberg 2010; Samara, Sinha, and Brady 2013; Reed and Chowkwanyun 2012). Obama's CNI program, like its predecessor, legitimates the current neoliberal political economic arrangements in two ways. First, it assumes that economic self-sufficiency is possible for all citizens without altering the institutional arrangements that give rise to poverty. The second way is by promoting the idea that place-based income mixing will lead to former public housing residents achieving economic self-sufficiency.

Like HOPE VI, CNI adopts as its primary goal the development of economic self-sufficiency among low-income residents (Smith et al. 2010). The HOPE VI program failed to produce the expected gains in income and employment opportunities for low-income residents, and it is not clear how CNI will improve upon this dismal record without overcoming structural barriers to economic opportunity (Joseph, Chaskin, and Webber 2007; Greenbaum et al. 2008). CNI, which seeks to change distressed neighborhoods into "neighborhoods of opportunity," assumes that the economy produces enough living wage jobs for everyone to attain self-sufficiency. It also assumes that economic self-sufficiency is just a matter of matching the poor in jobless neighborhoods to neighborhoods where jobs are abundant. Of course, this assumption does not factor in how many of these jobs pay a living wage. It would seem that no amount of spatial sorting can overcome the fact that the U.S. political economy fails to produce sufficient numbers of well-paid jobs. Only a national jobs and income support program can hope to make economic self-sufficiency even possible (Gans 2010).

CNI policy makers continue to believe in the elixir of top-down social mixing in housing and neighborhoods. While CNI is too new to have a track record, numerous scholarly evaluations of HOPE VI have called into question their shared assumption that spatial proximity with middle-income citizens would redound to the benefit of low-income residents. The reigning assumption is that public housing tenants, deficient in social capital, would benefit from either observing their middle-income neighbors as role models, or from being incorporated into the social networks of these neighbors. In doing so, they will be able to gain access to information about employment opportunities, which will lead to their self-sufficiency (Bolt and Kempen 2013). Even when poor and affluent residents share the same mixed-income development they do not have much contact with each other (Bolt and Kempen 2013; Joseph, Chaskin, and Webber 2007). Not only is there little social mixing in some destination neighborhoods, but the homeowners often blame the former public tenants for bringing their problems with them. For instance, in a few mixed-income developments in Chicago white and black homeowners criticized the "ghetto culture" of their subsidized neighbors (Khare, Joseph, and Chaskin 2014). These findings suggest that spatial proximity does not guarantee social incorporation nor does it overcome racial and class segregation (Greenbaum et al. 2008; Khare, Joseph, and Chaskin 2014).

In their review of HOPE VI developments, Joseph and his colleagues (2007) found that although social mixing did not lead to inclusive social networks, residents did report an increase in social control. For example, middle-class residents were able to establish and enforce social norms of order and decorum in many mixed-income developments (Joseph, Chaskin, and Webber 2007). For policy elites the problem of concentrated poverty in public housing was about the lack of social control, which was supposed to be remedied by scattering "problem families" into middle-class neighborhoods or job-rich suburbs. This dispersal had the added benefit of displacing visible poverty in the central city to locations where it was harder to see (Samara, Sinha, and Brady 2013; Wacquant 2008; Gans 2010). Because the dispersal policy did not overcome entrenched patterns of racial and class segregation, the relocation of former public tenants to adjoining working-class neighborhoods in the city or in inner-ring suburbs approximated a "contained dispersal" which did not threaten more distant affluent suburbs (Dwyer 2012; Hyra 2012).

Not only did HOPE VI facilitate social control through "contained dispersal," it also opened up former public housing sites on prime urban land for lucrative redevelopment that would benefit real estate developers and upper-income urban citizens (Samara, Sinha, and Brady 2013; Weber 2002; Imbroscio 2008; Hyra 2012; Goetz 2013a; Joseph, Chaskin, and Webber 2007; DeFilippis and Fraser 2010). HOPE VI represented a "massive transfer of public, state-controlled assets to private hands" (Samara, Sinha, and Brady 2013, 323). There is every indication that CNI, like its older cousin, is committed to the larger ideological purpose of privatizing public goods which is "to reinforce private property and individual self-reliance as the bases of citizenship and to further disenfranchise those who cannot achieve it for whatever reason" (Darcy 2013). Obama endorses the principle of individual self-reliance in his admiration for the new black professional class. Although this stratum faces racial barriers, he gushes, "you won't hear these men and women use race as a crutch or point to discrimination as an excuse for failure. In fact, what characterizes this new generation of black professionals is their rejection of any limits to what they can achieve" (2006, 241).

Class, Black Elites, and Obama's Urban Policy

The preoccupation of many scholars with highlighting the persistence of racial inequality in order to counter arguments about the dawn of a post-racial era in America has meant that these scholars have missed the extent to which Obama practices a class-inflected politics that questions the civic worth of poor blacks. Their emphasis on the respectability discourse discounts the extent to which black professionals have a political and material stake in marginalizing working-class blacks' ability to claim state benefits and urban land in the post-segregation era. Since the 1960s, middle-class blacks have become directors of public institutions like public housing authorities, public schools, police departments, and welfare programs where they manage the dispossession and social control of poor blacks (Reed 1999; Wacquant 2008). While not overlooking the power of the Clinton administration and a Republican-dominated Congress, it is African American intellectuals and policy entrepreneurs who have provided the key concepts, ideological justification, and policy design that preceded HOPE VI. Regardless of what his intentions may have been, William J. Wilson's ecological concepts of "social isolation" and "concentrated effects" of poverty helped to provide the intellectual groundwork for deconcentration of poverty policies (Wilson 1987; Bennett and

Reed 1999). While Wilson stressed the structural reasons for black dispossession, he also emphasized ghetto culture as a significant contributing factor to black poverty (Wilson 1987, 1996, 2009). In fact, the implications of his discussion of black middle-class flight from inner cities is that poor blacks who once had the "social buffer" provided by higher-income blacks during segregation could regain it through income mixing in engineered housing developments (Bennett and Reed 1999).

Another important black contributor to the deconcentration of poverty policies has been Vincent Lane, former director of Chicago Housing Authority. Lane applied Wilson's ideas about black middle-class flight and took advantage of "integration fatigue" among the black public to advocate for class integration of blacks in former public housing developments. His experiments in Chicago laid the policy groundwork for the "transformation of public housing" in the 1990s (Bennett and Reed 1999; Bennett 2006). Not surprisingly, many black directors of public housing authorities followed suit. Renee Glover, executive director of the Atlanta Public Housing Authority, has been a vocal supporter of HOPE VI which has led to the elimination of public housing in that city (Goetz 2013a, 2013b). In her chapter in this volume, Amy Khare points out that the influence of former real estate developer Valerie Jarrett and Obama's own experience working in the Chicago affordable housing development industry has been instrumental in shaping his commitment to mixed-income housing. In the for-profit and nonprofit sectors, black real estate firms, banks, and large churches have become partners of redevelopment in inner city neighborhoods in New York, Chicago, and Washington, D.C. (Hyra 2012, 2008).[3] In addition, upper-income black households have benefited from new housing opportunities in gentrifying neighborhoods in these cities to the detriment of lower-income black households (Hyra 2008, 2012; Boyd 2008; Pattillo 2007; Goetz 2011). It is difficult to minimize the influence of African American political elites and intellectuals in the crafting and implementation of public housing policy that has victimized poor blacks, or to attribute such influence solely to a politics of respectability discourse.

Due to the antidiscrimination housing and lending policies of the 1960s and 1970s, the black middle class had its housing and neighborhood options broadened in the context of class-stratified housing markets. Obama describes how new black professionals in Chicago now "can afford to live in neighborhoods of their choosing and send their children to the best private schools" (2006, 241). Following an earlier period, during which racial segregation dampened the effect of black income inequality on residential location, black income segregation in housing grew to three times that of their white counterparts (Reardon and Bischoff 2011). In the 1970s and 1980s, income segregation among African Americans increased precipitously as the growing black middle class was able to penetrate new suburban areas, leaving behind working-class blacks in the central city. The fact that this trend of rising income segregation ended "abruptly" in the 1990s is consistent with the idea that increased income-mixing at the census tract level resulted from the deconcentration of poor blacks and the growth of black gentrification in and near former black public housing sites (Reardon and Bischoff 2011; Hyra 2012). While it is true that the deconcentration of poor blacks has opened up development and housing opportunities for middle- and upper-income blacks in inner-city neighborhoods, it was assumed that the dispersal of poor black households would bring them into closer spatial proximity with affluent black households in the metropolitan area. Black income segregation has lessened slightly, but this has largely been due to poor blacks residing with the "near poor" rather than with affluent blacks (Dwyer 2012).

Conclusion

The seemingly endless and fruitless debate about whether or not President Obama has aided and abetted the dawn of a post-racial era and the consequent need to highlight the persistence of racial disparity misses some important links between Obama, black elites, and urban policy. In the face of overwhelming black support for Obama's election and administration, the critical role that black elites have played in Obama's urban policy has not been emphasized. This constituency approves of Obama's underclass rhetoric and benefits from the neoliberal housing policies such as HOPE VI and CNI that have opened up housing and development opportunities for its members. Mixed-income developments under HOPE VI and CNI have indeed become "neighborhoods of opportunity," but not so much for former public housing residents as for both black and white developers and higher-income homeowners now populating U.S. inner cities.

The inability to adequately account for the investment of black elites in social control policies has been underlined by the recent spate of police violence against poor black victims. On one level, the fact that most of the victims have been black has put an end to any silly talk about the dawning of a post-racial America. Unfortunately, this renewed visibility of racial disparity does not bring any more clarity about the underlying causes of unaffordable housing or police violence. In fact, it highlights the limitations of an analysis that explains urban inequality as principally a racial phenomenon. While the police killings of poor black victims in Ferguson, Missouri, Cleveland, Ohio, and Staten Island confirm a familiar discourse of a white political establishment abetting the killings of black men, the death of Freddie Gray in Baltimore does not fit this dominant narrative. The presence of a black mayor and, until recently, a black police superintendent in Baltimore, and the fact that three of the six officers indicted in the Freddie Gray killing were black has not altered the antiracism framework that seeks to explain the recurrent problem of police killing blacks as primarily racially motivated, a legacy of slavery and Jim Crow.

Contrary to this framework, the assessment by many residents of West Baltimore has been that Freddie Gray's death was "not a racial incident" but rather, one motivated by class. One of these residents, Taiwan Parker, commented that Baltimore police treat everyone in the poorest neighborhoods of Baltimore as if they were drug dealers and criminals (Inskeep 2015). In addition, another neighborhood resident wondered out loud why the problems of unemployment and homelessness in the city do not get the same response from protesters as police violence (Fessler 2015). These comments reveal that the analysis of these killings by black working-class residents in West Baltimore is far more astute than the analysis that emanates from an obtuse antiracism framework. These black citizens can more clearly see the class commitments of black city officials who view poor blacks as a threat to the maintenance of social order in Baltimore.

While stressing the importance of the problems of police violence and lack of accountability on the part of law enforcement officials, the fact that these problems have been framed as mainly a racial problem will unfortunately continue to produce the same ineffective political response of the last forty years. The reassertion of an antiracism narrative excludes a broader framework that could link black victims of police violence to the killing of brown and white people at the hands of the police and call for a class-based response to police unaccountability (Burch 2011). To echo political scientist Thomas Adams, the recurrent story of police killing of black people will not end until there is a political force that could mobilize an effective political response to the problems of unaffordable housing and the absence of police accountability (Adams 2014). This political force will need to employ an analysis that is not limited to seeing only black victims and white perpetrators, but a large dispossessed working class that has been marginalized by neoliberal policies produced by a multiracial elite.

Notes

1. The Promise Neighborhoods initiative is patterned after Harlem Children's Zone, which "features over 20 programs that represent a combination of structural and cultural interventions to help and empower individuals who live in these 97 blocks" (Wilson 2010, 43).
2. This point was made by Cedric Johnson about the respectability discourse employed by many black scholars as an explanation for social tensions within the black community. He argues that this discourse allows these black scholars to criticize black elites within a racial paradigm (personal communication).
3. Black policy elites' interest in black-led redevelopment as well as partnering with the state and large white development firms was signaled as early as the 1950s in Chicago and in other cities (P. Smith 2012).

References

Adams, Thomas. 2014. "Ferguson Violence Exposes America's Political Decay." *The Age*, August 20. Accessed July 25, 2015. http://www.theage.com.au/comment/ferguson-violence-exposes-americas-political-decay-20140820-10648b.html.

Bennett, Larry. 2006. "Transforming Public Housing." In *The New Chicago: A Social and Cultural Analysis*, ed. John P. Koval, Larry Bennett, Michael Bennett, Fassil Demissie, Roberta Garner, and Kiljoong Kim, 269–76. Philadelphia: Templeton University Press.

Bennett, Larry, and Adolph Reed Jr. 1999. "The New Face of Urban Renewal: The Near North Redevelopment Initiative and the Cabrini-Green Neighborhood." In *Without Justice for All:*

The New Liberalism and Our Retreat from Racial Equality ed. Adolph Reed Jr., 175–211. Boulder, Colo.: Westview Press.

Bolt, Gideon, and Ronald van Kempen. 2013. "Introduction Special Issue: Mixing Neighborhoods: Success or Failure?" *Cities* 35: 391–96.

Boyd, Michelle R. 2008. *Jim Crow Nostalgia: Reconstructing Race in Bronzeville*. Minneapolis: University of Minnesota Press.

Burch, Andrea. 2011. "Arrest-Related Deaths, 2003–2009—Statistical Tables." U.S. Department of Justice, Office of Justice Programs, Bureau of Justice Statistics. NCJ 235385. http://www.bjs.gov/content/pub/pdf/ard0309st.pdf.

Darcy, Michael. 2013. "From High-Rise Projects to Suburban Estates: Public Tenants and the Globalised Discourse of Deconcentration." *Cities* 35: 365–72.

Dawson, Michael. 2012. "Racial Tragedies, Political Hope, and the Tasks of American Political Science." *Perspectives on Politics* 10 (3): 669–73.

DeFilippis, James, and Jim Fraser. 2010. "Why Do We Want Mixed-Income Housing and Neighborhoods?" In *Critical Urban Studies: New Directions,* ed. Jonathan S. Davies and David L. Imbroscio, 135–47. Albany: State University of New York Press.

Donovan, Shaun. 2009. "From Despair to Hope: Two HUD Secretaries on Urban Revitalization and Opportunity." Prepared remarks for Secretary of Housing and Urban Development Shaun Donovan at the Brookings Institution Metropolitan Policy Program's Discussion. National Press Club. Washington, D.C., July 14.

Dwyer, Rachel E. 2012. "Contained Dispersal: The Deconcentration of Poverty in US Metropolitan Areas in the 1990s." *City & Community* 11 (3): 309–31.

Edelman, Peter. 2010. "The Next War on Poverty." *Democracy Journal* 15 (Winter): 21–33. http://democracyjournal.org/magazine/15/the-next-war-on-poverty/.

Fessler, Pam. 2015. "After Police Are Charged in Gray's Death, Baltimore Awaits Next Steps." *National Public Radio.* May 2. Accessed July 21, 2015. http://www.npr.org/2015/05/02/403831427/after-police-are-charged-in-gray-s-death-baltimore-awaits-next-steps.

Fraser, Carly. 2009. "Race, Post-Black Politics, and the Democratic Presidential Candidacy of Barack Obama." *Souls: A Critical Journal of Black Politics, Culture, and Society* 11 (1): 17–40.

Gans, Herbert J. 2010. "Concentrated Poverty: A Critical Analysis." *Challenge* 53 (3): 82–96.

Goetz, Edward G. 2011. "Gentrification in Black and White: The Racial Impact of Public Housing Demolition." *Urban Studies* 48 (8): 1581–1604.

———. 2013a. *New Deal Ruins: Race, Economic Justice and Public Housing Policy*. Ithaca, N.Y.: Cornell University Press.

———. 2013b. "The Audacity of HOPE VI: Discourse and the Dismantling of Public Housing." *Cities* 35: 342–48.

Goetz, Edward G., and Karen Chapple. 2010. "You Gotta Move: Advancing the Debate on the Record of Dispersal." *Housing Policy Debate* 20 (2): 209–36.

Greenbaum, Susan, Wendy Hathaway, Cheryl Rodriguez, Ashely Spalding, and Beverly Ward. 2008. "Deconcentration and Social Capital: Contradictions of a Poverty Alleviation Policy." *Journal of Poverty* 12 (2): 201–28.

Hackworth, Jason. 2007. *The Neoliberal City: Governance, Ideology, and Development in American Urbanism*. Ithaca, N.Y.: Cornell University Press.

Harris, Fredrick C. 2009. "Towards a Pragmatic Black Politics?" *Souls: A Critical Journal of Black Politics, Culture, and Society* 11 (1): 41–49.

———. 2012. *The Price of the Ticket: Barack Obama and the Rise and the Decline of Black Politics*. New York: Oxford University Press.

Hyra, Derek S. 2008. *The New Urban Renewal: The Economic Transformation of Harlem and Bronzeville*. Chicago: University of Chicago.

———. 2012. "Conceptualizing the New Urban Renewal: Comparing the Past to the Present." *Urban Affairs Review* 48 (4): 498–527.

Imbroscio, David. 2008. "'[U]nited and Actuated by Some Common Impulse of Passion': Challenging the Dispersal Consensus in American Housing Policy Research." *Journal of Urban Affairs* 30 (2): 111–30.

Inskeep, Steve. 2015. "Baltimore Is Not Ferguson. Here's What It Really Is." *National Public Radio.* April 29. Accessed July 21, 2015. http://www.npr.org/2015/04/29/402971487/residents-disappointed-at-how-rioters-tore-up-baltimore.

Joseph, Mark L., Robert J. Chaskin, and Henry S. Webber. 2007. "The Theoretical Basis for Addressing Poverty Through Mixed-Income Development." *Urban Affairs Review* 42 (3): 369–409.

Katz, Michael B., Mark J. Stern, and Jamie J. Fader. 2005. "The New African American Inequality." *The Journal of American History* 92 (1): 75–108.

Khare, Amy T., Mark L. Joseph, and Robert J. Chaskin. 2014. "The Enduring Significance of Race in Mixed-Income Developments." *Urban Affairs Review* (June): 1–30.

Klinkner, Philip A. 1999. "Bill Clinton and the Politics of the New Liberalism." In *Without Justice for All: The New Liberalism and Our Retreat From Racial Equality,* ed. Adolph Reed Jr. 11–28. Boulder, Colo.: Westview.

Mele, Christopher. 2013. "Neoliberalism, Race and the Redefining of Urban Redevelopment." *International Journal of Urban and Regional Research* 37 (2): 598–617.

Metzler, Christopher J. 2010. "Barack Obama's Faustian Bargain and the Fight for America's Racial Soul." *Journal of Black Studies* 40 (3): 395–410.

Obama, Barack. 2006. *The Audacity of Hope: Thoughts on Reclaiming the American Dream.* New York: Three Rivers Press.

———. 2009a. "A More Perfect Union: Race Speech, March 18, 2008." In *Words That Changed a Nation: The Most Celebrated and Influential Speeches of Barack Obama.* Seattle, Wash.: Pacific Publishing Studio, 37–54.

———. 2009b. "Remarks by the President at Urban and Metropolitan Policy Roundtable." White House, July 13.

O'Connor, Alice. 2001. *Poverty Knowledge: Social Science, Social Policy, and the Poor in Twentieth-Century U. S. History.* Princeton, N.J.: Princeton University Press.

Pattillo, Mary. 2007. *Black on the Block: The Politics of Race and Class in the City.* Chicago: University of Chicago Press.

Powell, John A. 2009. "Post-Racialism or Targeted Universalism?" *Denver University Law Review* 86: 785.

Reardon, Sean F., and Kendra Bischoff. 2011. "Income Inequality and Income Segregation." *American Journal of Sociology* 116 (4): 1092–153.

Reed, Adolph, Jr. 1999. "The 'Underclass' as Myth and Symbol: The Poverty of Discourse about Poverty." In *Stirrings in the Jug: Black Politics in the Post-Segregation Era,* ed. Adolph Reed Jr., 179–96. Minneapolis: University of Minnesota Press.

———. 2014. "Nothing Left: The Long, Slow Surrender of American Liberals." *Harper's Magazine* (March): 28–36.

Reed, Adolph, Jr., and Merlin Chowkwanyun. 2012. "Race, Class, Crisis: The Discourse of Racial Disparity and its Analytical Discontents." *Socialist Register* 48: 149–75.

Samara, Tony Roshan, Anita Sinha, and Marnie Brady. 2013. "Putting the "Public" Back in Affordable Housing: Place and Politics in the Era of Poverty Deconcentration." *Cities* 35: 319–26.

Sinclair-Chapman, Valeria, and Melanye Price. 2008. "Black Politics, the 2008 Election, and the (Im)Possibility of Race Transcendence." *PS: Political Science & Politics* 41 (4): 739–45.

Smith, Preston H. 1999. "'Self-Help,' Black Conservatives, and the Reemergence of Black Privatism." In *Without Justice for All: The New Liberalism and Our Retreat from Racial Equality,* ed. Adolph Reed Jr., 257–90. Boulder, Colo.: Westview Press.

———. 2012. *Racial Democracy and the Black Metropolis: Housing Policy in Postwar Chicago.* Minneapolis: University of Minnesota Press.

Smith, Robin, G., Thomas Kingsley, Mary Cunningham, Susan Popkin, Kassie Dumlao, Ingrid Gould Ellen, Mark Joseph, and Deborah McKoy. 2010. "Monitoring Success in Choice Neighborhoods: A Proposed Approach to Performance Measurement." The Urban Institute. http://www.urban.org/sites/default/files/alfresco/publication-pdfs/412092-Monitoring-Success-in-Choice-Neighborhoods-A-Proposed-Approach-to-Performance-Measurement.PDF.

Smith, Rogers M., and Desmond S. King. 2014. "Barack Obama and the Future of American Racial Politics." In Barack Obama and the Myth of a Post-Racial America, ed. Mark Ledwidge, Kevern Verney, and Inderjeet Parmar, 102–15. New York: Routledge.

Steinberg, Stephen. 2010. "The Myth of Concentrated Poverty." In The Integration Debate: Competing Futures for American Cities, ed. Chester Hartman and Gregory D. Squires, 213–28. New York: Routledge.

Wacquant, Loïc. 2008. "Ghettos and Anti-Ghettos: An Anatomy of the New Urban Poverty." Thesis Eleven 94 (1): 113–18.

Weber, Rachel. 2002. "Extracting Value from the City: Neoliberalism and Urban Redevelopment." Antipode 34 (3): 519–40.

Wilson, William J. 1987. The Truly Disadvantaged: The Inner City, the Underclass, and Public Policy. Chicago: University of Chicago Press.

———. 1996. When Work Disappears: The World of the New Urban Poor. New York: Vintage Books.

———. 2009. "More Than Just Race: Being Black and Poor in the Inner City." Poverty & Race 9 (3): 1–2, 9–11.

———. 2010. "The Obama's Administration's Proposals to Address Concentrated Urban Poverty." City & Community 9 (1): 41–49.

4

HOUSING POLICY AND THE MORTGAGE FORECLOSURE CRISIS DURING THE OBAMA ADMINISTRATION

RACHEL G. BRATT AND DAN IMMERGLUCK

President Obama took office in January 2009 amid the most serious financial crisis since the Great Depression. The mounting number of defaults and foreclosures were, understandably, the most pressing immediate housing concern facing the new administration. At the same time, and related to the mortgage foreclosure crisis, the massive dislocations of the financial industry were presenting enormous challenges. While these events clearly created a sense of urgency, the range of ongoing housing problems has not disappeared and has continued to be problematic, particularly for urban areas.

The context for this inquiry is the historically intense political schism between Republicans and Democrats, which appears to have worsened over the past decade. Since the Great Depression, when the federal government became actively involved with housing, there has been a split in the way in which Democratic and Republican administrations typically view what is, perhaps, the central question about housing policy: should the federal government be an active player in providing a range of assistance to households, particularly to those with lower incomes, to help them acquire and sustain long-term safe, secure, and affordable housing, and, if so, how?

During the President Franklin D. Roosevelt administration, for example, an aggressive and far-reaching set of programs were initiated to assist homeowners facing serious defaults, the public housing program was created, and support was provided to the banking and homebuilding industries, notably in the form of the Federal Housing Administration, which provided homeowners with mortgage insurance on fully amortized loans. With all these initiatives, an overriding goal was to stimulate the economy and to reduce unemployment.

In the presidential campaign of 1960, "the Republican platform was conspicuously silent on needs for low-rent public housing or housing for the poor" (Keith 1973, 138). With the Democrats prevailing, an explicit pro-housing and inner-city agenda came to fruition under the Kennedy and Johnson administrations. Below-market-interest-rate programs were created to promote homeownership, and there were new rental housing opportunities for low- and moderate-income households, with a particular focus on urban areas.

Republican administrations, for their part, can claim credit for promoting affordability of housing through the Section 8 program, which is now called the Housing Choice Voucher program. Although this program has been an enormous help to millions of households since its creation under the Nixon administration in 1974, its stimulus was, primarily, a desire on the part of the federal government to become less involved in the production, management, and long-term commitment to subsidize an affordable housing stock. Similarly, the Low Income Housing Tax Credit program, created during the Reagan administration, is another important subsidy, but here, too, there was an explicit assumption on the part of the government that "the genius of the market economy, freed of the distortions forced by government housing policies and regulations . . . can provide for housing far better than Federal programs" (U.S. President's Commission on Housing 1982, xvii).

Yet, for about the past four decades, and despite the growing general polarization between Republicans and Democrats, the distinctions between the two parties have become more blurred around the housing agenda. For example, the record of President Clinton was "mixed at best." While inroads on the housing problems facing low-income households were made, they were not nearly as substantial as had been hoped (Bratt 2002, 626).

The conclusions offered by Peter Marcuse and Dennis Keating are sobering: "Despite significant differences between liberal and conservative approaches to housing policy, those differences remain within a narrow spectrum. . . . Neither liberal nor conservative approaches to housing policy have come close to solving the housing problems facing the American people, even though liberal policies have been more ameliorative than the conservative ones" (2006, 155).

In addition to the historically stronger support for housing on the part of Democrats, Obama's record as a community organizer and senator, as well as his support for various housing initiatives articulated during the campaign, contributed to an upbeat, anticipatory mood. Shortly before the election, an article published in the National Housing Institute's online magazine noted the importance of Obama's community experiences and that "if rhetoric is a measure of intentions, [there is] reason for optimism" (Moberg 2007). Moreover, the article quoted an Obama fundraising letter as saying: "Together we have an incredible opportunity to bring politics back to our neighborhoods and communities, where people genuinely care about our common future and believe that we have the power to shape the kind of society in which we live" (Moberg 2007).

Specifically concerning mortgage issues, there were also good reasons for advocates to feel that Obama would aggressively deal with the unfolding crisis. Obama had been a strong supporter of anti-predatory lending regulations while an Illinois state senator. In addition, prior to the 2008 election, he formed a large housing policy advisory group, which included many leading figures from the nonprofit housing and housing policy communities. A few days after the election, the National Low Income Housing Coalition captured the sense of promise and enthusiasm among neighborhood activists and progressives by succinctly noting that "Obama's historic victory . . . was met with optimism in the housing advocacy community" (National Low Income Housing Coalition 2008, 4).

To sum up, on the one hand, the historical differences between Republicans and Democrats suggest at least some degree of optimism about the Obama administration's housing agenda. On the other hand, analyses of the housing records of recent presidents from both major parties might predict that housing policy under President Obama would not differ significantly from that of the prior administration, of George W. Bush. Which assessment is most valid?

The first part of this chapter explores the record of the Obama administration in maintaining and further developing the country's longstanding housing programs and in supporting or initiating new strategies to address housing problems facing low-income households. The second part presents a summary of the initiatives aimed at stemming the tide of foreclosures.

Ongoing Housing Challenges and New Initiatives

This section focuses on how several key housing indicators have changed during the Obama administration: funding for selected housing programs; the size of the homeless population; and how low-income households, particularly renters, have been faring. Given the scope of this chapter, several important issues are omitted, such as expiration of affordability restrictions and resident services in the U.S. Department of Housing and Urban Development's (HUD)–assisted developments. Also omitted is a discussion of the public housing program, which is covered in chapter 5. The section concludes with a brief review of three new Obama administration initiatives related to housing.

Funding for Housing

There are at least two ways to explore budgetary issues during the Obama administration. The first is a comparison between funding for key housing programs in the last budget prior to the start of Obama's presidency and his first budget, and the second is an assessment of changes in funding for these programs during his time in office.

Looking first at funding for the major federal housing subsidy programs (not including the off-budget Low Income Housing Tax Credit program), between President Bush's last budget, for selected key housing programs in FY 2009 ($35,722 billion), and President Obama's first budget for those same programs the following year ($39,922 billion), there was an increase of $4.2 billion (in real dollars), or more than 11 percent (see Table 4.1). (The figure used for the FY 2009 budget does not count the significant increase in funding, provided through the American Recovery and Reinvestment Act, to help stimulate the economy in the aftermath

TABLE 4.1. DIRECT FEDERAL APPROPRIATIONS FOR SELECTED HUD-ASSISTED HOUSING PROGRAMS, FY 2007–15 (IN $ MILLIONS)

	FY 2007(a)	FY 2008(a)	FY* 2009(b)	FY 2010(b)	FY 2011(c)	FY 2012(d)	FY 2013(e) Sequestration	FY 2014(e)	FY 2015	FY 2016
Total Tenant-Based Rental Assistance	$15,887	$15,702	$16,225	$18,184	$18,371	$18,914	$17,964	$19,177	$	$
Project-Based Rental Assistance (Section 8 contracts)	5,976	6,382	7,130 (2,000)	8,558	9,257	9,340	8,851	9,917		
Public Housing Operating Fund	3,864	4,200	4,455	4,775	4,617	3,962	4,054	4,400		
Public Housing Capital Fund	2,431	2,439	2,450 (4,000)	2,500	2,040	1,875	1,777	1,875		
Homeless Assistance Grants	1,442	1,586	1,677 (1,500)	1,865	1,901	1,901	1,933	2,105		
Choice Neighborhoods	—	—	—	65	65	120	114	90		
HOME	1,757	1,704	1,825 (2,250)	1,825	1,607	1,000	948	1,000		

Native American Housing Block Grants	624	630	635	690	649	650	616	650
Housing for persons with:								
Disabilities	237	237	250	300	150	277	156	126
AIDs	286	300	310	335	334	332	315	330
Elderly	735	735	765	825	399	375	355	384
Total Above	1,258	1,272	1,325	1,460	883	984	826	840
Total Selected Housing Programs	$33,239	$33,915	$35,722 ($9,750)	$39,922	$39,390	$38,746	$37,083	$ $40,054

Note: There are occasional discrepancies in funding levels for a given program for a given year, as presented in various HUD documents, issued in different years. To the best of our ability, we have used the most recent numbers.

*The American Recovery and Reinvestment Act of 2009 added funds for HUD. The data for FY 2009 shows these amounts in parentheses.

Sources: U.S. Department of Housing and Urban Development: (a) Fiscal Year 2009 Budget Summary. Accessed July 2, 2014. http://www.hud.gov/about/budget/fy09/fy09budget.pdf; (b) Fiscal year 2011 Budget, Investing in People and Places. Accessed July 2, 2014. http://hud.gov/budgetsummary2011/budget-authority-by-prog.pdf; (c) Fiscal Year 2013 Budget, Housing and Communities Built to Last. Accessed July 3, 2014. http://portal.hud.gov/hudportal/documents/huddoc?id=CombBudget2013.pdf; (d) HUD FY 2014 Budget, Meeting the Need for Quality Affordable Rental Housing; (e) Overview of FY 2015 President's Budget, March 4, 2014. Accessed July 3, 2014. http://portal.hud.gov/hudportal/documents/huddoc?id=FY2015BudgetPresFINAL.pdf.

of the Great Recession.) Yet, between President Obama's first budget, in FY 2010, and his most recent enacted budget for FY 2016 for the selected housing programs ($41,023 billion), the increase in funding for these key housing programs was rather modest, less than 3 percent, just over $1 billion (in real dollars).

Further examining funding changes in various budgetary line items, it is clear that there have been some programmatic "winners" and "losers." Between FY 2010 and FY 2016, there was about a 7 percent increase in tenant-based rental assistance; 21 percent increase in homeless grants; and a 25 percent increase in project-based rental assistance. The programs that sustained large declines during that same period include: a 50 percent reduction in the public housing capital fund; a 9 percent reduction in the public housing operating fund; 44 percent reduction in the HOME program; and a 35 percent reduction in housing for people with disabilities. And, although there was a significant increase in the Choice Neighborhoods program during the middle years of the Obama administration, the program was cut by more than half in FY 2016, compared with FY 2010. There were also fluctuations in the Native American Housing Block Grant program, declining for several years and then experiencing a 5 percent increase in FY 2016 compared with FY 2010. Similarly, funding for elderly housing experienced sharp declines for several years, but by FY 2016 it rebounded considerably, but still sustained a 13 percent loss in funding.

Although some of the programs with funding reductions (Choice Neighborhoods, HOME, elderly, and disability housing) involve relatively small dollar amounts, the declines are still enormously important for these smaller programs. In addition, the downward funding trend for the public housing operating and capital funds are serious both in terms of actual dollar amounts and for how they signal dwindling support for this critical source of low-rent housing. In contrast, it is possible that the increased funding for the homeless could be producing real dividends, in terms of declines in the homeless population, discussed below.

While the small overall budgetary increase for key housing programs during the Obama presidency may be explained by the intense interparty conflicts, the general antisocial welfare mood of the country, and the general budget-cutting atmosphere that is pervasive in the second decade of the millennium, it is certainly discouraging that funding for housing did not fare well during this period.

The Homeless

There has been a decline in the homeless population since President Obama took office. This continued a trend that started in at least 2007 of a fairly steady reduction in the number of homeless people. While there was a slight increase in 2010, the single night count of homeless people declined from 630,227 in 2009 to 564,708 in 2015, a decline of more than 10 percent. There was also improvement in the number of homeless people who were unsheltered, declining from 36 percent of the homeless population to 31 percent, in that same time period (Henry et al. 2015, 8).

Less than two years after the start of the Obama presidency, HUD collaborated with a nonprofit organization, Community Solutions, to work on the ambitious goal of providing permanent housing to 100,000 homeless people, to be achieved by July 2014. In an upbeat article, the *New York Times* announced, with reference to this initiative, "The Push to End Chronic Homelessness Is Working" (Bornstein 2014). Despite these improvements, it is clear that more vigorous efforts, accompanied by adequate funding, are needed. The stark number of homeless people—more than a half million—still represents a daunting challenge.

Rental Housing

Regrettably, President Obama's record in closing the gap between rental housing units available and affordable to extremely low-income households has not been encouraging. Given the disconnect between the cost of producing and maintaining housing that is affordable to lower-income households, "it is no surprise that the gap between the number of lower-income renters and the supply of affordable units continues to grow" (Joint Center for Housing Studies 2013, 7).

In 2010, there was a need for 6.8 million units affordable and available to extremely low-income households (those earning less than 30 percent of area median income); this figure rose to 7.2 million by 2014 (Arnold et al. 2014; Emmanuel 2016). In addition, in 2009 (shortly before Obama took office) there were some 7.1 million very low-income renter households (earning less than 50 percent of area median income) with "worst case housing needs" (households below this income that do not receive housing assistance, with severe cost burdens or who live in severely inadequate housing). This number increased to a record 8.5 million in 2011 and then began to decline, reaching 7.7 million in 2013, but still 9 percent higher than in 2009 and a startling 49 percent higher than in 2003 (HUD 2015).

How much is President Obama to blame for this series of negative findings? Many of these trends were either evident before he took office or the dire economic climate during his first term significantly added to the challenges facing low-income renter households. Yet, it is still troubling that through Obama's presidency, greater inroads or reversals in these trends were not made. The sequestration of funds, as mandated by Congress in 2013, the ongoing polarization between Republicans and Democrats, and the continued reluctance to significantly expand housing subsidies do not bode well for the rental housing agenda.

New Housing Initiatives

In view of the chaotic state of the housing and financial markets during much of President Obama's term in office, his focus on health care, immigration policy, critical foreign policy issues, and the deep partisan divisions, it is not surprising that new housing initiatives were not at the forefront. Yet, three such programs are noteworthy.

First, as the centerpiece and top priority of the housing advocacy agenda for about two decades, the National Housing Trust Fund (NHTF) was created just prior to the Obama presidency. The role of the NHTF is to provide a dedicated revenue source for affordable housing, principally to assist in the production, preservation, and rehabilitation of rental housing for extremely low-income households. Funding for NHTF was stalled significantly since contributions, which are based on the annual volume of business conducted by Fannie Mae and Freddie Mac, were suspended due to the difficulties these organizations faced during the financial crisis. However, the suspension was lifted in December 2015, the first contributions to the NHTF began in 2015, and the first distributions of funds—$174 million—were scheduled to be made in 2016.

Although created during the George W. Bush administration, the NHTF has received support from the Obama administration and was always on the policy agenda. Since President Obama's first budget request, in FY 2010, each year the administration requested $1 billion for the NHTF. However, these requests were never approved by Congress (National Low Income Housing Coalition 2014, 90).

The second new program discussed here, President Obama's Housing Choice Neighborhoods Initiative (CNI), is very much his own, although it is modeled after its predecessor, the HOPE VI program. Similar to HOPE VI, CNI is focused on significantly upgrading severely distressed public housing properties, while also including HUD-assisted, private housing properties and entire neighborhoods.

As discussed in chapter 10 by Amy Khare, CNI is a place-based initiative, aimed at transforming severely distressed public housing and HUD-assisted developments to create better housing opportunities (whether through demolition, rehabilitation, or new construction), while addressing a range of other neighborhood-based challenges, such as crime, education, supportive services, capital projects, and community facilities.

It would be hard to argue that Choice Neighborhoods represents a whole new strategy, since it builds upon prior initiatives such as HOPE VI and a range of locally developed comprehensive community initiatives. Yet, it is noteworthy that the Obama administration is attempting to put its mark on a holistic strategy to assist lower-income households living in publicly assisted housing by helping them address a range of economic and social problems.

The third major new housing initiative of the Obama Administration is the Rental Assistance Demonstration (RAD). Authorized in FY 2012, RAD assists public housing authorities and owners of private, HUD-assisted rental housing to use the Section 8 program (either Housing Choice Voucher contracts or project-based assistance) to raise private debt and equity for capital improvements. HUD has placed a cap on the number of units that can be converted from public housing to a Section 8 platform through RAD; no new funds for the conversions have been appropriated. As of December 2015, nearly 11,000 public housing units were on a wait-list for RAD conversions. The National Low Income Housing Coalition has raised a number of questions about the extent to which existing residents will be protected from displacement as a result of RAD conversions and whether public housing authorities will continue to control the management of the developments (Gramlich, 2016).

Responses to the Mortgage Crisis

In addition to swelling number of homeowners facing default and foreclosure, financial institutions were understandably nervous about income losses, and a wide range of investors, who had put a great deal of faith in an array of arcane financial instruments that had been based on shaky, high-risk mortgage assets, were realizing that their investments could be worthless. As problems worsened, local community officials and activists also began to articulate growing fears about how the mortgage crisis and mounting foreclosures would impact neighborhoods, due to an increase in vacant foreclosed properties.

Historical Context

Although the scale of the recent mortgage crisis and its effects on the global economy are largely unprecedented, we can learn—or should have learned—some lessons from previous mortgage and financial industry crises, despite their more limited scope and scale. For example, many of the problems that surfaced during the recent mortgage crisis were foreshadowed by experiences with HUD's Section 235 program. The Section 235 program was part of a major package of federal legislative initiatives, enacted in 1968, to promote and subsidize homeownership for lower-income households and to reverse longstanding patterns of redlining in inner city areas. The Section 235 program was the country's first major subsidized low- to moderate-income homeownership program, offering qualifying households federally insured mortgages (which were provided by private financial institutions) at interest rates as low as 1 percent. The overall experiences with the program were disappointing, as a series of abuses on the part of HUD, real estate agents, and mortgage companies all contributed to the troubling story that unfolded.

In addition, a now-familiar problem surfaced for the first time: defaulting homeowners faced new obstacles while trying to save their homes due to the structure of the secondary mortgage market and the relatively new practice of loans being sold from originators to investors. In short, there was a lack of protection for homeowners, particularly those in default; HUD was lax in enforcing its own guidelines for loan modifications; and there were a number of hidden financial incentives for originators and servicers not to assist homeowners in default (Bratt 1976, 2012, 146–69). All of these issues found new life in the first decade of the twenty-first century.

Two decades later, another set of financial industry problems surfaced, this time concerning savings and loan associations (S&Ls). As a direct result of the deregulation of financial institutions during the Reagan administration, S&Ls, which had been the traditional mortgage lender in the United States, were now permitted to engage in a range of commercial lending activities, which had largely been outside their normal area of expertise. The results were disastrous, as S&Ls became involved with a host of risky, poorly underwritten investments. While many S&Ls went out of business, the federal government provided massive financial assistance and instituted a number of reform measures, aimed at stabilizing the banking industry.

Mortgage Crisis, 2008

A variety of factors came together and conspired to create the 2008 mortgage crisis. These included a period of sustained low interest rates and "cheap" money, which fueled buyer demand and a virtual hysteria about "buying now"; large numbers of unprepared home purchasers; originators of loans taking little risk in carefully assessing the quality of loans; rating agencies that were not neutral parties in the selling of securities backed by mortgage loans; and a lax federal regulatory environment. Deregulation of the finance industry had started under President Reagan and continued under President Clinton, with the latter having supported repeal of the Glass-Steagall Act, which had separated the banking and investment functions of financial institutions. And, finally, during much of the early- and mid-2000s the lax regulatory environment provided fertile ground for investment firms to make extensive use of derivative instruments, many of which carried inordinate risk due to the weakness of the underlying loans (see, for example, Immergluck 2009, 2013; and Bratt 2012). The opaqueness and lack of transparency of these instruments, as well as their reliance on untested computer models, were a principal factor in the mortgage crisis.

As might be expected, many conservatives sought to blame the crisis on federal housing policies aimed at helping low- and moderate-income families, including the Community Reinvestment Act and the Affordable Housing Goals of the GSEs (Wallison 2011). This narrative has persisted despite ample evidence that such policies had little to do with spurring irresponsible, subprime lending (Immergluck 2009; Financial Crisis Inquiry Commission, 2011; Ghent, Hernández-Murillo, and Owyang 2012).

This section focuses on some of the more immediate responses to the mortgage default and foreclosure problem. Concerning the long-term regulatory responses, primarily through the reform legislation known as Dodd-Frank,[1] our brief summation is that the issuance of regulations has been slow and continuously resisted by members of Congress and the financial industry.

For example, while the Consumer Financial Protection Bureau (CFPB) has proven to be an assertive regulator, it has been continually investigated by a hostile Congress. Moreover, bills have been proposed to curtail key regulations, including the most important provision from a consumer-protection perspective—requiring lenders to ensure that borrowers have the ability to repay their mortgages. Over time, the CFPB's opponents appear to have given up on dissolving the agency entirely. However, they have proposed dozens of deregulations, in the hope that a few of them might get through. As Representative Carolyn Maloney (D-NY) has said, "it's like death by a thousand cuts for the CFPB" (*Housingwire* 2014). Thus, it remains to be seen how effective Dodd-Frank will be in preventing future reckless and abusive lending practices.

Another important issue that will not be discussed here is the impact of foreclosures on neighborhoods. Suffice to say that the early results of the three rounds of the Neighborhood Stabilization Program (NSP) appear disappointing (see chapter 13 by Deirdre Oakley and Jim Fraser).[2] Although federal funds have been available to enable cities and towns to purchase and rehabilitate foreclosed homes, the process appears to have been too slow and inflexible to reduce adverse neighborhood effects (Immergluck 2013).

Putting the foreclosure problem in perspective, between September 2008 and December 2015, CoreLogic estimates that foreclosures were completed on 6.1 million homes (CoreLogic 2016). This is approximately 8 percent of homes in the United States. (A substantially larger number of homeowners experienced mortgage delinquency or default, or began the foreclosure process, over this period.)

Federal Government Responses to Mounting Defaults and Foreclosures

As of December 2015, approximately 4.8 million households had received a permanent loan modification or a refinanced loan under the two major federal programs, the Home Affordable Modification Program (HAMP) and the Home Affordable Refinancing Program (HARP) (Federal Housing Finance Agency 2016; SIGTARP 2015, 101). Of these, over 3.4 million were assisted through the more successful HARP program, which was not aimed at seriously distressed borrowers, just borrowers who were unable to refinance their home due to being underwater. The total number of households receiving assistance was far fewer than the projected goal of 7 million to 9 million assisted homeowners.

Looking at the numbers of households assisted through HAMP loan modifications, the record is certainly disappointing: six years from the start of the program, just 887,000 households were actively participating. Although nearly 2.2 million loan modification trials were started, only about 1.4 million became permanent. And, of these, about one third re-defaulted (SIGTARP 2015, 140). In addition, about 70 percent of the households that had applied for loan modifications were rejected by their servicers (SIGTARP 2015, 101).

There have been four major federal strategies in terms of direct assistance to homeowners in default. These include counseling programs; voluntary modification programs, often with fairly narrow guidelines about eligibility; direct support to financial institutions to promote liquidity; and, to a much lesser extent, principal reduction efforts.

In reviewing the various initiatives, Immergluck noted that, in general, Bush administration efforts were weaker than Obama's, but even the latter have been insufficient (Immergluck 2013). We offer seven more specific observations about the array of programs aimed at stemming or remediating foreclosures, or dealing with nonperforming loans. The first two relate to the processes through which the programs were introduced and the general level of clarity about each initiative. The remaining five observations reflect the extent to which the financial sector represents a powerful interest group and the reluctance of the federal government to create programs that are not supported by this large and well-funded set of actors and institutions.

1. Programs were rolled out, rather timidly at first, with minimal direct benefits for homeowners.

The early measures were primarily focused on providing counseling. While this was helpful in many cases, it was too modest an intervention for the hundreds of thousands of households facing serious financial difficulties. In addition, President Bush set the tone, which was largely followed by the Obama administration (see observation 3, below), of creating loan modification programs that were designed by the financial industry and that heavily favored investors and lenders over borrowers. These initial programs were largely unsuccessful.

2. The programs were complicated, confusing, and the names of the programs were nondescriptive, readily forgettable, and easy to mix up.

Given the complexity of our mortgage finance system, a simple solution was, perhaps, unlikely. Regardless, the new initiatives were hard for consumers to understand and program names either did not explicitly describe the benefits being offered or were hard to distinguish from each other. In addition, program requirements often targeted a relatively narrow band of eligible households. These factors contributed to low levels of participation.

For example, under President Bush, we witnessed the creation of

- FHA Secure: refinancing program
- Hope Now Alliance: counseling; voluntary loan modifications
- National Foreclosure Mitigation Program: counseling
- HOPE for Homeowners: foreclosure prevention, primarily through initiatives to refinance loans through the Federal Housing Administration

The Obama initiatives included the Making Home Affordable Program, which consisted of several separate, although very similar-sounding programs aimed at borrowers at varying risk of foreclosure:

- Home Affordable Refinancing Program (HARP): a refinancing program for borrowers who were not in default and would benefit from a lower interest rate;
- Home Affordable Modification Program (HAMP): the principal loan–modification program for distressed borrowers in which loan payments would be reduced;

- Home Affordable Foreclosure Alternative: a program to provide incentives to lenders to allow severely "underwater" homeowners (where current market value of the home is less than the outstanding mortgage) to sell their homes by forgiving part of the balance due;
- And a variety of other programs that are ancillary to HAMP, such as the Unemployment Program, the Principal Reduction Alternative Program, and the Second Mortgage Program. These programs assist troubled borrowers to modify their mortgages when they are suffering from bouts of unemployment, have outstanding principal balances that exceed the value of their homes, and cannot afford a second mortgage.

In contrast to this confusing array of programs, during the Great Depression of the 1930s, there was a single, aggressive, simple, readily understandable refinancing option, provided by the Homeowners Loan Corporation. Qualifying homeowners could get fully amortized loans (which was not yet a standard practice in mortgage lending), at a fixed interest rate, for a longer loan period than was typical for that era.

3. Approaches were more sharply targeted to the needs of lenders/investors than to the needs of homeowners.

While it is not surprising that this characterized the Bush administration initiatives, President Obama did not offer a radical shift in approach; his appointment of a financial industry insider, Timothy Geithner, as Secretary of the Treasury presented a confusing message to those hoping for a significant change in direction.[3] Further, in January 2009, the Federal Reserve Bank began to buy Fannie Mae and Freddie Mac mortgage-backed securities. While this may have indirectly helped homeowners, the focus was on promoting liquidity to financial institutions and low interest rates. To the extent that homeowners benefited, they tended to have middle and upper incomes. Several years later, the Principal Reduction Alternative Program encouraged lenders to lower the amount of principal owed. But modifications had to make more financial sense to the lender than foreclosure or lenders were not obligated to implement them. Cost/benefit analyses were undertaken from strictly a lender/investor point of view; there was no requirement for impacts to be assessed based on net benefits to society or on homeowner or neighborhood needs. Even if it made overall financial sense to reduce principal, lenders were not required to do so.

4. The servicing industry was more oriented toward foreclosure, rather than loan modification.

The loan servicing business is based on consistency and volume. In contrast, loan modifications require specialized attention to each property and borrower. To do this well, case-by-case analyses are required and numerous guidelines and regulations must be followed. However, this type of individualized attention is costly and servicers are more prone to follow the simpler, less creative processes dictated by foreclosure.

5. There were few actual requirements placed on lenders/investors, and loan modification programs typically provided only small incentive payments to servicers.

In addition, sanctions for servicers not following HAMP guidelines, for example, were non-existent until June 2011, and even then they were modest. The combination of small incentives and the hesitancy to employ serious sanctions proved far too weak to reverse the strong proclivities of the mortgage industry to move forward with foreclosure in the event of delinquency and default.

6. A critical missing tool for addressing foreclosures was the stronger stick of bankruptcy "cram down" modification—a provision that would have allowed a bankruptcy court judge to reduce the principal amount owed on a primary residence.

Congress pushed back against this proposal, originally introduced by Senator Dick Durban (D-IL) in 2007, and while the Obama Administration initially endorsed it, it failed to make it a real priority and so the proposal died. If servicers and investors had been threatened with the possibility that a bankruptcy court judge might reduce the principal on the amount owed, this might have stimulated a stronger response from servicers. Moreover, bankruptcy judges would have been able to lower other nonmortgage debts as well, providing for a more successful approach to reducing a household's overall debt burden.

Of course, there are important questions about principal reduction. Although reducing the principal for those in serious default may not create a moral hazard by stimulating others to purposely default (just to get the principal reduction relief), is it equitable to provide this kind of relief for some and not for others? As with all non-entitlement programs aimed at providing a social good, this question vexed policy makers and, perhaps more importantly, contributed to a hostile political climate for proponents of principal reduction; nevertheless a full discussion is beyond the scope of this effort.

Might we have done better to offer principal reduction for everyone below a certain income/asset limit? Alternatively, should more efforts have been made to craft a simpler, more transparent initiative than the one offered by the Federal Housing Administration (FHA) Secure program, whereby loans advanced to cure defaults would be repaid upon sale, if a homeowner had positive equity? Or could nonprofits have been called upon to play a larger role by helping to acquire, on an interim basis, properties facing foreclosure with homeowners renting from the nonprofit and then having the option of reacquiring their home when finances stabilized (Bratt 2010).[4]

In conclusion, there may be some irony in the fact that the homeowners who may end up doing the best are those who are eligible for some of the restitution payments being made as a result of legal settlements between the federal and state governments and financial institutions. For example, states' attorneys general settled with the largest bank servicers to the tune of $26 billion over the 2010 "robo-signing" scandal—foreclosures taking place without following correct legal processes.[5]

7. Sales of nonperforming loans are being made to investors rather than to nonprofit organizations on behalf of homeowners.

Another disappointing aspect of President Obama's housing record involves the way in which HUD and the FHA along with Fannie Mae and Freddie Mac (government-sponsored enterprises, or GSEs), under the supervision of the Federal Housing Finance Agency (FHFA), has gone about selling loans that are in default, or non-performing. While these entities have had the option to sell the defaulting loans to nonprofit organizations that, in turn, would assist homeowners to retain occupancy of their homes, instead, most of the sales of these loans are providing investment opportunities for speculators. Although this allows the GSEs to remove nonperforming loans from their portfolios, it is detrimental both to the households who are losing their homes and it adds to the destabilization of neighborhoods, as homes become vacant due to foreclosure.

As a recent report noted, HUD and the FHFA

> are auctioning off, often at a discount, tens of thousands of Non-Performing Loans that they want to get off their books. The vast majority of these loans have gone to hedge funds and private equity firms, and in many cases the properties then end up in their hands. *Although Fannie Mae and Freddie Mac have been unwilling to offer principal reduction to struggling homeowners, they often offer steep discounts when they sell these mortgages to Wall Street speculators.* (Sen 2015, 1, emphasis in the original)

Out of the approximately 130,000 loans that HUD, Fannie Mae and Freddie Mac have sold off since 2012, only a small fraction—less than 2 percent—have gone to nonprofits. The vast majority has been sold to private equity firms and hedge funds (Sen 2015, 4).[6] And, particularly troubling is that the four largest purchasers of these HUD and FHFA loans may be "breaking laws, deceiving homeowners, and harming taxpayers more generally" (Sen 2015, 2).

Also disturbing is that, at the same time that HUD and the FHFA are providing private firms with lucrative investment opportunities, these agencies have been reticent, at best, and unwilling, at worst, to give preferential treatment to nonprofit organizations that are trying to assist foreclosed homeowners to retain occupancy of their homes as tenants, postforeclosure (Bratt 2016). Indeed, a recent editorial in the *New York Times* (2016) advocated that Federal housing agencies sell more of their foreclosed properties to nonprofits.

Despite President Obama finally being able to appoint his own choice to head the FHFA in 2014, Mel Watt, the agency has continued to be inflexible about offering GSE-foreclosed homes at sales prices that would be affordable to lower-income occupants. Moreover, HUD has very rarely approved foreclosed homes being conveyed with occupants, despite this being a permitted HUD policy and one that would benefit occupants of foreclosed homes, as well as the surrounding neighborhood (Bratt 2016).

In sum, the Obama Administration's responses to the mortgage crisis were too weak, too tentative, and too confusing. Its decision not to press hard for "cram down" bankruptcy modification early in the crisis, and its failure to push harder for effective servicer action in implementing HAMP were two major shortcomings. Also disappointing was the Obama administration's less than consumer-oriented approach to dealing with nonperforming loans and the disposition of foreclosed properties. To better prepare for any future crises, policy makers need to learn both from historical experiences and from the shortcomings of these efforts and craft a system that can provide a clearer, simpler, and more aggressive response to homeowner distress.

Conclusion

Although HUD, except through its governance of the FHA, was not a key player in the mortgage crisis, with much of the responsibility falling to the Treasury Department,[7] it is still the agency with the most direct involvement with the nation's overall housing agenda, as discussed in the first section of this chapter. As such, it is instructive to hear how President Obama summarized HUD's role over the course of about two-thirds of his term in office. In nominating a new secretary of HUD, Obama noted the major accomplishments of outgoing HUD secretary Shaun Donovan, who had headed the agency since the start of his administration.

The president highlighted increases in home sales and construction; declines in foreclosures; the number of households that are no longer "underwater" on their mortgages; and the $50 billion settlement by banks to compensate homeowners for being targeted by deceptive mortgage practices. The president acknowledged that these changes were "*in part* because of the outstanding work of Shaun Donovan" (emphasis added). Regardless of whatever role HUD played, it is likely that these changes were primarily due to improvements in the overall economy. Concerning accomplishments that were more fully within HUD's control, the president pointed to improvements in HUD's use of data to solve problems and save taxpayer dollars; efforts to build strong, sustainable neighborhoods; assisting 4.3 million families to buy a new home; and leading the recovery after Hurricane Sandy (Obama 2014).

Thus, the president's own summation of HUD's accomplishments, as he started the last one-third of his term in office, did not mention inroads being made to assist the most vulnerable members of the population. Although HUD's achievements are certainly commendable, particularly "efforts to build strong, sustainable neighborhoods," they fall far short of inspirational. The overriding conclusion of this inquiry is that the Obama housing record has been disappointing, both in terms of responses to the mortgage crisis and in making inroads on the more general set of housing issues.

Sadly, the optimism voiced by housing advocates at the start of his administration failed to materialize as fully as had been hoped. Despite some good efforts, the sharp distinctions between Republicans and Democrats, so apparent in other domestic and foreign policy areas, were not significant in the housing domain. Instead, the Obama record, while better than his predecessor, only represented a marginal improvement. The fundamental question of whether and how government should assist our most vulnerable residents to acquire and maintain decent, affordable homes was neither a dominant part of Obama's agenda, nor was it the focus of the ideological battles between the president and Congress. A more far-reaching, progressive housing strategy has not yet emerged as a federal priority.

Notes

1. Among the many components of this legislation, enacted in 2010, are the following: creation of the Federal Oversight Stability Council to safeguard the overall financial sector; limiting the ability of banks to set up "off-balance-sheet" entities, which can conceal risk; requiring greater regulation and transparency for trading of derivative products; instituting greater regulatory oversight of credit rating companies; and creating a new, independent Consumer Financial Protection Bureau. In addition, the legislation prescribed that no bank should be "too big to fail," and directed that large institutions would have to be broken up, if necessary.

2. The NSP program was created in 2008 and, in two subsequent funding rounds, has provided financial and technical assistance to states, local governments, nonprofits and a consortium of nonprofit entities on a competitive basis for the purchase and redevelopment of foreclosed and abandoned homes and residential properties. The goal of NSP is to mitigate the adverse neighborhood impacts of foreclosed and vacant properties.

3. Geithner was the president of the Federal Reserve Bank of New York during the Bush administration. In addition, Lawrence Summers, who had served as deputy secretary and secretary of the treasury during the Clinton administration, and had actively supported the view that derivative instruments issued by financial institutions did not need federal government regulation, was a close advisor to President Obama. Summers had been a leading candidate for the head of the Federal Reserve Bank, prior to his withdrawing his name for consideration, due to the opposition by several members of Congress.

4. Although on a small scale, a similar initiative is being carried out by Boston Community Capital, a nonprofit organization. Homes are purchased from lenders following a foreclosure and then sold back to the original homeowners, at the newly adjusted, lower market price (Dawan 2012). Another Boston program is focused on helping former owners and tenants to remain in their homes after foreclosure, but as renters (Bratt 2014, 2016).

5. In assessing their mortgages, JP Morgan has offered additional compensation for borrowers where irregularities were found (Silver-Greenberg and Protess 2013). In addition, JP Morgan settled various complaints related to its mortgage lending activities by making an additional $13 billion in payments—$9 billion in fees and $4 billion to struggling homeowners (Protess and Silver-Greenberg 2013).

6. The one exception to the general policy of essentially ignoring the role of nonprofits as potential buyers of nonperforming loans involves New Jersey Community Capital, a CDFI. The pilot, the Community Impact Pool program, facilitates the sale of groups of nonperforming loans in a given locale so that they can be restructured "to help keep families in their homes and enable distressed communities to flourish" (Wayne Meyer, President of NJCC, quoted by Lane 2015).

7. Despite HUD's modest official role in the response to the mortgage crisis, Secretary Donovan and others at HUD were still heavily involved, playing an important housing advocacy role in the design and delivery of programs.

References

Arnold, Althea, Sheila Crowley, Elina Bravve, Sarah Brundage, and Christine Biddlecombe. 2014. *Out of Reach 2014: 25 Years Later, the Affordable Housing Crisis Continues*. With preface by Barry Zigas. Washington, D.C.: National Low Income Housing Coalition.

Bornstein, David. 2014. "The Push to End Chronic Homelessness Is Working." *New York Times*, May 28. Accessed July 1, 2014. http://opinionator.blogs.nytimes.com/2014/05/28/the-push-to-end-chronic-homelessness-is-working/?_php=true&_type=blogs&_r=0.

Bratt, Rachel G. 1976. "Federal Homeownership Policy and Home Finance: A Study of Program Operations and Impacts on the Consumer." Ph.D. diss., Massachusetts Institute of Technology. http://hdl.handle.net/1721.1/64829.

———. 2002. "Housing for Very Low-Income Households: The Record of President Clinton, 1993–2000." *Housing Studies* 18 (4): 607–35.

———. 2010. "Fixing the Homeowner Default Trap." *Boston Globe*, February 28. http://archive.boston.com/bostonglobe/editorial_opinion/oped/articles/2010/02/28/fixing_the_homeowner_default_trap/.

———. 2012. "Home Ownership Risk and Responsibility Before and After the U.S. Mortgage Crisis." In *Beyond Home Ownership: Housing, Welfare and Society*, ed. Richard Ronald and Marja Elsinga, 146–69. New York: Routledge.

———. 2014. "Coalition of Occupied Homes in Foreclosure (COHIF): An Assessment of the Greater Four Corners Community Stabilization Project during the First Two Years." *Citizen's Housing and Planning Association*. June 12. Accessed September 29, 2014. http://www.chapa.org/housing-policy/research-reports/coalition-occupied-homes-foreclosure-cohif-assessment-greater-four.

———. 2016. "Post-Foreclosure Conveyance of Occupied Homes and Preferential Sales to Nonprofits: Rationales, Policies, and Underlying Conflicts." *Housing Policy Debate*. http://dx.doi.org/10.1080/10511482.2016.1143857.

CoreLogic. 2016. "National Foreclosure Report." January. http://www.corelogic.com/about-us/researchtrends/national-foreclosure-report.aspx#.Vye203puBDQ.

Dawan, Shaila. 2012. "Lender with an Unusual Offer: A Second Chance." *New York Times*, March 21. Accessed June 7, 2014. http://www.nytimes.com/2012/03/22/your-money/program-in-massachusetts-helps-those-facing-foreclosure.html?pagewanted=all&_r=0.

Emmanuel, Dan. 2016. "The National Need for Housing." 2016 Advocates' Guide. National Low Income Housing Coalition. http://nlihc.org/sites/default/files/2016_Advocates-Guide.pdf.

Federal Housing Finance Agency. 2016. "Refinance Report—Fourth Quarter 2015." http://www.fhfa.gov/AboutUs/Reports/ReportDocuments/4Q15-Refi-Report.pdf.

Financial Crisis Inquiry Commission. 2011. "The Financial Crisis Inquiry Report." Washington, D.C.: U.S. Government Printing Office. Accessed June 7, 2014. http://fcic-static.law.stanford.edu/cdn_media/fcic-reports/fcic_final_report_full.pdf.

Ghent, Andra C., Rubén Hernández-Murillo, and Michael T. Owyang. 2012. "Did Affordable Housing Legislation Contribute to the Subprime Securities Boom?" Working paper 2012–005B. Federal Reserve Bank of St. Louis. Accessed June 7, 2014. https://research.stlouisfed.org/wp/more/2012-005.

Henry, Meghan, Azim Shivji, Tanya de Sousa, and Rebecca Cohen. 2015. *The 2015 Annual Home- less Assessment Report (AHAR) to Congress. Part 1: Point-in-Time Estimates of Homelessness.* Washington, D.C.: U.S. Department of Housing and Urban Development. https://www. hudexchange.info/resources/documents/2015-AHAR-Part-1.pdf.

Housingwire. 2014. "House Republicans Struggle to Control CFPB." May 21. Accessed June 6, 2014. http://www.housingwire.com/articles/30081-house-republicans-struggle-to-control-cfpb.

HUD (U.S. Department of Housing and Urban Development). 2015. *Worst Case Housing Needs 2015 Report to Congress.* https://www.huduser.gov/portal//Publications/pdf/WorstCase Needs_2015.pdf.

Immergluck, Dan. 2009. *Foreclosed! High-Risk Lending, Deregulation, and the Undermining of Amer- ica's Mortgage Market.* Ithaca, N.Y.: Cornell University Press.

———. 2013. "Too Little, Too Late, and Too Timid: The Federal Response to the Foreclosure Crisis at the Five-Year Mark." *Housing Policy Debate* 23 (1): 199–232.

Joint Center for Housing Studies of Harvard University. 2013. *America's Rental Housing: Evolving Markets and Needs.* Cambridge, Mass.: Harvard University Press.

Keith, Nathaniel S. 1973. *Politics and the Housing Crisis since 1930.* New York: Universe Books.

Lane, Ben. 2015. "Fannie Mae picks non-profit for first small sale of non-performing loans." *Hous- ingWire.* September 2. http://www.housingwire.com/articles/34963-fannie-mae-picks-non -profit-for-firstsmall-sale-of-non-performing-loans.

Marcuse, Peter, and W. Dennis Keating. 2006. "The Permanent Housing Crisis: The Failures of Conservatism and the Limitations of Liberalism." In *A Right to Housing: Foundation for a New Social Agenda,* ed. Rachel G. Bratt, Michael E. Stone, and Chester Hartman, 139–62. Philadelphia: Temple University Press.

Moberg, David. 2007. "Obama's Third Way." *Shelterforce Online* 149 (Spring). Accessed August 2, 2014. http://nhi.org/online/issues/149/obama.html.

National Low Income Housing Coalition. 2008. "National Housing Trust Fund: Election Met with Optimism by Low Income Housing Advocates." *Memo to Members: The Weekly Newsletter of the National Low Income Housing Coalition* 13 (44). http://nlihc.org/sites/default/files/Memo 13-44.pdf.

———. 2014. *Advocates' Guide to Housing and Community Development Policy,* 90.

New York Times. 2015. "The Problem with House Prices." August 17. http://www.nytimes.com /2015/08/17/opinion/the-problem-with-house-prices.html.

New York Times. 2016. "The Racist Roots of a Way to Sell Homes." April 29. http://www.nytimes .com/2016/04/29/opinion/the-racist-roots-of-a-way-to-sell-homes.html.

Obama, Barack. 2014. "Remarks by the President at Nomination of Shaun Donovan as OMB Direc- tor and Mayor Julián Castro as Secretary of Housing and Urban Development, May 23, 2014." White House. Accessed July 1, 2014. http://www.whitehouse.gov/the-press-office/2014/05/23 /remarks-president-nomination-shaun-donovan-omb-director-and-mayor-juli-n.

Protess, Ben, and Jessica Silver-Greenberg. 2013. "Where Does JPMorgan's $13 Billion Go?" DealBook, *New York Times,* November 20. Accessed June 30, 2014. http://dealbook.nytimes .com/2013/11/20/where-does-jpmorgans-13-billion-go/.

Sen, Aditi. 2015. "Do Hedge Funds Make Good Neighbors? How Fannie Mae, Freddie Mac & HUD Are Selling Off Our Neighborhoods to Wall Street." The Center for Popular Democracy and the ACCE Institute. http://populardemocracy.org/sites/default/files/Housing%20Report %20June%202015.pdf.

SIGTARP (Office of the Special Inspector General for the Troubled Asset Relief Program). 2014. *Quarterly Report to Congress.* January 29. https://www.sigtarp.gov/Quarterly%20Reports /July_30_2014_Report_to_Congress.pdf.

Silver-Greenberg, Jessica, and Ben Protess. 2013. "JPMorgan Chase Faces a Full-Court Press of Federal Investigations." DealBook, *New York Times,* March 27. Accessed June 7, 2013. http:// dealbook.nytimes.com/2013/03/26/jpmorgan-chase-faces-full-court-press-of-federal-inves tigations/.

U.S. President's Commission on Housing. 1982. *The Report of the President's Commission on Housing*. Washington, D.C.: U.S. Government Printing Office.

Wallison, Peter J. 2011. "The True Story of the Financial Crisis." *The American Spectator,* May. Accessed June 7, 2014. http://spectator.org/archives/2011/05/13/the-true-story-of-the -financial-crisis.

5

PUBLIC HOUSING POLICY UNDER OBAMA
(SEE THE CLINTON ADMINISTRATION)

JANET SMITH

> For a half century, housing policy debates have often been about
> homeownership versus rental, public versus private, supply versus
> demand, and people versus place. This economic and housing crisis
> has brought these abstract arguments into sharp focus. For every
> family and neighborhood in America, it has revealed the dramatic gap
> between wages and housing prices, which easy credit through so-called
> "financial innovation" failed to close. It pulled back the curtain on
> the unsustainable nature of our growth—the great distances too
> many families have to travel simply to get to work or school—and
> rolled back nearly two decades of gains in urban cores
> of older industrial cities.
>
> —*Shaun Donavon, U.S. Department of Housing and Urban Development,*
> *May 2010,* HUD Strategic Plan 2010–2015, *iii*

The Obama administration stepped into a huge housing crisis upon taking office
in 2009 with steeply rising foreclosure rates and plummeting housing values. Compounding this situation was an already strapped nation of renters and owners living in housing that by federal standards was unaffordable.[1] While the immediate
focus was on stabilizing the for-sale market, the U.S. Department of Housing and
Urban Development reviewed its entire portfolio of programs as it developed a strategic plan for the agency—one that would guide the administration through its
first term and segue hopefully into its second. Taking a long view, the plan was to
define a new HUD for the next fifty years. This included "Improving Outcomes
for the Poorest Families," which had two measures of success: reducing the number of households with worst case housing needs and increasing the proportion of
HUD-assisted families in low-poverty and racially diverse communities (HUD
2010a).

To help meet HUD's goals, the Obama administration committed to continuing the transformation of public housing into mixed-income communities and to
finding ways to offset the estimated $26 billion to $32 billion backlog of capital
development needs—an amount that increased by several billion dollars since a

Democrat was last in the White House.[2] Two new initiatives were introduced: Choice Neighborhoods and the Preservation, Enhancement and Transition of Rental Assistance (PETRA) Act. Choice Neighborhoods to a certain extent is a new version of HOPE VI, a program developed during the Clinton era to transform public housing into mixed-income communities and which ended when the funding was zeroed out in the FY 2010 budget. However, as Khare illustrates in chapter 10, Choice Neighborhoods is also a much broader initiative; it does not just replace public housing with mixed-income developments, it also focuses on the surrounding neighborhood.

Proposed in February 2010, PETRA sought to help all the cash-poor federal affordable housing programs. The plan was to leverage as much as $27 billion in mostly private capital by converting public and existing HUD-assisted housing to a new form of project-based contract (HUD 2010b). In simple terms, the plan was to use the public and assisted housing, and more precisely its guaranteed rents, to raise funds from private investors for capital improvements (*Shelterforce* 2010). The argument behind the strategy was also simple: HUD needed at least that much for capital improvements and maintenance to prevent the further deterioration of its nearly 1.2 million public housing units. PETRA would also consolidate various rental assistance programs and wait lists and encourage regional mobility for voucher holders, which could potentially help public housing residents move into more economically and racially mixed communities. At the same time, it would require all developments to move toward becoming mixed-income.

This chapter examines decisions made by the Obama administration aimed at improving the quality of public and subsidized housing. I focus on the logic of PETRA, which was never brought to a vote in Congress, and the Rental Assistance Demonstration (RAD), which was proposed in its place and approved by Congress in 2012. While different programs, RAD is very similar to PETRA: it relies on converting public and assisted housing stock to a voucher-based form of rent assistance, which then can be used to leverage private funding to maintain and redevelop and eventually become mixed-income. Both the idea to transform public housing neighborhoods and to use the federal rent subsidy to leverage private investment originated in the Clinton era. While the latter was never implemented, the former was and many lessons have been learned. Tying the two approaches together, which is what the Obama administration has done through its Rental Assistance Demonstration program, represents a new form of public–private partnership that is being watched closely. While RAD represents a solution to dwindling financial support for public housing, it is also a risky proposition and has many longstanding advocates concerned that this truly is the end of public housing in the United States (see discussion in Stephens 2014). Since RAD is relatively new and public housing transformation is still a work in progress, my analysis focuses on the theory of change underpinning both and how HUD has developed each program to produce the early- and intermediate-term changes needed to achieve its goals.

Public Housing Transformation: Choice or No Choice?

The federal government began redeveloping public housing in earnest in 1989 when Congress created the National Commission on Severely Distressed Public Housing, which was charged with developing a national action plan to eliminate the conditions that made an estimated 86,000 units "severely distressed." It was during the Clinton administration that HOPE VI was introduced to redevelop the worst developments into low-density, mixed-income housing. The policy objectives were clear: (1) improve the living environment for residents of severely distressed public housing through the demolition, rehabilitation, reconfiguration, or replacement of obsolete projects (or portions thereof); (2) revitalize sites on which such public housing projects are located and contribute to the improvement of the surrounding neighborhood; (3) provide housing that will avoid or decrease the concentration of very low-income families; and (4) build sustainable communities.[3] Achieving these objectives required a lot more than the $5 billion Congress allocated for HOPE VI, so HUD required any local public housing authority (PHA) applying for the grant to use it to leverage additional dollars. Grants were up to $50 million per development, which, given the size of those deemed severely distressed, was not enough for PHAs to fulfill their plans, especially ambitious ones (e.g., the estimated cost of the redevelopment plan for Cabrini Green in Chicago, which would develop about 3,700 units, was $281 million).

HOPE VI was premised on a belief that "the intentional mixing of incomes and working status of residents" would "enhance the quality of life for residents while improving the economic viability of multifamily developments, particularly former public housing developments, and strengthen neighborhoods" (HUD 1997, 1). The underlying assumption was that mixing together market rate and public housing units would "promote the economic and social interaction of low-income families within the broader community, thereby providing greater opportunities for the upward mobility of such families" (HUD 1996, 1970, 8–19). Trying to make up for previous mistakes in the design and development of public housing, the intent was to undo the social isolation of very low-income families, mostly African American, and to redress the negative externalities produced in surrounding communities. Clearly, these were high expectations for the social outcomes of income mixing. Research to date suggests that there has been greater success on some aspects while less on others. For example, most agree that public housing residents have benefited from living in improved housing conditions. Also, these communities generally have seen an increase in income levels and rates of employment. However, whether that change was due to improvement in the economic status of public housing residents or simply their relocation to other neighborhoods is not really known (Levy, McDade, and Dumlao 2010).

What we do know is that, since 1993, there has been a net loss of more than 200,000 public housing units—far more than the number of severely distressed units estimated by HUD in the early 1990s (CBPP 2012). While many attribute this reduction in public housing units to the HOPE VI program, it is only partially to blame (or credit depending on point of view). Two additional changes in federal policy during the Clinton administration made this possible: the 1995 Rescissions Act and the Quality Housing and Work Responsibility Act (QHWRA) of 1998. The 1995 Rescissions Act suspended the one-for-one replacement rule that had previously required all PHAs to replace any units it tore down. As in the past, residents would have to be provided vouchers but there was no requirement to build a permanent unit.[4] The QHWRA required PHAs to remove from their inventory any development with 250 units or more with high vacancy rates (10 percent or higher) if modernization was more costly than providing tenants rent assistance in the private market. Furthermore, if redeveloped, the housing had to be mixed-income but it did not have to be owned by the PHA, allowing private developers who built replacement housing to own and operate it with public rental subsidies. While the developer had to guarantee the units would be available for use as public housing by low-income families for a minimum of forty years, the funding to keep it so was subject to annual budget negotiations.[5] There was nothing to assure the owner, whether a PHA or private company, that Congress would allocate the funds needed to fulfill HUD's side of the contract.

Between a Rock and Hard Place: Long-Term Federal Support for Public Housing

Reflecting on what had changed since the agency was created in 1965, HUD's 2010–15 plan recognized that while affordable housing was once primarily built, owned, and managed by government it now was in the hands of partners— nonprofit, local government, and the private sector. As the plan states:

> These new partners bring a new discipline to the housing industry, changing the way affordable housing is financed and how properties are managed. Our challenge now is to follow their lead, to restore the federal leadership that will take these innovations to scale, and to collaborate with these new partners that have become key civic institutions in neighborhoods across the country.[6]

Once the vanguard, public–private partnerships were now HUD's stock and trade. With PETRA and RAD, the Obama administration fully committed to using public funds to induce private capital investment. For the most part, the agency had no other option given the scale of the problem and the limited support over the years from Congress to fully fund the rehabilitation of public and subsidized housing. However, as stated above, this administration and HUD also believes there is something to learn from these partners, under the assumption that they shared the same vision and sought the same outcomes. In its revised mission statement, in addition to being committed to improving the lives and living conditions of its residents, HUD promised to its partners it would "be a flexible, reliable problem solver and source of innovation" and its commitment to the public was to "be a good neighbor, building inclusive and sustainable communities that create value and investing public money responsibly to deliver results that matter."[7] While not necessarily new territory for HUD it is for most of the private sector, given its housing investment track record.

HUD introduced PETRA a year after Obama had been in office. Perhaps it was too soon to ask the country to support a program that relied on the same people and institutions blamed for the housing crisis we were mired in. While many PETRA opponents did express concerns about this aspect of the program, they also focused on how it harkened back to the Public Housing Reinvestment Initiative, a proposal from George W. Bush's administration that was not approved by Congress. However, this actually was a Clinton-era idea, though it was never implemented. In 1994, during an extremely aggressive Republican-led 104th Congress, which was considering shutting down the agency based on concerns about inefficiency, raised by the Office of Management and Budget, the Clinton administration and HUD introduced its "reinvention" (Manegold 1995, 17; HUD 1995). Part of a three-pronged plan to overhaul the agency, one proposal was to create a "Housing Certificate Fund" (HCF). The HCF would consolidate the voucher and certificate programs and replace all project-based assisted housing programs so that "as contracts expire on existing project-based programs and as public housing is transformed from a project-based system, HCF will become the vehicle for providing portable subsidies for low-income Americans" (HUD 1995, 12). At the time, this proposal "significantly alienated traditional constituencies" because it potentially could have resulted in complete disinvestment of the entire stock if tenants moved out, which given the condition many likely would (Austin 1997).

When PETRA was introduced, HUD spent several months doing "outreach, interactive webcasts, stakeholder discussions, and PowerPoint presentations" to explain to its constituents the logic of why this initiative was needed. The presentations focused on how this approach was critical to the future of public housing and assuring its overall health and stability. They also pointed to urgency of getting funding quickly because the Obama administration had another funding challenge with expiring rental assistance contracts for about 38,000 subsidized units. This included developments funded through the Rent Supplement (Rent Supp) and Rental Assistance Payment (RAP) programs, which could not be renewed. Interestingly, the expiring Rent Supp and RAP contracts were the result of the Clinton administration's Multifamily Assisted Housing Reform and Affordability Act (MAHRA), which was in response to potential funding problems for Section 8 project-based contracts, many set to expire in 2000. Many Section 8 buildings were built in the 1980s when interest rates were in the double digits, which meant high carrying costs for the owners and higher rent subsidies for the federal government. Just as many homeowners were doing at the time, HUD wanted Section 8 property owners to refinance their mortgages and take advantage of the low interest rates. Owners had the option to stay in the program and refinance or pay up and "opt out." Unfortunately, many owners across the country and especially in hot housing markets opted out of the program and thousands of affordable units were lost from HUD's portfolio. Those that opted in were given new rent subsidies via the Rent Supp and RAP programs that under MAHRA were limited in time (twenty years) and could not be renewed (HUD 2013b).

HUD proposed PETRA partly in response to a problem it had created. However, PETRA was designed to do much more than help extend the rent assistance of a relatively small portion of its portfolio; it was to effectively transfer the future of its stock to private investors in order to save it now. Tenants, who initially seemed on board, soon opposed it, along with housing advocates, academics, and many members of Congress led by Representative Maxine Waters (Waters 2010). Their primary concern was that this scheme would not only privatize public and subsidized housing, it would make it vulnerable to foreclosure if for some reason Congress did not honor the rents in the future and, as happened under MAHRA, could be converted to market-rate rentals (*Shelterforce* 2010). In response, HUD promised that there were rules and guarantees in PETRA to assure that private investors had to keep housing affordable (for at least thirty years), tenants had to be consulted before conversion, and there was protection against foreclosure (HUD 2010b). However, there was no requirement or way to require Congress or the president to keep the rents funded. And under RAD there is no guarantee either.

After several months of negative public critique, PETRA went dormant. In late 2011 HUD introduced the Rental Assistance Demonstration program, which was easily approved by Congress in July 2012 with relatively little public outcry. RAD allows PHAs to use either project-based vouchers or project-based rental assistance to fund the operation of their public housing, which then can be used to borrow money to rehab the buildings (HUD 2012). While HUD claims that RAD is not a reprise of PETRA, it uses the same strategy to get private sector investment: long-term rent assistance as a guarantee, which in the case of RAD is up to twenty years—the same as MARHA and Section 8 in the past. The key difference is that it is a voluntary program rather than a policy affecting all HUD housing, and it is currently capped at 60,000 units—though HUD has a waiting list for another 117,000 (HUD 2014). Also, unlike PETRA there was relatively little promotion of RAD.

Some have described RAD as a "win-win-win" since it will preserve the housing stock and provide long-term affordable quality housing for low-income families, all without having to rely on Congress to increase funding (Hoekman and Griffith 2013). However, it also places a 50 percent cap on the number of project-based vouchers allowed in each RAD development in order to promote income mixing. The exception to this will be granted for units for households that are either elderly or have a person with a disability, or that agree to participate in supportive services programs. These units then can only continue getting rent assistance if occupied by a household in one of these categories. As a result, "some PHAs might urge half of the households to move to other developments, if available."[8] However, tenants may also choose to leave with a voucher—a feature some valued in PETRA because it promotes choice and could help reduce racial and economic segregation.[9]

Both Choice Neighborhoods and the Rental Assistance Demonstration continue the Clinton and Bush administration's shift toward relying on private investment to restore and even save public and subsidized housing. The Obama administration appears to have acquiesced to the permanent withdrawal of federal support for affordable housing for the poor and which Democrats in the past have expanded including Clinton when he first entered office (Hays 2012). In sharp contrast, Obama supported shoring up banks that were "too big to fail" and now is turning to them to loan the government money to fix up its public housing. This requires putting a lot of faith in the private sector to step up and the federal government to keep its promise and pay the rent.

Early evidence suggests that investors are interested in RAD, but it should be read as part of a longer cautionary tale (HUD 2013b). While HOPE VI did prove the private sector is willing to partner with HUD and local PHAs to redevelop public housing and even take some of the risk, it has also provided insights into some real and potential limits to these partnerships—some that HUD anticipated and some it did not but should have nonetheless. If RAD is expanded, serious consideration needs to be given to the lessons learned.

Change in Theory and Practice

In evaluation research, a theory of change describes how and why an initiative works (Connell and Kubisch 1998). As Weiss describes it, "the concept of grounding evaluation in theories of change takes for granted that social programs are based on explicit or implicit theories about how and why the program will work" and that through the evaluation process, these theories will be revealed (Weiss 1995). In practical work, it is recommended that an initiative should be designed with a comprehensive picture in mind of the early- and intermediate-term changes needed to reach the long-term goal being sought (Weiss 1995). In this case, with RAD as with HOPE VI, the goal is to secure private sector investment to rehabilitate public and subsidized housing.

The Clinton administration, to a certain extent, can take credit for making the early changes needed to move us toward the privatization of public and subsidized housing, particularly in outlining why it was needed and reframing the problem. This included emphasizing the benefits of giving local government more control in the process (they know best what is needed in their communities), the logic of mixed-income housing as a social policy as well as a financial strategy (it might change the culture of poverty and definitely will reduce the concentration of it), and the presumed benefits of bringing the private sector to the table to solve the public housing problem (these developers have built a lot of housing and know what is needed to make a successful development, evidenced by what they have already produced) (Smith 2013).

At the time, HUD itself needed to improve its performance, which included becoming more efficient and effective at what it was charged with doing.[10] Without going into the mechanics of retooling HUD to meet these expectations, I focus here on what was expected to change outside of the agency and specifically in the private sector in order to bring developers and lending institutions into the process of redeveloping public housing under HOPE VI and what is still needed if RAD is going to produce the results sought. Focusing on the financial aspects only, four key groups of actors have to change or adapt new behavior in very specific ways:

- Lending institutions have to accept the risk of financing mixed-income housing often in weak submarkets.
- Private sector developers have to get private investors to invest in these projects.
- Private investors/consumers have to put aside any prejudice or preconceived notion about living near low-income families and what makes a secure investment when buying a new home.
- PHAs have to commit to rehabilitating units if they can be and use vouchers as a substitute only when this is infeasible.

So what did HUD do to help make each group of actors change to assure private investment in public housing transformation? First, it changed its underwriting policy to allow mixed financing and specifically to let market conditions drive the housing mix and overall development, which meant allowing less public housing in the mix depending on how much market-rate housing might be needed to make it successful. As a result, the income and tenure profiles of mixed-income public housing developments vary widely. However, a common feature across most is the limited number of public housing units in the mix. While in part due to the social policy rhetoric and concern that too much public housing would essentially reproduce the problems that the transformation was trying to fix, the amount of replacement public housing is more likely the result of negotiations between developers and PHAs about what is financially feasible and profitable. Research suggests that location also matters with hot markets more likely to have less public housing, even though federal underwriting would allow more.[11] All this was possible under HOPE VI as long as there were vouchers to make up the difference between the replacement housing and original units. The same is true for RAD, which only allows half the units in each development to be converted to project-based vouchers. By default, this means a potential of at least a 50 percent reduction in actual hard units with affordable rents guaranteed.

Second, to help for-profit developers get private investment into HOPE VI developments, HUD allowed PHAs to use the low-income housing tax credit (LIHTC) to subsidize development of the "affordable units" in the mix (i.e., those units with price points between the market and public housing). While adding more layers to the financing, this does bring in private investment; however, it also means a potential loss of tax revenue (assuming investors did not invest but paid taxes on the money they invested) and it is a very secure investment when compared to making a straight equity loan. Also, when combined with the public housing development funds and rent subsidy, both assured the developer that the majority of the development and its long-term costs were covered (or at least the revenue sources were known). This meant that the majority of units on average were in some way "guaranteed" by the federal government—the public housing rent through annual allocation and the LIHTC through oversight by the Internal Revenue Service.

While HOPE VI grantees were able to leverage and steadily increase the amount of investment coming from other sources, the highest it got was $2.63 per HOPE VI dollar (GAO 2002). However, most of that was from other federal sources—80 percent according to HUD—which raises several questions, most importantly, why didn't we see more "true" private sector investment? One answer might be the availability of the LIHTC, which the National Commission on Severely Distressed Public Housing explicitly said should not be used because it would take resources away from other development—and it did. In communities with a large number of HOPE VI projects like Chicago, the majority of LIHTC allocations were held and given directly to the housing authority (Smith 2013). The same is happening in RAD already, with 83 of 132 projects using LIHTC. Furthermore, these tax credit units are not always that affordable and they do not adjust with income, so many developers rely on housing choice vouchers to cover rents.[12]

Although the LIHTC is technically private investors putting money into affordable housing, it is really a very safe form of investment and usually made—because the investors are necessarily interested in the issue but because they can get a good return on their investment. The LIHTC in HOPE VI and now in RAD means controlled private investment with significant tax benefits to incentivize investors. This is not the same as having investment from banks or a real estate investment trust, which take the risk that their investment might lose money. The LIHTC in effect does the opposite—investors put money in and federal oversight makes sure the developer keeps the units occupied or pay a penalty. Occupancy is important because it is part of the compliance review, which in turn then determines whether the tax credit agreement is being fulfilled (i.e., the funds are being used for the purposes intended).

Third, HUD did very little to directly incentivize higher-income people to move into mixed-income developments, leaving it to the local development team to market their units. However, it did lift the total development cost ceiling to ensure developers could produce quality housing for all income groups in the mix. Since no systematic study of the market response to mixed-income housing has been completed on how much profit developers have made, we do not know how successful developers have been in attracting nonsubsidized renters and buyers or whether some locations have fared better than others. What we do know is that developers generally did not take a lot of risk when it came to the market portion of the development mix. As noted already, the underwriting process allowed the mix to be determined to some extent by the developer's read of the market. Assuming more market rate units would be needed in areas lacking a market, developers could justify building more. However, while that made sense from the perspective of FHA underwriting, it ran contrary to the fact that most developers likely saw such sites as highly risky ventures. In fact, the U.S. GAO, after reviewing several HOPE VI grants issued in the first five years, found that while there was success in "economically viable locations," it was less optimistic about sites that were "physically isolated or suffered from extreme economic distress" (GAO 1998, 25). It concluded that "the current HOPE VI funding model may not be adequate to revitalize some of the nation's most severely distressed sites" (GAO 1998, 26). And the same concerns are raised by RAD, which has no guarantee that banks will loan money to invest in public or subsidized housing. If past is prologue, then we can expect risk-averse lenders to be willing to invest in safe markets and avoid certain locations all together.

Finally, based on the number of units demolished since the introduction of HOPE VI and more importantly since rescinding one-for-one replacement and QHWRA, there is little reason to believe that this trend will not continue with RAD. However, unlike the severely distressed units that HOPE VI addressed and the large developments that QHWRA required to be demolished if not feasible to rehab, the remaining stock is relatively speaking in fairly good condition. Based on a 2010 report, the average cost for capital repairs was estimated to be just $19,029 per unit, with a median of $15,374 per unit (Finkel et al. 2010). In comparison to the average cost of building new replacement housing, this is a deal! This may explain why the Obama administration is relying on a radical approach to funding the rehabilitation of federal affordable housing even if the likelihood of its success relies on various actors behaving in a contrary fashion.

Conclusion

Historically, Democrats have been on the side of public housing when compared to Republicans (Hays 2012). That changed with the Clinton administration. While it is understandable why some attribute this shift to neoliberalism and blame Democrats for embracing it, we should also consider how both the Clinton and Obama administrations were being pragmatic about finding new sources of funding when it was clear Congress was not a fan of public and subsidized housing. Unlike Clinton, the Obama administration is generally committed to preserving what housing we have, favoring rehabilitation over demolition, and is not as focused on vouchering people out, though RAD does try to strike a balance by giving people choice.

Still, there is a fundamental premise embraced by both administrations that cannot be ignored: the assumption that mixed-income development is a solution to poverty—something that has still not been proven through years of HOPE VI research (Levy, McDade, and Dumlao 2010). At a time when the United States has the highest ever reported level of "worst case housing needs"—8.48 million very low-income renter households, which is a 43.5 percent increase since 2007 (HUD 2013a)—strategies like RAD that reduce the availability of subsidy to keep people in affordable housing, especially if it has been renovated, are short-sighted. Clearly, there is a political calculus applied in every policy decision. In the case of public and subsidized housing, it appears that the Obama administration believes that reducing housing for those with the most need will somehow help reduce poverty. That sounds much more like a position a Republican would take.

Notes

1. Based on 2011 data, the U.S. Department of Housing and Urban Development estimated that 8.48 million, or 43.9 percent, of all low-income households were "worst case," with most cost burdened, that is, paying more than 30 percent of their income toward their housing costs including utilities, taxes, and insurance. This was a 43.5 percent increase over 2007 (HUD 2013a).
2. The low-end estimate is from the U.S. Department of Housing and Urban Development (HUD 2013b). The high-end estimate is from the National Housing Law Project (NHLP 2016).
3. Quality Housing and Work Responsibility Act of 1998. Pub. L. No. 105–276.
4. The U.S. Department of Housing and Urban Development had lost about 25 percent of its budget at the time, so vouchers were definitely a cost-effective way to house more people.
5. Quality Housing and Work Responsibility Act of 1998.
6. Fiscal Year 1993 Appropriation Act, H.R. 5679, Pub. L. 102-389, 2.
7. Ibid., 4.
8. National Low Income Housing Coalition to Office of General Counsel, Department of Housing and Urban Development, comments on Rental Assistance Demonstration, April 23, 2012. http://nlihc.org/sites/default/files/NLIHC_RAD_Comments_4-23-12.pdf.
9. Poverty & Race Research Action Council to U.S. House Financial Services Committee, May 25, 2010. http://www.prrac.org/pdf/PETRA_Letter_to_House_Financial_Services_Committee.pdf.
10. This is a larger subject than can be addressed here. For early lessons learned, see GAO (1998).
11. The Federal Housing Administration assumed that more market-rate housing was needed in the mix in weak markets while strong markets needed less.
12. This is not unique to public housing transformation but rather a common problem with the LIHTC, which sets rents at a fixed rate that is often too high for many working poor families—the target market—let alone most public housing residents. Current research suggests that up to 70 percent of extremely low-income LIHTC tenants also have a housing choice voucher or some form of rent assistance. See Furman Center for Real Estate and Urban Policy (2012).

References

Austin, Diane. 1997. "Federal Housing Policy: The Road Ahead." *Shelterforce Online.* http://www.nhi.org/online/issues/91/feds.html.

Center on Budget and Policy Priorities (CBPP). 2012. *National Federal Rental Assistance Facts.* Washington, D.C.: Center on Budget and Policy Priorities. http://www.cbpp.org/sites/default /files/atoms/files/4-13-11hous.pdf.

Connell, James P., and Anne C. Kubisch. 1998. "Applying a Theory of Change Approach to the Evaluation of Comprehensive Community Initiatives: Progress, Prospects, and Problems." In *New Approaches to Evaluating Community Initiatives,* Vol. 2, *Theory, Measurement, and Analysis,* ed. Karen Fulbright-Anderson, Anne C. Kubisch, and James P. Connell, 15–44. New York: Aspen Institute.

Finkel, Meryl, Ken Lam, Christopher Blaine, R. J. de la Cruz, Donna DeMarco, Melissa Vandawalker, Michelle Woodford, Craig Torres, and David Kaiser. 2010. *Capital Needs in the Public Housing Program.* Revised final report for the U.S. Department of Housing and Urban Development. Bethesda, Md.: Abt Associates. http://portal.hud.gov/hudportal/documents /huddoc?id=PH_Capital_Needs.pdf.

Furman Center for Real Estate and Urban Policy. 2012. "*What Can We Learn about the Low-Income Housing Tax Credit Program by Looking at the Tenants?*" Moelis Institute policy brief (October). http://furmancenter.org/files/publications/LIHTC_Final_Policy_Brief_v2.pdf.

GAO (U.S. General Accounting Office). 1998. *HOPE VI: Progress and Problems in Revitalizing Distressed Public Housing.* Washington, D.C.: GAO/RCED-98–187. www.gao.gov/assets/ 230/226004.pdf.

———. 2002. *HOPE VI Leveraging Has Increased, but HUD Has Not Met Annual Reporting Requirement.* Washington, D.C.: GAO/RCED-03–91. http://www.gao.gov/assets/240/236351.pdf.

Hays, R. Allen. 2012. *The Federal Government and Urban Housing.* 3rd ed. SUNY Series in Urban Public Policy. New York: State University of New York Press.

Hoekman, Scott, and John Griffith. 2013. "HUD's Rental Assistance Demonstration: A Bold Plan for Preserving Affordability in an Era of Austerity." *HUD User* (Summer). https://www .huduser.gov/portal/periodicals/em/summer13/highlight1.html.

HUD (U.S. Department of Housing and Urban Development). 1995. *HUD Reinvention: From Blueprint to Action.* March. https://books.google.com/books?id=ALDLOl8kxh8C&pg=PA7 3&lpg=PA73&dq=reinvention+blueprint+hud&source=bl&ots=uGRvox1_kv&sig=1V4CSS ok3IocQoU1deFDLMfAczg&hl=en&sa=X&ved=0ahUKEwi5qvqx3M7MAhVI3IMKHY3C D6AQ6AEIPjAG#v=onepage&q=reinvention%20blueprint%20hud&f=false.

———. 1996. "Public/Private Partnerships for the Mixed-Finance Development of Public Housing Units." *Federal Register* 61 (86): 19708–19.

———. 1997. "FHA's Mixed-Income Housing Underwriting Guidelines," Directive H 97–12. http:// portal.hud.gov/hudportal/HUD?src=/program_offices/administration/hudclips/notices /hsg/97hsgnotices.

———. 2010a. *FY 2010–2015 HUD Strategic Plan.* http://portal.hud.gov/hudportal/HUD?src=/pro gram_offices/cfo/stratplan.

———. 2010b. "Myth v. Facts: Setting the Record Straight about PETRA." http://portal.hud.gov /hudportal/documents/huddoc?id=PETRAMythsvsFacts.pdf.

———. 2012. "RAD Final Notice Overview." http://docsfiles.com/pdf_section_8_powerpoint .html.

———. 2013a. *Worst Case Housing Needs 2011: Report to Congress Summary.* Washington, D.C.: U.S. Department of Housing and Development. https://www.huduser.gov/Publications/pdf /HUD-506_WorstCase2011_reportv3.pdf.

———. 2013b. *Rental Assistance Demonstration: Information on Initial Conversions to Project-Based Vouchers.* GOA-14-402. Washington, D.C.: U.S. Government Accountability Office. http:// www.gao.gov/assets/670/662736.pdf.

———. 2014. "Applications beyond the 60,000 Cap (as of 5/31/14)." http://portal.hud.gov/hudpor tal/documents/huddoc?id=PendingRADApps_053114.pdf.

Levy, Diane, Zach McDade, and Kassie Dumlao. 2010. *Effects from Living in Mixed-Income Communities for Low-Income Families—A Review of the Literature.* Washington, D.C.: The Urban

Institute. http://www.urban.org/sites/default/files/alfresco/publication-pdfs/412292-Effects -from-Living-in-Mixed-Income-Communities-for-Low-Income-Families.PDF.

Manegold, Catherine. 1995. "Secretary Proposes Reshaping HUD to Save It," *New York Times,* March 20.

National Housing Law Project (NHLP). 2016. "What NHLP Is Working on This Winter." *NHLP Housing Law Bulletin* (March). http://www.nhlp.org/March2016.

Shelterforce. 2010. "The End of Public Housing." October 17. http://www.shelterforce.org/arti cle/2024/the_end_of_public_housing.

Smith, Janet. 2013. "The End of Public Housing as We Knew It." *Urban Research & Practice* 6 (3): 276–96.

Stephens, Alexis. 2014. "Risks vs. Rewards: Inside HUD's Favorite New Program," *Next City,* October 9. https://nextcity.org/daily/entry/public-housing-privatized-hud-rad-section-8.

Waters, Maxine. 2010. "Congresswoman Waters Expresses Concerns about Changes in Public Housing Programs." Press release. https://waters.house.gov/media-center/press-releases /congresswoman-waters-expresses-concerns-about-changes-public-housing.

Weiss, Carol H. 1995. "Nothing as Practical as Good Theory: Exploring Theory-Based Evaluation for Comprehensive Community Initiatives for Children and Families." In *New Approaches to Evaluating Community Initiatives,* Vol. 1, *Concepts, Methods, and Contexts,* ed. J. P. Connell, A. C. Kubisch, L. B. Schorr, and C. H. Weiss, 65–92. Washington, D.C.: Aspen Institute.

6

IMMIGRANTS AND THE OBAMA URBAN POLICIES
Tarnishing the Golden Door

CHRISTINE THURLOW BRENNER

Progressive Obama urban policies designed to create economic opportunity, provide high-quality educational opportunities, and spark community revitalization were built with borders that often marginalized or omitted immigrant newcomers. The Obama administration's strategic decision to pursue health care reform in his first term spent his political capital at the cost of many other important policy goals, most noticeably comprehensive immigration reform. In the absence of comprehensive reform and a pathway to citizenship for the 12 million undocumented persons currently residing in the United States, other federal urban policies have kept urban immigrant communities in the shadows.

This chapter chronicles how the Obama urban policy agenda ignored immigrants, resulting in the loss of the human capital potential newcomer immigrants represented, underserving immigrant youth who were English language learners in a time of high-stakes testing, excluded immigrant entrepreneurs from capital access unless they sold 51 percent of their business to a U.S. partner, and expanded the immigrant-exclusionary measures of the Clinton-era 1996 PROWA by omitting immigrants' health care access under the Affordable Care Act. Immigrant settlement patterns of the twenty-first century find more immigrants moving directly to metropolitan regional suburbs (51 percent) than to central cities; however, targeted federal urban policies developed during Obama's presidency frequently discount immigrant newcomers as future partners in the American dream.

Immigrant Population Trends during the Obama Presidency

Immigration to the United States soared in the past two decades. The net gain of 11 million immigrants between 1990 and 2000 was a peak migration point for the country.[1] The twenty-first century saw a similar net increase, albeit at a somewhat lower level of 8 million, from the years 2000 to 2010. As a share of the total U.S. population, immigrants (both legal and unauthorized) represented 13 percent of the total population throughout the Obama presidency (2009–16). This is only a slight increase from 2000, when immigrants represented an 11 percent share of the total population. There were 41.3 million foreign-born immigrants residing in the United States, according to the 2013 American Community Survey.

The foreign-born population holds various citizenship statuses. Forty-two percent of all immigrants have become naturalized U.S. citizens, which requires learning English, passing the citizenship and personal background tests, and swearing allegiance to the United States. Once naturalized, they hold the same rights and responsibilities as U.S.-born citizens, including the right to vote and pay taxes. An additional 31 percent are legal permanent residents, and hold a green card, which grants them the right to work and attend school in the country. The unauthorized population comprises the final 27 percent of the immigrants living in the United States. They represent persons who either crossed into the country without inspection at a border crossing or are visa over-stayers.

Metropolitan areas endure as strong magnets for immigrants. Traditional gateway cities like New York, Los Angeles, Miami, and Chicago continue to attract the largest numbers of foreign-born; however the immigrant proportion of the total urban area population varies among these communities.[2] Urban border communities, while smaller in total population than other major cities, have, not surprisingly, some of the highest percentages of foreign-born as a share of their total population.[3] The advent of new destination immigrant urban areas in the late twentieth century brought foreign-born newcomers to many Southern and Western cities like Atlanta, Charlotte, Raleigh, Nashville, and Las Vegas (Singer and Glades 2014). The pull factor of manufacturing and housing construction drew immigrants to these growing areas. Obama's ascendancy to the presidency during the height of the Great Recession negatively impacted immigration to high-growth areas as new construction dropped precipitously and manufacturing firms cut back on production (McCabe and Meissner 2010).

Suburbanization of immigration was first noted in the 2000 census when 52 percent of immigrants resided in urban ring suburbs. Jones-Correa identified thirty-five "melting pot" metros where immigrants moving to the suburbs were entering predominantly white enclaves and still comprised minority incursions into these areas (Jones-Correa 2008). The 2009 American Community Survey confirmed this trend as more immigrants chose to settle in small towns and suburbs. This growth was driven by Latinos, both immigrants and citizens, who comprised one-third of all suburban growth (13.3 million versus 2.5 million blacks and two million Asians) (Travernise and Gebeloff 2010).

Mexico continues to be the primary sending country for U.S. immigrants, comprising 29 percent of the total flow of new residents (Hipsman and Meissner 2013). China and India, at 5 percent of total immigrants, represent the next largest countries of origin. The Philippines recently slipped to fourth place in sending countries, following India's immigration surge.[4]

Obama's Comprehensive Immigration Reform Goals

President Obama's commitment to comprehensive immigration reform that was present in his electoral campaign was quickly swallowed up in the priorities of the new administration. Immigration was one of the seven named transition teams created prior to his inauguration; however, the economy, still reeling from the Great Recession and the need for Wall Street reforms, reauthorization of No Child Left Behind, reform of student loans for higher education, and most notably health care reform edged out immigration reform. These issues notably evolved during his presidency. Health care reform was central to the first two years of his term, culminating in the passage of the Affordable Care Act in March 2010. Wall Street regulation and tax reform, and the pay-as-you-earn student loan forgiveness program received heightened attention in the latter part of 2010 through 2014.[5]

Piecemeal approaches to immigration reform were often introduced as a part of other legislation. President Obama chose to support some of these initiatives, such as the 2009 reauthorization of the State Children's Health Insurance Program (SCHIP), which allowed states the option to lift the five-year waiting period for immigrant children's eligibility for SCHIP, and which was one of the first bills passed and signed into law during Obama's first year in office.

The Obama policy document, "Building a 21st Century Immigration System," was released in May 2011. It outlined four principles for comprehensive immigration reform. First, the federal government's responsibility to secure the borders. Second, business accountability for exploiting unauthorized workers and undermining American workers. Third, strengthening economic competitiveness by pursuing reform that reflects our values and diverse needs, including provisions for seasonal agricultural workers, children brought to the country at a young age, family reunification, supporting immigrant entrepreneurship, and encouraging immigrants who receive their higher education in the United States or who serve in the armed forces to become citizens. The final principle was that to enter a pathway for citizenship unauthorized migrants would need to pay taxes, pay a penalty, learn English, pass criminal background checks, and "go to the back of the line" (White House 2011). This policy document formed the basis for a series of meetings across the United States with business and community leaders, faith leaders, and law enforcement officials to muster a call to action for comprehensive immigration reform.

Obama's "Now Is the Time" speech delivered in late January 2013, early in his second term in office, reiterated his views on comprehensive immigration reform in the post–Affordable Care Act environment.

> Now is the time. I'm here because most Americans agree that it's time to fix a system that's been broken for way too long. I'm here because business leaders, faith leaders, labor leaders, law enforcement, and leaders from both

parties are coming together to say now is the time to find a better way to welcome the striving, hopeful immigrants who still see America as the land of opportunity. Now is the time to do this so we can strengthen our economy and strengthen our country's future. . . . So that's what comprehensive immigration reform looks like: smarter enforcement; a pathway to earned citizenship; improvements in the legal immigration system so that we continue to be a magnet for the best and the brightest all around the world. It's pretty straightforward. (Obama 2013b)

Comprehensive immigration reform as envisioned by President Obama held great promise for urban areas.

Overview

This chapter explores President Obama's statements, press releases, speeches, and administrative guidance to examine the administration's actions related to reforming immigration policies. The primary outcome of this analysis reveals a dearth of attention paid to immigrants living in urban areas and the absence of an urban policy that is inclusive of immigrant newcomers. This section examines the types of presidential communications and the presence of official comments on immigration and urban policy, with special attention to where the two policies are linked. Communications include weekly radio addresses, blogs, videos, photos, administrative guidance, and other methods of disseminating information.

Weekly Presidential Radio Addresses: Immigrants and Economic Development

Immigration does not emerge in the Saturday radio addresses until Obama's second term in office. President Obama, like his predecessors, finds the weekly radio address to the nation as an effective way to concentrate on emergent issues and clearly communicate his personal perspective of the issue. Sixteen weekly addresses highlight the topic of immigration policy. Initially it is introduced as part of a litany of challenges the country faces during his second term,

And we can step up to meet the important business that awaits us this year: creating jobs, boosting incomes, fixing our infrastructure and our immigration system, promoting energy independence while protecting our planet from the harmful effects of climate change, educating our children, and shielding them from the horrors of gun violence. (Obama 2013a)

In February, 2013 Obama links the concepts of raising the minimum wage to ensure "hard work leads to a decent living" and recognizing the hard work of immigrants. He identifies the need to "harness the talents and ingenuity of hard-working immigrants" with comprehensive immigration reform and specifies the parameters of that reform: "securing our borders, establishing a responsible path to earned citizenship, and attracting the highly skilled entrepreneurs and engineers that will help create job" (Obama 2013c).

The importance of an immigration system "that actually works for families and businesses" is promoted in his March 9, 2013 address (Obama 2013d). This theme is reinforced in his address given in May 2013, preceding his trip to Mexico and Costa Rico, where he notes the importance of not only reuniting families but also reiterates the goal of "attract[ing] the highly skilled entrepreneurs and engineers who will help create good paying jobs and grow the economy" (Obama 2013e). Subsequent addresses in 2013 emphasize Obama's self-described common sense approach to immigration policy reform that include enforcement, an earned path to citizenship, and updating the legal immigration system. Through the summer of 2013, he often returns to the point that comprehensive immigration reform portends positive economic growth and a more stable financial future for the nation. Obama appeals directly to the American people, when Congress reconvenes after its summer recess in the fall of 2013 and again after their winter break in January 2014, about the need for the legislature to work on comprehensive immigration reform.

Urban policy issues are captured in 16 of 286 Saturday radio addresses; however, interestingly Obama never approaches the issues from an urban framework. Rather he talks about the experiences of persons living in cities and towns across America, and the impact of proposed changes, and constructs his arguments exclusively from a national perspective. Gun violence, postdisaster recovery, homeland security, the impact of the Recovery Act, raising the minimum wage, economic development that creates jobs and benefits entrepreneurs, and protecting citizens from power plants spewing carbon pollution are never given an exclusively urban trope. Neither are they linked in any overt way with immigration policy.

Indeed the only tangential linkage comes around the discussion of economic development and the benefit of highly skilled immigrant entrepreneurs who can create jobs, albeit not exclusively in urban areas. Recent research by economists Peri, Shih, and Sparber find that the co-location of low- and high-skilled immigrants during the past decade expanded local economic development and had a net positive impact on younger native workers with limited postsecondary education (Peri, Shih, and Sparber 2013). Obama's emphasis on immigrants who are highly skilled engineers and entrepreneurs tracks with Peri's analysis that "jobs and production created by highly educated immigrants . . . more than compensates for the competition generated from less-skilled immigrants" (Peri 2014).

Obama's emphases on the desirability of high-skilled immigrants like engineers presume an easy segue from foreign training and education into the American labor market. Recent work by the Governor's Task Force on Immigrant Healthcare Professionals in Massachusetts refutes that view and supports the blocked mobility thesis (Bonacich and Modell 1980), finding there are multiple institutional barriers for immigrants' professional recertification.[6] "These challenges include difficulties in obtaining recognition of professional experiences and credentials earned from educational institutions abroad, acquiring professional-level English skills, navigating costly or time-consuming recertification processes, and building professional networks and U.S. job search skills" (Batalova, McHugh, and Morawski 2014, 1).

The particular emphasis on highly skilled immigrant professionals is consistent with changing patterns of immigrant visas issued at foreign posts during the Obama administration. Numerically, immigrant relatives and family-sponsored preference visas outweigh employment visas eighteen to one. However, employment-based visas have seen a 52.7 percent change over the five-year period from 2009 to 2013, while immigrant relative visas decreased by 9.7 percentage points and family-sponsored visas increased by less than 10 percentage points (see Table 6.1).

Included in the employment-based visas is a special category for immigrant investors (EB-5 visa), created by Congress in response to the 1990 recession. These visa holders comprise less than 1 percent of all visas issued worldwide each year, according to the State Department. Immigrant investors must invest, without borrowing, in qualifying commercial enterprises, either $1 million or $500,000 in a high-unemployment or rural area *and* within two years of the investment create ten full-time jobs.[7] The number of investor visas almost doubled between 2011 and 2012 (3,340 to 6,628) and by 2013 the EB-5 visas issued grew from 0.3 percent of all visas to 0.9 percent (n = 8,543). The growth of immigrant investors paralleled the economic recovery following the Great Recession.

The Obama administration advocated for this visa category as borrowing remained tight following the Great Recession (Grimaldi, Loten, and O'Connell 2013). From 2009 to 2011 the number of EB-5 visa applicants quadrupled to more than 3,800 (McGeehan and Semple 2011). New flexibility introduced through administrative rule-making in 2011 saw the number of immigrant investor visas rise to over 7,000 by 2013. The vast majority of the immigrant investor visas were granted for regional target areas with high unemployment, which were primarily in postindustrial urban areas. Some controversy surrounded the program post–Great Recession as critics labeled it a "cash-for-visa scheme"; however, numerous urban building projects would not have occurred without this infusion of foreign capital (McGeehan and Semple 2011).

Obama's use of administrative rule changes allowed him to advance urban redevelopment policy goals that benefited immigrants and the American public at large through job creation. Singer and Glades (2014) note there is a lack of reliable data to analyze the effectiveness of the program; however, they estimate that between 2010 and 2012 approximately $2.5 billion in investments and over 40,000 direct full-time jobs were created. The contribution to regional economic development in the United States through foreign direct investment via the EB-5 visa program represents only a small portion of the foreign direct investment made in the

TABLE 6.1. IMMIGRANT VISAS ISSUED AT FOREIGN SERVICE POSTS FY 2009 TO 2013

Visa Category	2009	2010	2011	2012	2013	5-Year Percentage Change 2009 to 2013	Actual Change
Immigrant Relatives	227,517	215,947	216,856	235,616	205,435	−9.7	(22,082)
Family-Sponsored Preference	176,273	200,567	192,891	189,128	189,020	7.2	12,747
Employment-Basis Preference	13,846	12,701	15,099	19,137	21,144	52.7	7,298
Diversity Immigrants	46,761	49,771	49,507	33,125	51,080	9.2	4,319
Special Immigrants*	4,325	3,043	1,861	5,219	6,424	48.5	2,099
Vietnam AmerAsian Immigrants	48	23	35	75	12	−75.0	(36)
Armed Forces Special Immigrants	0	0	0	0	0	0	0
Total	468,770	482,052	476,249	482,300	473,115	0.9	

* Special immigrant totals include returning residents, Iraqi and Afghan translators, and certain Iraqis or Afghans employed by or on behalf of the U.S. government.

Source: Author's own calculations. From U.S. Department of State, Annual Visa Statistics, http://travel.state.gov.

United States each year;[8] however, the targeting of high-unemployment areas for investments of $500,000 has the potential to link with urban economic recovery programs. These linkages are tenuous in many areas; nevertheless, they represent opportunities to strengthen regional economic recovery in future iterations of the EB-5 visa (Singer and Glades 2014).

News Conferences, Immigration Reform, and Economic Growth

Immigration and urban policy were jointly mentioned in only one news conference, held December 19, 2012, in the aftermath of the tragic shootings in Newtown, Connecticut. Obama affirms Americans' constitutional right to bear arms and acknowledges there are regional and urban-rural differences in the traditions of gun ownership. He hones in on the critical lesson from Newton being the recognition of what is really important to the American people, finding a way to move forward through compromise in the legislature and with the executive office.

> But right now what the country needs is for us to compromise, get a deficit reduction deal in place, make sure middle class taxes don't go up, make sure that we're laying the foundations for growth, give certainty to businesses large and small, not put ourselves through the some sort of self-inflicted crisis every 6 months, allow ourselves time to focus on things like preventing the tragedy in Newton from happening again, focus on issues like energy, immigration reform, and all the things that will really make a determination as to whether our country grows over the next 4 years, 10 years, 40 years. (Obama 2012)

Effective communicators use the opportunity of a news conference and questions from the press to refocus the public's attention. Obama's frustration with congressional inaction on legislative initiatives the White House supports is clear in this statement, with his reference to "self-inflicted crisis" and his desire to move toward compromise.

News conferences switch the locus of communication control from the president to the press. The questions posed at news conferences usually focus on the dominant issues in the public eye. Additionally we see a repetition of the theme that immigration reform and economic growth share a linked fate for the future of the nation. The 2013 report jointly released by the Americas Society/Council of the Americas and Partnership for a New American Economy that examined county-level census data from 1970 to 2010 found that "for every 1,000 immigrants living in a county, 46 manufacturing jobs are created or preserved that would otherwise not exist or would have moved elsewhere" (Vigdor 2013). The economic recovery policy Obama espouses in the Jobs-Driven National Emergency Grant program clearly has an immigration component; what is lacking is an urban focus.

Tucking Immigrant-Focused Policy into Economic Recovery Programs

The nexus of national economic recovery following the Great Recession and the role of immigrants in that recovery does not achieve a central focus in the Obama administration. Presumably privileging immigrant newcomers over native workers would be politically difficult to sell to the American people; however, that does not mean immigrants were left totally out of the recovery equation.

The Jobs-Driven National Emergency Grant (JD NEG) program, sponsored by the Department of Labor, is an example of how a recovery program can include immigrants while attending to the reemployment needs of natives. The program, available in 2014 to states and federally certified tribes, provided funding for new or expanded workplace-based training partnerships or occupational training to receive industry-recognized credentials in demand fields. In their application for funds, states determined the category of dislocated workers eligible to receive services, including dislocated workers; dislocated workers with an emphasis on the long-term unemployed; recipients of unemployment insurance profiled as likely to exhaust their benefits; recently separated veterans; and foreign-trained immigrant workers facing barriers in their trained profession.

The Department of Labor awarded $154.7 million in grants to thirty-two states, Puerto Rico, and one indigenous tribe in the summer of 2014. Table 6.2 shows that the top state-level priority for job-driven training was dislocated workers, particularly the long-term unemployed. Those likely to lose their unemployment insurance benefits were included in the training grants of 79 percent of the states receiving funding. Slightly more than half of the states targeted returning veterans for job training under the grant.

The decentralized nature of state-level decision-making regarding the category of qualified workers allowed twenty-three states to opt out of serving their immigrant population. Only one-third of the states that received funding under the JD NEG program included foreign-trained immigrant workers facing barriers in their trained profession as program recipients.

Obama's neoliberal market-driven solutions to the economic recovery of the United States vis-à-vis immigrants mirror the embedded policy initiatives being pursued by the European community. Generalist programs such as JD NEG contain permissive clauses to include high-skilled immigrants, yet the decentralized nature of U.S. federalism requires progressive leadership from states. Partisan congressional gridlock characteristic of the Obama presidency constrained national leadership on programs that benefit foreign-trained, high-skill immigrants' entry into the U.S. job market, often resulting in a loss of human capital potential in many urban areas of the country.

Press Briefings, Fact Sheets, and Integration Policy Initiatives

Press briefings are often used to announce new policies or to release reports that contain information about the status of existing policies. Examining the press brief-

TABLE 6.2. NUMBER AND PERCENTAGE OF STATES, INCLUDING WORKER CATEGORY IN JOB-DRIVEN NATIONAL EMERGENCY GRANTS 2014 (N = 34)

	Category of Worker Included in Grant				
	Dislocated	Dislocated, Long-term Unemployed	Unemployment Benefits Nearly Exhausted	Returning or Recently Separated Veterans	Foreign-Trained Immigrant*
Number of States	34	32	27	18	11
Percentage of States Including Worker Category**	100.0	94.1	79.4	52.9	32.4

* States include Idaho, Illinois, Maine, Maryland, Massachusetts, Michigan, Minnesota, New York, Oregon, Pennsylvania, and Texas.

** Totals to more than 100 percent because some states included multiple categories.

Source: Author's own calculations from http://www.doleta.gov/layoff/jd_neg_award_summary.

TABLE 6.3. NUMBER AND PERCENTAGE OF ENGLISH LANGUAGE LEARNERS
(ELL) ENROLLMENT (IN 1,000S) BY CITY AND SUBURBAN TYPE IN 2011

	City			Suburban			Total City and Suburban*
	Large	Mid-size	Small	Large	Mid-size	Small	
Number of ELLs	1,211	430	394	1,439	97	68	3,640
ELLs as a Percent of Enrollment by City Size	16.7	12.6	10.9	9.4	6.4	7.6	11.7

Note: The remaining ELLs reside in towns and rural areas (n=336 towns and 414 rural areas). ELLs represent 6.2 percent of total enrollment in towns and 3.9 percent of total rural enrollment.

Source: U.S. Department of Education, National Center for Education Statistics, Common Core of Data (CCD), "Public Elementary/Secondary School Universe Survey," 2008–9, 2009–10, 2010–11, and 2011–12; and "Local Education Agency Universe Survey," 2010 and 2011–12.

ings held during the Obama administration provides insight into the centrality of policy issues and can show change over time.

Fact sheets distributed during press briefings are used to highlight the key components of presidential policy. For example, the fact sheet released after the first national gathering on immigrant integration held in July 2014 describes the White House's guiding principles on successful civic, economic, and linguistic integration. (See Table 6.3.) Embedded in the fact sheet are links to multiple policy initiatives and programs the White House was pursuing to advance the primary goal of immigrant integration. While comprehensive immigration reform remained elusive throughout the Obama administration, the president established a taskforce in November 2014, whose goal was to develop a federal immigrant integration strategy that allowed new Americans to contribute to society to their fullest potential and help build stronger communities.

> Therefore, I am establishing a White House Task Force on New Americans, an interagency effort to identify and support State and local efforts at integration that are working and to consider how to expand and replicate successful models. The Task Force, which will engage with community, business, and faith leaders, as well as State and local elected officials, will help determine additional steps the Federal Government can take to ensure its programs and policies are serving diverse communities that include new Americans. (White House 2014)

It is clear that none of the initiatives has an explicitly urban focus; however, the economic initiatives have the most promise for benefiting immigrants living in urban areas.

Proclamations Reinforcing Values

Presidential proclamations draw attention to important events and highlight the values and diversity of our national heritage. The majority of the forty-four proclamations issued during Obama's presidency honor the religious and ethnic heritage of Americans. A few of the proclamations prohibit entry into the United States by aliens who have committed human rights violations or foreign officials who support human trafficking. Obama demonstrates his support for "commonsense" immigration reform in the proclamation issued in October 2013 for national entrepreneurship day. He again uses this opportunity to emphasize the added value immigrants bring to the country's economic growth.

> America is home to a long and storied line of immigrants who sought opportunity on our shores—from entrepreneurs of the industrial revolution to startup founders of the digital age. This June, the Senate passed a commonsense immigration reform bill that would provide startup visas for immigrant entrepreneurs; eliminate backlogs for employment-based visas; and remove visa caps for those with advanced degrees in science, technology, engineering, and mathematics. These principles are consistent with ensuring our country remains a land of opportunity while fostering economic growth and innovation. (Obama 2013f)

Additional support for immigrant human capital as a means to grow the economy is also seen in a parallel shift during the Obama years in the type of immigrant visas issued by the United States. Immigrant relatives and family-sponsored preference visas dominate in numbers of visas issued from 2009 through 2013; however, the five-year percentage change in number of visas issued decreased by 9.7 percentage points for relatives and saw a small increase of 7.2 percentage points for family sponsored visas. During the same time period employment-based preference visas increased by 52.7 percentage points, as shown in Table 6.1.

Emphasis on immigrants as part of the American economic recovery effort, both through programs like JD NEG grants and the emphasis on employment-based visas are central to the Obama administration's immigration policy, which has had positive spillover impacts in urban areas.

Urban Education of Immigrant Youth

English-language acquisition by immigrant youth is critical for successful integration into American communities. Local public schools assume the primary responsibility for accomplishing this task, which is financed by the federal government

TABLE 6.4. U.S. DEPARTMENT OF EDUCATION LANGUAGE
ACQUISITION STATE GRANTS 2009–14

Year	Budget Expenditure
2009 Actual	$730,000,000
2010 Actual	$750,000,000
2011 Actual	$733,530,000
2012 Actual	$732,143,628
2013 Budget*	$732,100,000
2014 Estimate	$732,100,000

Note: The amount shown for FY 2013 excludes the 0.612 percent
across-the-board increase in Pub. L. No. 112–175, the 0.2 percent across-the-
board decrease required by Pub. L. No. 113-6, and the sequester reduction of
5 percent required by the Budget Control Act of 2011.

Source: U.S. Department of Education Budget Summary and Background
Information 2009–14.

through Title III of the Elementary and Secondary Education Act, as reauthorized
in 2001. Approximately 9 percent of the total youth enrolled in America's public
schools were English learners (ELs) during the Obama presidency, according the
National Center for Education Statistics.

The need for an urban education policy that adequately addresses the language
acquisition needs of youth in major urban centers and large suburban districts has
been clearly present during Obama's years in office. It was most recently emphasized in the May 8, 2014, U.S. Department of Education and U.S. Department of
Justice jointly issued letter to local education agencies (districts) reminding them of
their legal obligation to provide equal access to all children residing within their
district.[9]

Eighty-three percent of all ELs lived in cities and their surrounding suburban areas, with only 8 percent in small towns and 9 percent in rural areas of the
country in 2011, the most recent year for which data is available. Table 6.3 shows
that ELs are concentrated in major urban areas with populations of 250,000 or
more and the large suburban districts that surround those cities.

Funding for language acquisition state grants was essentially flat from 2009
through 2014 at $732.1 million dollars, as shown in Table 6.4. These are formula
grants that distribute funds "based on each State's share of the Nation's English
Learners (ELs) and recent immigrant students."[10] Additionally, the Obama admin-

istration's Department of Education reserved $47.5 million per year "for competitive grants in order to support the development and implementation of high-quality programs for ELs, including dual-language and transitional bilingual programs."[11]

Obama's educational focus during his second term was not on immigrants or K–12 education, but rather on education and training that leads to a job, as discussed in the prior section. The increases in education funding for immigrants were not aimed at K–12 youth, but rather at postsecondary interventions, primarily in the technical and skill training offered in community colleges. Even in postsecondary enrollment, Latino adults (over age twenty-six) and Latino youth (eighteen to twenty-five years of age) cite lack of English language skills as a major reason they are not doing well in school, 58 percent and 43 percent, respectively (Lopez 2009). From the end of the Bush presidency in academic year 2007–8 to the second term of the Obama presidency (academic year 2011–12), the number of English learners in the public schools increased by 5.7 percentage points, from 4.15 million to 4.39 million students. Inadequate funding for public school language acquisition disadvantages English-learning school-aged immigrant youth.

Immigration Enforcement, Raids, and Deportation

The groundwork for federal partnerships with state and local law enforcement agencies has been in place since the passage of the 1996 Illegal Immigration Reform and Immigrant Responsibility Act through provisions of Section 287(g). The Department of Homeland Security (DHS), under the authority of Section 287(g), entered into memorandums of agreement (MOA) with various local and state law enforcement agencies to deputize them. Local and state agencies receive training from the DHS and agree in return to accept "detainers" for alleged unauthorized immigrants held in their custody as well as gaining access to federal immigration databases that may assist them in detaining and interrogating alleged criminals. Thirty-four local law enforcement agencies in seventeen states participate in the program (DHS n.d.).

This policy has been controversial throughout the Obama presidency. Immigration advocacy groups and faith- and community-based groups, among others, have complained of police profiling of Latinos and others resulting in arrests and detainers being issued for minor crimes like traffic violations. Detainers, when exercised by Immigration and Customs Enforcement (ICE), have led to increased internal deportations,[12] frequently separating unauthorized immigrant parents from their U.S. citizen children. Concerns about inconsistent application of the provisions of 287(g) led Department of Homeland Security secretary Janet Napolitano to standardize the MOAs with local agencies.

The new MOA aligns 287(g) local operations with major ICE enforcement priorities—specifically, the identification and removal of criminal aliens. To address concerns that individuals may be arrested for minor offenses as a guise to initiate removal proceedings, the new agreement explains that participating local law enforcement agencies are required to pursue all criminal charges that originally caused the offender to be taken into custody. (DHS 2009b)

The Obama administration shifted immigration enforcement policies early in his first term. The 2010 Morton memo, issued by the assistant secretary of ICE, directed ICE officers that

in light of the large number of administrative violations the agency is charged with addressing the limited enforcement resources the agency has available, ICE must prioritize the use of enforcement personnel, detention space and removal resources to ensure that removal the agency does conduct promote the agency's highest enforcement priorities, namely national security, public safety and border security. (Morton 2010)

The Morton memo also revealed for the first time the federal financial resources available for removal of unauthorized immigrants—400,000 per year, which represented less than 4 percent of the estimated total unauthorized immigrants residing in the United States (Morton 2010).

Workplace enforcement raids were a hallmark of the Bush administration. High-profile raids struck fear into immigrant communities, where many families had members with varying degrees of legal status. E-Verify, the principle federal database used to authenticate an individual's work authorization, was consistently cited for inaccuracies,[13] and the strategy to pursue the migrants working without legal authorization penalized individuals not corporations.

The Obama administration shifted enforcement policies to focus on employers who hired unauthorized workers. Secretary Napolitano's 2009 directive outlined "that ICE will focus its resources in the work site enforcement program on the criminal prosecution of employers who knowingly hire illegal workers in order to target the root cause of illegal immigration" (Failkowski 2012). The targeting of employers, managers, and owners led to increased audits and investigations. For example, from 2008 to 2009 immigration audits increased from 503 to 8,000 (Failkowski 2012).

Policy Initiatives through Administrative Guidance

President Obama, thwarted by the inaction of a polarized Congress, tasked several executive agencies with developing progressive immigration policy initiatives that could be implemented through executive action. The Department of Justice (DOJ) and DHS played pivotal roles in developing options for the president to consider.

Critically, the policy initiatives suggested were designed as administrative guidance for the employees of the executive agencies. Why did this matter? It was important because had the agencies chosen to suggest administrative rules, rather than guidance, the rules would have been subject to the public and interagency review and comment process required under the 1946 Administrative Procedures Act (APA). Administrative guidance was within the purview of the agencies, and importantly it did not rise to the standard of administrative rulemaking (Wadhia 2010).

Deferred action, as recommended by the DOJ and DHS, fell into the category of prosecutorial discretion. Cox and Rodriguez find that "the Executive [President Obama] still has de facto delegated authority to grant relief from removal on a case-by-case basis. The Executive simply exercises this authority through its prosecutorial discretion, rather than by evaluating eligibility pursuant to a statutory framework at the end of removal proceedings" (Cox and Rodriguez 2009).

Deferred action became the avenue through which President Obama could provide relief from deportation to groups of unauthorized immigrants. By applying the principle of deferred action on the macro level Obama in essence created categorical groups of unauthorized immigrants who would receive protection from deportation for a period of time. Widows and widowers of U.S. citizens and their unmarried children under twenty-one years of age were granted deferred action in June 2009 through DHS guidance.[14] The guidance in effect "suspended removal proceedings against a particular individual or group of individuals for a specific timeframe" (Wadhia 2010, 263).

In June 2012, the Secretary of Homeland Security Janet Napolitano announced that certain people who came to the United States as children and meet several key guidelines may request consideration of deferred action for a period of two years, subject to renewal, and would then be eligible for work authorization. Deferred Action for Childhood Arrivals (DACA) required an application, evidence of residency, and payment of an administrative fee (DHS 2012). This group of unauthorized immigrants eligible for DACA was the same target group that had long sought legislative relief through the Development, Relief, and Education for Alien Minors (DREAM) Act.

Seventy-seven percent of the 818,500 DACA applications received between 2012 and 2014 were approved by U.S. Citizenship and Immigration Services (USCIS). The denial rate is very low, approximately 4 percent.

On November 20, 2014, U.S. Secretary for Homeland Security Jeh Johnson issued a memorandum expanding the categories of administrative relief available to unauthorized immigrants. The new group covered by this memo was parents of DACA-eligible immigrants. Deferred Action for Parental Accountability (DAPA) applications were put on hold based on a February 2015 judicial decision from the U.S. District Court for the Southern District of Texas (Brownsville). The case is before the U.S. Supreme Court with a summer 2016 decision anticipated.[15]

The net impact of DACA and DAPA on urban areas was to allow many families to remain together and receive relief from the omnipresent fear of deportation and family separation. DACA and DAPA support the president's values of family unification and counterbalance the high levels of deportations under his administration.

Conclusion

The nexus of immigration and urban policy during Obama's presidency is intermittent at best, based on an examination of official communications from the White House and executive agencies during his two terms in office. Skilled immigrants who contribute to the economic recovery of urban areas received the highest priority in entry during the Obama administration, a clear shift from prior policies that privileged family reunification. Federal programs that could assist skilled immigrants experiencing barriers in reentering their profession are not universally available due to the decentralized federal system that allows states to determine how to allocate formula grants. Finally, funding for important programs such as English acquisition for school-aged youth was flat during the Obama years.

The missed opportunities to advance immigrants' contributions to urban areas may be a reflection of the financial constraints the country faced following the Great Recession. Or it may reflect the inability of the White House to act due to partisanship in a Congress that continually preempted comprehensive immigration reform. Or, it may be the reflection of a White House too distracted by health care reform, complicated international crises, and other issues. Regardless of the reasons, immigrants living in urban areas and the large suburbs surrounding major cities were not integrated into a comprehensive national urban strategy during the Obama presidency.

Notes

1. Net immigration reflects the difference between actual immigration to the United States minus immigrant deaths and emigration.
2. Miami has the largest national share of immigrants in its urban population (38.2 percent); LA is close with 34.2 percent foreign-born, ranking third nationally. New York City ranks eighth nationally with 28.6 percent immigrant population, and Chicago's immigrant population is 17.6 percent of its total population, placing it at 37 in national urban rankings.
3. El Centro, California, ranks fourth nationally with 32.4 percent immigrants; McAllen-Edinburg in south Texas ranks seventh highest with 29.5 percent foreign-born residents, and El Paso, Texas, is tenth with a 26.1 percent immigrant population.
4. El Salvador, Vietnam, Cuba, and Korea each send 3 percent of total U.S. immigrants, respectively. The Dominican Republic and Guatemala, at 2 percent each, complete the list of the top ten sending countries.
5. Based on the author's analysis of President Obama's weekly radio addresses, 2009 through 2014.
6. Unpublished results of the Massachusetts Governor's Task Force on Immigrant Healthcare Professionals. Available from author. Author is a member of the taskforce.
7. Jobs created must be for U.S. citizens, lawful permanent residents, or other immigrants authorized to work in the United States (excluding the investor's spouse and children).
8. Foreign direct investment in the United States was $230.2 billion in 2011 and $166.4 billion in 2012, according to the U.S. Bureau of Economic Analysis. The World Bank describes

foreign direct investment as "the net inflows of investment to acquire a lasting management interest (10 percent or more of voting stock) in an enterprise operating in an economy other than that of the investor. It is the sum of equity capital, reinvestment of earnings, other long-term capital, and short-term capital as shown in the balance of payments." See http://data.worldbank.org/indicator/BX.KLT.DINV.WD.GD.ZS.

9. Equal access obligations for states and local education agencies are informed by U.S. Supreme Court cases, including *Brown v Board of Education*, 347 U.S. 483 (1954), *Plyler v Doe*, 457 U.S. 202 (1982), and *Martinez v Bynum*, 461 U.S. 321, 328 (1983).

10. National Center for Education Statistics, Common Core of Data (CCD), "Public Elementary/Secondary School Universe Survey," 2008–9, 2009–10, 2010–11, and 2011–12, https://nces.ed.gov/ccd/pubschuniv.asp; and "Local Education Agency Universe Survey," 2010–11 and 2011–12. https://nces.ed.gov/ccd/pubagency.asp.

11. U.S. Department of Education, Fiscal Year 2012 Budget Summary—February 14, 2012. Section IIA Elementary and Secondary Education, English Learner Education. https://www2.ed.gov/about/overview/budget/budget12/summary/edlite-section2a.html#ela. Funds are currently authorized under Title III of the Elementary and Secondary Education Act (ESEA). Quote is in the report under the section on English Learners.

12. One-third of all ICE deportations were internal (ICE 2014). https://www.ice.gov/doclib/about/offices/ero/pdf/2014-ice-immigration-removals.pdf.

13. In 2009, 11,932 authorized workers were erroneously classified as final nonconfirmation (FNC), 6.3 percent of all worker queries that year (Westat 2012).

14. Additional conditions applied, including whether the widow/widower resided in the United States and had been married for less than two years prior to the spouse's death (DHS 2009a).

15. Case 1:14-cv-00254 Document 145 Filed in TXSD on February 16, 2015. U.S. District Judge Andrew S. Hanen ruled that the deferred-deportation program should not move forward while a lawsuit filed by twenty-six states challenging it was being decided. The plaintiffs represent the following states: Alabama, Arizona, Arkansas, Florida, Georgia, Idaho, Indiana, Kansas, Louisiana, Maine, Michigan, Mississippi, Montana, Nebraska, Nevada, North Carolina, North Dakota, Ohio, Oklahoma, South Carolina, South Dakota, Tennessee, Texas, Utah, West Virginia, and Wisconsin.

References

Batalova, Jeanne, Margie McHugh, and Madeleine Morawski. 2014. "Brain Waste in the U.S. Workforce: Select Labor Force Characteristics of College-Educated Native-Born and Foreign-Born Adults." Washington, D.C.: Migration Policy Institute.

Bonacich, Edna, and John Modell. 1980. *The Economic Basis of Ethnic Solidarity: Small Business in the Japanese American Community*. Berkeley: University of California Press.

Cox, Adam B., and Christina Rodriguez. 2009. "The President and Immigration Law." *Yale Law Journal* 119: 458. http://ssrn.com/abstract=1356963.

DHS (U.S. Department of Homeland Security). 2009a. "DHS Establishes Interim Relief for Widows of U.S. Citizens." Press release. https://www.dhs.gov/news/2009/06/09/dhs-establishes-interim-relief-widows-us-citizens.

———. 2009b. "Secretary Napolitano Announces New Agreement with State and Local Immigration Enforcement Partnerships & Adds 11 New Agreements." Press release. https://www.dhs.gov/news/2009/07/10/secretary-announces-new-agreement-state-and-local-immigration-enforcement.

———. 2012. "Secretary Napolitano Announces Deferred Action Process for Young People Who Are Low Enforcement Priorities." Press release. https://www.dhs.gov/news/2012/06/15/secretary-napolitano-announces-deferred-action-process-young-people-who-are-low.

———. n.d. "Delegation of Immigration Authority Section 287(g) Immigration and Nationality Act." Accessed April 3, 2016. https://www.ice.gov/factsheets/287g.

Failkowski, Elise. 2012. "The Administration's New Workforce Enforcement Initiatives: Focus on Employer Compliance Will Increase Audits and Investigations." *Business Law Today,* January 2. http://www.americanbar.org/publications/blt/2010/01/02_fialkowski.html.

Grimaldi, James V., Angus Loten, and Vanessa O'Connell. 2013. "Chinese Investors Get Picky over U.S. Visa-for-Cash Deal." *Wall Street Journal,* March 19. http://www.wsj.com/articles/SB10001424127887324445904578285863761735122.

Hipsman, Faye, and Doris Meissner. 2013. "Immigration in the United States: New economic, social, political landscapes with legislative reform on the horizon." *Migration Information Source.* April 16. http://www.migrationpolicy.org/article/immigration-united-states-new-economic-social-political-landscapes-legislative-reform.

ICE (Immigration and Customs Enforcement). 2014. "ICE Enforcement and Removals Report." https://www.ice.gov/doclib/about/offices/ero/pdf/2014-ice-immigration-removals.pdf.

Jones-Correa, Michael. 2008. "Immigrant Incorporation in Suburbia: The Role of Bureaucratic Norms in Education." In *New Faces in New Places,* ed. Doug Massey, 308–40. New York: Russell Sage Foundation.

Li, Peter S. 1992. "Ethnic Enterprise in Transition: Chinese Businesses in Richmond, B.C., 1980–1990." *Canadian Ethnic Studies* 24 (1): 120–38.

Lopez, Mark Hugo. 2009. "Latinos and Education: Explaining the Attainment Gap." Pew Research Center, Hispanic Trends. http://www.pewhispanic.org/2009/10/07/latinos-and-education-explaining-the-attainment-gap.

McCabe, Kristen, and Debra Meissner. 2010. "Immigration and the United States: Recession Affects Flows, Prospects for Reform." *Migration Information Source.* January 20. http://www.migrationpolicy.org/article/immigration-and-united-states-recession-affects-flows-prospects-reform.

McGeehan, Patrick, and Kirk Semple. 2011. "Rules Stretched as Green Cards Go to Investors." *New York Times,* December 18. http://www.nytimes.com/2011/12/19/nyregion/new-york-developers-take-advantage-of-financing-for-visas-program.html.

Morton, John. 2010. "Civil Immigration Enforcement: Priorities for the Apprehension, Detention and Removal of Aliens," June 30. https://www.ice.gov/doclib/news/releases/2010/civil-enforcement-priorities.pdf.

Obama, Barack. 2012. "The President's News Conference." *American Presidency Project.* December 19. http://www.presidency.ucsb.edu/ws/?pid=102775.

———. 2013a. "Weekly Address: Working Together in the New Year to Grow Our Economy and Shrink Our Deficits." January 5. White House, Office of the Press Secretary. https://www.whitehouse.gov/the-press-office/2013/01/05/weekly-address-working-together-new-year-grow-our-economy-and-shrink-our.

———. 2013b. "Remarks by the President on Comprehensive Immigration Reform." Del Sol High School, Las Vegas, Nev. January 29. http://www.whitehouse.gov/the-press-office.

———. 2013c. "Weekly Address: Following the President's Plan for a Strong Middle Class." February 16. White House, Office of the Press Secretary. https://www.whitehouse.gov/the-press-office/2013/02/16/weekly-address-following-president-s-plan-strong-middle-class.

———. 2013d. "Weekly Address: End the Sequester to Keep Growing the Economy." March 9. White House, Office of the Press Secretary. https://www.whitehouse.gov/the-press-office/2013/03/09/weekly-address-end-sequester-keep-growing-economy.

———. 2013e. "Weekly Address: Fixing our Immigration System and Expanding Trade in Latin America." May 4. White House, Office of the Press Secretary. https://www.whitehouse.gov/the-press-office/2013/05/04/weekly-address-fixing-our-immigration-system-and-expanding-trade-latin-a.

———. 2013f. "743 - Proclamation 9052 - National Entrepreneurship Month, 2013." http://www.presidency.ucsb.edu/ws/?pid=104364.

Peri, Giovanni. 2014. Does Immigration Hurt the Poor? *Pathways.* http://inequality.stanford.edu/_media/pdf/pathways/summer_2014/Pathways_Summer_2014_Peri.pdf.

Peri, Giovanni, Kevin Shih, and Chad Sparber. 2013. "STEM Workers, H1B Visas and Productivity in U.S. Cities." February. University of California–Davis, Department of Economics working paper. http://dx.doi.org/10.1086/679061.

Singer, Audrey, and Camille Glades. 2014. "Improving the EB-5 Investor Visa Program: International Financing for U.S. Regional Economic Development." Washington, D.C.: Brookings Institute.

Travernise, Sabrina, and Robert Gebeloff. 2010. "Immigrants Make Paths to Suburbs, Not Cities." *New York Times,* December 14. http://www.nytimes.com/2010/12/15/us/15census.html?_r=0.

U.S. Department of State. 2009–15. Annual Reports of the Visa Office. https://travel.state.gov/content/visas/en/law-and-policy/statistics/annual-reports.html.

Vigdor, Jacob L. 2013. "Immigration and the Revival of American Cities: From Preserving Manufacturing Jobs to Strengthening the Housing Market." American Society/Council of the Americas and Partnership for a New American Economy. December 12. http://www.as-coa.org/articles/immigration-and-revival-american-cities.

Wadhia, Shoba Sivaprasad. 2010. "Role of Prosecutorial Discretion in Immigration Law." *Connecticut Public Interest Law Journal* 9 (2): 243.

Waldinger, Roger D. 1986. *The Eye of the Needle: Immigrants and Enterprise in New York's Garment Trades.* New York: New York University Press

Westat. 2012. "Evaluation of the Accuracy of E-Verify Findings." Report submitted to U.S. Department of Homeland Security. https://www.uscis.gov/sites/default/files/USCIS/Verification/E-Verify/E-Verify_Native_Documents/Everify%20Studies/Evaluation%20of%20the%20Accuracy%20of%20EVerify%20Findings.pdf.

White House. 2011. "Building a 21st Century Immigration System." Policy document. May 1. https://www.whitehouse.gov/sites/default/files/rss_viewer/immigration_blueprint.pdf.

———. 2014. "Presidential Memorandum—Creating Welcoming Communities and Fully Integrating Immigrants and Refugees." November 21. http://www.whitehouse.gov/the-press-office/2014/11/21/presidential-memorandum-creating-welcoming-communities-and-fully-integra.

7

OBAMA'S EDUCATION POLICY

More Markets, More Inequality, New Urban Contestations

PAULINE LIPMAN

When President Obama appointed Arne Duncan U.S. Secretary of Education in 2009, one of Duncan's first acts was to fly to Detroit to announce federal support for the city's struggling school system—on the condition that Detroit follow Chicago's model of education reform. Duncan came to Washington from Chicago, where he was CEO of Chicago Public Schools from 2001 to 2009. Chicago has been a laboratory and incubator of neoliberal education policies focused on top-down accountability, high-stakes testing, school closings and privatization, mayoral control, and business practices in schools. The goals of these policies are to open up public education to the market and reorient schooling to U.S. economic competitiveness (Hursh 2007; Weiner 2012).

In this chapter, I situate President Obama's education policy at the intersection of neoliberal urban political economy, race, and economic crisis—particularly the fiscal crisis of cities. I propose that Obama's K–12 education agenda expands and accelerates the neoliberal restructuring of public education that began with President Reagan. The policies stemming from this framework have had particularly negative consequences for low-income students and students of color in urban school districts. More broadly, I argue Obama's education policies are constitutive of wider processes of neoliberal urban restructuring. The Obama administration capitalized on the economic crisis and fiscal crisis of cities to accelerate the neoliberalization of urban public education, and thus the city itself. I conclude by noting that education has become a focal point of urban political-economic contestations over inequality and racial exclusion.

The Obama Education Agenda

President Obama accelerated the neoliberal shift in federal education policy first set out in the National Commission on Excellence in Education's 1983 report, *A Nation at Risk: The Imperative for Educational Reform* (National Commission 1983). The report, commissioned by President Reagan, put the blame for the faltering U.S. economy on public schools. To restore the United States' global economic dominance, *A Nation at Risk* called for a top-down system of education accountability, higher standards for course-taking, and tying teachers' salaries to student performance. Many argued the document was largely aimed at producing a "manufactured crisis" (Berliner and Biddle 1996) to warrant radical restructuring of public education. Education scholar Gene Glass called *A Nation at Risk* a "political document determined more by ideology than by a careful review of the literature" (Glass 1987, 9).

Thus began a concerted, business-led, market-driven, bipartisan campaign against public education, teachers' unions, and teacher professionalism (Weiner 2012). But it was left to George W. Bush to institutionalize this neoliberal agenda with No Child Left Behind (NCLB), the 2002 reauthorization of the federal Elementary and Secondary Education Act (ESEA). NCLB established tough accountability measures and sanctions to hold students, teachers, schools, and school districts accountable for improving academic achievement. The act facilitated management through target setting and comparison by those distant from schools and classrooms, and established testing metrics to underpin education markets. Schools that did not meet annual achievement thresholds faced reconstitution or replacement with publicly funded but privately operated charter schools. NCLB also funneled tax dollars to private education services contracted to improve student performance.

More than a decade after Bush's launch of NCLB, public schools, particularly in cities, are dominated by business methods and market logics—high-stakes standardized tests, top-down accountability, "school choice," privatization, management by CEOs, and so on. Much research indicates these policies have watered down curriculum, particularly for low-income students and students of color, who disproportionately attend low-performing schools (Berliner 2011; Hursh 2011; Lipman 2004), undermined teacher morale and professionalism (Valli and Buese 2007), and intensified inequitable opportunities to learn for low-income students of color and second-language learners (Darling-Hammond 2007; Valenzuela 2005). They have opened a vast new market in education management organizations, charter schools, and private education services, and have been a boon to technology and testing companies and publishers of text books, curricula, and teacher training allied with tests and standards (Burch 2009).

Despite the evidence against these policies and growing public opposition to them, President Obama not only fully embraced markets and business practices, but seized on the economic crisis, particularly the fiscal crisis of cities and states, to escalate their implementation, embedding them in federal education funding requirements, competitive grants, and new initiatives. Three interrelated themes run through Obama's education program: more markets, privatization, and top-down accountability; competitive allocation of resources; and the pervasive influence of an interlocking network of corporate consulting groups, neoliberal think tanks, billionaire venture philanthropies (particularly the Bill and Melinda Gates

Foundation and the Eli Broad Foundation), and the private organizations and projects they sponsor. Education historian Diane Ravitch tartly dubbed the Obama administration, "Bush's third term in education" (2009).

From the beginning, President Obama unequivocally signaled his intentions by appointing Arne Duncan to head the U.S. Department of Education (DOE) over education policy scholar Linda Darling-Hammond (Hursh 2011). Duncan then filled top positions in the DOE with staffers from the Gates Foundation, graduates of the Broad Foundation's education leadership programs, and individuals with ties to the corporate-funded NewSchools Venture Fund, dedicated to training entrepreneurs to run schools. According to a recent estimate, since 2008 the Gates Foundation has spent at least $2 billion, the Walton Family Foundation at least three-quarters of a billion, and Broad half a billion dollars to promote charter schools, standards and testing, performance pay for teachers based on student test scores, elimination of teacher tenure, and other corporate-driven initiatives (Pelto 2014).

Obama's policy agenda incorporated these and other venture philanthropists' favored projects. For example, Duncan made the Gates-funded Turnaround Challenge (a toolkit for school turnarounds) a DOE handbook for turning around low-performing schools, and Gates' Common Core State Standards are now national policy. Alternative teacher certification programs (e.g., Teach for America, funded by Gates) and education leadership programs, funded by Gates and Broad to recruit and train business people to run urban schools and school districts (e.g., New Leaders, the Broad Center for the Management of School Systems and its training programs), were part of the DOE's portfolio of "best practices" (Barkan 2011; Saltman 2010). Through these programs, neoliberal "reformers" have trained hundreds of teachers, administrators, and school district leaders with the goal of advancing their education agenda (Weis 2013).

Obama unveiled his education program in a speech to the Hispanic Chamber of Commerce in spring 2009 (Obama 2009a). Linking U.S. economic competitiveness with achievement of "the American dream," he claimed, "The future belongs to the nation that best educates its citizens." Echoing the crisis rhetoric of *A Nation at Risk,* he warned, "We've let our grades slip, our schools crumble, our teacher quality fall short, and other nations outpace us." To address this emergency, he outlined key education planks: invest in early childhood education through competitive grants, more accountability and standards, alternative teacher preparation programs and performance pay; expand charter schools; and turn around low-performing schools. He also promised to expand access to higher education by increasing student grants and tuition tax credits.

To leverage this agenda, a few months later, Obama announced Race to the Top (RTTT), his signature $4.35 billion competitive education grant to states. Funding for RTTT comes from the Education Recovery Act, part of the American Recovery and Reinvestment Act of 2009—the economic stimulus. In 2010, the administration codified the RTTT agenda in *A Blueprint for Reform,* Obama's proposal to overhaul the Elementary and Secondary Education Act (ESEA), which is the principal source of federal funding for K–12 schools serving children in poverty. The DOE began implementing the *Blueprint* piecemeal with competitive Title I School Improvement grants and other initiatives. The following sections briefly summarize these Obama education initiatives.

Race to the Top

To have a shot at securing RTTT grants, states had to raise their caps on charter school expansion and agree to tie teacher evaluation and compensation to student test scores (Stan Karp 2010). RTTT was administered in three phases. Ten states and the District of Columbia received grants in phases one and two, and an additional seven states were awarded smaller grants in phase three. However, the carrot of federal funding in a period of economic recession leveraged all but four state legislatures to align their laws with RTTT guidelines advancing RTTT goals nationally. In 2012, RTTT competition was expanded to local education agencies. The DOE awarded sixteen cities, metropolitan areas, and consortia of charter schools a total of over $400 million over four years (U.S. Department of Education 2015), making RTTT an explicitly urban initiative. RTTT was developed with support from the Gates Foundation, and Gates and other key venture philanthropies' favorite policies were written into it (Barkan 2011; Saltman 2010). To ensure that proposals would be aligned with its program, Gates awarded planning grants to help states write their proposals.

The Blueprint for Education Reform

A Blueprint for Reform codified and extended RTTT and proposed a similar funding structure based on competitive grants. The *Blueprint* has six sections:

1. *College- and Career-Ready Students:* Education is to make students career ready through rigorous national standards (e.g., the Common Core Standards), rewards for successful schools, and strong accountability with intervention for the lowest performing 5,000 schools, including closing, reconstitution, takeover by the state or an outside operator, and conversion to a charter school.

2. *Great Teachers and Great Leaders:* Improve teaching and education leadership and equitable distribution of excellent teachers through performance pay based partly on student test scores ("value added"), alternative teacher and administrator certification programs (e.g., Teach for America and New Leaders).

3. *A Complete Education:* Improve literacy and science, technology, engineering, and mathematics (STEM) education.

4. *Meeting the Needs of English Learners and Other Diverse Learners:* A statement of the problem; no goals or new initiatives.

5. *Successful, Safe, and Healthy Students:* Extended learning time, family engagement in schools, data to track health and safety, and Promise Neighborhoods, interlocking networks of schools and social service agencies in low-income communities.

6. *Fostering Innovation and Excellence:* Scale up charter schools, school choice, and on-line learning.

Title I School Improvement Grants and Privately Funded Initiatives

To improve the "persistently lowest-performing schools," the DOE provided funds for four interventions:

- *Turnaround:* Replace the principal and at least 50 percent of the staff
- *Restart:* Close or convert the school and replace it with a private operator, charter operator, charter management organization, or education management organization
- *Close:* Close the school and transfer the students to a higher-achieving school
- *Transformation:* Replace the principal and revamp the instruction, institute teacher performance pay, extend learning time, and provide additional technical assistance

Several other small Obama initiatives were largely funded by private interests. ConnectED is a partnership of the Federal Communications Commission and corporate sponsors—Apple, Microsoft, Sprint, Verizon, and other technology companies—to connect classrooms and libraries with the Internet. Corporate sponsors select the recipients and make all decisions.

My Brother's Keeper is an interagency partnership of state and local officials, the private sector, and philanthropies, the stated goal of which is to advance the achievement of boys and young men of color. In announcing this project, President Obama noted, "I'm going to pen this presidential memorandum directing the federal government not to spend more money, but to do things smarter to implement proven solutions" (Obama 2014). While the memorandum called for relaxing zero-tolerance discipline policies that have led to disproportionate expulsions and suspensions of male students of color, it framed African American young men and boys as problems to be fixed through technocratic entrepreneurial strategies, thus reinforcing neoliberal racial discourses and solutions (Dumas 2015).

Examining Obama's Education Policies

In many ways, Obama's national education agenda was an urban education agenda. RTTT, the *Blueprint*, School Improvement Grant guidelines, My Brother's Keeper and other policies are particularly consequential for urban school districts with high concentrations of low-income students and students of color and disproportionately large numbers of schools deemed persistently low-performing. What is the evidence for these policies? What interests drive them? And what are their implications for urban education?

An Ideological Agenda Shaped by Corporate Interests

> This competition will not be based on politics or ideology or the preferences of a particular interest group. Instead, it will be based on a simple principle—whether a state is ready to do what works. (Obama 2009b)

Despite President Obama's claim to eschew ideologically driven policy and rely on sound evidence, his education initiatives indicate otherwise. An assessment of the *Blueprint* by a group of respected education researchers (Mathis and Welner 2010) found the use of credible research was "extraordinarily weak," with only 15 percent of references from peer-reviewed, independent sources (13). Instead, the editors note, the *Blueprint* relies on think tanks, ideologically driven reports, corporate consulting groups, and contractors with a financial interest in the recommendations. "Overall, the document is of little or no value for those who seek evidence of the soundness of the Obama administration's proposed legislation" (10). In their assessment of the section on college and career readiness, Ravitch and Mathis (2010) conclude it is "rife with inaccuracies, misrepresentations, and misunderstandings of cited sources" (18). "The document starts with a pre-determined end (the *Blueprint*) and back-fills support for these positions. While it presents itself as a research document, it is in fact a political document" (12). In a review of the section "Great Teachers and Great Leaders," a leading teacher education researcher calls it a "partisan political text," not grounded in research (Shaker 2010, 30). In sum, the *Blueprint* continues a pattern of ideologically driven neoliberal policy that goes back to the Reagan administration.

Both Race to the Top and the *Blueprint* were heavily influenced by neoliberal think tanks (Ravitch and Mathis 2010, 18; Saltman 2010) and venture philanthropies (particularly Broad and Gates) that have leveraged billions of dollars to steer U.S. education to markets, accountability, and workforce preparation (Barkan 2011; Saltman 2010; Scott 2009). The Broad Foundation wrote in its 2009–10 annual report, "The election of President Barack Obama and his appointment of Arne Duncan, former CEO of Chicago Public Schools, as the U.S. secretary of education, marked the pinnacle of hope for our work in education reform. In many ways, we feel the stars have finally aligned" (Broad 2009–10, 9).

Obama's policies were also heavily influenced by corporations that stand to gain economically. Nearly half the research references in the "College and Career Readiness" section of the *Blueprint* are to organizations that would gain from the proposed policies (Ravitch and Mathis 2010). A well-known case is the Common Core

State Standards (CCSS) (adopted by forty-six states and the District of Columbia as of May, 2016). The Gates Foundation, led by former Microsoft CEO Bill Gates, spent more than $200 million to develop Common Core and organize political support for it nationally. Microsoft and other technology companies stand to make millions from new online testing and computer upgrades to roll out the standards in schools across the United States (Layton 2014). California alone estimated its costs for implementing the CCSS at $3 billion (Hepler 2014). Common Core requires new textbooks, staff development, and student and teacher assessments marketed by Pearson. In the neoliberal policy environment, Pearson's multinational educational publishing conglomerate has expanded to producer of global education testing products and services and key influence in the global education policy process. Ravitch noted, "With the U.S. Department of Education now pressing schools to test children in second grade, first grade, kindergarten—and possibly earlier . . . Pearson will control every aspect of our education system" (Ravitch 2012). The Thomas B. Fordham Institute estimated the national cost for compliance with Common Core will be between $1 billion to $8 billion, and the profits will go almost directly to publishers (Fleisher 2012). In February, 2014, Microsoft announced that Pearson's Common Core classroom materials would be loaded on Microsoft's tablet, giving Microsoft an edge over Apple's iPad, the main tablet in K–12 classrooms. Pearson and Microsoft are also collaborating on a digital education model that combines Pearson's Common Core System of Courses with Microsoft technology to create personalized learning programs geared to the new College and Career Readiness Standards, another boon to both corporations (*PRWeb* 2014).

Business Logics and Markets

Business logics, technocratic interventions, and market mechanisms dominate Obama's education initiatives. The DOE continued to hinge school improvement on a business model of top-down accountability and testing that the nonpartisan National Research Council (2011) and many other researchers (see Berliner 2013) have concluded has not worked to improve academic achievement or close the racial achievement gap. Moreover, it has produced inequitable opportunities to learn for low-income students of color (Darling-Hammond 2007), including a narrowed curriculum focused on low-level skills, inappropriate assessment of English language learners and students with special needs, and incentives to exclude low-scoring students in order to achieve test score targets (245). Competitive performance pay for teachers tied to student test scores was another favored Obama policy despite evidence of its lack of validity and harm to teacher collaboration (Baker et al. 2010).

Charter schools are the principle vehicle for education markets in the United States. Nationally, by 2014, the number of students enrolled in charter schools had nearly doubled under the Obama presidency (Journey For Justice 2014, 3). The administration incentivized the expansion of charter schools through its competitive grants, despite acknowledging in the *Blueprint* charter schools' mixed results.

The most comprehensive national study of charter schools found that overall they do not perform better than traditional neighborhood schools (CREDO 2009).[1] Nor did the *Blueprint* explain why charters would help high-poverty urban school districts when research shows that, overall, charter schools serve lower percentages of English-language learners and special education students and increase racial segregation (Rotberg 2014). They also employ less-experienced, less-qualified teachers and administrators who are paid less and have a higher turnover rate (Fabricant and Fine 2012). The DOE's claim that charter schools are a source of innovation is also dubious. While some standalone charters take advantage of increased flexibility to support innovative teaching and learning, many charter school chains replicate rigid practices. School turnarounds were another Obama DOE strategy imported from the corporate playbook, yet researchers have cautioned there is little conclusive research supporting their efficacy (Scott 2008; Mintrop and Sunderman 2009).

Expansion of markets (charter and turnaround schools) in urban areas is tied to closing neighborhood schools. Over the past decade, Detroit, New York, and Chicago have closed more than a hundred public schools each; Columbus, Pittsburgh, St. Louis, Houston, Philadelphia, Washington, D.C., Kansas City, Milwaukee, and Baltimore have closed more than twenty-five (Journey For Justice 2014). As of the fall of 2014, every traditional neighborhood public school in New Orleans had been closed. Since President Obama came into office, cities across the United States closed schools in unprecedented numbers. These school closings have had a vastly disproportionate impact on African American students. In the 2013 mass school closings in Chicago, 79 percent of students affected were African American, although 40.5 percent of students are African American. In Philadelphia, more than 80 percent were African American, although African Americans are 58 percent of the district (Lee 2013). In Washington, D.C., 93 percent were African American, although they make up 72 percent of the district (Khalek 2013). Detroit's wave of school closings has also primarily affected African American students.

Strong on Competition and Incentives, Weak on Equity

Overall, the Obama administration employed competitive strategies rather than funding based on need to improve K–12 schools. In place of substantive supports for teaching, Obama offered competitive performance pay for raising test scores. This shifts responsibility for student achievement onto teachers, obfuscating the opportunity gap and poverty penalty faced by schools in low-income urban communities and intensifying competition within schools. Berliner (2013) summarizes what "virtually every scholar of teaching and schooling knows," school effects account for only about 20 percent of the variation in student scores on achievement tests, and "teachers are only a part of that constellation of variables associated with 'school'" (5). Urban teachers are also paid less than many suburban teachers. Although the *Blueprint* acknowledges this disparity, it proposes no policies to address it. Instead Obama offered fast-track alternative teacher certification programs (e.g., Teach for America) that place noncredentialed and novice teachers in economically disadvantaged schools, where they have twice the turnover rate as teachers from traditional teacher education programs (Weis 2013, 7).

President Obama did not used federal policy to target significant new federal funding to schools with high concentrations of low-income students, despite the obvious need (Martire 2013). Urban schools generally have greater needs yet less per-pupil funding than suburban schools. Competitive grants (RTTT), rather than guaranteed funding streams, benefit some urban districts but not others and do not address dramatic funding inequities (Education Trust 2006).[2] In 2011–12, the per-pupil funding for instruction in Chicago was $8,376. In the affluent suburb of New Trier it was $12,725 (Illinois State Board of Education n.d.). The disparity translates into a significant education opportunity gap. Over seventy studies report the need for additional funding of 20 percent to 40 percent to meet the needs of low-income children (Ravitch and Mathis 2010, 16). Low-income children have larger class sizes, higher student-to teacher ratios, a less-rigorous curriculum, and less experienced teachers (Barton 2004), and this education opportunity gap has increased since 2000 (Berliner 2013). In the absence of a larger federal role, the solution to these inequities is left up to the states and cities.

Beyond school funding, much research demonstrates that economic inequality and the hardships of poverty are the *most* significant factors affecting educational outcomes (Anyon 2014; Berliner 2013; Rothstein 2008). The *Blueprint* acknowledges this reality but the research base for Obama's interventions (networks of social services, more parent engagement, and longer school days) is weak (Glass, Barnett, and Welner 2010), and the interventions locate responsibility in families' supposed deficiencies and their need to do more. The DOE's principle education program to address poverty, Promise Neighborhoods, was modeled entirely on the Harlem Children's Zone (HCZ), which is organized around a network of charter schools, social service providers, and private investors. In the first three rounds of competition, beginning in 2010, the administration awarded $100 million in competitive planning and implementation grants to replicate the HCZ in cities and rural areas. Despite the HCZ's popular acclaim, it has had mixed results and relies heavily on millions of dollars in private funding (Croft and Whitehurst 2010). In short, the *Blueprint* does not address structural causes of poverty and its consequences for children. Rather, it reproduces the discourse of individual responsibility, racialized pathologization of poverty and "human capital" deficiencies, and market solutions that underlies other racialized neoliberal urban policies (DeFilippis and Fraser 2010; Goetz 2013; Imbroscio 2008; Lipman 2009; Reed 1999).

Promise Neighborhoods are part of Obama's Promise Zones, Neighborhood Revitalization Initiative, which combines Promise Neighborhoods grants with Choice Neighborhoods grants funded by the Department of Housing and Urban Development and the Department of Justice's Byrne Criminal Justice Innovation program. Promise Zone grants replicate the administration's competitive strategy, with winners having preferred access to additional federal grants over other high-poverty neighborhoods. Not only is there no strong evidence for the Promise Zone strategy, it is clearly inadequate in the face of structural causes of high levels of child poverty, homelessness, inadequate health care, long-term parent unemployment, and so on. At the same time, Obama's school closing and turnaround policies continue to levy a poverty penalty on low-income students who are most likely to be in low-performing schools.

Narrowing Education to Economic Goals

Obama's education policy narrowly focused on preparing economically productive individuals (i.e., labor force development to serve U.S. economic competitiveness). Common Core, geared to U.S. economic competitiveness, stresses academics in kindergarten, excludes curriculum on democratic citizenship, marginalizes literature and the arts, and undermines teachers' pedagogical decision making. Even policies to expand preschool include testing and a narrow focus on school-ready skills, despite counter recommendations of early childhood experts. This narrow economic focus displaces other important educational goals—full human development and thoughtful civic participation.

Indeed, Obama's Educate to Innovate Campaign seems to be a capital accumulation strategy, rather than an education agenda. DOE partnerships with the corporate sector were designed to retool schooling for high-priority workforce and economic sectors (science, technology, engineering, and mathematics—STEM), establish curriculum standards, and use data to align schooling with corporate labor needs (Obama 2009c). The Educate to Innovate Campaign was funded by over $700 million in public–private partnership dollars (Obama 2009c). "Change the Equation," an expansion of Educate to Innovate, was a "CEO-led" coalition of more than a hundred CEOs of technology and petroleum companies[3] to expand math and science in 100 "high-need" communities. The corporations stand to benefit handsomely from publicly funded workforce training. As Obama explained, "They've got a self-interest in it. Xerox is going to do really well if we've got a whole bunch of engineers and scientists and math majors who are clamoring to work for some of America's most innovative businesses" (Obama 2010).

As urban schools scramble to create STEM programs, the promise they will lead to high-paying jobs rings hollow. Instead the emphasis on STEM is more likely to benefit U.S. global corporations than urban students (Gutstein 2009). Despite the claim that STEM education will increase education and career opportunities for underrepresented groups, the typical job of the future is not in high tech but in low-wage service work.[4] The combined total of all STEM jobs in 2009 was 6 percent of U.S. employment, and wages varied widely (Cover, Jones, and Watson 2011). Nor does more education increase wages overall—the U.S. workforce is more educated since the 1970s yet wages have remained stagnant. Education can democratize the competition for jobs, but it does not create new or better-paying ones (Weiner 2012). That requires policies to support living wages, strong unions, and government protections for workers.

Education Policy and Neoliberal Urbanism

Cities have become strategically central laboratories for neoliberal experimentation (Brenner and Theodore 2002). The overarching goal of these experiments (e.g., tax abatements, enterprise zones, public–private partnerships, property redevelopment schemes, and new strategies of social control) is to mobilize urban space for market-oriented economic growth and elite consumption practices (Hackworth 2007; Harvey 2001). In *The New Political Economy of Urban Education* (Lipman 2011), I argue that current neoliberal education policies are constitutive of neoliberal urban restructuring and marketing of urban space. Specifically, education markets are part of a broad agenda of urban privatization, and policies to close schools, primarily in low-income urban communities of color, and to turn them over to private operators, contribute to racialized processes of displacement, gentrification, and commodification of black urban space.

In gentrifying areas, closing schools serving low-income students of color and replacing them with rebranded selective enrollment and specialty schools for a new upper-middle-class clientele is a way to push out current residents and attract real estate investment and affluent home buyers (Lipman 2004). Research in Chicago (Lipman 2011), Detroit (Pedroni 2011), New Orleans (Buras, Randels, and Salaam 2012), and Philadelphia (Cucciara 2008) demonstrates this relationship between school closings, displacement, and gentrification (see also Burdick-Will, Keels, and Schuble 2012; Davis and Oakley 2013). In other, deeply disinvested, mainly African American areas, the concentration of school closings and their replacement with charter school chains and education management organizations instantiates state abandonment and transfer of public assets to private hands. Some deeply disinvested Chicago community areas now have almost no neighborhood public schools left (Sarah Karp 2013). Charter schools, most run by large charter school operators, are the only option.

Whatever their failings, public schools are integral to community life, often the glue that binds urban neighborhoods. Closing them or turning them over to private operators weakens these bonds, affecting the community as a whole. Many closed urban schools were anchors in communities faced with decades of public and private disinvestment. They frequently provided resources in short supply— health clinics, adult education and exercise classes, English classes, arts and sports programs, and computer labs. Thus their closing degrades the community as a whole. The loss of a school also means the loss of unionized jobs frequently held by community residents, further impoverishing affected communities (Lee 2013). In contrast, charter schools are largely nonunion and are neither rooted in, accountable to, nor necessarily open to students where they locate.

The Obama administration's support for charter schools as "a force for innovation" (Obama 2009b) has helped to fuel the growth of the charter school industry. From 2000 to 2012, the percentage of charter schools grew from 1.7 to 5.8 percent, and the total number increased from 1,500 to 5,700 (NCES and IES 2014). The publicly funded and subsidized charter school industry is a vast new market with opportunities to make money through charter school management fees, tax credits, investment in charter school real estate and charter school bonds, education services and materials, marketing, and all the speculative spin-offs of these investments. In New York City, hedge funds are at the "epicenter" of the charter school market (Hass 2009). One analysis reports they stand to make millions of dollars from investments in the Harlem Children's Zone charter schools alone (Miner 2010). Low-income children are both the commodities of investors and customers for the charter school market. From the vantage point of African American and Latino/a urban communities, the loss of neighborhood public schools and concentration of charter schools constitutes private expropriation and commodification of public space.

Downloading the 2007 financial crisis onto cities has presented an opportunity for further neoliberal experimentation (Peck 2012). Urban austerity politics displace the crisis of banks and financial institutions onto workers, the poor, and the middle class through wage and benefit cuts, cuts in public services particularly to low-income communities, and privatization of public infrastructure and institutions. Education is a prime target of this expanded neoliberalization of the city. This was the context for Arne Duncan's visit to Detroit in early 2009 and for Obama's competitive education grants. The Obama administration utilized the economic crisis to accelerate market-driven education policies while city governments mobilize discourses of fiscal crisis to close schools as "the only solution" to budget deficits. As these education policies intersect with other urban austerity policies, their impact on low-income communities of color is compounded. This is particularly so in African American community areas where school closings are concentrated and where the state has relinquished responsibility for social welfare while intensifying policing and surveillance.

Conclusion

Cities have become "the battlefield" over neoliberal education policies (Journey For Justice 2014, 4). The congealed consequences of a decade of high-stakes testing, top-down accountability, blaming teachers and teacher unions, school closings, and privatization erupted in the historic 2012 Chicago teachers strike and the rebirth of the Chicago Teachers Union as an anti-neoliberal, grassroots union in alliance with parents and students. Mass school closings have spawned oppositional coalitions of parents, students, and teachers in cities across the United States. A national backlash against high-stakes testing is also taking shape. This national convergence is zeroing in on federal policy. The Journey 4 Justice Alliance, a coalition of community organizations in twenty-one cities, is pressing the DOE's Office of Civil Rights to investigate school closings in black and Latino/a communities as civil rights violations. The coalition also compelled the DOE to make community-driven school transformation a fifth option for urban school improvement grants. Local grassroots education movements and teacher unions are beginning to link education to organizing for affordable housing, living wages, and racial justice as part of an emergent urban social movement (e.g., Caref et al. 2015; Fulfill the Promise 2014).

President Obama did not invent neoliberal education policies, but he incentivized markets, privatization, and vocationalization of education, leveraging urban and state fiscal crises to accelerate this agenda. The policies he championed reinforce existing educational inequalities, deprofessionalize teaching and school leadership, undermine public education, and contribute to gentrification, destabilization, and commodification of low-income urban communities of color. In essence, the role for government in Obama's education agenda was to facilitate public–private partnerships, privatization, and the work of managerial technicians who are deployed to facilitate markets and apply technical solutions to "fix" urban schools and urban children of color. However, the social movement these policies have triggered is becoming a focal point of urban political contestations over inequality and the remaking of the city for capital accumulation and racial exclusion.

Notes

1. The CREDO study found 17 percent of charters were superior to traditional neighborhood schools, 37 percent significantly worse, and nearly half no different. A 2015 update (CREDO 2015) found charters performed marginally better but that analysis has been critiqued for unsubstantiated claims and methodological flaws (Maul 2015).
2. In 2006, the Education Trust reported that nationally, state and local funds provide $825 per student less in the highest poverty districts than in the most affluent districts and $908 less in the districts that educate the most students of color compared with districts that educate the fewest students of color (6).
3. The Board of Directors is comprised of chairmen and CEOs of Intel Corporation, Time Warner Cable, Xerox, Eastman Kodak Company, Sally Ride Science, and Exxon Mobil.
4. In 2012, the Bureau of Labor Statistics projected that five of the ten occupational groups that will add the most jobs will not require a high school education, three will require high school, and one a two-year associate's degree (cited in Anyon 2014, 37).

References

Anyon, Jean. 2014. *Radical Possibilities: Public Policy, Urban Education, and a New Social Movement*, 2nd ed. Critical Social Thought. New York: Routledge.

Baker, Eva L., Paul E. Barton, Linda Darling-Hammond, Edward Haertel, Helen F. Ladd, Robert Linn, Diane Ravitch, Richard Rothstein, Richard J. Shavelson, and Lorrie A. Shepard. 2010. "Problems with the Use of Student Test Scores to Evaluate Teachers." Economic Policy Institute. http://www.epi.org/publication/bp278/.

Barkan, Joanne. 2011. "Got Dough? How Billionaires Rule Our Schools." *Dissent* (Winter): 49–57. https://www.dissentmagazine.org/article/got-dough-how-billionaires-rule-our-schools.

Barton, Paul E. 2004. "Why Does the Gap Persist?" *Educational Leadership* 62 (3): 8–13. http://www.ascd.org/publications/educational-leadership/nov04/vol62/num03/Why-Does-the-Gap-Persist%C2%A2.aspx.

Berliner, David C. 2011. "Rational Responses to High-Stakes Testing: The Case of Curriculum Narrowing and the Harm That Follows." *Cambridge Journal of Education* 41 (3): 287–302.

———. 2013. "Effects of Inequality and Poverty vs. Teachers and Schooling on America's Youth." *Teachers College Record* 115: 1–26.

Berliner, David C., and Bruce J. Biddle. 1996. *The Manufactured Crisis: Myths, Fraud, and the Attack on America's Public Schools.* New York: Basic Books.

Biddle, Bruce J., and David C. Berliner. 2003. "What Research Says about Unequal Funding for Schools in America." *Policy Perspectives.* WestEd. https://www.wested.org/online_pubs/pp-03-01.pdf.

Brenner, Neil, and Nik Theodore. 2002. "Cities and the Geographies of 'Actually Existing Neo-liberalism.'" *Antipode* 34 (3): 349–79.

Broad Foundation. 2009. *Annual Report.* http://www.broadeducation.org/asset/1129-2009.10%20annual%20report.pdf.

Buras, Kristen L., Jim Randels, Kalamu ya Salaam, and Students at the Center. 2012. *Pedagogy, Policy, and the Privatized City: Stories of Dispossession and Defiance from New Orleans.* New York: Teachers College Press.

Burch, Patricia. 2009. *Hidden Markets: The New Education Privatization.* Critical Social Thought. New York: Routledge.

Burdick-Will, Julia, Micere Keels, and Todd Schuble. 2013. "Closing and Opening Schools: The Association between Neighborhood Characteristics and the Location of New Educational Opportunities in a Large Urban District." *Journal of Urban Affairs* 35 (1): 59–80.

Caref, Carol R., Kurt Hilgendorf, Jankov Pavlyn, Sarah Hainds, and Josh Conwell. 2015. *A Just Chicago: Fighting for the City Our Students Deserve.* Chicago: Chicago Teachers Union.

Carey, Kevin. 2005. "The Funding Gap 2004: Many States Still Shortchange Low-Income and Minority Students." The Education Trust. http://www.cgu.edu/pdffiles/the%20funding%20gap%202004%20many%20states%20still%20shortchange%20low-income%20and%20minority%20students%20--%20ed%20trust.pdf.

Cover, Ben, John I. Jones, and Audrey Watson. 2011. "Science, Technology, Engineering, and Mathematics (STEM) Occupations: A Visual Essay." *Monthly Labor Review,* May: 3–15. http://www.bls.gov/opub/mlr/2011/05/mlr201105.pdf.

CREDO (Center for Research on Education Outcomes). 2009. "Multiple Choice: Charter School Performance in 16 States." Stanford, Calif.: Stanford University.

———. 2015. "Urban Charter School Study: Report on 41 Regions." Stanford, Calif.: Stanford University. https://urbancharters.stanford.edu/download/Urban%20Charter%20School%20Study%20Report%20on%2041%20Regions.pdf.

Croft, Michelle, and Grover J. Whitehurst. 2010. "The Harlem Children's Zone, Promise Neighborhoods, and the Broader, Bolder Approach to Education." Brookings Institute. http://www.brookings.edu/research/reports/2010/07/20-hcz-whitehurst.

Cucciara, Maia. 2008. "Re-Branding Urban Schools: Urban Revitalization, Social Status, and Marketing Public Schools to the Upper Middle Class." *Journal of Education Policy* 23 (2): 165–79.

Darling-Hammond, Linda. 2007. "Race, Inequality and Educational Accountability: The Irony of 'No Child Left Behind.'" *Race, Ethnicity and Education* 10 (3): 245–60.

Davis, Tomeka, and Deirdre Oakley. 2013. "Linking Charter School Emergence to Urban Revitalization and Gentrification: A Socio-Spatial Analysis of Three Cities." *Journal of Urban Affairs* 35 (1): 81–102.

DeFilippis, James, and Jim Fraser. 2010. "Why Do We Want Mixed-Income Housing and Neighborhoods?" In *Critical Urban Studies: New Directions,* ed. Jonathan S. Davies and David L. Imbroscio, 135–47. Albany: State University of New York Press.

Dumas, Michael. 2015. My Brother as "Problem": Neoliberal Governmentality and Interventions for Black Young Men and Boys. *Educational Policy* 30(1): 94–115.

Education Trust. 2006. *The Funding Gap 2006*. https://edtrust.org/resource/the-funding-gap-2/.

Fabricant, Michael, and Michelle Fine. 2012. *Charter Schools and the Corporate Makeover of Public Education: What's at Stake?* New York: Teachers College Press.

Fleisher, Lisa. 2012. "Textbook Sales Likely to Rise on New Rules." *Wall Street Journal*, May 29. http://www.wsj.com/articles/SB10001424052702303674004577434430304060586.

Fulfill the Promise: The Schools and Communities our Children Deserve. 2014. Schools and Communities United. Milwaukee, Wisc. http://www.schoolsandcommunitiesunited.org/wp-content/uploads/2014/05/Fulfill-the-promise-SCU-report-and-excerpt.pdf.

Glass, Gene V. 1987. "What Works: Politics and Research." *Educational Researcher* 16 (3): 5–10.

Glass, Gene V., Stephen Barnett, and Kevin G. Welner. 2010. "A Review of Successful, Safe, and Healthy Students." In *The Obama Education Blueprint: Researchers Examine the Evidence*, ed. William J. Mathis and Kevin G. Welner, 63–76. The National Education Policy Center Series. Charlotte, N.C.: Information Age.

Goetz, Edward, G. 2013. "The Audacity of Hope VI: Discourse and the Dismantling of Public Housing." *Urban Studies* 35: 342–48.

Gutstein, Eric. 2009. "The Politics of Mathematics Education in the US: Dominant and Counter Agendas." In *Culturally Responsive Mathematics Education*, ed. Brian Greer Swapna Mukhopadhyay, Sharon Nelson-Barber, and Arthur B. Powell, 137–64. New York: Routledge.

Hackworth, Jason. 2007. *The Neoliberal City: Governance, Ideology, and Development in American urbanism*. Ithaca, N.Y.: Cornell University Press.

Harvey, David. 2001. *Spaces of Capital: Towards a Critical Geography*. London: Routledge.

Hass, Nancy. 2009. "Scholarly Investments." *New York Times*, December 4. http://www.nytimes.com/2009/12/06/fashion/06charter.html.

Hepler, Lauren. 2014. "Common Core Cash-in? Handicapping Silicon Valley's Race for K–12 Classrooms." *Silicon Valley Business Journal*, April 1. http://www.bizjournals.com/sanjose/news/2014/04/01/common-core-cash-in-handicapping-silicon-valleys.html?page=all.

Hursh, David. 2007. "Assessing No Child Left Behind and the Rise of Neoliberal Education Policies." *American Educational Research Journal* 44 (3): 493–518.

———. 2011. "More of the Same: How Free Market Capitalism Dominates the Economy and Education." In *The Phenomenon of Obama and the Agenda for Education*, ed. Paul R. Carr and Brad J. Porfilio, 3–22. Critical Constructions: Studies on Education and Society. Charlotte, N.C.: Information Age.

Illinois State Board of Education. n.d. "eReport Card Public Site." http://webprod.isbe.net/ereportcard/publicsite/getsearchcriteria.aspx.

Imbroscio, David. 2008. "'United and Actuated by Some Common Impulse of Passion': Challenging the Dispersal Consensus in American Housing Policy Research." *Journal of Urban Affairs* 30 (2): 111–30.

Journey For Justice Alliance. 2014. "Death by a Thousand Cuts: Racism, School Closures, and Public School Sabotage." http://www.j4jalliance.com/wp-content/uploads/2014/02/J4JReport-final_05_12_14.pdf.

Karp, Sarah. 2013. "A Sign of Stability." *Catalyst Chicago* 24 (3): 11–15. http://catalyst-chicago.org/2013/04/sign-stability/.

Karp, Stan. 2010. "School Reform We Can't Believe In." *Rethinking Schools* 24 (3). http://www.rethinkingschools.org/archive/24_03/24_03_NCLBstan.shtml.

Khalek, Rania. 2013. "Racist School Closings in Washington, DC." *Truthout*, May 31. http://www.truth-out.org/news/item/16672-racist-school-closings-in-washington-dc.

Layton, Lyndsey. 2014. "How Bill Gates Pulled Off the Swift Common Core Revolution." *Washington Post*, June 7. http://www.washingtonpost.com/politics/how-bill-gates-pulled-off-the-swift-common-core-revolution/2014/06/07/a830e32e-ec34–11e3–9f5c-9075d5508f0a_story.html.

Lee, Trymaine. 2013. "Mass School Closings' Severe Impact on Lives of Black, Latino Students." *MSNBC.* http://nbclatino.com/2013/10/15/mass-school-closings-severe-impact-on-lives-of-black-latino-students/.

Lipman, Pauline. 2004. *High Stakes Education: Inequality, Globalization, and Urban School Reform.* Critical Social Thought. New York: Routledge.

———. 2009. "The cultural politics of mixed income schools and housing: A Racialized Discourse of Displacement, Exclusion, and Control." *Anthropology & Education Quarterly* 40 (3): 215–36.

———. 2011. *The New Political Economy of Urban Education: Neoliberalism, Race, and the Right to the City.* Critical Social Thought. New York: Routledge.

Martire, Ralph M. 2013. "'For Each and Every Child'—Why Funding Reform Is Crucial to Enhancing Student Achievement." Center for Budget and Tax Accountability. http://www.ctbaonline.org/sites/default/files/reports/ctba.limeredstaging.com/node/add/repository-report/1386523017/PPT_2013.08.12_Presentation%20NCSL%20Atlanta%20%5Beducation%5D.pdf.

Mathis, William J., and Kevin G. Welner, eds. 2010. *The Obama Education Blueprint: Researchers Examine the Evidence.* Charlotte, N.C.: Information Age.

Maul, Andrew. 2015. "Review of Urban Charter School Study 2015. National Education Policy Center." http://nepc.colorado.edu/%20thinktank/review-urban-charter-school.

Miner, Barbara. 2010. "Ultimate Superpower: Supersized Dollars Drive 'Waiting for Superman' Agenda." *NOTwaitingforsuperman.org.* http://www.notwaitingforsuperman.org/Articles/20101020-MinerUltimateSuperpower.

Mintrop, Heinrich, and Gail L. Sunderman. 2009. "Predictable Failure of Federal Sanctions-Driven Accountability for School Improvement—And Why We May Retain It Anyway." *Educational Researcher* 38 (5): 353–64.

National Commission on Excellence in Education. 1983. *A Nation at Risk: The Imperative for Educational Reform.* Washington, D.C.: United States Department of Education. http://www2.ed.gov/pubs/NatAtRisk/index.html.

National Research Council. 2011. *Incentives and Test-Based Accountability in Education.* Washington, D.C.: National Academies.

NCES and IES (National Center for Education Statistics and Institute for Education Sciences). 2014. *The Condition of Education 2014.* Washington, D.C.: U.S. Department of Education. http://nces.ed.gov/pubs2014/2014083.pdf.

Obama, Barack. 2009a. "Remarks by the President to the Hispanic Chamber of Commerce on a Complete and Competitive American Education." Video and transcript. *This Week with Barack Obama.* March 10. http://thisweekwithbarackobama.blogspot.com/2009/03/president-obamas-speech-on-education.html.

———. 2009b. "Remarks by the President on Education." The White House. July 24. http://www.whitehouse.gov/the_press_office/Remarks-by-the-President-at-the-Department-of-Education/.

———. 2009c. "Educate to Innovate." The White House. November 23. http://www.whitehouse.gov/issues/education/k-12/educate-innovate.

———. 2010. "Remarks by the President at the Announcement of the 'Change the Equation' Initiative." The White House. September 16. http://www.whitehouse.gov/the-press-office/2010/09/16/remarks-president-announcement-change-equation-initiative.

———. 2014. "Remarks by the President on 'My Brother's Keeper' Initiative." The White House. February 27. https://www.whitehouse.gov/the-press-office/2014/02/27/remarks-president-my-brothers-keeper-initiative.

Peck, Jamie. 2012. "Austerity Urbanism: American Cities under Extreme Economy." *City* 16 (6): 626–55.

Pedroni, Thomas C. 2011. "Urban Shrinkage as a Performance of Whiteness; Neoliberal Urban Restructuring, Education, and Racial Containment in the Post-industrial, Global Niche City." Special Issue. *Discourse: Studies in the Cultural Politics of Education* 32 (2): 203–15.

Pelto, Jonathan. 2014. "Funding 'Education Reform': The Big Three Foundations." *The Progressive: Public Schools Shakedown.* June 24. http://www.publicschoolshakedown.org/funding -education-reform.

PRWeb. 2014. "Global Leader Pearson Creates Leading Curriculum, Apps for Digital Learning Environments." February 20. http://www.prweb.com/releases/2014/02/prweb11601976.htm.

Ravitch, Diane. 2009. "Obama Gives Bush a 3rd Term in Education." *Huffington Post,* July 14. http://www.huffingtonpost.com/diane-ravitch/obama-gives-bush-a-3rd-te_b_215277.html.

———. 2012. "The United States of Pearson." Diane Ravitch's Blog. https://dianeravitch. net/2012/05/07/the-united-states-of-pearson-2/.

Ravitch, Diane, and William J. Mathis. 2010. "A Review of College- and Career-Ready Students." In *The Obama Education Blueprint: Researchers Examine the Evidence,* ed. William J. Mathis and Kevin G. Welner, 9–22. Charlotte, N.C.: Information Age.

Reed, Adolph, Jr. 1999. The "Underclass" as Myth and Symbol: The Poverty of Discourse about Poverty. In *Stirrings in the Jug: Black Politics in the Post-Segregation Era,* ed. Adolph Reed Jr., 179–96. Minneapolis: University of Minnesota Press.

Rotberg, Iris C. 2014. "Charter Schools and the Risk of Increased Segregation." *Phi Delta Kappa International,* July 14. http://www.edweek.org/ew/articles/2014/02/01/kappan_rotberg.html.

Rothstein, Richard. 2008. "Whose Problem Is Poverty?" *Educational Leadership* 65 (7): 8–13.

Saltman, Kenneth J. 2010. *The Gift of Education: Public Education and Venture Philanthropy.* Education, Politics, and Public Life. New York: Palgrave Macmillan.

Scott, Caitlin. 2008. "A Call to Restructure Restructuring: Lessons from the No Child Left Behind Act in Five States." Washington, D.C.: Center on Education Policy. http://cep-dc.org/ displayDocument.cfm?DocumentID=175.

Scott, Janelle T. 2009. "The Politics of Venture Philanthropy in Charter School Policy and Advocacy." *Educational Policy* 23 (1): 106–36.

Shaker, P. 2010. "A Review of Great Teachers and Great Leaders." In *the Obama Education Blueprint: Researchers Examine the Evidence*, ed. William J. Mathis and Kevin G. Welner, 23–32. Charlotte, N.C.: Information Age.

U.S. Department of Education. 2015. "Awards—Race to the Top District." http://www2.ed.gov /programs/racetothetop-district/awards.html.

Valenzuela, Angela, ed. 2005. *Leaving Children Behind: How "Texas-style" Accountability Fails Latino Youth.* SUNY series, The Social Context of Education. Albany: State University of New York Press.

Valli, Linda, and Daria Buese. 2007. "The Changing Roles of Teachers in an Era of High-Stakes Accountability." *American Educational Research Journal* 44 (3): 519–58.

Weiner, Lois. 2012. *The Future of Our Schools: Teachers Unions and Social Justice.* Chicago: Haymarket Books.

Weis, Elaine. 2013. "Mismatches in Race to the Top Limit Educational Improvement: Lack of Time, Resources, and Tools to Address Opportunity Gaps Puts Lofty State Goals Out of Reach." Economic Policy Institute. http://www.epi.org/publication/race-to-the-top-goals/.

8

UNIONS IN THE OBAMA ERA
Laboring under False Pretenses?

NIK THEODORE

Via Chicago

On January 29, 2009, President Barack Obama signed his first bill into law, the Lilly Ledbetter Fair Pay Act. Speaking at the bill signing for this equal-pay legislation, Obama told those in attendance that this act would "send a clear message that making our economy work means making sure it works for everybody" (quoted in Stolberg 2009). This bill signing, occurring just nine days after Obama took office, appeared to herald the beginning of a new era for labor and workers' rights in the United States. After decades of malign neglect, if not the deliberate thwarting of labor rights, by the executive branch of government, the Obama presidency appeared poised to rebalance employment relations and redress the prolonged erosion of worker power. The battle lines, so to speak, were quickly drawn. Labor unions, including the American Federation of Labor-Congress of Industrial Organizations (AFL-CIO), the Service Employees International Union (SEIU), and the American Federation of Teachers (AFT) supported the bill, as did a number of women's rights organizations, including the National Organization of Women (NOW), 9to5, and Women Employed. Those opposed included organizations that have had a history of activism against policies that strengthen the rights of workers, notably the U.S. Chamber of Commerce, Eagle Forum, National Association of Manufacturers, and Associated Builders and Contractors. With the signing of the Lilly Ledbetter Fair Pay Act, however, the message seemed clear: the faith labor unions had demonstrated in strongly backing Obama's candidacy would be rewarded—the labor movement would have a stronger voice in national economic policy under the Obama administration.

This moment also seemed to confirm at least two aspects of Obama himself. First, that his prior experience as a community organizer—which has been elevated to near-mythical status by those on both sides of the partisan divide, lauded by the Left and reviled by the Right—made a deep ideological and emotional impression on the new president, sensitizing him to the plight of the disadvantaged. And second, that Obama would be the first "urban president," an executive who would view the world from the vantage point of the modern American metropolis. With inequality at its highest level since the Great Depression (Stierli et al. 2014) and the unemployment rate soaring during the 2007–9 financial crisis, problems of economic hardship and entrenched poverty would be back on the national agenda, and under the leadership of an activist president progressive policies would be enacted to expand economic opportunity.

Barack Obama arrived in Chicago to work as a community organizer following the historic election of Mayor Harold Washington. He accepted a position with the Developing Communities Project, a faith-based organization on the city's South Side that was committed to grassroots organizing in the tradition of Saul Alinsky. During his three-year stint as an organizer, Obama worked in neighborhoods that had been ravaged by deindustrialization, as wave after wave of plant closings and layoffs swept through the region. On his first day of work at the Developing Communities Project, Barack Obama was taken to the site of the shuttered Wisconsin Steel facility, where more than 3,000 unionized workers had permanently lost their jobs—literally overnight—when its parent company Envirodyne suddenly closed the plant. In his memoir, he recalled the scene: "We sat there in silence, studying the building. It expressed some of the robust, brutal spirit of Chicago's industrial past, metal beams and concrete rammed together, without much attention to comfort or detail. Only now it was empty and rust-stained, like an abandoned wreck" (Obama 2004, 224). That night, organizer Obama attended a community meeting where former Wisconsin Steel workers told of their struggles: lost pensions, the shame of unemployment, family hardships, deepening poverty. Now, some twenty years later, President Obama would have an opportunity to pursue policies that would benefit working families and the unemployed throughout the United States, beginning with the enduring problem of earnings discrimination against women.

This chapter examines the state of labor policy in the Obama era in the months and years following the signing of the Lilly Ledbetter Fair Pay Act. The next section considers the historic connections between unions and cities, and examines the trajectory of unionization in the period since the election of President Ronald Reagan in 1980. It explains how Reagan administration policies contributed to declining union membership in the urban centers of the Northeast and Midwest, thereby eroding the political power of these pro-labor, heavily Democratic cities. The Reagan presidency is cast as a key period in which labor-management relations were remade, and one from which labor unions have never fully recovered. The section that follows takes up the politics of labor law reform during the Obama presidency, with a focus on the failure of the Employee Free Choice Act to pass Congress and the rise of state-level legislation to curb collective bargaining and otherwise limit the influence of labor unions. Organized labor counted on President Obama's pro-union stance help achieve sweeping reforms to the nation's labor laws. Instead, probusiness, antiunion interests have seen their power grow in state after state, while federal legislation to address unions' top policy priority—enacting laws to restore the ability of unions to organize workers—has languished. The final section explores the rise of alternative labor organizations, including worker centers and other community-based workers' rights organizations. Reductions in union density along with the inadequate enforcement of labor standards have contributed to the spread of regulatory voids in a restructuring U.S. economy, leading to widespread problems of wage theft and other economic hardships. A range of workers' rights organizations have emerged in an attempt to regulate labor markets "from the bottom up" (Peck and Theodore 2012), often with the tacit support of labor unions. Against a rising tide of antiworker policies, workers' rights organizations and worker center-union collaboration represent some of the few opportunities to ensure that workers in low-wage industries, in particular, have the benefits of worker representation, even if this occurs outside the traditional union model. The chapter concludes with reflections on labor politics in the late stages of the Obama presidency.

Union Cities, Union Decline

Unionization in the United States has been, and continues to be, a largely urban phenomenon. Throughout the twentieth and early twenty-first centuries, cities have been the sites of numerous labor struggles over scope of employment rights and protections; they remain centers of economic activity, so much so that they can be legitimately regarded as regional drivers of national economic prosperity (Katz 2010); and they have been the locus of community-labor activism, including the formation of worker centers and other types of worker organizations that have helped workers shore up faltering labor standards (Turner and Cornfield 2007; Milkman and Ott 2014). While important labor organizing campaigns have been won in nonurban sectors, such as agriculture, and in nonurban locations, such as the rural, industrializing South, the fact remains that urban areas offer the most promising arenas for a revitalized and inclusive labor movement.

To be sure, though, if there is to be revitalization, the U.S. labor movement has its work cut out for it. Between 1950 and 1990, the U.S. labor force more than doubled, increasing from 62.2 million workers to 125.8 million workers (Lee and Mather 2008), and rising to 153.9 million in 2012 (U.S. Census Bureau 2012). Unionization levels, on the other hand, did not keep pace. There were approximately 14 million unionized workers in 1950. This figure rose to nearly 21 million in 1979, before falling to 16.7 million in 1990, 16.3 million in 2000, and 14.3 million in 2012 (Hirsch and Macpherson 2014). As a share of the U.S. labor force, union density declined from approximately 30 percent in 1950 to just 11.2 percent in 2012, including just 6.6 percent of the private sector workforce (Hirsch and Macpherson 2014). Moreover, if 1979 represented the high-water mark of unionization in terms of the absolute numbers of covered workers, it also was a time in which the terrain of labor organizing was to radically change. The election of President Ronald Reagan in 1980 impacted the union movement in at least three crucial ways: (1) the

administration's policies accelerated the pace of deindustrialization, thereby eroding a key source of labor movement membership within manufacturing and related
activities, as well as political power within major industrial cities; (2) the administration withdrew resources for pro-poor and pro-development urban policies, thus
weakening the economic position of many U.S. cities, particularly in the industrial
heartland of the Midwest and Northeast; and (3) the Reagan election ushered in
an era of virulent antiunionism, the legacies of which endure to this day. The
remainder of this section briefly considers these developments and what they have
meant for the power of labor unions in the twenty-first century.

Reaganomics was based on an abiding faith in tax cuts for the wealthy, deregulation, reductions in social spending, and the promotion of "free trade." Among
the administration's key economic strategies was the lowering of many import tar-
iffs on foreign-made goods in an effort to stimulate global trade. This created an
influx of lower-priced goods manufactured abroad into U.S. consumer markets, and
U.S. trade deficits soared. It also accelerated the exodus of manufacturing plants
from the United States and contributed to the spatial reorganization of economic
activity within the country, principally from the atrophying Rust Belt to the boom-
ing Sun Belt. Deindustrialization, the systemic loss of manufacturing capacity
and jobs, more severely impacted northern cities than southern cities, African
Americans more than whites, and unionized workers more than those without
labor representation (Bluestone 1983). The states of Illinois, Wisconsin, Indiana,
Michigan, and Ohio alone lost one million manufacturing jobs, or 19.3 percent, during the period from 1979 to 1986 (Markusen and Carlson 1989). In Chicago, job
losses at Wisconsin Steel were among the 128,986 net manufacturing job losses in
the decade beginning in 1979, a staggering loss of 36 percent (Ranney 2003). The
population declines that followed these job losses, particularly in core industrial
cities such as Buffalo, Detroit, and St. Louis, contributed to the diminishing political influence of urban centers on the national stage. The influence of labor unions
in national politics declined as well. Deindustrialization had eliminated tens of
thousands of unionized jobs, most of these concentrated in the major cities of northern metropolitan areas. Consequently, unions had fewer resources to contribute
to electoral and policy campaigns, and their ability to mobilize the electorate was
reduced by the population outflows from these cities.

Upon taking office, President Reagan oversaw a massive increase in military
spending, which generated more than one million new jobs that disproportionately
benefited "gunbelt" states such as California, Arizona, Texas, and Utah (Markusen et al. 1991), while implementing a series of significant spending cuts, targeting
transfer payments to cities and dramatically reducing appropriations for a range
of urban services and programs, including economic development, public transportation, social services block grants, public service jobs, and job training services
(Fainstein and Fainstein 1989). These cuts had far-reaching effects on the economic
and social viability of urban areas, and further shifted the balance of electoral power

from traditionally Democratic Midwestern cities to the Republican-leaning Sun Belt. At a time of significant job losses, especially in older industrial cities, budget cuts withdrew revenues for initiatives aimed at attracting and retaining jobs and industry, while at the same time reducing funding for social services, job retraining programs, and other forms of assistance designed to help unemployed workers and families in need. By the close of his second term, Reagan had slashed federal spending to local governments by 60 percent, setting in motion a spiral of fiscal decline that constrained municipal decision-making for decades (Dreier 2011).

The presidents who followed Reagan did little to reverse spending priorities or to elevate urban concerns on the national policy agenda. Despite a couple of high-profile urban initiatives, most notably the Empowerment Zone program, federal contributions to municipal budgets continued to decline, falling from 17.5 percent in 1977 to just 5.4 percent in 2000 (Wilson 2010). So when President Obama took office, his administration faced a legacy of antiurban policy-making and funding decisions, and many cities struggled to cope with the fiscal fallout from shifting federal priorities (Newman and Ashton 2004; Peck 2014; Weber 2010). While it may indeed be the case, as Hilary Silver has argued, that "President Obama has a 'stealth urban policy' implicit in his budgetary priorities" (2010, 6), most notably the spending priority areas identified in the American Recovery and Reinvestment Act (ARRA) and the Affordable Care Act (ACA), the absence of an explicit urban agenda, and the presidential leadership necessary to see it through, has been a glaring omission throughout President Obama's first and second terms.

Finally, the Reagan era helped entrench and normalize a pattern of overt hostility to labor unions and to workers' rights issues more generally. Shortly into President Reagan's first term, the Professional Air Traffic Controllers Organization (PATCO) went on strike seeking increased pay, improved working conditions, and a thirty-two-hour workweek. More than 13,000 air traffic controllers walked off the job. But the walkout had violated a law banning strikes by government workers, allowing Reagan to fire 11,345 striking air traffic controllers who had ignored an order to return to work within forty-eight hours. Replacement workers were hired and the union was decertified as the legal bargaining unit for the controllers. Reagan's actions sent shock waves throughout the labor movement. In the aftermath of the PATCO debacle, the use of strikes in response to workplace grievances was sharply curtailed (Figure 8.1), and labor unions grew more cautious, even in the face of increasingly aggressive employer actions aimed at undermining organized labor. Speaking more than two decades after PATCO, Federal Reserve Board Chairman Alan Greenspan (2003, italics added; see also McCartin 2011) summarized the broader significance of Reagan's actions for U.S. labor law:

> Perhaps the most important, and then highly controversial, domestic initiative was the firing of the air traffic controllers in August 1981. The President invoked the law that striking government employees forfeit their jobs,

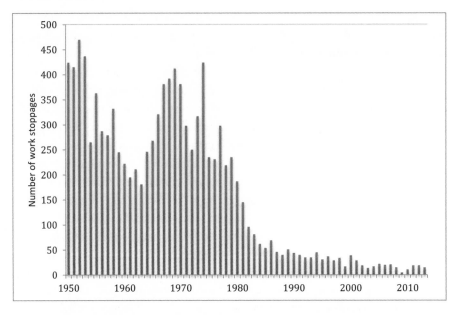

Figure 8.1. Work stoppages involving 1,000 or more workers, 1950–2013. Source: U.S. Bureau of Labor Statistics, Major Work Stoppages, Work stoppages involving 1,000 or more workers, 1947–2013. http://www.bls.gov/news.release/wkstp.t01.htm.

an action that unsettled those who cynically believed no President would ever uphold that law. President Reagan prevailed, as you know, *but far more importantly his action gave weight to the legal right of private employers, previously not fully exercised, to use their own discretion to both hire and discharge workers.*

The Employee Free Choice Act and "the Demise of a Civilization"

Increasingly emboldened by a president whose demonstrated commitment to restraining the power of the American worker had been without parallel in the twentieth century, employers became more brazen in their efforts to undercut unionization and to weaken workers' rights. "Reaganomics reflected the rise of Sunbelt capitalism—of right-to-work-state businessmen who, unlike their Northern counterparts, had never cottoned at all to unions or regulations. . . . And though Reaganomics may have begun in the backwaters of American capitalism, it soon spread to Wall Street" (Meyerson 2004). Middle-class jobs were targeted, with countless jobs subcontracted, offshored, or otherwise undermined in the drive for low wages and increased flexibility (on employers' terms). The rise of contingent work, and with it systemic insecurity for an increasing share of the U.S. workforce, was just one sign that the social compact between business and labor had been broken.

The assault on union organizing began to gather pace during the Reagan era and has continued ever since. Employer retaliation and other forms of coercion have increased in U.S. workplaces, including the firing of workers thought to be union supporters. A fact-finding report by the Commission on the Future of Worker-Management Relations (Dunlop 1994, 70) reported that

- In the early 1950s, approximately 600 workers were reinstated each year because of a discriminatory discharge during a [union] certification campaign. By the late 1980s, this number was near 2,000 a year.
- Adjusted for the number of certification elections and union voters, the incidence of illegal firing increased from one in every 20 elections adversely affecting one in 700 union supporters to one in every four elections victimizing 1 in 50 union supporters.

These startling figures represent a failure of labor law to protect the rights of workers seeking unionization, and they provide insight into some of the causes behind the precipitous decline of union membership in the United States. Overt employer resistance to organized labor has had a chilling effect on the ability of workers to exercise their rights in the workplace, particularly in the context of a restructuring economy in which workers must cope with employment instability and income insecurity. In analyzing the complex interplay between the economic, regulatory, and political forces that have contributed to the breakdown of labor law, Dorian Warren (2010) highlights the role of "regulatory capture" by business interests of the government agencies charged with enforcing labor and employment laws. Regulatory capture has substantially eroded the ability of the National Labor Relations Board (NLRB) to oversee and govern labor-management relations. In response, labor unions have prioritized labor-law reform, seeing reform as a necessary first step toward restoring the rights of U.S. workers to collectively bargain with their employers. Warren explains:

> Increasing employer hostility to workers' rights and unionization efforts, and the ineffectiveness or disinclination of the NLRB to redress this hostility, have driven organized labor to promote labor law reform, to fix what they consider to be a broken system. . . . Their hope is to reverse labor's organizational fortunes by changing the rules of union recognition and collective bargaining, making it easier to overcome management opposition to organizing drives, and increasing the penalties on employers for violating the law. (849)

Key to reforming labor law, from the perspective of labor unions, has been amending the National Labor Relations Act (NLRA) to allow workers to more easily decide whether or not to form a union, and to make this decision without employer coercion. The NLRA provides the framework of regulations through which employees' legal rights to unionize and collectively bargain with their employer are exercised. Section 7 of the NLRA establishes the "right to self-organization, to form, join or assist labor organizations, to bargain collectively through representatives of their own choosing, and to engage in other concerted activities for the purpose of collective bargaining or other mutual aid or protection." Generally, employers are required to collectively bargain with workers over the terms and conditions of their employment if the majority of workers vote in favor of unionization in an election conducted by the NLRB. Unions, however, contend that the Taft-Hartley Labor Act of 1947, which amended the NLRA, provides employers too much leeway within the scope of the law to violate workers' right to organize. Taft-Hartley established the employer free speech clause that permits employers' agents to openly campaign against worker self-organization so long as they do not discriminate against workers who support unionization. Unions further contend that given the considerable latitude employers have been granted to engage in antiunion campaigning, the NLRB election process has ceased to function as a means of democratically deciding whether or not workers want to collectively bargain with their employer.

Estimates provided by the NLRB indicate that that there is a sound basis to the charge that employers routinely violate workers' right to organize. According to the NLRB, employers illegally retaliate against 20,000 workers every year for trying to organize a union (Greenhouse 2004). But employer coercion does not stop there. Employers are becoming increasingly savvy in their antiunion activities, devising ways to pressure employees into voting "no" in representation elections (Bronfenbrenner 2000; Logan 2006). Some of these tactics fall within the bounds of legality. Many others exist in the gray areas of the law, making unfair labor practice charges difficult, if not impossible, for unions to substantiate. These include thinly veiled threats of layoffs made during union organizing campaigns, as well as bogus warnings of plant closings and facility relocations should unions be victorious (Mehta and Theodore 2005). Such tactics, as well as many other forms of employer free speech that are directed against unions, are protected under the NLRA, yet they also serve to create a workplace environment characterized by subtle—as well as overt—coercion of union supporters. Many employers take their antiunion tactics even further, for example, when they strategically fire known union supporters. In such cases, while unions may be unable to provide the NLRB with sufficient evidence demonstrating employer retaliation for union activities, the impact of these types of antiunion behavior is clearly understood at the worksite where it has a chilling effect on unionization campaigns.

Buoyed by the success of "card check" procedures, through which a union can be certified if the majority of employees in a bargaining unit sign authorization forms indicating they would like union representation, especially the SEIU Justice for Janitors campaign, which saw tens of thousands of janitors organized in major U.S. cities, unions began pressing for federal legislation that would reform the NLRA. In March 2007, the Employee Free Choice Act (EFCA), which would provide for union recognition through card check, as well as stiffer penalties for employers that violate labor laws, passed in the House on a 241 to 185 vote. The business community quickly mobilized, pouring millions of dollars into legislative campaigns and vigorously opposing the legislation through lobbying efforts. Bernard Marcus, cofounder of Home Depot, summarized the views held by many business leaders, that EFCA was a "hostile takeover by organized labor" and contending that it marked "the demise of a civilization" (Marcus 2008; Silverstein 2009). Three months later, in June 2007, the legislation stalled in the Senate, falling nine votes short of the sixty needed to invoke cloture and prevent a threatened filibuster by Republicans.

One of the bill's cosponsors, then-Senator Barack Obama, remained confident of its eventual passage: "We will pass the Employee Free Choice Act. It's not a matter of if—it's a matter of when. We may have to wait for the next president to sign it, but we will get this thing done." Following the 2008 election of President Obama, EFCA was reintroduced in Congress, though Democratic support had waned somewhat following sustained opposition from business groups and rightwing advocacy organizations. Never able to muster a filibuster-proof sixty votes in the Senate, despite there being sixty Democratic senators at one point, EFCA languished in Congress. For its part, the Obama administration focused on other economic policy priorities, leaving labor-law reform largely untouched. After spending a quarter-billion dollars to elect President Obama and other Democrats in 2008, organized labor was left searching, in the words of one labor leader, for "a Plan B" (quoted in Meyerson 2010).

To be sure, the passage of EFCA, Harold Meyerson writes,

> was a heavy lift in the Senate—but without Obama's hands-on leadership, it stood no chance. "We wanted a jobs bill and EFCA right off the bat," Teamster President James P. Hoffa says. "Everyone expected it." Instead, Obama asked labor to wait until health care had been enacted. (2010)

Over the course of the ensuing year, the primary domestic policy priority of the Obama administration was the passage of health care reform legislation. Following a bruising and protracted lobbying effort, the ACA was signed into law in March 2010. But by this point the political winds had shifted in Washington and the president had expended enormous political capital to see the passage of ACA through a contentious Congress, whose relationship with the administration had grown increasingly acrimonious. The moment for EFCA, even the strongest supporters on Capitol Hill would concede, had passed.

Reflecting on the broader implications of EFCA's demise, Meyerson (2010) opined: "The failure to reform labor law almost certainly means that the half-century decline of unions in America . . . will continue apace. It means that the corresponding stagnation—and periodic decline—in the incomes of working- and middle-class Americans will likely continue as well." Moreover, the defeat of EFCA occurred within a broader context of mounting antiunion politics at the state level. An attack on collective bargaining in Wisconsin, a state that not only had been a union stronghold for decades but also the birthplace of the public sector union AFSCME (the American Federation of State, County and Municipal Employees union), was launched under the guise of an emergency response to the fiscal crisis. In early 2011, Governor Scott Walker, a newly elected Republican who had garnered substantial campaign funding and support from national antiunion advocacy organizations, signed into law a bill that eliminated collective bargaining for 175,000 public sector employees working for state and municipal governments, prohibited public employees from striking, and required various pay and benefits concessions. Shortly thereafter, Ohio enacted legislation that similarly would eliminate collective bargaining and the right to strike for approximately 350,000 public sector workers. Though signed into law by Governor Kasich, voters repealed the law following a massive union-funded effort that poured in more than $26 million and mobilized more than 17,000 volunteers to defeat the measure (Kroll 2011).

The defeat of antiunion legislation in Ohio has by no means staunched the efforts of lawmakers to reduce the influence of unions. Between 2011 and 2014, state legislators introduced more than 3,950 bills regarding collective bargaining and other issues specifically pertaining to labor unions (NCSL 2014). Though the vast majority of these bills stalled in legislative chambers, many were signed into law, including a number of bills that restrict collective bargaining and undermine existing labor agreements. After years of relative inactivity, right-to-work legislation (which prohibits union security agreements that govern the extent to which a union can require employees' membership, payment of union dues, or fees as a condition of employment) returned to the top of the agenda for antiunion lawmakers. In 2012, right-to-work legislation was introduced in nineteen states, while in 2013 legislation was introduced in twenty-one states and the District of Columbia (NCSL 2012, 2013). During these two legislative sessions, right-to-work legislation was passed in five states: Michigan became the twenty-fourth right-to-work state, Indiana expanded its right-to-work provisions to cover all private sector employment (where previously only school employees were covered), Tennessee first moved to require employers to post notices of the state's right-to-work law and then prohibited waivers of rights to join or refrain from joining a union, and South Carolina enacted harsher penalties for violations of the state's right-to-work law.

Worker Centers and the Revitalization of the Labor Movement

The challenges facing organized labor are daunting, especially given the spread of antilabor legislation at the state level and few, if any, substantial labor-law reforms at the federal level that might restore the ability of workers to organize. Unions will need to organize at least one million new workers each year if they are to maintain the *current* level of union density. But even this statistic, as sobering as it is, may understate what it takes to rebuild union density, and with it, the power of organized labor. Dan Clawson (2003, 13) has observed that "historically labor has not grown slowly, a little bit each year. Most of the time unions are losing ground; once in a while labor takes off. . . . Each period of upsurge redefines what we mean by the 'labor movement.'" In the Obama era, one of the unexpected developments has been the continued rise of so-called alt-labor: worker centers and other workers' rights groups that organize workers outside traditional labor union structures. Perhaps even more unexpected has been the way many unions have embraced these new, upstart organizations as part of the labor movement.

Confronted by the problem of wage theft and violations of labor standards (Bernhardt et al. 2008), workers in low-wage industries have begun to organize to redress workplace violations and raise wages. In cities across the country, carwash workers, day laborers, domestic workers, restaurant workers, taxi workers, temporary staffing industry employees, and others have formed industry-specific organizations aimed at improving employment conditions and providing workers a voice in the workplace. Similar efforts are under way in rural areas where farmworkers and workers in food production are organizing to improve pay and working conditions. There are now more than 200 worker centers nationally (Eidelson 2013), operating in a range of industries and organizing workers using a variety of tactics. In addition to these efforts, retail and fast-food workers have launched a series of high-profile campaigns to raise wages and demand dignity on the job. Recently, unions have begun to throw their support behind these "alternative" labor organizations and campaigns. In 2006, the AFL-CIO and the National Day Laborer Organizing Network signed an agreement creating the National Worker Center–AFL-CIO Partnership (Theodore 2010). This partnership between the largest federation of labor unions and the largest alliance of worker centers signaled the formal recognition of a shared agenda to defend workers' rights. The partnership has since expanded to include domestic workers, guest workers, taxi workers, and workers in other sectors.

Worker centers have moved into the institutional void created by declining union density and inadequate enforcement of employment laws, and they confront head-on at least two limitations facing the traditional labor movement. First, unlike unions that seek to establish collective bargaining units at a given workplace, worker centers tend to organize *across* multiple worksites. Growing sectors of urban economies, such as care work, taxi driving, and construction are characterized by contingent employment relations and substandard working conditions. Worker centers seek to reregulate industries from the bottom up through direct worker organizing, policy advocacy, and other strategies that highlight these conditions. Population densities within urban areas provide worker centers with a key point of leverage in industries that are growing but fragmented—large numbers of workers employed across dozens, hundreds, and even thousands of workplaces can be a powerful force for social change when they transcend the confines of any given employer and act collectively. The passage of domestic workers' bills of rights in several states, the defense of the right to search for work in public spaces by day laborers, as well as successful unionization drives by taxi drivers and carwash workers are evidence of worker-center strategies in action.

Second, guided by a social movement ethos, most worker centers have developed flexible structures and models of worker-led governance. Unlike unions that are subject to a raft of laws that constrain their ability to organize, worker center models more closely resemble that of community organizing, where the ability to rapidly respond to changing conditions on the ground is prioritized. Here again, operating in dense urban environments presents strategic advantages. Workers can share information across sectors of the economy, and tactics to address substandard conditions at a given worksite can ripple through an industry as workers organize and employers are forced to raise standards or risk damage to their reputations and competitive positions. For these reasons, cities have been the principal sites for the development of worker-center strategies and the locus of organizing efforts to reduce economic inequality.

Predictably, perhaps, as the impact of alt-labor has increased, calling into question low-road employment practices and shaping public opinion about inequality, business groups have begun to step up their attacks on worker centers (Uetricht 2013). With the likelihood of proworker labor-law reform receding in the waning time of the Obama presidency, and with it any hope of a substantially altered labor landscape that favors union organizing, probusiness advocacy organizations have targeted worker centers, seeking to undermine this key site of worker activism. Whether this ultimately slows the development of these organizations remains to be seen; worker centers and their allies have realized a number of tangible gains, including improvements in government enforcement of workplace protections, the recovery of millions of dollars in unpaid wages, the redressing of racial and gender discrimination in the workplace, and the empowerment of workers in low-wage industries. For worker centers, these are still early days—organizations will need to continue to develop their capacities to reach deeper into problem sectors of the economy. But in the absence of transformative reforms to U.S. labor laws— something that seems increasingly improbable in the closing months of the Obama administration—alt-labor may offer one of the few pathways for worker representation for large numbers of workers.

Conclusion: Workers' Rights in the Latter Stages of the Obama Presidency

In 2014, after a period of relative quiet in terms of labor and employment law reform, President Obama signed two employment-related executive orders, one guaranteeing a minimum wage of $10.10 for federal contractors, and the other banning federal contractors from discriminating against workers on the basis of gender identity. As important as these measures are, however, they do little to reverse the erosion of workplace standards or the growth of economic inequality. As a result, rising inequality may well be one of the uncomfortable legacies of the Obama presidency.

In late 2013, President Obama delivered a speech in which he identified economic mobility as "the defining challenge of our time: Making sure our economy works for every working American" (Obama 2013). In this speech, delivered well into his second term, President Obama chose to echo remarks he made during his first few weeks in office on the occasion of the signing of the Lilly Ledbetter Fair Pay Act. On both occasions, he called on policymakers to ensure that the economy works for all. As has typically been the case, Obama's speech was stirring, calling attention to astonishing degrees of income inequality:

> The top 10 percent no longer takes in one-third of our income—it now takes half. Whereas in the past, the average CEO made about 20 to 30 times the income of the average worker, today's CEO now makes 273 times more. And meanwhile, a family in the top 1 percent has a net worth 288 times higher than the typical family, which is a record for this country.

But in the realm of domestic policy, it must be said, President Obama has failed to transform economic relations in the United States. Were the challenges significant? Yes, without question. Were they insurmountable? Probably not. Riding a wave of popular support, Obama was granted a unique opportunity—a mandate, one might say—to not only shape public discourse on economic inequality but also to champion policies that improve the standing of working Americans. Reforming labor law—ensuring that workers are able to exercise their rights to representation in the workplace—was a vital step toward reducing inequality, a step that ultimately was not taken.

References

Albert, Kyle. 2014. "Labor Union Political Strategy in an Era of Decline and Revitalization." *Sociological Inquiry* 84 (2): 210–37.

Bernhardt, Annette, Ruth Milkman, Nik Theodore, Douglas Heckathorn, Mirabai Auer, James DeFilippis, Ana Luz González, Victor Narro, et al. 2009. *Broken Laws, Unprotected Workers: Violations of Employment and Labor Laws in America's Cities.* New York: National Employment Law Project.

Bluestone, Barry. 1983. "Deindustrialization and Unemployment in America." *The Review of Black Political Economy* 12 (3): 27–42.

Brady, David, Regina S. Baker, and Ryan Finnigan. 2013. "When Unionization Disappears: State-Level Unionization and Working Poverty in the United States." *American Sociological Review* 78 (5): 872–96.

Bronfenbrenner, Kate. 2000. *Uneasy Terrain: The Impact of Capital Mobility on Workers, Wages, and Union Organizing.* Report submitted to the U.S. Trade Deficit Review Commission, September 6.

Clawson, Dan. 2003. *The Next Upsurge: Labor and the New Social Movements.* Ithaca, N.Y.: Cornell University Press.

Dreier, Peter. 2011. "Reagan's Real Legacy." *The Nation*, February 4. http://www.thenation.com/article/158321/reagans-real-legacy#.

Dunlop, J. T. 1994. *Fact-Finding Report:* Commission on the Future of Worker-Management Relations. Washington, D.C.: U.S. Department of Labor and Department of Commerce.

Eidelson, Josh. 2013. "Alt-Labor." *American Prospect*, January 29. http://prospect.org/article/alt-labor.

Fainstein, Susan S., and Norman Fainstein. 1989. "The Ambivalent State Economic Development Policy in the US Federal System under the Reagan Administration." *Urban Affairs Review* 25 (1): 41–62.

Greenhouse, Steven. 2004. "How Do You Drive Out a Union? South Carolina Factory Provides a Textbook Case." *New York Times*, December 14, A26.

Greenspan, Alan. 2003. "Remarks by Chairman Alan Greenspan." *The Reagan Legacy*, Ronald Reagan Library, Simi Valley, California, April 9. http://www.federalreserve.gov/boarddocs/speeches/2003/200304092/default.htm.

Hirsch, Barry T., and David A. Macpherson. 2014. "Union Membership, Coverage, Density, and Employment." http://www.unionstats.com/.

Katz, Bruce. 2010. "Obama's Metro Presidency." *City & Community* 9 (1): 23–31.

Kroll, Andy. 2011. "Bye bye, SB 5: Anti-Union Law Repealed in Ohio." *Mother Jones*, November 8. http://www.motherjones.com/mojo/2011/11/issue-2-sb-5-ohio-repeal.

Lee, Marlene A., and Mark Mather. 2008. "U.S. Labor Force Trends." *Population Bulletin* 63 (2): 3–15. http://www.prb.org/pdf08/63.2uslabor.pdf.

Logan, John. 2006. "The Union Avoidance Industry in the United States." *British Journal of Industrial Relations* 44 (4): 651–75.

Marcus, Bernard. 2008. "A Hostile Takeover of American Business." *Bloomberg Businessweek*, September 22. http://www.businessweek.com/stories/2008-09-22/employee-free-choice-act-labor-vs-dot-businessbusinessweek-business-news-stock-market-and-financial-advice.

Markusen, Ann, and Virginia Carlson. 1989. "Deindustrialization in the American Midwest: Causes and Responses." In *Deindustrialization and Regional Economic Transformation: The Experience of the United States*, ed. Lloyd Rodwin and Hidehiko Sazanami, 29–59. Boston: Unwin Hyman.

Markusen, Ann, Peter Hall, Scott Campbell, and Sabina Deitrick. 1991. *The Rise of the Gunbelt: The Military Remapping of Industrial America*. New York: Oxford University Press.

McCartin, Joseph A. 2011. *Collision Course: Ronald Reagan, the Air Traffic Controllers, and the Strike that Changed America*. Oxford: Oxford University Press.

Mehta, Chirag, and Nik Theodore. 2005. *Undermining the Right to Organize: Employer Behavior during Union Representation Campaigns*. Washington, D.C.: American Rights at Work.

Meyerson, Harold. 2004. "Class Warrior." *Washington Post*, June 9. http://www.washingtonpost.com/wp-dyn/content/article/2004/06/09/AR2005033112101.html.

———. 2010. "Why Can't Labor Get a Little More Help From Its Friends?" *American Prospect*, March 27. http://prospect.org/article/why-cant-labor-get-little-more-help-its-friends-0#main-content.

Milkman, Ruth, and Ed Ott, eds. 2014. *New Labor in New York: Precarious Workers and the Future of the Labor Movement*. Ithaca, N.Y.: Cornell University Press.

Morris, Lorenzo. 2012. "Behavioral Pragmatism: President Obama's Approach to Unemployment." *The Review of Black Political Economy* 39 (1): 137–54.

NCSL (National Conference of State Legislatures). 2012. *Right-to-Work Legislation*. http://www.ncsl.org/research/labor-and-employment/2012-right-to-work-legislation.aspx.

———. 2013. *Right-to-Work Legislation*. http://www.ncsl.org/research/labor-and-employment/2013-right-to-work-legislation.aspx.

———. 2014. *Collective Bargaining and Labor Union Legislation Database*. http://www.ncsl.org/research/labor-and-employment/collective-bargaining-legislation-database.aspx.

Newman, Kathe, and Philip Ashton. 2004. "Neoliberal Urban Policy and New Paths of Neighborhood Change in the American Inner City." *Environment and Planning A* 36 (7): 1151–72.

Obama, Barack. 2004. *Dreams from My Father: A Story of Race and Inheritance.* New York: Three Rivers Press/Random House.

———. 2013. "Remarks by the President on Economic Mobility." http://www.whitehouse.gov/the-press-office/2013/12/04/remarks-president-economic-mobility.

Peck, Jamie. 2014. "Pushing Austerity: State Failure, Municipal Bankruptcy and the Crises of Fiscal Federalism in the USA." *Cambridge Journal of Regions, Economy and Society* 7 (1): 17–44.

Peck, Jamie, and Nik Theodore. 2012. "Politicizing Contingent Work: Countering Neoliberal Labor Market Regulation . . . from the Bottom Up?" *South Atlantic Quarterly* 111 (4): 741–61.

Ranney, David. 2003. *Global Decisions, Local Collisions: Urban Life in the New World Order.* Philadelphia: Temple University Press.

Silver, Hilary. 2010. "Obama's Urban Policy: A Symposium." *City & Community* 9 (1): 3–12.

Silverstein, Ken. 2009. "Labor's Last Stand: The Corporate Campaign to Kill the Employee Free Choice Act." *Harper's,* July. http://harpers.org/archive/2009/07/labors-last-stand/.

Stierli, Markus, Anthony Shorrocks, James B. Davies, Rodrigo Lluberas, and Antonios Koutsoukis. 2014. *The Global Wealth Report 2014.* Zurich: Credit Suisse.

Stolberg, Sheryl Gay. 2009. "Obama Signs Equal-Pay Legislation." *New York Times,* January 29. http://www.nytimes.com/2009/01/30/us/politics/30ledbetter-web.html?_r=0.

Theodore, Nik. 2010. *Realigning Labor: Toward a Framework for Collaboration between Labor Unions and Worker Centers.* Washington, D.C.: Neighborhood Funders Group.

Turner, Lowell, and Daniel B. Cornfield, eds. 2007. *Labor in the New Urban Battlegrounds: Local Solidarity in a Global Economy.* Ithaca, N.Y.: Cornell University Press.

Uetricht, Micah. 2013. "Big Business Aims to Crush Worker Centers." *In These Times,* July 30. http://inthesetimes.com/working/entry/15378/big_business_aims_to_crush_worker_centers.

U.S. Census Bureau. 2012. *Labor Force, Employment, and Earnings: Labor Force Status.* http://www.census.gov/compendia/statab/cats/labor_force_employment_earnings/labor_force_status.html.

Warren, Dorian T. 2010. "The American Labor Movement in the Age of Obama: The Challenges and Opportunities of a Racialized Political Economy." *Perspectives on Politics* 8 (3): 847–60.

Weber, Rachel. 2010. "Selling City Futures: The Financialization of Urban Redevelopment Policy." *Economic Geography* 86 (3): 251–74.

Wilson, William Julius. 2010. "The Obama Administration's Proposals to Address Concentrated Urban Poverty." *City & Community* 9 (1): 41–49.

9

A WORK STILL IN PROGRESS

The Achievements and Shortcomings of the Affordable Care Act

J. PHILLIP THOMPSON

On March 23, 2010, President Obama signed the Patient Care and Affordable Care Act (ACA) into law. The act was an historic accomplishment. Called Obama's principal legacy, comprehensive health care reform had been tried and abandoned by several earlier Democratic regimes, most recently the Clinton administration. The act made several major advances in fixing a broken health care system. Among them were efforts to slow down excessive and increasing health care costs; making quality in health services more equitable and transparent (the bill forced insurance companies to accept people with preexisting conditions and banned them from charging higher premiums for people with serious health problems); and, perhaps most importantly, providing more affordable health insurance for tens of millions of uninsured lower-income Americans (Daschle and Nather 2010, 187).

The ACA did not do several important things. It did not work out a means for financing long-term care at a time when nearly 80 million baby boomers are hitting retirement age. It did little to hold down exorbitant monopoly costs for prescription drugs. Instead, the Obama administration cut a deal with the Pharmaceutical Research and Manufacturers of America (PhRMA) that reduced prescription drug costs 50 percent for seniors falling into the infamous doughnut hole.[1] But, in exchange for PhRMA's political support of the ACA, Democrats agreed not to import FDA-approved cheaper foreign prescription drugs. They also agreed not to use Medicare's bargaining power to negotiate for lower drug costs. Lawmakers also eliminated the "public option," the public health insurance plan that would compete with private insurance companies. The public option was actually a scaled-down version of a national mandatory health insurance "single payer" system advocated during the Clinton era; in eliminating it, Democrats sought to meet conservative criticism that a single-payer system represented "socialism" and "government takeover." Conservatives ultimately proved equally opposed to market competition from a government-run "public option" program.

The ACA did not set up a national exchange to enable the uninsured to easily enroll for health insurance. Instead, it created fifty exchanges that are, at the time of this writing, either run by state governments (thirteen plus Washington, D.C.), the federal government in lieu of an operational state exchange (nineteen states), or something in between. The success of state-run exchanges will ultimately depend on the competence and political will of state governments to operate fairly and effectively. In many cases this will be unlikely. The ACA does not end racial disparities in the medical delivery system. Title VI of the Civil Rights Act of 1964 bans discrimination on the basis of race or national origin by entities that receive federal funds (almost all hospitals receive large amounts of federal Medicare and Medicaid funding). Yet the law does not prohibit "economic" discrimination. Since African Americans (and many other minority groups) are disproportionately poor, the "economic" exception creates a giant loophole for hospitals to discriminate against low-income minorities. Deborah Stone writes that

> the virtually complete transformation of hospital accommodations from wards to private and semi-private rooms; the migration of hospitals out of center cities into suburbs; the migration of health care itself out of hospitals and into nursing homes, ambulatory clinics, and homes, where compliance with civil rights law was much, much harder to monitor, if it applied at all—each of these shifts in industrial organization was in part stimulated by a desire to evade the watchful eye of the Department of Health Education and Welfare's Office for Civil Rights. (Stone 2005, 72)

The ACA does little to combat racial disparities caused by doctors and hospitals that discriminate with impunity.

The ACA also set in motion new organizations and processes that are ongoing. There is a new Independent Payment Advisory Board to review and make recommendations regarding Medicare spending. The board was created to bring professional judgment, as opposed to political lobbying, to Medicare funding decisions. However, hospitals and physicians are leery of the board and even this early in the game have succeeded in reducing its budget. There is a new Patient-Centered Outcomes Research Institute (PCORI) that will conduct comparative effectiveness research on the best ways to improve health outcomes while reducing costs. Potentially, if they survive, these boards could help move the conversation about health care from much of the misleading rhetoric that characterized the debate over the creation of the ACA to actual evidence in achieving results.

Political Mobilization and the ACA

Much has been written about right-wing mobilization against passage of the ACA during the congressional recess in August, 2009. It was then that conservative (often Tea Party) activists surprised Democrats who were holding town meetings with their constituents. Vulnerable Democrats in Republican-leaning states, the so-called Blue Dog Democrats, were particularly unnerved, and this led to many parts of the original bill, such as the public option, being scrapped.

Why did the Left not mobilize more strongly in support of the proposed bill?

The lapse on the Left is nothing new. Health care advocacy has long lacked the participation of the poor themselves. For example, there are more than 60 million Medicaid recipients in the United States, and not a single national organization representing them. Moreover, as is often the case, labor unions were far more interested in protecting the narrow interests of their members during the ACA deliberations than they were in building a broad movement with Medicaid recipients, seniors, and the uninsured (Jacobs and Skocpol 2012, 105). Even more fundamentally, a major contradiction existed in low-income community organizing between advocates, such as labor unions, which generally avoided raising issues of race, and many African American (and some Latino) community groups. Many such groups, typically local and underfinanced, insisted that racial disparities and prejudice be highlighted. The administration itself, likely hoping to minimize even greater conservative opposition, avoided highlighting race and poverty during the battles over passage of the ACA. This, despite the unmistakable racist undertones of the Right wing's mobilization against the ACA. By avoiding direct confrontation with racist mobilization on the Right, Democrats lost the opportunity to engage African Americans and Latinos highly sensitive to racism.

Opportunities for Mobilization through Expanding Insurance Coverage

One of the major and most unrecognized achievements of the ACA, despite problems in Left mobilization during the legislative process, was the bill's creation of many opportunities and incentives for mobilizing poor people who, once mobilized, could later reform the bill after initial passage. A good example is the ACA's expansion of health insurance coverage for uninsured people. The process of signing people up for health insurance presents an opportunity for registering new voters and educating potential recipients about the need to get involved in policy and political activities. The roughly 30 million uninsured Americans are disproportionately young and minority; they represent a large segment of the nonvoting population.

There are many who discount the significance of such low-income community organizing. New York Senator Charles Schumer ruffled feathers when he argued that the Obama administration made a political mistake focusing on expanding health care when so few of its intended beneficiaries vote: "The Affordable Care Act was aimed at the 36 million Americans who were not covered," Schumer said. "It's been reported that only a third of the uninsured are even registered to vote. In 2010, only about 40 percent of those registered voted. So even if the uninsured kept with the rate, which they likely didn't, you would still only be talking about 5 percent of the electorate" (Schumer 2014). Casting beyond this kind of status quo politics is precisely what made the ACA more than the sum of its parts. While many health care advocates or labor unions have not yet made the connection, some do.

Political battles are occurring in the states (more than twenty) refusing to expand Medicaid, leaving nearly 6 million eligible people without health insurance. Tom Wolf, a Democrat, ousted Governor Tom Corbett of Pennsylvania, an ACA opponent, and promptly launched an expansion of Medicaid. Others got the message. At the time of this writing, Republican governors in Tennessee, Utah, and Wyoming are fighting their own Republican-led legislatures to expand Medicaid.

Community Benefits Requirements

A vague community benefit requirement for nonprofit hospitals has been on the IRS books since the late 1960s. In addition, twenty-three states have long required nonprofit hospitals to provide community benefits (Somerville, Nelson, and Mueller 2013). How much hospitals were required to spend on community benefits varied, as did state monitoring of whether hospitals actually complied with the spirit of the regulation. In Cleveland, Ohio, one director of a local hospital said that the hospital initially viewed community benefit requirements as superfluous to the hospitals' mission. It met the requirements by conducting superficial award banquets for community leaders, marches against hunger, and other "one off" events. Later, the hospital leadership, under pressure from community leaders, decided that it was in the hospitals' interest to become an economic anchor for the surrounding neighborhood.

The hospital had found it difficult to recruit nurses and doctors who wanted to trade a long and arduous commute for a walk to work, but were prevented from making the move by crime in the neighborhood. Additionally, the city had a choice of hospitals to which to send city employees. Boosting Cleveland's economy would help the hospital win favor with the city administration, which in turn could help the hospital gain more business. The hospital used its community benefits money to help more than a hundred local minority and women-owned businesses secure and execute contracts with the hospital, particularly during its $1.2 billion expansion. The experience was transformative for the culture of the hospital internally, as well as for the hospital's reputation in the city.[2]

Not all hospitals are as community-oriented as University Hospitals of Cleveland. New York State charged an 8.95 percent surcharge on hospital bills to provide for an "Indigent Care Pool" to help financially strapped patients pay their hospital bills. A study by the Community Service Society of New York found that hospitals were collecting money from the Indigent Care Pool while doing nothing to help low-income patients, and even foreclosing on their homes for unpaid bills: "Even hospitals that reported they had spent nothing on financial aid, or had filed hundreds of liens against patients' homes, were allowed to collect without questions from the charity care pool, which distributes more than $1 billion a year" (Bernstein 2012).

In 2010, ACA Section 2007 strengthened federal community benefit requirements by requiring all nonprofit hospitals to, among other things, conduct a

Community Health Needs Assessment and Implementation Plan. Advocates argued that in return for billions of dollars in federal tax subsidies, not-for-profit hospitals ought to do more to help the low-income communities that support them. Under the ACA, nonprofit hospitals must conduct participatory assessments to determine the health needs of their communities and respond to those needs by developing implementation or community service plans and providing "community benefits" beyond the types of medical services that can also be provided by for-profit institutions. These requirements are intended to encourage comprehensive health planning and innovation by hospitals, health systems, and communities. There are 2,894 nonprofit community hospitals in the United States.

As of this writing, it is unclear how the IRS will enforce the new community benefit requirements. Advocates for the ACA community benefit legislation suggested that nonprofit hospitals devote a minimum of 3 to 5 percent of annual revenues to community benefit activities. How much hospitals are currently spending on community benefits varies widely, from nothing in some cases to nearly $2 billion annually by Kaiser Permanente. Another uncertainty about using the ACA community benefit requirements concerns the IRS's ongoing distinction between "community benefit" (directly related to health improvement) and "community building" (addressing social determinants of health) expenditures. The Department of Health and Human Services (HHS) does not regard social determinants of health such as employment or decent housing as eligible for Medicaid funding because such factors do not *directly* contribute to health. Yet, there is ample evidence that these social determinants of health have a *bigger* impact on health in the aggregate than do medical interventions that are considered direct contributors to health (and are eligible for funding with community benefit money). Health ethicist Norman Daniels writes:

> The public, encouraged by scientists and the media, is fascinated by every new biomedical discovery and has come to believe that our "success" in improving population health is entirely or largely the result of exotic science. . . . The idea that scientific medicine is responsible for our health blinds us to socioeconomic inequality as a source of worse population health. (Daniels 2008, 102)

The core problem is political. Most in Congress, today and historically, blame poverty and long-term unemployment on the poor themselves and are unwilling to "incentivize irresponsibility." In real life, however, it is not possible to separate the anxiety and depression that stem from unemployment or homelessness from negative health outcomes like high blood pressure or alcoholism (self-medication) leading to liver disease. In the federal system, treating high blood pressure and liver disease is a legitimate health expense, but providing jobs or ensuring adequate housing for the poor is not. Thus, for political reasons, the IRS (like HHS) is put in the position of drawing the line between social psychological causes of illness stemming from social conditions and "physical" causes of illness attributable, presumably, to nonsocial "individual" factors. Medical evidence is moving swiftly in the opposite direction, linking social and individual causes of illness (Wilkinson and Pickett 2010).

In an effort to wrest rules from irrationality, the IRS has sought wriggle room: the IRS has not categorized efforts to address underlying social determinants of health as qualifying for community benefit expenses, but community benefits might be eligible for funding if hospitals can show that community-building activities can be linked to health improvement. Reporting instructions now indicate that some community-building activities may also meet the definition of community benefit if they can draw a link to health improvement by meeting the IRS's test for "community health improvement services." Hospitals can establish an investment as a "community health improvement service" if it responds to a demonstrated community need. One way to establish a demonstrated community need is by documenting that it arose from a request by a public agency or a community group. Though it falls short of sound public health reasoning in order to appease the current Republican congressional majority, the IRS's sensible test is commendable. It lets local communities and local officials determine what social factors contribute to good (or bad) health.

It will take strong community advocacy to ensure that community benefits requirements are implemented, as has been the case with other legislation, such as the Community Reinvestment Act and the Voting Rights Act, opposed by powerful political actors. However, the resources that the Collective Bargaining Agreement (CBA) provision of the ACA could potentially provide for community-based action targeting unemployment, inadequate housing, toxic environmental conditions, unhealthy foods, and other community issues are substantial. Like many other aspects of ACA, the CBA provision opens up ground for future political mobilization, and its outcome is not predetermined. To date, community-development groups and community-based organizations outside of the health advocacy community appear to know little about the ACA community benefit requirements—hospitals are receiving little local pressure to engage with communities or put programs in place.

Medicaid Reform

What many consider Medicaid consists of two different programs. One is called CHIP. CHIP serves children whose parents earn too much for Medicaid but not enough for private insurance. The other, Medicaid, serves low-income, elderly, and disabled people. Medicaid is not a poor peoples' or "welfare" program only; the elderly and disabled accounted for about a quarter of Medicaid enrollees in 2010, and they accounted for 64 percent of the spending on benefits. Another important point about Medicaid is that "States have the authority to set and administer their own eligibility criteria; reimbursement rates; policies for participation of doctors, hospitals and managed care plans; and to an ever larger extent, thanks to a flurry of waivers from federal standards, their own benefit packages and coverage policies" (Stone 2005, 70–71). The ACA expanded Medicaid eligibility to include adults under 65 years old making less than 133 percent of the federal poverty level—about $30,700 for a family of four.

The federal government will pay 100 percent of the Medicaid expansion costs through 2016, and 90 percent of the costs thereafter. States must pay the balance. This amounts to the Feds paying 93 percent of the costs between 2014 and 2022 (Angeles and Broaddus 2012). The effect of the Medicaid expansion is thus twofold. There are strong incentives for states to expand Medicaid both as a way of satisfying elderly and disabled constituents (at a time when baby boomer voters are retiring in large numbers), as well as hospitals and nursing homes seeking additional funding. On the other hand, expanding Medicaid will eventually cost states money, even if the share is small compared to the federal portion. States are incentivized to both expand coverage and control costs. Later in the article I examine what this process looks like in a part of Brooklyn, New York City. Before doing so I take a detour into long-standing arguments about race and health in the United States, as these arguments shape the politics of Medicaid reform in Brooklyn, and will in many other parts of the country.

Race and Public Health

African Americans and whites (and often other groups) tend to understand race differently. For African Americans, race has, as sociologist Michele Lamont suggests, "as powerful an effect on the structuration of everyday life as do economic forces" (Lamont 1997). Racism is not just a view about black people, or nonwhite people, racism is a viewpoint that connects ones' station in life to hereditary characteristics (including culture). Seeing race as part of an underlying hereditary perspective social hierarchy is a pervasive worldview that not only explains black/white economic differences, but also why poor whites are poor; why some blacks are richer than other blacks; and why some whites are richer than other whites. It thereby encompasses not only "race," as commonly understood, but also offers an alternative explanation of "class" hierarchies than the sociological or Marxian view. The core concept of race, understood this way, is much harder to eradicate than personal racism or even structural racism as it continually arises in new cultural forms, such as that the "underclass" are deemed poor because of their inherited inferior "culture" rather than skin color. Racism is part of a more deeply and broadly antiequalitarian social outlook than usually imagined. The inheritance idea, increasingly fused with biological determinism during the mid-nineteenth century, turned out to be a seamless means of explaining and justifying not only slavery and the eradication of indigenous peoples, but inequalities wrought by capitalism generally.

Influential academics brought the inheritance view to intellectual prominence in the 1960s and 1970s and provided a social scientific defense of sustained inequality. University of Chicago political scientist Ed Banfield was one such intellectual. Banfield believed that social position was determined by the disposition of individuals and groups themselves, particularly their capacity to think long-term (or lack thereof) (Banfield [1930] 1974). Short of taking babies away from parents, such capacities were culturally inherited and difficult, if not impossible, to change: "No one knows how to change the culture of any part of the population—the lower class or the upper, whites or Negroes, pupils or teachers, policemen or criminals" (Banfield [1930] 1974). Banfield's notion of "class" was that it was largely comprised by inherited characteristics. Banfield, and his former student and colleague James Q. Wilson, created a dehumanized image of low-income blacks as lacking in capacity for moral dialogue, or for thinking beyond the short-term (Banfield and Wilson [1947] 1963). The policy implications, and influence, of the Banfield and Wilson approach were immense. Banfield favored repealing the minimum wage, reducing the school leaving age, intensive birth control guidance of the "incompetent poor," and "stop and frisk" policing, to alter the incentive structure for people culturally predisposed to violate acceptable social norms (Banfield [1930] 1974, 269). Many of the ideas later publicized by William Julius Wilson's "The Truly Disadvantaged," such as that of a degenerate slum culture, women-headed households due to lack of attachment of black men to the labor force, outmigration of black middle-class "role models" from the inner-city ghetto, were earlier put forward by Banfield and Wilson.

What has all this got to do with race and public health? The ideologies and public policies espoused by Banfield, James Q. Wilson, and others demean African Americans and other marginalized groups, blaming and punishing them for their problems. Such low social status and lack of social support undermine health:

> When we're stressed or depressed or feeling hostile, we are far more likely to develop a host of bodily ills, including heart disease, infections and more rapid ageing. (Wilkinson and Pickett 2010)

What Is a Healthy Ideology for Poor Black People?

Demeaning notions of African Americans, indigenous Americans, and other marginalized groups are impossible to eradicate without fundamentally reworking dominant cultural narratives in the United States. For example, James Q. Wilson depicted Andrew Jackson—who was, frankly, genocidal—as a great moral leader (Wilson 1983, 245, 248). Wilson's example illustrates the general problem African Americans (not to mention indigenous people) face in constructing a healthy self-image. The soul-crushing effect of dehumanization has been a primary theme of black protest and criticism for nearly two hundred years. In the 1830s, Sarah Grimke, a feminist abolitionist, wrote that it was easy for [white] people, who are "alive to bodily pain" to apprehend the physical sufferings of slavery. Fewer, she argued, appreciated the slaves' "mental and spiritual degradation" (quoted in Davis 2014, 203). A sense of hopelessness and self-hatred, or an uncontrollable rage, are two consequences of mental and spiritual degradation among blacks.

Developing a positive black morality (of "self" and "other") is key to improving the health of black communities. This has been convincingly demonstrated in the work of social epidemiologist Sherman James. In his nuanced study, James examined a group of working-class blacks in eastern North Carolina, testing them both for social attitudes and for health status. He found that lower-income blacks who believe in the American Dream were considerably more stressed than those who believe that the U.S. system was biased against them. James captured the American Dream aspiration in the term "John Henryism," a reference to the fabled African American railroad and tunnel worker strongman, who in the early 1870s was said to have won a steel-driving contest using nothing but a nine-pound hammer, with a steam-powered mechanical drill. After the contest, John Henry died of mental and physical exhaustion.[3] James likened those low-income blacks pursuing the American Dream to John Henry:

> The John Henryism hypothesis assumes that lower socioeconomic status individuals in general, and African Americans in particular, are routinely exposed to psychosocial stressors (chronic financial strain, job insecurity, subtle and or perhaps not so subtle insults linked to race or social class) that require them to use considerable energy each day to manage the psychological stress generated by these conditions. (James 1994)

James found that "John Henry" workers were *three times* more likely to suffer hypertension than other low-income black workers. James concluded that John Henryism, though understandable, exacted a high cost on black life, shortening life spans considerably. James's work makes a strong case for seeking an alternative to the dominant American culture and morality, which is what many blacks concluded long ago. Race, for many African Americans, became an inherently political *verb* to describe the unjust social conditions that cause black social isolation and suffering.

While James demonstrated *social* causes for stress and related disease such as hypertension in black communities (as opposed to the medical professions' historical focus on individual risk factors such as eating too much salt), Jonathan Metzl, a psychiatrist and cultural studies scholar, has shown how race and gender shape categories and frames that medical professionals use to diagnose mental illness. In effect, the medical profession itself has often been a source of racial anxiety. In the 1960s, with the advent of the civil rights and black power movements, the official medical diagnosis of schizophrenia changed, suddenly foregrounding "masculinized hostility, violence, and aggression," and another disorder, "blaming other people for their problems" (Metzl 2009, 98). Using the new science, the FBI diagnosed Malcolm X with, "pre psychotic paranoid schizophrenia." Robert Williams, the leader of the Monroe, North Carolina, chapter of the NAACP who organized armed black self-defense after a series of violent racist attacks, according to the FBI, "has previously been diagnosed as schizophrenic and has advocated and threatened violence" (Metzl 2009, 122). Africans Americans continue to be disproportionately diagnosed as schizophrenic—as opposed to depressed or angered because of oppression. A recent study of the treatment of mentally ill veterans found that African Americans were four times more likely than whites to be diagnosed with schizophrenia. The researchers found no significant differences among the veterans regarding severity of illness, combat exposure, financial status, substance use, or a host of other variables: "the only factor that was truly important was race" (Metzl 2009, 188). Metzl argues that "even in an era dominated by neuroscience, diagnosis remains a projective act, one that combines scientific understanding with a complex set of ideological [and] . . . political assumptions (Metzl 2009, xvii).

The pioneering black social psychologist Kenneth Clark maintained that blacks' self-esteem required, unlike John Henryism, an unflinching condemnation of America's dominant values and institutions, with sustained outreach to white Americans to encourage core humanistic and equalitarian values (Clark 1974). Yet, creating a healthy ideology requires not just words, but institutional reinforcement. Building separate black institutions for creative and healthy development has thus been an adaptive strategy for insuring positive and healthy black development. Just *how* separate these black institutions should be has long been a subject of lively debate in black communities (Dawson 2001). The upside of lacking a nurturing home in the nation's narrative, or a strong defense in the halls of science, or the absence of solidarity with suffering poor whites, was that African Americans were forced to create their own language, concepts, song, and institutions, and to search for deeper sources of identity than the nation-state, or the pursuit of common economic interests. In this search they discovered, some argue, the deeper meaning of freedom and democracy, which is the ability to *create* meaning for themselves and their nation.[4] The lack of space to imagine and realize their humanity, and the striving to create such spaces, has been a key generative force in black music and art, and politics.

Racism in society produces anxiety among African Americans. This racist oppression cannot be ignored without destroying a healthy personality, making one fit to "be put in an institution." Or, as was seen tragically in December, 2013, in Brooklyn, New York, when Abdullah Brinsley, a mentally disturbed African American, shot his girlfriend and killed two cops in Brooklyn claiming payback for recent police killings of unarmed blacks, and then committed suicide—it can lead to uncontrollable rage and insanity. A healthy alternative, many black activists have come to believe, is for blacks to engage in nonviolent protest, and in constructive efforts to change the social ills that hamper human development. This is what King and others meant by constructive "maladjustment."

Given all this, it may perhaps now be easy to interpret the largely critical response in African American communities to former Mayor Michael Bloomberg's efforts to improve the health of black and other low-income communities by ordering a reduction in the size of soda bottles.[5] Mayor Bloomberg, a billionaire many times over, went to extreme lengths to oppose community benefits agreements on projects that required more than a minimum wage (Tishman 2014). He also promoted the notorious "stop and frisk" program, ruled illegal by the state's highest court, that led to the harassment of nearly 6 million innocent black and Latino citizens over the course of his mayoralty. For Bloomberg to claim that black health problems stem from soda, rather than the inequality that underlines chronic health problems and unhealthy behavior in these communities, was too much for many to tolerate.

It is in this political climate in New York City that the New York State Health Department plans to implement Medicaid reform. The department has had the good sense to acknowledge that they do not know how to improve the community's health, and that Medicaid reform efforts should be locally led. They are also under pressure to keep down Medicaid costs. This has produced an unusual convergence of interests between the state and many low-income communities of color. The state has an interest in encouraging actual improvements in community health so as to reduce the use of expensive hospital care. The community, in the case of Brooklyn discussed below, wants to improve its health, mainly, and ironically, by reducing what it perceives as the sickness of the broader society. Community leaders also hope to demonstrate the power of a low-income black community to improve its own health by undertaking social change initiatives. This may well lead to many confrontations with state, city, and federal agencies, but for once the overarching demand for fiscal prudence is working on the side of the community activists. Short of eliminating Medicaid and similar programs, there is little alternative to improving community health as a means of holding down costs significantly. The process under way can be seen in efforts to save and change Interfaith Medical Center in Central Brooklyn.

Interfaith Medical Center

Medicaid comprises the second largest share of the New York State budget, after public education. In 2014, the state spent $26.6 billion of its own revenue on Medicaid; the federal share was $39.37 billion, while New York City paid $9.4 billion toward Medicaid. In 2014, New York State (NYS) reached an agreement with the Department of Health and Human Services allowing the state to receive up to $8 billion from the federal government to initiate cost-saving reforms in Medicaid that the state projects will save $17 billion in Medicaid spending over time. The first $1 billion increment of the money was released to NYS in 2013. To qualify for funds from this program, hospitals had to be deemed "safety net," and they had to agree to form coalitions with community health and service providers (which could include other hospitals). Future Medicaid payments will be allocated by HHS based on benchmarks the state achieved in realizing its promised $17 billion in reduced spending. The pressure is on the state to deliver on its promised reductions. The state initiated a reform initiative, called the Delivery System Reform Incentive Payment Program (DSRIP). As of this writing, similar Medicaid reform efforts are under way in California, Texas, Massachusetts, New Jersey, and Kansas.

There are different ways states can approach saving money in Medicaid. One approach is to ration services, most explicitly by closing hospitals that serve poor people. Another approach is to address the problems that lead low-income communities, and communities of color in particular, to incur disproportionate levels of chronic illness in the first place, which ultimately translates into higher Medicaid costs. Factors leading to racial disparities in rates of chronic illness include lack of primary care, high levels of unemployment and underemployment, instability in housing and lack of decent housing, violence, poor education, lack of healthy food, and lack of education. These linkages are increasingly understood in public health literature. The question arises, why not address the underlying causes of poor health and expensive treatment? If voters were, as rational choice theorists suggest, "utility maximizers," then they would have supported large-scale social interventions long ago. Why has this not happened? It is very similar to the "mass incarceration" problem. Why is the nation spending so much on mass incarceration despite much evidence that incarceration, particularly of nonviolent offenders, is counterproductive and expensive (Gottschalk 2015)? Public health policy embeds a fatalism that poor people, and the black poor in particular, are beyond improvement. This notion has deep roots in urban policy, as shown in reference to Banfield and Wilson, and in American thinking going back to slave times.

New York State has closed twenty hospitals since 2000, mostly "safety net" hospitals, often in poor communities of color. Safety net hospitals rely on Medicaid to fund themselves. By closing hospitals, the state hopes to reduce Medicaid spending. New York State closed hospitals that they thought were mismanaged, or located in areas the state considered "over-bedded." The hospital closings have been highly controversial. Closings entail layoffs. In many poor communities, hospital jobs are important for the economic stability and well-being of surrounding neighborhoods—frequently they are the largest employer. Closing a hospital in a poor community may not even save Medicaid money. Medicaid recipients might simply go elsewhere for care, or they might forego care until problems become worse and more expensive to treat (as in an emergency room). During the 2013 New York mayoral race, hospital closings were one of the main campaign issues. Current mayor Bill deBlasio strongly criticized his main rival, Christine Quinn, for not fighting hospital closings vigorously, including the closure of St. Vincent's Hospital right in her city council district.

In late 2012, Interfaith Medical Center in the predominately African American and West Indian portion of Central Brooklyn went into bankruptcy, largely due to mismanagement. Most observers expected the state to close down the hospital, with hundreds of jobs lost. Two labor unions representing workers at the hospital, Local 1199 and the New York State Nurses Association, asked this author to study the issue and make recommendations to the unions on what should happen with Interfaith. Specifically, our team was asked to consider health needs in the community surrounding Interfaith, and to recommend a future course for the facility (Thompson et al. 2014). Labor and community activists formed an ongoing local coalition to advocate on behalf of workers in the hospital and for the health needs of the community. Sensing community concern, all the elected officials of Central Brooklyn joined the coalition, including two members of Congress, several state legislators, and several city council members, as well as the borough president of Brooklyn.

Our team's study of community health needs found that the community surrounding Interfaith has unmet medical needs for prenatal care, circulatory diseases, and asthma, but these needs were not being met by Interfaith—their main focus has been on mental health care. More importantly, we found largely unmet needs for preventative health care, quality housing, and jobs in the community. In Central Brooklyn, such problems often begin with employment. Unemployment and underemployment are stressful conditions to live under, and lead to other forms of instability such as lack of housing, lack of quality food, depression, and various forms of "self-medication," like drug and alcohol abuse. Unemployment and underpay also contribute to drug dealing, violence, incarceration, and associated mental disorders. High levels of crime then discourage walking and use of open space, making health worse. Fresh food is not easily found around Interfaith, and housing quality is poor though expensive. Bad housing leads to roaches, rodents, and mold, which in turn contribute to asthma. In short, poverty and chronic illnesses are closely linked.

The Interfaith plan is to initiate a comprehensive community-led approach to tackle these issues together. Initial strategies include repurposing the hospital, creating preventative health care jobs in the community, improving housing with an infusion of labor pension funds, retrofitting buildings for energy efficiency and asthma reduction, and using hospital and other anchor institution procurement to attract local manufacturing and create additional jobs. The goal and method is to engage community residents in taking responsibility for their own health outcomes, and to incentivize them by creating mechanisms for community residents to share in the savings of health improvements.

Our report called for the governor to appoint a majority of hospital workers and community residents on the governance board of the hospital. The goal in this request was to empower the community to develop and implement its own plan to improve community health, while making Interfaith the center for coordinated improvement efforts across the area. We also recommended the state fund Interfaith as a demonstration project to show how social improvements can improve health (and eventually reduce costs). Both of our recommendations fall within the state's own Medicaid (DSRIP) reform process, which includes all the hospitals in Brooklyn. Elected officials in Central Brooklyn sent a letter to the governor in support of the plan, as did ministers and community leaders in Brooklyn. The elected officials said that having an analysis and plan enabled them to do their jobs more effectively. At one point, Letitia James, the third-highest-ranking politician in the city said, "we don't need to be convinced about the plan, just give us our marching orders." The coalition, at the request of the elected officials, prepared a "to do" list for city, state, and federal legislators from Central Brooklyn, respectively.

The DSRIP process in Brooklyn has led to the formation of several health coalitions in the borough. Interfaith is in coalition with several larger hospitals and more than 250 community organizations. DSRIP has created, indeed required, a large-scale participatory process, unlike any seen in New York City in decades. The coalitions have established governance structures that will decide on strategies for improving health and holding down Medicaid costs in different parts of Brooklyn. Future Medicaid funding will be drawn down by the coalitions and divided according to a complex formula based on eligible patients served and the type of service rendered. It is in these coalitions that much of the future direction of health care will be fought over and decided. The stakes are high in this process. The Interfaith community coalition is committed to a broad social change agenda; they believe that the broader society is the root cause for disproportionate health problems in Central Brooklyn. Medicaid funding, while purporting to address social determinants of health, favors medical interventions (similar to the "community building" exclusion in community benefit funding discussed earlier). However, future Medicaid waivers might allow for innovation in addressing social problems.

What the Interfaith project demonstrates is that the battle over the ACA is still taking place and, if anything, is expanding. While local inner-city communities were not mobilized (for the most part) during the legislative process, they are mobilizing in some communities as the effects of health reform affect their jobs and neighborhoods. With strongly divergent views on the causes and solutions for community illness, there will no doubt be many confrontations during the process. Yet there is potential in this process for genuine community participation, and if community demands for addressing social causes of poor health are met, there can be funding for community interventions and organizing that ultimately will come from Medicaid savings. In this way, the ACA provides an opening to push back against oligarchy—increasing corporate domination of politics and policy. Obama saw this potential, and I suspect it will be an ever-increasing credit to his legacy. The closing words are the president's, from his April 1, 2014, speech on the ACA:

> That's what the Affordable Care Act, or Obamacare, is all about—making sure that all of us, and all our fellow citizens, can count on the security of health care when we get sick; that the work and dignity of every person is acknowledged and affirmed. . . . And, yes, at times this reform has been

contentious and confusing, and obviously it's had its share of critics. That's part of what change looks like in a democracy. Change is hard. Fixing what's broken is hard. Overcoming skepticism and fear of something new is hard. . . . We are on our way. And if all of us have the courage and the wisdom to keep working not against one another, not to scare each other, but for one another—then we won't just make progress on health care. We'll make progress on all the other work that remains to create new opportunity for everybody who works for it, and to make sure that this country that we love lives up to its highest ideals. That's what today is about. That's what all the days that come as long as I'm President are going to be about. That's what we're going to be working towards. (Obama 2014)

Notes

1. The "doughnut hole" refers to people who are forced to pay prescription drug costs out-of-pocket when they exceeded their initial Medicare coverage but fall short of coverage for catastrophic illness. Out-of-pocket costs came to more than $3,500 in some cases.
2. Authors' notes from interview with Steve Standley, chief administrative officer of University Hospitals, January 27, 2012. See also Serang, Thompson, and Howard (2013).
3. "That the real John Henry was a diminutive man, consigned to convict-lease labor under the post–Civil War Black Codes, who had died of overwork and silicosis along with at least one hundred other convicts constructing the railroad tunnel system through the Allegheny Mountains had disappeared from view" (Foley 2010).
4. This is, I suspect, what Hannah Arendt called true "politics."
5. The proposal was struck down in 2014 by the state's highest court.

References

Angeles, January, and Matt Broaddus. 2012. "Federal Government Will Pick Up Nearly All Costs of Health Reform's Medicaid Expansion." Center for Budget and Policy Priorities. http://www.cbpp.org/cms/?fa=view&id=3161.

Baldwin, James. 1965. "The American Dream and the American Negro." *New York Times Magazine*, March 7. https://www.nytimes.com/books/98/03/29/specials/baldwin-dream.html.

Baldwin, James, and Richard Avedon. 1964. *Nothing Personal*. New York: Atheneum.

Banfield, Edward C. (1930) 1974. *The Unheavenly City Revisited: A Revision of The Unheavenly City.* Boston: Little, Brown.

Banfield, Edward C., and James Q. Wilson. (1947) 1963. *City Politics*. Cambridge, Mass.: Harvard University Press.

Bernstein, Nina. 2012. "Hospitals Flout Charity Aid Law." *New York Times*, February 12. http://www.nytimes.com/2012/02/13/nyregion/study-finds-new-york-hospitals-flout-charity-rules.html.

Blassingame, John W., and John R. McKivigan, eds. 1992. *The Frederick Douglass Papers*. New Haven, Conn.: Yale University Press.

Brown, Chip. 1994. "Escape from New York." *New York Times*, January 30. http://www.nytimes.com/1994/01/30/magazine/escape-from-new-york.html?pagewanted=all.

Clark, Kenneth B. 1974. *Pathos of Power*. New York: Harper and Row.

Cohen, Geoffrey L., and David Sherman K. 2014. "The Psychology of Change: Self-Affirmation and Social Psychological Intervention." *Annual Review of Psychology* 65: 333–71.

Crouch, Colin. 2011. *The Strange Non-Death of Neoliberalism*. Malden, Mass.: Polity.

Dahl, Robert Alan. 1985. *A Preface to Economic Democracy*. Quantam Book. Berkeley: University of California Press.

Daniels, Norman. 2008. *Just Health: Meeting Health Needs Fairly*. New York: Cambridge University Press.

Daschle, Thomas, and David Nather. 2010. *Getting It Done: How Obama and Congress Finally Broke the Stalemate to Make Way for Healthcare Reform*. New York: Thomas Dunne.

Davis, David Brion. 2014. *The Problem of Slavery in the Age of Emancipation*. New York: Knopf.

Dawson, Michael C. 2001. *Black Visions: Roots of Contemporary African-American Political Ideologies*. Chicago: University of Chicago Press.

Douglass, Frederick. 1975. *The Life and Writings of Frederick Douglass: Early Years, 1817–1849*. New York: International Publishers.

Eversley, Shelly. 2001. "The Lunatic's Fancy and the Work of Art." *American Literary History* 13 (3): 445–68.

Foley, Barbara. 2010. *Wrestling the Left: The Making of Ralph Ellison's Invisible Man*. Durham, N.C.: Duke University Press.

Geronimus, Arline T., and J. Phillip Thompson. 2004. "To Denigrate, Ignore, or Disrupt: Racial Inequality in Health and the Impact of Policy-induced Breakdown of African American Communities." *DuBois Review* 1 (2): 247–49.

Gottschalk, Marie. 2005. "Organized Labor's Incredible Shrinking Social Vision." In *Healthy, Wealthy, and Fair: Health Care and the Good Society*, ed. James A. Marone and Lawrence R. Jacobs, 137–75. New York: Oxford University Press.

———. 2015. *Caught: The Prison State and the Lockdown of American Politics*. Princeton, N.J.: Princeton University Press.

Hacker, Jacob, and Paul Pierson. 2010. *Winner-Take-All Politics: How Washington Made the Rich Richer—and Turned Its Back on the Middle Class*. New York: Simon and Schuster.

Harcourt, Bernard E. 2001. *Illusion of Order: The False Promise of Broken Windows Policing*. Cambridge, Mass.: Harvard University Press.

Jackson, Thomas F. 1993. "The State, the Movement, and the Urban Poor: The War on Poverty and Political Mobilization in the 1960s." In *The Underclass Debate*, ed. Michael Katz, 403–39. Princeton, N.J.: Princeton University Press.

Jacobs, Lawrence R., and Theda Skocpol. 2012. *Health Care Reform and American Politics: What Everyone Needs to Know*. New York: Oxford University Press.

James, Sherman A. 1994. "John Henryism and the Health of African-Americans." *Culture, Medicine, and Psychiatry* 18 (2): 163–82.

Karatani, Kojin. 2005. *Transcritique: On Kant and Marx*. Translated by Sabu Kohso. Cambridge, Mass.: MIT Press.

Kawachi, Ichiro. 2005. "Why the United States Is Not Number One in Health." In *Healthy, Wealthy, and Fair: Health Care and the Good Society*, ed. James Marone and Lawrence Jacobs, 19–36. New York: Oxford University Press.

Kelley, Robin D. G. 1999. "A Poetics of Anticolonialism." *Monthly Review* 51 (6): 1. http://monthlyreview.org/1999/11/01/a-poetics-of-anticolonialism/.

———. 2002. *Freedom Dreams: The Black Radical Imagination*. Boston: Beacon Press.

King, Martin Luther, Jr. 1961. "The American Dream." In *A Testament of Hope: The Essential Writings and Speeches of Martin Luther King, Jr.*, ed. James M. Washington, 208–16. New York: HarperSanFrancisco.

Lamont, Michele. 1997. "Colliding Moralities Between Black and White Workers." In *From Sociology to Cultural Studies*, ed. Elizabeth Long, 263–85. New York: Blackwell.

Lessig, Lawrence. 2011. *Republic Lost: How Money Corrupts Congress—and a Plan to Stop It*. New York: Twelve.

Mansbridge, Jane J. 2001. "Complicating Oppositional Consciousness." In *Oppositional Consciousness: The Subjective Roots of Social Protest*, ed. Jane J. Mansbridge and Aldon Morris, 238–64. Chicago: University of Chicago Press.

McAdam, Doug, and Karina Kloos. 2014. *Deeply Divided: Racial Politics and Social Movements in Postwar America*. New York: Oxford University Press.

McEwen, Bruce S., and Peter J. Gianaros. 2010. "Central Role of the Brain in Stress and Adaptation: Links to Socioeconomic Status, Health, and Disease." *Annals of the New York Academy of Sciences* 1186: 190–222.

Metzl, Jonathan. 2009. *The Protest Psychosis: How Schizophrenia Became A Black Disease*. Boston: Beacon Press.

Mills, Charles W. 1998. *Blackness Visible: Essays in Philosophy and Race*. Ithaca, N.Y.: Cornell University Press.

Obama, Barack. 2014. "President Obama Delivers a Statement on the Affordable Care Act." April 1, 2014. https:www.whitehouse.gov/photos-and-video/video/2014/04/01/president-obama-delivers-statement-affordable-care-act.

Putnam, Robert D. 2000. *Bowling Alone: The Collapse and Revival of American Community*. New York: Simon and Schuster.

Rosavallon, Pierre. 2013. *The Society of Equals*. Cambridge, Mass.: Harvard University Press.

Said, Edward. 1990. "Reflections on Exile." In *Out There: Marginalization and Contemporary Cultures*, ed. Russell Ferguson, Martha Gever, Trinh Minh-ha, and Cornel West, 357–66. Documentary Sources in Contemporary Art 4. Cambridge, Mass.: MIT Press.

Schumer, Charles. 2014. "Senator Charles Schumer Delivers Remarks at the National Press Club." in *Congressional Quarterly*: Sage.

Sellers, Charles. 1991. *The Market Revolution: Jacksonian America, 1815–1846*. New York: Oxford University Press.

Serang, Farzana, J. Phillip Thompson, and Ted Howard. 2013. "The Anchor Mission: Leveraging the Power of Anchor Institutions to Build Community Wealth." College Park: The Democracy Collaborative at the University of Maryland. http://community-wealth.org/content/anchor-mission-leveraging-power-anchor-institutions-build-community-wealth.

Somerville, Martha H., Gayle D. Nelson, and Carl H. Mueller. 2013. "Hospital Community Benefits after the ACA: The State Law Landscape." Baltimore, Md.: The Hilltop Institute. http://community-wealth.org/sites/clone.community-wealth.org/files/downloads/paper-somerville-et-al-Hilltop.pdf.

"Special Issue: Racial Inequality and Health." 2011. *Du Bois Review* 8(1):1–307.

Stannard, David E. 1992. *American Holocaust: The Conquest of the New World*. New York: Oxford University Press.

Stone, Deborah. 2005. "How Market Ideology Guarantees Racial Inequality." In *Healthy, Wealthy, and Fair: Health Care and the Good Society*, ed. James A. Marone and Lawrence R. Jacobs, 65–90. New York: Oxford University Press.

Strong, Tracy B. 2012. *Politics without Vision: Thinking without a Banister in the Twentieth Century*. Chicago: University of Chicago Press.

Thompson, J. Phillip, Barbara Caress, Mariana Arcaya, Stacey Sutton, Saleema Moore, and Dara Yaskil. 2014. "Caring for Today: Planning for Tomorrow." New York: SEIU Local 1199.

Tishman, Maggie. 2014. "Achieving Inclusive Economic Development in New York City." Master's thesis, MIT. http://hdl.handle.net/1721.1/90109.

Wald, Priscilla. 1995. *Constituting Americans: Cultural Anxiety and Narrative Form*. Durham, N.C.: Duke University Press.

Wilkinson, Richard G., and Kate Pickett. 2010. *The Spirit Level: Why Greater Equality Makes Societies Stronger*. New York: Bloomsbury.

Wilson, James Q. 1968. *Varieties of Police Behavior: The Management of Law and Order in Eight Communities*. Publication of the Joint Center for Urban Studies. Cambridge, Mass.: Harvard University Press.

———. 1983. *Thinking About Crime*. Rev ed. New York: Vintage Books. First published in 1975 by Basic Books.

10

STILL SWIMMING, TIDES RISING

Community Change, Spatial Interventions, and the Challenge
of Federal Place-based Antipoverty Public Policies

AMY T. KHARE

There are several Obama administration policies that foreground *place*. One of these is the place-based housing and neighborhood redevelopment initiative known as Choice Neighborhoods. This chapter analyzes the Obama administration's signature place-based policy and its attempts to catalyze changes in urban environments. In so doing it asks about the role of federal policy in revitalizing urban communities; about how urban communities are conceptualized; and about how place-based policy priorities compliment and contrast the historical trajectory of federal investments. I conclude with a set of arguments about how the path dependency of policies arising from the U.S. Department of Housing and Urban Development may illuminate a broader set of trends within the Obama administration's urban policy agenda.

Conceptions of Community within Place-based Public Policies

One way to understand the Obama administration's place-based initiatives is to draw on the sociological literature that considers conceptions of community. This allows us to better understand how such place-based policies prioritize *spatial* interventions as a means of addressing urban poverty.

Within the sociological literature there is disagreement on what constitutes community. The disparate definitions and possibilities raise ambiguities, present contradictions, and create conflicts. "Community" is sometimes described as a place, sometimes as a group of people, and often it is a vague, intricate, and convoluted combination of both. When we look at place-based antipoverty policies in the light of this literature, we see that those policies tend to conflate concepts of community. They often speak of building, supporting, creating, intervening, and even protecting community. But in these cases there is rarely clarity about *which* (sense of) community is the target of the proposed intervention. Thus, it is necessary to explore the variety of propositions about the meaning of community to understand how these different ideas are influential in framing the Obama administration's place-based antipoverty policies.

Place-based conceptions of community begin with the significance of spatially defined arrangements, such as the density of the physical environment or the boundaries of a neighborhood (Chaskin 1997; Sampson 1999). People-based notions account for how socially constructed groups form and are influenced by common interests, relationships, and institutional arrangements (Castells 1983; DeFilippis, Fisher, and Shragge 2010; Fisher and Kling 1997). If placed-based definitions of community emphasize the *local,* however debatable the boundaries, people-based conceptions tend to examine how communities exist both within and beyond geographic constraints. Both conceptions assume that individuals within communities share some degree of common identification, whether living on the same block or sharing the experience of immigrating to a new country. Debates exist, however, about the extent to which macro political economic forces matter to meta-level undercurrents *within* communities (Sites, Chaskin, and Parks 2007).

Within the sociological tradition, theories of why communities matter remain tied to early ecological conceptions of communities as constituted by unbiased dynamics in which different social groups compete and cooperate with one another for access to valued goods, services, amenities, and relationships, all within a bounded locality. Thus, the sociological view implicitly merges with a place-based perspective. Scholars in the urban ecological orientation have worked from assumptions that the lack of social order in cities reflects heterogeneous relations and social organization, and that communities' intrinsic evolutionary logics allow them to develop through mutually dependent processes of "invasion" and "succession" (Burgess [1925] 1967, 47). Subcomponents of place-communities (such as ethnic enclaves) are thought to function in symbiotic or competitive relationship to one another and ultimately contribute to creating balanced systems. These theories further assume that impartial processes shape communities in neutral ways, rather than that political or economic actors external to the local areas intentionally facilitate inequitable processes (Park [1925] 1967; Wirth 1938).

Subsequent sociological theories of social disorganization conceptualized how urban place-communities lack residents who share common values and informal social control expectations, which presumably contributes to rising crime and disorder (Anderson 1990). Ecological perspectives influenced later social capital arguments that conceptualize how social relationships, such as "weak ties" (Granovetter 1973), facilitate the obtainment of functional, instrumental, and coping resources (Portes 1998; Wellman and Leighton 1979). While these arguments explicitly center on notions of communities as forms of social support, much of the empirical work considers how local ecosystems of concentrated disadvantage matter in ways that are constraining. Even later structuration arguments that consider how economic, political, and social structures of society exacerbate inequality and segregation in urban communities maintained a tie to these early ecological influences through their focus on "underclass culture" (Wilson 1987, 3). By failing to consider or challenge power differentials, these and other arguments from the sociological tradition maintain conceptions of communities as places of scarcity and thus arguably in need of interventions in order to establish social norms, organization, and resources.

The origins of U.S. place-based interventions are found in the late nineteenth-century settlement house movement, when reformers organized to provide services to new immigrants in urban low-income neighborhoods. Throughout the growth of modern U.S. cities, policies such as Urban Renewal, Model Cities, and Empowerment Zones sought to reshape physical and social environments of severely distressed neighborhoods where the opportunities for low-income households were greatly challenged. Policy advocates argued that place-based interventions were necessary in order to address intergenerational poverty, reduce the risk of diseases and mortality, curb violence, and prevent disconnection from educational opportunities and the labor market (Katz 2010). Recent empirical evidence suggests that growing up in neighborhoods that are concentrated with poverty contributes to the persistence of poverty across generations, and the designed interventions into particular places have sought to create a different set of opportunities for low-income children and young families (Chetty, Hendren, and Katz 2015; Sharkey 2013).

A central dilemma rests in policy design and implementation efforts when the targeted community is conceptualized as either a local place or as a community of people with shared experiences. In either case, federal policy directives may leave the definition of community arguably vague in order to allow for local interpretation—as is the case in other social policy frameworks that allow for state and municipal-level flexibility in order to meet the interests of local political constituencies (i.e., block grants for cash assistance, state provision of child welfare services).

The Obama administration's place-based initiatives launched between 2009 and 2015 have defined urban communities from the perspective of both people-communities and place-communities, in effect blurring the distinctions between particular localities and particular subpopulations. While one might see certain sophistication in these policy initiatives that are generally, on the surface, more holistic in design, it is nonetheless important to move beyond the policy rhetoric to analyze the funding arrangements, program models, and performance measurements that drive the local implementation of federal policies. In the case example explored here (Choice Neighborhoods), the policy aims to transform the physical environment of areas where distressed HUD-assisted housing is located. The target of the intervention is the housing and the space of the neighborhood. Of secondary concern are the communities of people living in these places. Social integration and economic mobility of low-income relocated populations, the majority of whom are racial minorities, remains a lower priority within the policy design. The evidence of the prioritization on place over people can be seen in the arrangement of resources and distribution of funding aimed at catalyzing changes for households and groups of residents, an argument that will be demonstrated in subsequent sections of this chapter.

Specifying the Obama Administration's Antipoverty Place-based Public Policies

The Obama administration demonstrated its faith in place-based initiatives by investing $365 million in approximately one hundred cities between 2009 and 2012 (Office of Urban Affairs n.d.). These initiatives center on how to strategically invest federal resources into urban neighborhoods, schools, and transit corridors, primarily for the purposes of revitalization and redevelopment.

Within this broad policy agenda, there are several place-based initiatives aimed at addressing the structural and cultural factors associated with concentrated poverty in urban areas of high racial segregation (Wilson 2010). The hope was that deliberately aligning interventions in these areas would have an economic impact on the broader cities in which these initiatives were launched. Additionally, these initiatives can be viewed as a form of political leverage, since resources are targeted to political constituencies (i.e., urban residents, racial minorities) who organized to elect President Obama.

The White House memo titled "Developing Effective Place-Based Policies for the FY 2011 Budget" defines the Obama administration's place-based policies this way:

> Place policies target the prosperity, equity, sustainability and livability of places—how well or how poorly they function as places and how they change over time. Place policy leverages investments by focusing resources in targeted places and drawing on the compounding effect of cooperative arrangements. (Orszag et al. 2009)

The memo describes three principles of place-based polices: (1) asserting measurable goals to evaluate the effectiveness of federal intervention; (2) federal interagency coordination and public–private partnerships at the community level; and (3) interjurisdictional and regional approaches to coordination. This last principle demonstrates that, by design, place-based public policies are aimed at federal investments in regions; the *urban* thus transcends traditional definitions of cities and neighborhoods to focus on broader areas of the metropolitan region.

The first of the Obama administration's policies, Promise Neighborhoods, makes grants available for distressed neighborhoods which they can use to plan and implement interventions tied to schools, early childhood, afterschool, parent education, and youth development (U.S. Department of Education n.d.). The second initiative, Choice Neighborhoods, invests federal resources to catalyze mixed-income neighborhood revitalization where HUD-assisted housing exists

(HUD, n.d., "Choice Neighborhoods"). In 2014, the White House launched another place-based initiative, Promise Zones, which aims to align federal resources and provide technical assistance in order to support the revitalization and economic development of twenty high-poverty communities (HUD n.d., "Promise Zones").

Arguably, many of the Obama administration initiatives that aim to stimulate change in urban communities, such as Choice, are pitched to transform local environments and facilitate improved socioeconomic mobility for citizens living in these low-income neighborhoods. The framework of the new initiatives centers on how to strengthen the connection between policies aimed at the health, education, and well-being of people as well as the places that are dependent, in part, on the actions of the citizens living and working in them.

According to some observers, however, these place-based initiatives implicitly prioritize spatial conceptions of community, and in doing so may fall short of providing adequate resources to move the marker on outcomes focused on human capital development. Specifically, low-income families living in targeted areas where place-based initiatives have been launched could greatly benefit from a host of public programs, including prioritized access to physical and mental health services (through the Affordable Care Act), early childhood programs (such as Head Start and Early Intervention), cash assistance, childcare subsidies, food and nutrition programs, and an array of other social welfare supports that provide relief from poverty.

In sum, federal entitlement programs, while less robust than in the pre-Clinton years, continue to provide time-limited cash assistance and services to citizens, some of whom live in the areas targeted for place-based initiatives. For this reason, federal policy alignment between the new place-based policies and the historic social welfare programs needs to be considered in order to confront enduring urban poverty. The dual challenge of both transforming people's lives and the places in which they reside will now be expanded upon through a policy analysis of HUD's signature place-based Choice Neighborhoods Initiative.

Choice Neighborhoods Initiative: A Continuation of the Prior Policy Path?

Public policies since the mid-1990s, such as the federal HOPE VI and Choice Neighborhoods Initiative (Choice), are intended to deliver affordable rental units in mixed-income housing developments[1] and to catalyze neighborhood redevelopment by privatizing public property in select urban areas. In general, the new mixed-income developments utilize a lower density of units, a mix of residents from diverse economic backgrounds, and a design approach that better integrates housing into the surrounding neighborhood (Cisneros and Engdahl 2009; Joseph, Chaskin, and Webber 2007).

Mixed-income development strategies represent a market-driven policy approach to urban neighborhood redevelopment (Fraser, Oakley, and Bazuin 2012; Hanlon 2010).[2] Government incentives are used to encourage private sector actors to develop the affordable housing and related social services that were previously provided directly by the state. The underlying rationale for these privatization reforms is that market investment into the built environment of places long associated with concentrated poverty is necessary because the public sector interventions have failed. If urban neighborhoods are to be radically reshaped, according to this vision, a significant portion of public housing units and the renters living in them will need to be replaced with market-rate housing and related amenities that show potential for economic development.[3]

As the most highly embraced response to concentrated poverty and racial segregation of areas where public and assisted housing sites are located, HOPE VI and Choice are policies that reflect the movement to privatize housing that was previously considered solely as the responsibility of the public domain. Privatization of public housing occurs through the shift from direct state provision of subsidized rental housing and related social services to the private sector.[4] Private sector actors may include for-profit corporations or nonprofit organizations that now are doing work that was previously performed by the government. These entities are positioned between the state and citizens; in this way, they mediate policy directives and the needs of local residents. Government-issued contracts and fiscal regulations stimulate a response by private sector entities that, in turn, become the primary suppliers of affordable housing and services previously delivered by the state.

Choice is an outgrowth of HOPE VI. It maintained the priority of privatizing public housing through physical redevelopment. Proposed in 2009 as part of the annual appropriations bill that provided funding to HOPE VI, Choice must be considered a contemporary iteration, rather than a radical departure from prior HUD policy, given the continued movement to further privatize HUD-assisted housing. Still, there are important distinguishing elements of Choice, most pointedly the extension of the Obama administration's framework for interagency coordination. In this next section, the policy design of Choice is compared with its predecessor, HOPE VI, in order to show the lack of a critical juncture in HUD policy development.

HOPE VI: Inherited Policy Landscape as the Origin of Choice

HOPE VI was focused on the demolition of dilapidated public housing projects, the relocation of residents who lived in public housing, and the privatization of public housing through contracting out the development and ownership of subsidized housing and services (Katz 2011; McCarty 2012). Between 1992 and 2010, HUD awarded approximately $6.7 billion in HOPE VI funding to local public housing authorities.[5] In each of the first five years of the program, Congress authorized approximately $550 million. Starting in FY 2003, under the Bush administration, the level of funding dropped significantly. By the time President Obama took office in January 2009, annual appropriations of HOPE VI had been substantially decreased to approximately $120 million a year.

HOPE VI has had many iterations over eighteen years, but the primary purpose of the program remained a deconcentration of poverty through dispersal of low-income households and the redevelopment of lower-density and mixed-income housing. HOPE VI used mixed-finance strategies to generate housing tenure diversity within developments that illuminated key New Urbanist principles, such as low-rise townhomes and pedestrian-friendly street designs. These principles were presumed to create interactive social environments.

To understand how the origins of Choice occurred in the broader context of public housing policy, it is important to detail the evolution of the funding for HOPE VI and Choice. Beginning in 2010 in an effort to refine the HOPE VI program, the Obama administration began calling for an end to HOPE VI and a shift of funding to its newly proposed Choice Neighborhoods Initiative. In August 2011, HUD awarded the first five Choice implementation grants to neighborhoods where the redevelopment of assisted housing developments had already experienced significant investment. With approximately $450 million in federal funding, HUD has awarded fifteen implementation grants and sixty-three planning grants since 2011. Planning grantees receive a maximum of $500,000 for two years and implementation grantees receive a maximum of $30.5 million for five years (HUD 2015a). Given the level of funding, Choice should be considered a boutique program compared to other HUD programs of the past, including HOPE VI, and the newly initiated Rental Assistance Demonstration (RAD) program.

Four points are relevant to understanding the evolution in funding from HOPE VI to Choice (see Table 10.1). First, Obama's HUD officials repeatedly requested more money than Congress allocated. Second, despite efforts by HUD leadership, Choice funding replaced HOPE VI funding rather than creating a larger share of federal funding directed at HUD-assisted housing redevelopment efforts. As HUD Secretary Donovan stated in the earliest public announcement of HUD's plan to build on HOPE VI, "public housing transformation is still our priority at HUD. That's why our FY 2010 budget request for Choice Neighborhoods would be $250 million—more than double the funding we have for HOPE VI this year" (Donovan 2009). This request for an expansion in budget appropriations did not transpire and the funding for Choice remains at similar levels as previous HOPE VI annual allocations. Third, the funding for Choice has not reached an equal level of annual funding allocations that existed in the first five years of HOPE VI (approximately $500 million per fiscal year), thus HUD has not reversed the previous trends under Bush that retracted original funding levels. Finally, Choice has not been made permanent through statutory law, despite the introduction of bills in committees of both the House of Representatives and the Senate. For now, Choice continues to operate through an annual HUD appropriation bill, resulting in future uncertainty once the Obama administration is no longer in office. In this way, the program still shows vulnerability to congressional authority that could elect to end the program.

TABLE 10.1. OBAMA ADMINISTRATION'S ANNUAL REQUEST AND
APPROPRIATIONS: HOPE VI AND CHOICE (IN $ MILLIONS)

Fiscal Year	HUD Request to Congress	HOPE VI Appropriation	Choice Appropriation
FY 2009	(Under Bush administration)	$120	$0
FY 2010	$250	$135	$65
FY 2011	$250	$28	$65
FY 2012	$250	$0	$120
FY 2013	$150	$0	$114
FY 2014	$90	$0	$90
FY 2015	$400*	$0	$80
FY 2016	$250	$0	$125
FY 2017	$200	$0	TBD

* The FY 2015 president's budget request also included the *Opportunity, Growth and Security Initiative*, a $56 billion separate legislative package to be supported through defense and non-defense programs. This package proposed to allocate an additional $280 million to Choice beyond the HUD budget request of $120 million. Thus, the total request for Choice was $400 million.

Sources: U.S. Department of Housing and Urban Development, Public and Indian Housing, Choice Neighborhoods, "2011 Summary Statement and Initiatives." Accessed February 2, 2015. http://www.hud .gov/offices/cfo/reports/2011/cjs/FY2011ChoiceNeighborhoods.pdf; U.S. Department of Housing and Urban Development, Public and Indian Housing, Choice Neighborhoods, "2013 Summary Statement and Initiatives." Accessed February 2, 2015. http://portal.hud.gov/hudportal/documents/huddoc?id=choice -neighb.pdf; U.S. Department of Housing and Urban Development, FY 2011 HOPE VI Funding Informa- tion. Accessed February 2, 2015. http://portal.hud.gov/hudportal/HUD?src=/program_offices/public _indian_housing/programs/ph/hope6/grants/fy11; U.S. Department of Housing and Urban Develop- ment, "Overview of FY2015 President's Budget." Accessed May 17, 2016. http://portal.hud.gov /hudportal/documents/huddoc?id=FY2015BudgetPresFINAL.pdf; U.S. Department of Housing and Urban Development, Public and Indian Housing, Choice Neighborhoods, "2016 Summary Statement and Initiatives." Accessed May, 2016. https://portal.hud.gov/hudportal/documents/huddoc?id=6-FY16CJ -Choice.pdf; National Low Income Housing Coalition, "FY17 Budget Chart." Accessed May 19, 2016. http://nlihc.org/sites/default/files/NLIHC_HUD-USDA_Budget-Chart.pdf.

Choice: Policy Diversion or Policy Enhancement?

The Choice program aims to redevelop distressed HUD-assisted housing and "transform neighborhoods of concentrated poverty into sustainable mixed-income communities, with a focus on improved housing, successful residents, and vibrant neighborhoods" (HUD 2015b) Choice program objectives fall in the categories of housing, people, and neighborhood.[6] HUD extends funding opportunities beyond public housing authorities (the exclusive recipients of HOPE VI) to local governments, nonprofit organizations, and for-profit developers (provided the for-profit entity applies jointly with a public agency). Projects that had previously received a HOPE VI award were not permitted to apply for Choice funds. HUD required grantees to ensure lease-compliant residents had a right to return to replacement housing and comply with a one-for-one hard unit replacement policy.[7] Key elements of the policy design of both HOPE VI and Choice show some diversion in the policy framework (see Table 10.2).

Choice is designed to move beyond HOPE VI in six key ways. First and foremost, Choice attempted multilayered coordination among city agencies, housing authorities, developers, community stakeholders, and elected officials. Its goal of integrating this complex web of partners is to reform local institutions, public agencies, and community-based resources—such as schools and health care services—as well as to leverage new investments that contribute to neighborhood revitalization. Choice reflects the idea that local systems supporting low-income community members were in need of radical change. Choice appears to offer a broader scope of authority, accountability, leadership, and investment for urban place-based initiatives across other public agencies, as well as outside of the public domain, in third-sector and for-profit ventures. This collaborative governance model was shown to be effective in engaging diverse sets of actors across different domains (housing, transportation, health care, education, and criminal justice) in certain cities, such as Boston, where mayoral and other elected officials used their political leadership to garner external support (Urban Institute and MDRC 2015). Lessons learned through Choice are described as applicable for municipal-level leadership and governing arrangements that could reform the historical silos within city government and across public agencies, nonprofit organizations, and for-profit ventures. Questions remain about the possible effects of these partnerships extending beyond the Choice neighborhoods to other areas of the city and other low-income populations (Urban Institute and MDRC 2015).

Second, Choice encourages a more diverse set of local actors to collaborate. With HOPE VI, eligible grantees could only be public housing authorities, who then would subcontract to private entities. Choice grantees can include nonprofit and for-profit developers who partner with public entities. In this way, Choice reflects the Obama administration's interest in spurring coalitions between nontraditional

TABLE 10.2. COMPARISON OF KEY ELEMENTS OF HOPE VI TO CHOICE

Policy Elements	HOPE VI	Choice
Legislative establishment & authority	Consolidated Appropriations Act of 1993 (originally the Urban Revitalization Demonstration); authorizing legislation within the Quality Housing and Work Responsibility Act of 1998	Consolidated Appropriations Act of 2010; no statutory authorization bill established; rather funded through appropriations
Federal appropriations	Annual appropriations bills until FY 2011; HUD authorized program guidelines and grant administration through annual NOFA	Annual appropriations bill starting in FY 2010; HUD authorized program guidelines and grant administration through annual NOFA
HUD-assisted housing replacement policy	No 1-for-1 replacement policy for all demolished units, resulted in demolition of more than 100,000 units but rebuilding of only about 50% of those	1-for-1 replacement policy for demolished units (including vacant and occupied)
Use of funds and partnerships	Public capital and operating subsidies for PHAs, with pass-through grants to private developers	Public capital and operating subsidies for PHAs, local governments, nonprofit and for-profit developers who partner with public entity
Revitalization strategy	Focus on large-scale demolition, including demolition-only grants of public housing buildings, rehabilitation, new construction	Demolition, rehabilitation, and new construction of HUD-assisted housing, including project-based Section 8 buildings
Resident relocation strategy	HUD required PHA resident relocation plan prior to implementation	HUD required resident relocation plan, with a focus on phased demolition and smooth relocation; tracking of original tenants over the course of the redevelopment

Policy Elements	HOPE VI	Choice
Community vs. housing development focus	Focus on housing demolition and rebuilding of housing units	Focus on housing demolition and rebuilding of housing, mixed-use buildings, recreation, and other neighborhood amenities
Community and supportive services	Cap at 15%	Cap at 15% for services; added critical community improvement program capped at 15% to be allocated to neighborhood change and infrastructure reforms
Intended beneficiary of HUD-assisted housing*	AMI at 80%	AMI at 120%
Resident engagement strategy	Required during planning stage at the outset of the grant application	Required during planning and implementation stage, over the 5 years of the grant

* HUD policy increased the AMI from 80 percent to 120 percent in order to create more market demand in these neighborhoods through subsidizing housing (rental and for sale) for a wider spectrum of income-eligible residents who could receive housing benefits. The argument for subsidizing at this higher cap is that Choice neighborhoods need to attract residents who otherwise have the financial means to live in more affluent neighborhoods, but who may be attracted to living in these neighborhoods if provided with economic incentives tied to their housing.

affiliates who may have shared interests but have not yet aligned their resources and expertise.

Third, Choice diversifies the type of eligible HUD-assisted housing stock to be targeted for redevelopment. Expanding the target housing beyond traditional public housing results in more competition for applicants and greater possibilities for redeveloping aging properties that otherwise may lack capital resources (such as the project-based Section 8 properties). In the first round of implementation grants, two of the five grantees included owners of project-based Section 8 housing properties (Urban Institute 2013).

Fourth, Choice moves further than HOPE VI to target entire neighborhoods for redevelopment. It does this by focusing on a larger area than the housing development footprint. Program applicants self-define the physical boundaries of the targeted area, guided by HUD eligibility criteria that requires the neighborhood to be challenged economically (defined by metrics such as low-performing schools, excessive crime, and high housing vacancy rates).[8] Here, we see that Choice maintains a spatial definition of "community" and suggests the revitalization of distressed housing may result in neighborhood transformation. Choice's theory of change suggests that the intervention's aim to redevelop distressed housing will have a spillover effect, increasing the economic value of housing on surrounding blocks.

Fifth, Choice requires a one-for-one replacement of subsidized units torn down as part of the redevelopment process. Lease-compliant residents are intended to have more options to return, since the grantee must ensure that there are available units on site. This focus on responsible redevelopment and the preservation of affordable housing options demonstrates that Choice architects sought to remedy the challenges in eradicating the subsidized housing stock raised by critics of HOPE VI. However, it should be noted that Choice grantees may request an exception to the one-for-one replacement housing rule, and grantees can petition to replace up to half of the housing units with tenant-based vouchers in housing markets with adequate supplies of affordable rental housing. Evidence is needed in order to demonstrate a causal relationship between the policy expectation of one-for-one replacement and the capacity for original residents undergoing relocation to return to the new housing.

Finally, Choice builds on historically comprehensive community initiative models. These models are designed to help neighborhood-based organizations work together and promote comprehensive change by linking to resources beyond a neighborhood. Choice grantees can elect to include in their budget "critical community improvements" (CCIs) that aim to address neighborhood needs beyond the HUD-assisted housing development (Pendall and Hendey 2013). HUD's criterion for what constitutes a CCI includes economic development activities that attract or improve commercial businesses, property improvement loans or grants targeted for homeowners, and public park improvements. The inclusion of CCIs shows how Choice moves beyond conceptualizing these places as mixed-income housing developments to entire neighborhoods that are integrated into the fabric of the broader city and region.

While these six features distinguish Choice from HOPE VI, the overarching framework of privatizing public housing continues to dominate HUD's policy agenda. Choice expands the use of market-based policy tools by engaging private owners of multifamily HUD-assisted housing projects and using financing arrangements demanding even more layering of both public and private sources.[9] Regarding the engagement of private owners, Senate leaders concerned about additional subsidies targeting private sector owners ensured that at least half of the funding be set aside for projects where public housing authorities serve as the lead entity.[10] Private developers must apply jointly with a government authority, thus ensuring the creation of a public–private partnership to manage the grant. To date, three of the seventeen grantees are private developers, and all the grantees have at least one core development partner that is a private corporation. Regarding the financing, after the initial round of Choice funding (FY 2010) the subsequent years (FY 2012 and FY 2013) required a firm commitment by Choice grantees to leverage additional matching funds. Choice applicants had to provide evidence of commitments from other stakeholders to provide significant financial assistance, such as private capital for housing redevelopment or grant funding for supportive services.

Choice appears to cross the spatial and social construction of community since the target of intervention is on the three program areas of housing, neighborhood, and people. But we continue to see that Choice prioritizes physical housing redevelopment over comprehensive community improvements and interventions focused on social and economic mobility of relocated residents. In other words, the spatial conception of community remains the priority.

The architects of Choice limited the role of federal policy in local community change efforts by remaining wedded to focusing on housing redevelopment, with 60 percent to 80 percent of Choice budget allocations directed toward housing. HUD restricts funding for the neighborhood and people domains of the program. The CCI budget is allowed up to 15 percent of the total Choice budget, which amounts to approximately $7 million per site (Urban Institute and MDRC 2015). In their applications, grantees describe how they intend to use the CCI funding to promote various community change efforts, such as crime reduction programs, strategies for neighborhood block-level organizing, the attraction of grocery stores, and the creation of recreational space. Ambitious neighborhood improvements, such as these, require a higher level of financial investment, and without significant non-Choice funding commitments the CCIs may have a limited impact.

Furthermore, Choice restricts community- and resident-supportive programming, since funding must be capped at 15 percent for investing in "people" activities. The policy that seeks to reform local public agencies and community-based services (such as in the realm of education, health care, and workforce development) will likely necessitate a higher allocation of resources, and possibly a different framework of federal interagency blending of resources, priorities, and technical assistance. Thus, redevelopment of HUD-assisted housing through market-based incentives is reflective of Choice's primary aim and continues HUD's focus on bricks-and-mortar solutions to concentrated urban poverty.

Possible Directions in Federal Antipoverty Place-based Public Policy

What then does HUD's signature place-based policy, Choice Neighborhoods Initiative, suggest about the role of the federal government in revitalizing urban communities during this era? How do Obama's policy priorities complement the historical trajectory of federal investments? How do they stand in contrast?

While Choice resolves some of the inherent challenges of HOPE VI, the focus on place-based policy continues to overtly prioritize changes to the spatial environment (seeing communities as bound by space) while leaving unresolved conflicts over how federal resources may be reallocated to more equitably support all citizens regardless of income, housing tenure, and geographic location. Choice reflects a path-dependent trajectory of prior policies that promote spatial interventions to address structural economic, political, and social problems. At its core, Choice's theory of change suggests that physical housing redevelopment is the key intervention for addressing concentrated poverty and racial segregation in urban communities.

Alternative policy reforms that could disrupt the historical trajectory of housing and urban development policy may have proved too politically challenging during a period when other policy initiatives (such as the Affordable Care Act and the economic stimulus package) took priority. Additionally, it may be that HUD political leadership wanted to continue HOPE VI in order to meet the desires of their core constituencies (i.e., public housing authorities, mayors, and private developers) rather than take a more novel approach to crafting a new set of policy priorities. HUD leadership may have been aware of the limitations of HOPE VI (such as discrimination in the rental market faced by tenants who relocated with vouchers) but faced statutory barriers too cumbersome to expediently recalibrate policy priorities.[11]

What is left unresolved in this moment is whether the opportunity for policy change will allow movement toward a new antipoverty policy framework. Growing economic inequality and poverty suggests that a new framework is needed, and efforts are being made to create heterogeneous networks and multidimensional coalitions at multiple scales (local, national, and even global). While Choice in some ways exemplifies a policy designed to establish interagency, multisectorial governance structures that may demonstrate potential for blending people and place approaches for local community change, it is not funded as such. An alternative framework might better account for "place-conscious" initiatives that move *across* spatial and political boundaries to work within a *regional context* to address intergenerational poverty (Turner et al. 2014). The intersectionality of public policies aiming to transform both urban places and the opportunities of citizens living and working in metropolitan areas can be more strategically aligned and sustainably funded. Choice makes an important movement toward strengthening the interventions aimed at both people and place, though considering budgetary arrangements, remains wedded to the proposition that the greatest return on investment comes from physical housing transformation.

The reforms that have emerged from the Obama administration thus take their place within a longer history of federal urban development policies, policies that increasingly use government incentives to stimulate market responses toward the redevelopment of urban neighborhoods while failing to address structural economic disadvantage, racial inequities, fiscal crisis, depopulation of cities, and growing violent crime. As O'Connor demonstrates in her 1999 piece, "Swimming against the Tide: A Brief History of Federal Policy in Poor Communities," policy efforts at the federal level to support urban community development have been mired in short-term programs, replicating the same ineffective solutions "while failing to address the structural conditions underlying community decline" (O'Connor 1999, 78).

Place-based and market-driven initiatives like Choice are different in that they are being implemented during a period in history when economic inequality is at its highest and there is a growing tendency—across academic disciplines and activist movements—to question the very structure of capitalism itself. Policy interventions seeking to initiate lasting changes for individuals and families living in areas of pervasive racial segregation, high crime, failed public housing, and economic disinvestment face an enormous task and necessarily mean high rates of expenditure. The levels of cross-sectorial coordination required are themselves daunting. An urban policy agenda that aims toward momentous macro-level structural changes to address historical urban decline are needed, as are policies that transcend neighborhood spatial boundaries.

Change for urban communities requires federal investment in more than local housing development strategies—it requires that low-income citizens have greater access to quality resources, amenities, and programs allowing for self-development; that they have knowledge about their rights as citizens and consumers; and that they politically organize to influence the community change processes. Looking at the history of community-development efforts coming out of federal policies, the Obama administration's place-based initiatives may well have made a modicum of difference for some neighborhoods and some of the people living in them. Moving beyond policies that prioritize the conceptions of communities as place-based to a set of policy initiatives that more equitably embrace and provide social welfare support universally for all citizens regardless of income, housing tenure, and geographic location would be a start toward addressing the deeper historical and vastly broader structural inequities that afflict many more.

Notes

1. There are a variety of definitions of mixed-income housing. I use the definition proposed by the Mixed-Income Research Design Group: "All intentional efforts to generate socioeconomic diversity in a targeted geographic area" (Briggs et al. 2009, 10). The mix may include rental and homeownership units; may mix by floor, building, or neighborhood block; and may include households living in subsidized units earning anywhere from no income to up to 120 percent of area median income.

2. The market-based nature of this strategy is best explained by recognizing the financing arrangements required to make it successful. The mixed finance model entails the use of HUD funds with other public and private funding sources for the development and rehabilitation of developments that include public housing units. The units may be solely or partially owned by a PHA or they may be owned by private corporations. This form of privatization assumes that it is possible to leverage private sector capital to produce public housing units. There is considerable debate about the extent to which the market rate for sale and rental units that do not receive public subsidies should be considered public or subsidized (Urban Institute 2009; HUD 2001).

3. At this writing, there are 1.12 million public housing units, 60 percent of which are located in areas with low or moderate poverty rates. Public housing, a nonentitlement program,

serves approximately 2.2 million low-income people, whose incomes may not exceed 80 percent of the local median income at the time of move into public housing. Since the mid-1990s, approximately 285,000 units have been removed due to deterioration, only one-sixth of which have been replaced with new units (Center on Budget and Policy Priorities 2015).

4. While the government retains ownership of the land on which the housing is built, for-profit corporations or nonprofit organizations own the housing units. Public housing authorities typically lease the land to private entities for a small fee (Marcuse and Keating 2006).

5. HOPE VI includes 262 revitalization grants, totaling nearly $6.3 billion, as well as 285 demolition grants and 35 planning grants totaling nearly $392 million and $15 million, respectively (HUD n.d., "Choice Neighborhoods").

6. According to the notice of funds availability, the Choice policy aims include the following: "1) Transform distressed public and assisted housing into energy-efficient, mixed-income housing that is physically and financially viable over the long-term. 2) Support positive outcomes for families who live in the target development(s) and the surrounding neighborhood, particularly outcomes related to resident's health, safety, employment, mobility, and education. 3) Transform neighborhoods of poverty into viable, mixed-income neighborhoods with access to well-functioning services, high-quality public schools and education programs, high-quality early learning programs and services, public assets, public transportation, and improved access to jobs" (HUD 2010).

7. Replacement units located off site were required to be in areas with a poverty rate of 40 percent or lower and a minority population that is less than 20 percentage points higher than the total percentage of minorities in the MSA. Grantees were able to request that up to 50 percent of replacement units be provided through tenant-based vouchers rather than hard units (HUD 2010).

8. HUD identified eligible neighborhoods as those with a poverty rate of at least 20 percent and at least one of the following: a violent crime rate over the last three years at least 1.5 times the rate for the city/county as a whole, a long-term vacancy/substandard home rate at least 1.5 times the rate for the city/count as a whole (averaged over three years or in the most recent year), a low-performing public school, and public or HUD-assisted housing that meets the definition of "severely distressed" (HUD 2010).

9. Housing eligible for Choice redevelopment awards include project-based Section 8, Section 9, Section 202, and Section 811.

10. The Senate-passed version of H.R. 3288 directed HUD to set aside at least half of the funding for projects where the public housing authority (PHA) serves as the lead entity, noting concern of broadening the program to other HUD-assisted housing developments.

11. For example, HOPE VI legislative does not permit more than 15 percent of the grant to be allocated to community and social services, which results in a priority being placed on housing development over interventions addressing a wide range of other needs (public safety, education reform, etc.). Choice is wedded to this model unless statutory reform occurs.

References

Anderson, Elijah. 1990. *Streetwise: Race, Class, and Change in an Urban Community*. Chicago: University of Chicago Press.

Briggs, Xavier de Souza, Greg Duncan, Katherine Edin, Mark Joseph, Robert D. Mare, John Mollenkopf, Mary Patillo, et al. 2009. "Research Design for the Study of Mixed-Income Housing." California Center for Population Research, University of California–Los Angeles. http://escholarship.org/uc/item/4jc6s3ks.

Burgess, Ernest W. (1925) 1967. "The Growth of the City: An Introduction to a Research Project." In *The City*, ed. Robert E. Park and Ernest W. Burgess, 47–62. Chicago: University of Chicago Press.

Castells, Manuel. 1983. *The City and the Grassroots: A Cross-Cultural Theory of Urban Social Movements*. Berkeley: University of California Press.

Center on Budget and Policy Priorities. 2015. "Policy Basics: Introduction to Public Housing." Accessed on May 19, 2016. http://www.cbpp.org/research/policy-basics-introduction-to-public-housing.

Chaskin, Robert J. 1997. "Perspectives on Neighborhood and Community: A Review of the Literature." *Social Service Review* 71 (4): 521–47.

Chetty, Raj, Nathaniel Hendren, and Lawrence F. Katz. 2015. "The Long-Term Effects of Exposure to Better Neighborhoods: New Evidence from the Moving to Opportunity Experiment." Equality of Opportunity Project Working Paper. Cambridge, Mass.: Harvard University.

Cisneros, Henry, and Lora Engdahl. 2009. *From Despair to Hope: HOPE VI and the New Promise of Public Housing in America's Cities.* Washington, D.C.: Brookings Institution.

DeFilippis, James, Robert Fisher, and Eric Shragge. 2010. *Contesting Community: The Limits and Potential of Local Organizing.* Piscataway, N.J.: Rutgers University Press.

Donovan, Shaun. 2009. Prepared remarks for Brookings Institution Metropolitan Policy Program's discussion, "From Despair to Hope: Two HUD Secretaries on Urban Revitalization and Opportunity." National Press Club, Washington, D.C. http://portal.hud.gov/hudportal/HUD?src=/press/speeches_remarks_statements/2009/speech_07142009.

Fisher, Robert, and Joe Kling. 1997. "Community Organization, New Social Movement Theory, and the Condition of Postmodernity." In *Integrating Knowledge and Practice: The Case of Social Work and Social Science,* ed. David J. Tucker, Charles Garvin, and Rosemary Sarri, 105–15. Westport, Conn.: Praeger.

Fraser, James, Deirdre Oakley, and Joshua Bazuin. 2012. "Public Ownership and Private Profit in Housing." *Cambridge Journal of Regions, Economy & Society* 5 (3): 397–412.

Granovetter, Mark S. 1973. "The Strength of Weak Ties." *American Journal of Sociology* 78 (6): 1360–80.

Hanlon, James. 2010. "Success by Design: HOPE VI, New Urbanism, and the Neoliberal Transformation of Public Housing in the United States." *Environment and Planning* A 42 (1): 80–98.

HUD (U.S. Department of Housing and Urban Development). 2001. "HOPE VI Guidance: Mixed-Finance Public Housing Development." http://portal.hud.gov/hudportal/documents/huddoc?id=DOC_10114.pdf.

———. 2010. "HUD's Fiscal Year (FY) 2010 NOFA for the Choice Neighborhoods Initiative–Round 1 NOFA." 2. Accessed on February 1, 2015. http://portal.hud.gov/hudportal/documents/huddoc?id=DOC_9823.pdf.

———. 2015a. "FY2015 Choice Neighborhood HUD Request to Congress: D-3." Accessed on February 1, 2015. http://portal.hud.gov/hudportal/documents/huddoc?id=FY15CJ_CHOICE_NEIGH.pdf.

———. 2015b. "Choice Neighborhoods 2015 Grantee Report." Accessed on May 19, 2016. http://portal.hud.gov/hudportal/documents/huddoc?id=CNGranteeReport2015.pdf.

———. n.d. "Choice Neighborhoods: Overview." Accessed February 1, 2015. http://portal.hud.gov/hudportal/HUD?src=/program_offices/public_indian_housing/programs/ph/cn.

———. n.d. "Promise Zones: Overview." Accessed February 1, 2015. http://portal.hud.gov/hudportal/HUD?src=/program_offices/comm_planning/economicdevelopment/programs/pz.

Joseph, Mark L., Robert J. Chaskin, and Henry S. Webber. 2007. "The Theoretical Basis for Addressing Poverty through Mixed-Income Development." *Urban Affairs Review* 42 (3): 369–409.

Katz, Bruce. 2011. "The Origins of HOPE VI." In *From Despair to Hope: HOPE VI and the New Promise of Public Housing in America's Cities,* ed. Henry Cisneros and Lora Engdahl, 15–30. Washington, D.C.: Brookings Institution.

Katz, Michael B. 2010. "Narratives of Failure? Historical Interpretations of Federal Urban Policy." *City & Community* 9 (1): 13–22.

Marcuse, Peter, and Dennis Keating. 2006. "The Permanent Housing Crisis: The Failures of Conservatism and the Limitations of Liberalism." In *A Right to Housing: Foundation for a New*

Social Agenda, ed. Rachel G. Bratt, Michael E. Stone, and Chester W. Hartman, 139–62. Philadelphia: Temple University Press.

Massey, Douglas S., and Nancy A. Denton. 1993. *American Apartheid: Segregation and the Making of the Underclass.* Cambridge, Mass.: Harvard University Press.

McCarty, Maggie. 2011. "HOPE VI: Public Housing Revitalization Program: Background, Funding, and Issues." In *Public Housing: Background and Issues,* ed. Sara M. Larsen, 65–93. Housing Issues, Laws and Programs. Hauppauge, N.Y.: Nova Science.

O'Connor, Alice. 1999. "Swimming against the Tide: A Brief History of Federal Policy in Poor Communities." In *Urban Problems and Community Development,* ed. Ronald F. Ferguson and William T. Dickens, 77–138. Washington, D.C.: Brookings Institution.

Office of Urban Affairs. n.d. "Neighborhood Revitalization Initiative." *Whitehouse.gov.* Accessed February 1, 2015. http://www.whitehouse.gov/administration/eop/oua/initiatives/neighborhood-revitalization.

Orszag, Peter R., Melody Barnes, Adolfo Carrion, and Lawrence Summers. 2009. "Developing Effective Place-Based Policies for the FY 2011 Budget." August 11. Memorandum. https://www.whitehouse.gov/sites/default/files/omb/assets/memoranda_fy2009/m09-28.pdf.

Park, Robert E. (1925) 1967. "The City: Suggestions for the Investigation of Human Behavior in the Urban Environment." In *The City,* ed. Robert E. Park and Ernest W. Burgess, 1–46. Chicago: University of Chicago Press.

Pendall, Rolf, and Leah Hendey. 2013. "A Brief Look at the Early Implementation of Choice Neighborhoods." Report prepared for the Annie E. Casey Foundation. Washington, D.C.: Urban Institute.

Portes, Alejandro. 1998. "Social Capital: Its Origins and Applications in Modern Sociology." *Annual Review of Sociology* 24 (August): 1–24.

Sampson, Robert J. 1999. "What 'Community' Supplies." In *Urban Problems and Community Development,* ed. Ronald F. Ferguson and William T. Dickens, 241–79. Washington, D.C.: Brookings Institution.

Sharkey, Patrick. 2013. *Stuck in Place: Urban Neighborhoods and the End of Progress toward Racial Equality.* Chicago: University of Chicago Press.

Sites, William, Robert J. Chaskin, and Virginia Parks. 2007. "Reframing Community Practice for the 21st Century: Multiple Traditions, Multiple Challenges." *Journal of Urban Affairs* 29 (5): 519–41.

Turner, Margery Austin, Peter Edelman, Erika C. Poethig, and Laudan Y. Aron. 2014. "Tackling Persistent Poverty in Distressed Urban Neighborhoods: History, Principles, and Strategies for Philanthropic Investment." White paper. Urban Institute. http://www.urban.org/research/publication/tackling-persistent-poverty-distressed-urban-neighborhoods.

Urban Institute. 2009. "The Uncharted, Uncertain Future of HOPE VI Redevelopments: The Case for Assessing Project Sustainability." Washington, D.C.: Urban Institute.

———. 2013. "Developing Choice Neighborhoods: An Early Look at Implementation in Five Sites." Washington, D.C.: U.S. Department of Housing and Urban Development.

Urban Institute and MDRC. 2015. "Choice Neighborhoods: Baseline Conditions and Early Progress." *Huduser.gov.* https://www.huduser.gov/portal/publications/reports/choice-neighborhoods-baseline.html.

U.S. Department of Education. n.d. "Promise Neighborhoods Overview." Accessed May 19, 2016. https://www.hudexchange.info/programs/promise-zones/promise-zones-overview/.

Wellman, Barry, and Barry Leighton. 1979. "Networks, Neighborhoods, and Communities: Approaches to the Study of the Community Question." *Urban Affairs Review* 14 (3): 363–90.

Wilson, William J. 1987. *The Truly Disadvantaged: The Inner City, the Underclass, and Public Policy.* Chicago: University of Chicago Press.

———. 2010. "The Obama Administration's Proposals to Address Concentrated Urban Poverty," *City & Community* 9 (1): 41–49.

Wirth, Louis. 1938. "Urbanism as a Way of Life." *American Journal of Sociology* 44 (1): 1–24.

II

COMMUNITY DEVELOPMENT IN THE AGE OF OBAMA

KATHE NEWMAN

Community development refers to a broad array of approaches to improve communities. Embedded in community-development practice is a tension about which approach best addresses poverty. Is change made through democratic processes by increasing access for marginalized groups; is it made by changing places and or people through redevelopment and social service delivery; or is it made through economic inclusion? Debates, funding, and the political and economic context shape how these approaches are realized, and approaches that support economic inclusion have been emphasized for nearly fifty years. Because access to credit has played a central role in these approaches, finding income streams has been a focus of policy and practice. As community-development organizations sought access to credit, changes within the financial system made credit more accessible but for some that access has come with higher risks. In the wake of the financial crisis, the community-development field has been challenged to address the problems created during the foreclosure crisis, which include weaving borrowers back into financial markets, and addressing the myriad of other challenges communities face. Community-development organizations are also challenged to expand their areas of activity and expertise to meet a wide array of community needs.

The chapter is organized in three main sections. The first section discusses community development and economic inclusion. The second provides an overview of the changes in the financial system that have extended credit to borrowers with less than prime credit, and the final section considers trends in the field of community development. The remainder of the chapter discusses community-development efforts to foster economic inclusion in the wake of economic restructuring and declining federal resources and changes in the banking and finance industry that increase access to financing for many, and concludes with some observations about creative community responses to the continuing problems the community-development field faces.

Economic Inclusion

Economic inclusion has been a dominant community-development approach since the 1960s. The programmatic objective is to increase low-income community access to credit, which is used for housing, business development, education, transportation, and a wealth of other activities. The flow of capital out of urban neighborhoods and the withdrawal of state funding since the 1970s created a push to locate alternative capital flows to fund affordable housing and economic development. This shift occurred in tandem with federal efforts to encourage market-based solutions to social problems (Fainstein and Gray 1997).

Doing so required creating an infrastructure between investors and communities. The federal government and philanthropic community created an intermediary community-development infrastructure that joins communities (borrowers/sites of investment) with investors to improve low- and moderate-income communities by expanding access to credit. While some financial institutions write down risk through financial engineering in the secondary markets, the community-development finance industry attracts investors, who may capture higher returns elsewhere, by absorbing risk and or guaranteeing financial returns. This happens in a few ways. The community-development finance community shapes policy to create and preserve programs, it builds reserves of patient capital by engaging private philanthropy and other financial partners in pooling resources for long-term low investment, and it builds community-development technical capacity to successfully implement projects. These activities give the community-development finance industry an important and powerful role in shaping community-development practice (McDermott 2004; Vidal 1997).

The federal government adopted economic inclusion approaches in the 1970s. In the wake of continued inner-city disinvestment it considered how to fund inner-city development. To attract private investment, it leveraged 7.4 million federal dollars to create the Opportunity Funding Corporation (OFC) ("Opportunity Funding Corp" n.d.). OFC's objective was to attract private investment to spur economic development in low-income communities. Programs included supporting banks in these communities and working with local development corporations to identify projects for investment while OFC identified private investment dollars ("Opportunity Funding Corp" n.d.). OFC also envisioned creating a secondary market for economic development loans, similar to the role that the government-sponsored enterprises play in residential lending. Instead, OFC created two venture capital funds: Syndicated Communications, Inc. (SYNCOM) in 1977 and Fulcrum Venture Capital Corporation in 1978 that funded business development (Bunn 1984, 62; Doctors and Lockwood 1971). Today OFC and Opportunity Finance Network (OFN), a community-development finance industry association formed in 1995 that now has more than 200 members, provides support for the growing community-development finance industry. OFN advocates for national programs that provide income streams and thus liquidity to the community-development finance industry. These programs include the CDFI Fund, New Markets Tax Credits, Small Business Loan Fund, and the CDFI Bond Guarantee program. CDFIs also have access to Federal Home Loan Bank system loans, which provide reliable income streams (Opportunity Finance Network 2015).

As these programs broadened access to business investment in the 1970s, the Federal Home Loan Bank (FHLB) increased capital flows for home mortgage lending by expanding the number of Neighborhood Housing Services (NHS) organizations. The NHS idea, to provide community loans and technical assistance, came out of Pittsburgh community efforts to access capital in 1968. Initially, the FHLB trained S&L loan officers to make loans in urban areas with the objective of increasing access to credit. In 1973, the FHLB worked with the U.S. Department of Housing and Urban Development (HUD) to replicate the NHS model. Within a few years, the Federal Reserve Board, FDIC, and the Comptroller of the Currency joined them in the Urban Reinvestment Task Force to extend residential credit. The effort accessed credit from the 1974 Community Development Block Grant, NHS's revolving loan fund, and finally from Congress when it transformed the taskforce into the Neighborhood Reinvestment Corporation in 1978 (FDIC 1978; Anglin and Montezemolo 2004; CQ Almanac 1978; AllGov 2015). Today the Neighborhood Reinvestment Corporation is known as NeighborWorks America, a multifaceted organization with certified NeighborWorks housing counselors, community-development corporations (CDCs), and community-development financial institutions (CDFIs), its own secondary loan market, and a well-developed community-development training and technical assistance system (AllGov 2015).

Within a decade, what emerged in the 1970s as an effort to identify income streams to fund community economic development and housing had become a national effort to increase capital access for low-income communities and to provide technical assistance to build individual and community capacity. The Ford Foundation and developer James Rouse created similar organizations at the end of the 1970s and early 1980s. The Ford Foundation created the Local Initiatives Support Corporation (LISC) in 1979 to increase access to investment dollars and to provide technical assistance; insurance companies and private foundations provided the initial investment dollars (Teltsch 1986; Williams 1986). An earlier Ford Foundation discussion paper suggested the need for such organization in light of the reduction in federal community-development funding and a desire to increase CDC capacity (Anglin and Montezemolo 2004). Quoting Ford Foundation's Mitchell Sviridoff, who led LISC's creation, "There is no way we could replace the billions of dollars government has provided in this area in the past. . . . We do hope we can help community organizations make more effective use of what they will receive from government and in the process, help them increase their self-sufficiency and attract additional private dollars" (Teltsch 1981). A few years after LISC incorporated, Enterprise Community Partners emerged in 1982 with a similar structure and the objective of providing all people with the "opportunity for affordable hous-ing" (Enterprise Community Partners 2016; McDermott 2004). LISC and Enter-prise have grown exponentially since these initial efforts, with local offices in cities and towns around the country. They have built a capacity to shape public policy and developed close relationships with financial institutions and local community-development organizations.

As with the broader financial system, the community-development financial system needs to attract investment dollars to lend. The low-income housing tax credit (LIHTC) has been a primary source of affordable housing funding since 1986. The idea sprang out of a partnership between LISC and the Cleveland Housing Network, and the 1986 federal tax law created the national program (Domhoff 2005; Guthrie and McQuarrie 2005, 26–27; National Equity Fund 2015). Because LISC, Enterprise, and other firms syndicate the tax credits, which means that they bring tax credit investors together with the projects that use them, the LIHTC gave the intermediaries an "institutional power they never before had" (Guthrie and McQuarrie 2005, 30; Liou and Stroh 1998). That institutional power enables them to shape national community-development approaches.

Foundations and intermediaries further coordinated their activities to increase capacity through the National Community Development Initiative, created in 1991 to expand economic inclusion. Later referred to as Living Cities, the effort brings large philanthropies and financial institutions together to pool their investments. "Today, Living Cities is made up of 22 of the world's largest foundations and finan-cial institutions and represents the largest philanthropic collaborative dedicated to improving cities and the lives of low-income people in them" (Farias cited in Reardon 2011; McDermott 2004, 172). While earlier approaches funded organiza-tions that developed their objectives individually, these later approaches pool fund-ing to achieve a greater effect, centralizing resources into particular programs.

The U.S. Treasury Department further institutionalized the community-development financial infrastructure with the creation of the Community Develop-ment Financial Institutions (CDFI) Fund in 1994, which provides financing, liquid-ity, and technical assistance (Taub 1994; Community Development Financial Institutions Fund 2016). The 2016 federal budget request for CDFI is $233.5 million (U.S. Treasury 2016). The 2010 Small Business Jobs Act authorized the CDFI Bond Guarantee program, which allows the Treasury Department to issue "up to 10 bonds per year, each at a minimum of $100 million" (Lowry 2012, 17). The Federal Financing Bank buys them. Qualified entities issue money to CDFIs, which use the bonds for loans to community and community economic development projects in low-income and underserved areas (Lowry 2012).

Community-development finance plays a fundamental role in modern community-development practice in two ways. First, it has become an impor-tant community-development funding mechanism and its use has fueled the development of a now well-developed community-development financial intermediary sector. These organizations access public and private dollars, shape public policy to expand income flows to fund affordable housing and community economic development, and build community-development capacity by providing technical assistance. Second, it has been important in shaping the communities in which community-development actors work.

Economic Inclusion II

As the community-development finance system was building capacity to intermediate between capital and community, changes within the finance system made credit more accessible. The banking and finance industry moved from a traditional banking system that relied on FDIC-protected deposits in traditional depository banking institutions such as savings and loans, which had access to the Federal Reserve Discount Window, to a more flexible institutional arrangement that accessed capital through global financial markets. The changes included a shift from a local to a global financial system that connected home mortgage borrowing to global capital markets, policy changes that permitted new styles of lending including subprime and nontraditional loans, and new tools and processes such as credit scoring and automated underwriting, which made it easier to more finely assess risk and price credit and to originate loans more quickly and inexpensively.

Subprime loans, which have higher interest rates and fees to offset the risk of lending to borrowers with less-than-prime credit, expanded credit access in the 1990s. "In 1994, the $35 billion in subprime mortgages represented less than 5 percent of all mortgage originations. By 1999, subprime lending had increased to $160 billion—almost 13 percent of the mortgage origination market" (Bunce et al. 2000, 257). Technical innovations including credit scoring and automated underwriting made it possible to more finely assess risk and respond to loan demand and legislative changes during the 1980s made it possible for lenders to originate loans with higher interest rates and flexible terms (Mansfield 2000). The Resolution Trust Corporation's efforts to move underperforming, complicated assets off the books of the failing S&Ls helped to contribute to the development of the secondary markets for subprime lending (Ashton 2009). These and other developments made it possible to originate loans more quickly with fewer staff and to borrowers with different credit profiles (Poon 2009; Cordell, Huang, and Williams 2012). While some initially saw subprime lending as a potential way to democratize credit, high loss rates in the 1990s and 2000s challenge that aspiration (Chomsisengphet and Pennington-Cross 2006).

Mortgage demand grew again as the Federal Reserve lowered interest rates in the early 2000s and investors looking for safe and reliable investments sought out mortgage-backed securities (Levitan and Wachter 2012). To maintain lending volume as interest rates rose, lenders expanded the share of subprime and nontraditional mortgages such as interest-only mortgages, which allowed borrowers to pay only the interest or some portion of it for a set period of time. "Between the end of

2001 and 2006, nontraditional lending instruments such as option ARMs [adjustable-rate mortgages] offering negative amortization and interest-only mortgages with nonamortizing features went from under five percent of all nonprime originations to over fifty percent" (McCoy, Pavlov, and Wachter 2009, 504). As housing prices increased, more flexible loan products made it possible for borrowers to purchase by lowering monthly payments and or underwriting rules. This style of lending assumed that borrowers could refinance or sell their properties, but these actions became hard to do when credit dried up and housing prices declined. Loose underwriting at the height of the speculative lending boom and fraud further contributed to poor loan performance. While many people accessed low-cost credit during this period, some borrowers found themselves in foreclosure. The recession, declining housing prices, and tightened underwriting contributed to continuing housing market challenges in some places.

Some communities have since struggled with boarded-up housing, housing-price decline, and the individual household challenges that are associated with foreclosure, frequent moves, impaired credit, and debt. These problems are experienced locally and individually and it is hard to assess the individual and community costs. Community-development organizations have responded in a myriad of ways. They have provided home loan counseling and credit repair, negotiated home purchases with financial institutions, rehabbed and marketed homes, become property managers when homes do not sell, tried to understand which homes in their neighborhood were in foreclosure, and explored what they could do to preserve their neighborhoods. The community-development finance system's intermediary position between capital and community enabled them to help people work through the foreclosure and subsequent financial crisis through new institutional and financial arrangements.

A daunting question remains about what produced the crisis and how the community-development field handles home homeownership in response. Whereas economic inclusion was the objective for decades, economic inclusion through the mainstream financial institutional structure led to less than positive outcomes for many. While some blame overly ambitious borrowers, another narrative is emerging that suggests that the demand for investment products—in short, speculation—drove demand. The speculation is related to the change from traditional to modern banking. In the past half-century, banking and finance changed from a predominantly local activity, in which depository banks made loans based on deposits, to a global financial system that connects borrowers and investors across the world. Securitization, the process of pooling income streams and issuing securities based on those income streams, made it possible for global investors to invest in a variety of instruments backed by any manner of underlying collateral. Property is difficult to invest in because it is rooted in place, and investing in it traditionally meant knowing a lot about it (Coakley 1994). Securitization makes it easier to invest in property because investors can easily purchase financial products such as securities while knowing little or nothing about the properties that make up the underlying collateral (Gotham 2006). While this can make borrowing less expensive and more accessible, there are concerns about how these processes expanded credit access, especially at the height of the speculative boom.

The government-sponsored enterprises (GSEs) originated the majority of mortgage-backed securities (MBS) until the mid-2000s, when private financial institutions, such as investment banks, increased their share. Historically, GSEs only securitized loans that met their cautious underwriting standards and their securities had the implicit backing of the U.S. government. Private institutions such as investment banks securitized some loans that did not meet those criteria, such as larger loans. Over time these private securitizers developed methods of securitization and credit enhancement that made it possible to pool and securitize the income streams from a variety of more risky mortgage products. The ability to sell secondary market financial products with high-cost underlying home mortgage collateral made it easier to sell more high-cost mortgages. Levitan and Wachter conclude that "the growth of private-label securitizations resulted in the oversupply of underpriced housing finance" (Levitan and Wachter 2012, 7). And they view the financial crisis as "caused by excessive supply of housing finance" (Levitan and Wachter 2012, 5).

The financial system had changed such that many communities were economically included. While most people were aware that housing prices had increased and housing demand was increased, few people realized what the landscape of housing finance looked like. Few knew that the share of nontraditional loans had grown dramatically or that nontraditional loans were used in the subprime market. Housing and community-development organizations and researchers typically use the Home Mortgage Disclosure Act (HMDA) to follow lending patterns, but HMDA provides little information about nontraditional loan terms and does not track loans through foreclosure. With no national foreclosure database and few if any state or local foreclosure databases, it was difficult to see foreclosure patterns before the crisis made them visible.

Making this lending even more opaque, some processes that made this style of lending possible took place in what is now referred to as the "shadow" banking sector. While difficult to define, the shadow banking sector is often defined as lending processes and or institutions that do not use FDIC deposit insurance or the Federal Reserve's Discount Window. FDIC insurance helps to prevent bank runs since consumers have little fear that money deposited in an FDIC-insured bank will disappear. The Discount Window allows lenders to borrow short term, often overnight at slightly higher rates, in the event that they run short, which helps to keep the banking system functional. The shadow banking system exceeded the amount of dollars commercial banks made in 1996 (Luttrell, Rosenblum, and Thies 2012). Because shadow banking institutions and processes do not directly use governmental protections, they could be considered more private and were subject to less regulation. In the wake of the foreclosure and financial crisis, researchers have learned more about this sector but few community-development actors or researchers understood the relationship between these banking system changes and urban and community development before the crisis.

Community Response to the Foreclosure Crisis

Community-development actors are diverse and they have responded to the foreclosure and financial crisis in different ways. Some community-development efforts have focused on getting vacant and abandoned housing back into use. These are place-based efforts that are committed to reducing abandonment as a neighborhood stabilization strategy. State and local actors like the National Vacant Properties Campaign work on policy to identify abandoned housing and to move those properties back into use. An increased interest in land trusts and land banking has accompanied these efforts. It is unclear whether land trusts will become central community-development tools. It is also unclear whether new strategies will emerge to reuse land that various entities have banked.

Some organizations have focused on loan counseling and supporting individual borrowers. While some CDCs provide housing counseling through the NeighborWorks umbrella, consumer agencies also offer home mortgage counseling. These community-development approaches focus on individuals rather than places. In some cases there is overlap within institutions but these are distinct efforts with different objectives and often-different funding streams. The Center for New York City Neighborhoods (CNYCN) offers a hybrid approach. It organized housing counseling and legal services efforts related to the foreclosure/financial crisis. CNYCN trains their networked counselors and facilitates communication between community-level service providers and financial institutions.

It has been difficult to understand the extent of the foreclosure crisis, to find funding and support for borrowers and communities, and to know what policies would improve lending in the future. The federal government addressed the foreclosure crisis by providing resources through the Neighborhood Stabilization Program and by instituting a variety of loan programs, but the effects have been limited. Communities meanwhile quickly became versed in foreclosure processes, learned how to gather data about foreclosure to understand what was happening in their neighborhoods and where it was happening, learned about securitization as they attempted to help borrowers, sought to purchase vacant homes, and tried to translate property conditions on the ground to financial institutions that serviced loans for amounts that far exceeded actual property value. But in many places it was difficult to find out what properties were in foreclosure or what had become REO—real estate owned by a financial institution. It was difficult to know which borrowers were in trouble until the foreclosure process started. And if community organizations successfully negotiated to purchase properties, which often meant not accessing properties with securitized mortgages, they still had to rehabilitate the property and find new buyers, which has been difficult in the credit market with many credit-impaired borrowers. Because of its intermediary role between capital and community, the community-development finance industry has played an important strategic role in resolving the foreclosure crisis. Industry actors have worked with borrowers and financial institutions to understand the foreclosure crisis, buy properties, provide loan counseling, support financial literacy, initiate larger projects to purchase loan pools and groups of properties and to restructure loans.

The foreclosure crisis overwhelmed many local community-development networks. More than seven years into the process it remains difficult to understand what properties are in foreclosure, which borrowers need assistance, and what strategies can best help individuals and communities. Even as community-based organizations responded to the foreclosure crisis, they continued to address a broad range of community needs. While many community-development actors depend on the state and private community-development infrastructure, many need more funding than these systems provide or they need funding for different purposes. Without state or philanthropic funding to meet their operational and or programmatic objectives, they have turned to an increasingly creative array of strategies to understand community problems, consider solutions, and create revenue streams through social business creation.

Other Community-Development Efforts

The demands on community-development organizations today are high. In addition to addressing the foreclosure and financial crises, community organizations find themselves continuing their bifurcated shadow state role. The state has continued to devolve responsibility to community organizations and the state and private actors rely on community organizations to represent communities and to relay information to communities. Community-based organizations meanwhile work on an array of topical issues including parks, community economic development, community food security, crime, housing development, education, small business development, financial literacy, education as a second language (ESL), tutoring, adult education, addressing a seemingly endless list of ongoing community needs.

In the last few years, there has been increasing interest in partnering community organizations with institutions such as schools and medical centers. Community-based organizations and health care institutions are expanding connections to improve health, reduce health care costs, and reduce the costs associated with repeated hospitalization. There is a burgeoning movement to partner community-based organizations with local schools to provide support to families to address nonschool barriers that make it hard for children to do well in school. Community schools provide a suite of support services for children and adults that include some mix of health care, tutoring, food, nutrition and access, ESL classes, and job training and GSE courses. The U.S. Department of Education's Full-Service Community

Schools Program supports these initiatives, as do some private funders. The federal government's Promise Neighborhoods Initiative embodies similar ideas. Promise Neighborhoods and many of the other efforts discussed above depend on ambitious data collection and analysis that requires that community-development organizations also have high-level research capacity.

Meanwhile, in communities across the country, community-based organizations have adopted an eclectic and pragmatic set of programs to address community needs. Elijah's Promise is a community organization that has evolved from a local soup kitchen into a creative and comprehensive community food organization in New Brunswick, New Jersey. It provides culinary job training, creates jobs, provides food education, runs a café, and opened a market for produce and products made in New Jersey. The mix of activities ensures that people who need food get it, that education and training form the backbone of efforts to move people from poverty, and that their business efforts generate money to support programs while providing job opportunities. Elijah's Promise redistributes income and wages within the community through donations, sales, and volunteers who glean produce, chop, cook, serve food, clean up, compost waste, and donate food and other materials. They address food insecurity and the poverty that is at the heart of it. Elijah's Promise is just one of many double and triple bottom line businesses that now add revenue-generating programs to fund poverty alleviation and a broad array of programs to address it. These efforts are made possible by countless volunteer efforts and donated materials. Elijah's Promise and community-development organizations across the country are creating creative and pragmatic approaches to address community needs within the actually existing conditions in which they work. But none of this is easy and community-based organizations find themselves taking on many new areas of work as demands increase and resources shrivel. These efforts also entail organizational risk.

Community Development in the Age of Obama

In many ways, community development in the age of Obama reflects the systems and processes that were put into place decades ago as the country experienced economic restructuring and the government turned increasingly to markets to meet social needs. As the state withdrew from social funding, private philanthropy and community organizations stepped in. Given that many communities and individuals lacked access to credit, increasing access to it became an important focus of community-development work. Alongside these developments, transformations in the mainstream financial sector incorporated people and many communities where community-development organizations work into the economic system. For some this was a positive development but for many individuals and communities, they have since struggled with the effects of the foreclosure and financial crisis. And the community-development field has adapted to provide much needed services for individuals and communities in a difficult financial environment.

Community-development organizations have also expanded their range of services, have become ever more important information conduits into communities, and developed new programmatic strategies to generate revenue to meet community needs. But the breadth of service provision and the need to create revenue-generating "businesses" to sustain services stretches community-development organizations in ways that increase the risk of organizational failure. Community-development organizations continue to operate in a context of increasing need and decreasing resources.

References

AllGov. 2015. "NeighborWorks America." http://www.allgov.com/departments/independent-agen cies/neighborworks-america?agencyid=7447.

Anglin, Roland V., and Susanna C. Montezemolo. 2004. "Supporting the Community Development Movement: The Achievements and Challenges of Intermediary Organizations." In *Building the Organizations that Build Communities: Strengthening the Capacity of Faith- and Community-Based Development Organizations,* ed. Roland V. Anglin, 55–72. Washington, D.C.: Department of Housing and Urban Development. http://www.huduser.org/publica tions/pdf/BuildOrgComms/SectionI_Paper4.pdf.

Ashton, Philip. 2009. "Appetite for Yield: The Anatomy of the Subprime Mortgage Crisis." *Environment and Planning A* 41 (6):1420-1441.

Bunce, Harold L., Debbie Gruenstein, Christopher E. Herbert, and Randall M. Scheessele. 2000. "Subprime Foreclosures: The Smoking Gun of Predatory Lending?" Paper presented at the U.S. Department of Housing and Urban Development conference "Housing Policy in the New Millennium," Crystal City, Virginia.

Bunn, Curtis. 1984. "Pumping Dollars into Black Ventures." *Black Enterprise* 15 (3): 60–62. https:// books.google.com/books?id=wV8EAAAAMBAJ&pg=PA60&lpg=PA60&dq=ofc+venture +capital+funds&source=bl&ots=RPd19PXALm&sig=GiL7tP53deIw-LYZxNWOJeo_vyM &hl=en&sa=X&ei=6YC1VMn7KLK1sQT5jYLoBg&ved=0CEUQ6AEwBA#v=onepage&q =ofc%20venture%20capital%20funds&f=false

Chomsisengphet, Souphala, and Anthony Pennington-Cross. 2006. "The Evolution of the Subprime Mortgage Market." *Federal Reserve Bank of St. Louis Review* 88 (1): 31–56.

Coakley, J. 1994. "The Integration of Property and Financial Markets." *Environment and Planning A* 26 (5): 697–713.

Community Development Financial Institutions Fund. 2016. "What Does the CDFI Fund Do?" https://www.cdfifund.gov/Pages/default.aspx.

Cordell, Larry, Yilin Huang, and Meredith Williams. 2012. "Collateral Damage: Sizing and Assessing the Subprime CDO Crisis." Working paper No. 11–30/R. Federal Reserve Bank of Philadelphia.

CQ Almanac. 1978. "Neighborhood Preservation." Washington, D.C.: Congressional Quarterly, 154–55. https://library.cqpress.com/cqalmanac/document.php?id=cqal77-1202014.

Doctors, Samuel, and Sharon Lockwood. 1971. "Opportunity Funding Corporation: An Analysis." *Law and Contemporary Problems* 36 (2): 227–37. http://scholarship.law.duke.edu/lcp/vol36 /iss2/6.

Domhoff, G. William. 2005. "The Ford Foundation in the Inner City: Forging an Alliance with Neighborhood Activists." *Who Rules America?* http://www2.ucsc.edu/whorulesamerica /local/ford_foundation.html.

Enterprise Community Partners. 2016. "Our Founders." *Enterprisecommunity.com.* http://www .enterprisecommunity.com/about/history/about-our-founders.

Fainstein, Susan, and Mia Gray. 1997. "Economic Development and Strategies for the Inner City: The Need for Governmental Intervention." In *The Inner City: Urban Poverty and Economic*

Development in the Next Century, ed. Thomas D. Boston and Catherine L. Ross, 29–38. New Brunswick: Transaction.

FDIC (Federal Deposit Insurance Corporation). 1978. "Housing and Community Development Amendments of 1978." https://www.fdic.gov/regulations/laws/rules/8000-4600.html.

Gotham, Kevin F. 2006. "The Secondary Circuit of Capital Reconsidered: Globalization and the US Real Estate Sector." *American Journal of Sociology* 112 (1): 231–75.

Guthrie, Doug, and Michael McQuarrie. 2005. "Privatization and the Social Contract. Corporate Welfare and Low-Income Housing in the United States since 1986." *Research in Political Sociology* 14: 15–51.

———. 2008. "Providing for the Public Good: Corporate-Community Relations in the Era of the Receding Welfare State." *City & Community* 7 (2): 113–39.

Levitan, Adam J., and Susan M. Wachter. 2012. "Explaining the Housing Bubble." *Georgetown Law Journal,* 100 (4): 1177–1258. Available at Social Science Research Network Electronic Paper Collection, http://papers.ssrn.com/sol3/papers.cfm?abstract_id=1669401.

Liou, Thomas, and Robert Stroh. 1998. "Community Development Intermediary Systems in the United States: Origins, Evolution, and Functions." *Housing Policy Debate* 9 (3): 575–94.

Lowry, Sean. 2012. "Community Development Financial Institutions (CDFI) Fund: Programs and Policy Issues." *Congressional Research Service.* 7–5700 R42770. https://www.fas.org/sgp/crs/misc/R42770.pdf.

Luttrell, David, Harvey Rosenblum, and Jackson Thies. 2012. "Understanding the Risks Inherent in Shadow Banking." Staff papers no. 18. Federal Reserve Bank of Dallas. http://www.dallasfed.org/assets/documents/research/staff/staff1203.pdf.

Mansfield, Cathy L. 2000. "The Road to Subprime 'HEL' Was Paved with Good Congressional Intentions: Usury Deregulation and the Subprime Home Equity Market." 51 S.C.L. Rev. 473.

McCoy, Patricia, Andrey Pavlov, and Susan Wachter. 2009. "Systemic Risk through Securitization: The Result of Deregulation and Regulatory Failure." *Connecticut Law Review* 41 (4): 493–541.

McDermott, Mark. 2004. "National Intermediaries and Local Community Development Corporation Networks: A View from Cleveland." *Journal of Urban Affairs* 26 (2): 171–76.

National Equity Fund. 2015. "Who We Are." *Nfinc.org.* http://www.nefinc.org/whoweare.html.

Opportunity Finance Network. OFN's Public Policy Work. Accessed January 12, 2015. http://ofn.org/ofns-public-policy-work#CDFI-Opportunity-Agenda.

Opportunity Funding Corporation. n.d. "Opportunity Funding Corporation: Facts and History. http://ofc.thurgoodmarshallfund.net/index.php/about/facts-and-history.

Poon, Martha A. 2009. "From New Deal Institutions to Capital Markets: Commercial Consumer Risk Scores and the Making of Subprime Mortgage Finance." *Accounting, Organizations and Society* 34 (5): 654–74.

Pozsar, Zoltan, Tobias Adrian, Adam Ashcraft, and Hayley Boesky. 2010. "Shadow Banking." Staff report no. 458. Federal Reserve Bank of New York.

Reardon, Patrick T. 2011. "Six LISC and Institute Leaders Reflect on Living Cities. LISC Institute for Comprehensive Community Development. http://www.instituteccd.org/news/3135.

Straka, John W. 2000. "A Shift in the Mortgage Landscape: The 1990s Move to Automated Credit Evaluations." *Journal of Housing Research* 11 (2): 207–32.

Taub, Richard. 1994. *Community Capitalism: The South Shore Bank's Strategy for Neighborhood Revitalization.* Boston: Harvard Business School Press.

Teltsch, Kathleen. 1981. "Funds Are Packaged to Aid Communities." *New York Times,* June 7.

———. 1986. "Foundation Helps Renew City Areas." *New York Times,* December 7. http://www.nytimes.com/1986/12/07/us/foundation-helps-renew-city-areas.html?smid=pl-share.

U.S. Treasury. 2016. Community Development Financial Institutions Fund. https://www.treasury.gov/about/budget-performance/budget-in-brief/Documents/11.%20CDFI%20FY%202016%20BiB%20Final.pdf.

Vidal, Avis C. 1997. "Can Community Development Re-invent Itself? The Challenges of Strengthening Neighborhoods in the 21st Century." *Journal of the American Planning Association* 63 (4): 429–38.

Williams, Winston. 1986. "Rebuilding from the Grass Roots Up." *New York Times,* December 21.

12

THE INCOMPLETENESS OF COMPREHENSIVE
COMMUNITY REVITALIZATION

TODD SWANSTROM

Jane Jacobs famously argued that cities cannot be understood using the methods of the hard sciences; the internal workings of cities are not like billiard balls in motion that can be analyzed using linear causal models or statistical techniques.

> Cities happen to be problems in organized complexity, like the life sciences. They present "situations in which a half-dozen or even several dozen quantities are all varying simultaneously *and in subtly interconnected ways.*" (Jacobs 1961)[1]

Based on a comprehensive study of neighborhood dynamics in Chicago, Robert Sampson recently concluded that neighborhoods cannot be understood by isolating variables using statistical controls and then adding up the individual causal relationships. Rather, neighborhoods need to be studied as systems (within larger systems) characterized by feedback loops, tipping points, and organizational capacities that drive neighborhood change. Policy interventions need to take this into account. "Communities can serve as a unit not just of social science theory and method, but of holistic policy intervention that prioritizes the interconnected social whole" (Sampson 2012, 421).

Comprehensive approaches to neighborhood revitalization are now widely accepted by community-development practitioners and are embedded in national urban policy. Partly this consensus reflects acceptance of the fact that government cannot do it alone. Governments need to partner with private businesses and non-profits in order to turn neighborhoods around. The consensus on a comprehensive approach stems also from the recognition that "siloed" policy interventions fail, especially in distressed neighborhoods. New housing alone will not turn around a distressed neighborhood. Unless the other elements that support housing demand are improved, such as crime rates, schools, transportation, and jobs, building new housing may only lead to vacant housing units in other parts of the community.

Based on a holistic understanding of neighborhoods, the following elements are necessary, if not alone sufficient, for successful neighborhood revitalization:

1. The initiative must be based on a plan that simultaneously addresses the social deficits and problems in the community at the same time that it leverages the assets of the area in a market-savvy fashion.
2. The plan must grow out of an extensive process of civic engagement so that all major stakeholders in the community accept it as legitimate, or at least do not oppose it.
3. The plan must have the support and collaboration of public, private, and nonprofit organizations, inside and outside the community, with sufficient resources to accomplish the major objectives and sustain itself over the long term. (Comprehensive community-revitalization initiatives generally require at least three years to produce significant results.)

To devise and implement a comprehensive revitalization plan satisfying the three elements outlined above requires considerable community capacity. It requires expertise in both economic and social policy, the ability to meaningfully engage low-income (often politically alienated) residents, and the capacity to keep multiple institutional partners focused on the collaboration over many years.

Community capacity has two main components: (1) organizational and (2) civic. *Organizational* capacity is the ability of individual organizations to sustain themselves, adapt to new circumstances, and deliver services efficiently and effectively in support of the plan. *Civic* capacity refers to the ability of organizations to collaborate with each other, strategically aligning resources in support of the community plan.[2] Civic capacity requires independent organizations to solve collective action problems without the coercive power of the state but rather through relations of trust and mutual self-interest. It is very easy for civic collaborations to unravel when leadership changes or institutions see their self-interest differently. Civic collaborations are especially challenging when confronting issues that require the redistribution of resources.

The Obama administration has embraced a comprehensive, collaborative approach to neighborhood revitalization. At the same time, the administration recognizes a serious "capacity gap" between what needs to be done for comprehensive community initiatives to succeed and what local actors on the ground are capable of doing. To address this capacity gap, the administration has implemented a series of capacity-building initiatives. In this chapter I review the comprehensive community-building and capacity-building policies of the Obama administration, examine how they are working on the ground in one community, and draw lessons from that experience for national urban policy.

The Origins of Comprehensive, Collaborative Approaches in Urban Policy

From the New Deal to the War on Poverty urban policy was driven by public agencies that did not stress local citizen engagement in planning and tended to focus on one policy silo at a time. Public housing, begun in 1937, was controlled by local public housing authorities run by boards appointed by local elected officials and concentrated on the physical improvement and affordability of housing. Urban Renewal, begun in 1949, also was also controlled by top-down public agencies and focused on physical improvements and economic development. Neither program gave local residents much of a say and neither one approached revitalization holistically, focusing primarily on physical improvements and/or economic development.

The comprehensive approach to urban revitalization can be traced to the 1960s War on Poverty.[3] As would be the pattern many times in the ensuing fifty years, national foundations pioneered comprehensive, collaborative approaches to neighborhood revitalization and the federal government followed with policies designed to spread the philanthropic initiatives across the nation.[4] In the 1960s, the Ford Foundation's Gray Areas Project funded nonprofit corporations in a number of cities that took a broader approach to revitalization, integrating social services with job training and physical redevelopment. Drawing from the community organizing tradition, many of these projects empowered local residents to guide the planning. Robert Kennedy was influenced by these ideas and his early support of community-development corporations (CDCs) grew out of this work. Lyndon Johnson embraced a comprehensive approach as part of his War on Poverty. The Economic Opportunity Act of 1964 established the Community Action Program (CAP) with the goal of "maximum feasible participation" by low-income residents of the community. CAP blew up politically when mayors objected to losing control over federal monies, but the idea of comprehensive services for poor communities remains to this day in community action agencies (CAAs) around the country. Model Cities, begun in 1966, is another example of a comprehensive approach to community revitalization that included extensive citizen participation.

The act establishing the U.S. Department of Housing and Urban Development (HUD) in 1965 articulated a broad mission for the new cabinet-level department:

> The Congress hereby declares that the general welfare and security of the nation and the health and living standards of our people require, as a matter of national purpose, sound development of the nation's communities and metropolitan areas in which the vast majority of people live and work.
>
> To carry out such purpose . . . the Congress finds the establishment of an executive department is desirable . . . to encourage the solution of problems of housing, urban development, and mass transportation through State, county, town, village and private action, including promotion of interstate, regional, and metropolitan cooperation. (Quoted in Brophy and Godsil 2009, 123)

The rightward movement of Congress and resistance by federal agencies and local governments to taking direction from the federal government gradually pushed HUD away from its original mission to a focus on housing, especially low-income housing. The switch to market-based mechanisms, such as housing vouchers, eliminated requirements for local planning based on citizen engagement.[5] The folding of seven categorical grant programs into the Community Development Block Grant (CDBG) program in 1974 permitted localities to take a comprehensive approach, but it put decision-making power in the hands of local elected officials and had weak requirements for civic engagement. An important exception to the withdrawal of the federal government from direct support of comprehensive community initiatives is the Empowerment Zone/Enterprise Community (EZ/EC) initiative passed by Congress in 1993. EZ/EC incorporated market-based incentives, but it also required a comprehensive approach with extensive citizen engagement.[6]

Starting in the late 1980s, national foundations began investing heavily in comprehensive community initiatives (CCIs).[7] They funded local initiatives directly and indirectly through intermediaries, such as the Local Initiatives Support Corporation (LISC), Enterprise Community Partners, and Living Cities. According to Anne Kubisch in *Voices from the Field III,* foundations invested over $1 billion in CCIs between 1990 and 2010 (Kubisch 2010, 10).[8]

Foundation funding is crucial because it often serves as social venture capital that enables communities to staff an initiative, engage citizens, and devise a plan. Over 90 percent of the funding for CCIs, however, comes from the public sector (Kubisch 2010, 10).[9] Government funding for housing and community development has evolved from direct government provision and categorical grants with tight restrictions to a set of complex policy tools that can be challenging for even sophisticated organizations. Direct production of housing by HUD fell from 248,000 units in 1977 to only 18,000 by 1996. But during this same period alternative funding mechanisms emerged that enabled private and nonprofit developers to build low-income housing. The passage of the low-income housing tax credit (LIHTC) in 1986 was a watershed. By 2005 the LIHTC program was funding more than 130,000 new apartment units annually (Erickson 2009, xii–xv). The LIHTC program is supplemented by federal historic preservation tax credits, and many states have enacted their own low-income and historic tax credit programs that piggyback on the federal credits. Besides CDBG, CCIs can access funds from the HOME Investments Partnership Program, which requires that at least 15 percent of funds be set aside for community-based nonprofits.[10] Through various programs run by the U.S. Department of the Treasury, including the New Markets Tax Credit program, Community Development Financial Institutions (CDFIs) provide funds for community health centers, charter schools, and economic development projects in low-income communities. The Community Reinvestment Act (CRA) requires that federally regulated lending institutions "meet the credit needs of their communities." Comprehensive community initiatives can call on banks for grants, low-interest loans, or other contributions that help them receive favorable CRA ratings from federal regulators. (CRA is discussed in more detail later.)

The challenge of the new federal policy toolbox is that local groups require substantial expertise and sophisticated networking to access these subsidies and utilize them effectively, especially when many projects involve a half a dozen or more subsidies. As David Erickson has documented, decentralized housing networks composed of public, private, and nonprofit actors have evolved to creatively solve problems and coordinate action in the complicated new policy environment (Erickson 2009).[11] A LIHTC application requires significant up-front investment in time and money for specialized consultants, actually selling the tax credits requires an intermediary with national investment connections, and the project must be monitored for many years or investors will lose their tax break.

A sophisticated community-development system has evolved since the 1980s to increase the capacity of local communities to do comprehensive community development. Community-development corporations (CDCs) are key actors in the system, growing from a handful in the 1960s to 4,600 by 2005 (NCCED 2005). CDCs often play the role of coordinating the many actors in a community around a plan. Many CDCs are small and underfinanced, however. National intermediaries such as LISC, Enterprise, and NeighborWorks have worked to build the organizational capacity of CDCs. In 1991, seven foundations funded the National Community Development Initiative (NCDI), a ten-year effort to increase the capacity of CDCs in twenty-three cities around the country. Including all three phases, approximately $254 million was raised, with $101 going to grants and the rest as loans.[12] LISC has funded CCIs in almost one hundred neighborhoods in twenty-four metropolitan areas around the nation and has established an Institute for Comprehensive Community Development that disseminates knowledge on best practices. Local intermediaries, such as Neighborhood Progress, Inc. in Cleveland, also enhance the capacity of communities to do comprehensive community development.[13]

Obama Urban Policy: A Comprehensive Approach

As a former community organizer in Chicago, Obama clearly understands the problems of distressed urban neighborhoods. Early in his campaign for the presidency Obama spoke in Anacostia, a poor neighborhood in Washington, D.C., advocating that the federal government replicate the Harlem Children's Zone program in twenty cities. "If poverty is a disease that infects the entire community in the form of unemployment and violence, failing schools and broken homes, then we can't just treat those symptoms in isolation. We have to heal that entire community" (quoted in MacGillis 2007).

Urban policy, however, has not been a high priority of the Obama administration. The president said little about urban issues in his reelection campaign, and funding for urban programs continues to decline.[14] Much of the blame must go to a deadlocked Congress and the unwillingness of Republicans to support any new funding for cities. The Democrats did control both houses of Congress from 2009 to 2011, but they were preoccupied with the economic crisis and the Great Recession strained the federal budget.

Within political and fiscal constraints, however, the Obama administration has initiated a series of bold pilot programs designed to increase the capacity of local actors to devise and implement comprehensive community-revitalization initiatives. For the most part, these programs have not included new funds but have reallocated existing authorized funding to competitive grant programs that incent comprehensive approaches. Collaborating with other departments, including the Department of Transportation (DOT) and the Environmental Protection Agency (EPA), HUD Secretary Shaun Donovan worked to put the "ud" back in HUD and his successor, Julián Castro, will probably follow a similar path.[15]

A month after taking office, President Obama issued an executive order creating the White House Office of Urban Affairs, whose central mission was to coordinate federal departments and agencies around comprehensive urban revitalization strategies. Eight months after Obama took office, the White House issued a memorandum to all departments and agency heads calling for "locally driven," "place based" policies that "break down federal 'silos'" (Orszag et al. 2009). In September of 2010 the administration announced the White House Neighborhood Revitalization Initiative (NRI). Acknowledging that little new funding would get through Congress, NRI was framed as a strategy, not a program, which would "improve alignment among Federal departments that direct resources to neighborhoods in distress" (Office of Urban Affairs 2011).

As part of the NRI the Obama administration initiated a series of grant programs to support comprehensive community initiatives (Table 12.1). The Sustainable Communities Initiative (SCI), a collaboration of HUD, DOT, and EPA, received $100 million in FY 2010 and $95 million in FY 2011.[16] The goal of SCI was to break down the silos that prevent federal agencies from collaborating in support of plans that link neighborhoods and regions in a sustainable fashion. Ultimately, collaborations in seventy-four metropolitan areas were funded.[17] Recognizing the need for capacity building, the SCI included planning grants as well as implementation grants. The planning grants were designed to help metropolitan areas enhance their civic capacity to collaborate around regional plans for sustainability. Depending on availability, metropolitan consortia could then apply for implementation grants. Planning grants for local actors to convene and construct comprehensive community revitalization plans were also built into other grant programs, such as Promise Neighborhoods and Choice Neighborhoods.

One program that explicitly addressed the capacity gap is the Strong Cities, Strong Communities (SC2) program, a collaboration of fourteen federal agencies led by the White House. As of this writing, fourteen cities have been chosen to participate in SC2. SC2 cities do not receive any direct federal funding, but winning cities do receive technical advice and expertise from federal interagency teams that

TABLE 12.1. OBAMA ADMINISTRATION COMPREHENSIVE COMMUNITY REVITALIZATION INITIATIVES

Initiative	Primary Administrative Agency	Mission
Choice Neighborhoods	HUD	Building on the work of HOPE VI Choice requires applicants to develop a "comprehensive neighborhood revitalization strategy" based on extensive community involvement.
Promise Neighborhoods	Education	Inspired by the Harlem Children's Zone, it supports cradle-to-career services for children in distressed neighborhoods.
Community Health Centers	Health and Human Services	Supports community-controlled organizations that provide health and related services to medically underserved communities.
Byrne Criminal Justice Innovation	Justice	Supports cross-sector partnerships to address the drivers of crime in persistent "hot spot" locations which are thwarting progress toward neighborhood revitalization.

will help them access federal resources as part of comprehensive revitalization plans. Mid-career professionals in federal government will be placed in the cities to facilitate the connections. Another capacity building program is the Building Neighborhood Capacity Program (BNCP), which provides capacity building assistance to eight neighborhoods around the nation (BNCP n.d.).

The Obama administration programs address all three of the elements discussed earlier that are necessary for successful comprehensive community revitalization. Funding for the new generation of urban programs, however, is completely inadequate to reach all, or even most, distressed communities and knit them back into the metropolitan fabric. As pilot programs, however, they should be carefully evaluated to determine if they represent valid models for expanded urban programs when political and fiscal conditions for progressive urban policy improve. Looking at the experience of one community can help us to understand the promise and the pitfalls of the Obama administration's approach.

24:1: Lessons from the Field

Suburban poverty is a new frontier for comprehensive community initiatives. As Alan Berube and Elizabeth Kneebone demonstrate, more poor people now live in suburbs than in central cities, and suburban poverty is growing much faster than urban poverty (Kneebone and Berube 2013). 24:1 is a comprehensive community initiative in an inner-ring suburban school district just outside the St. Louis that is poor (28.9 percent poverty rate in 2010), with a declining (down 9 percent from 2000 to 2010), largely black (83 percent African American in 2010) population, and a weak housing market.[18]

Margaret Weir argues that disadvantaged suburbs suffer from low levels of organizational and civic capacity. They have the same poverty and isolation from economic opportunities that hold down many inner-city neighborhoods, but they have the added disadvantage of low "political-organizational endowments," encompassing such factors as "the fiscal capacity of political jurisdictions, the presence of public services such as clinics and hospitals, and the array and capacity of nonprofit organizations, which deliver many key social-welfare services" (Weir 2011, 244). Local foundations are not as heavily invested in suburbs as they are in central cities (Reckhow and Weir 2012). Fragmented suburban governments weaken civic capacity by increasing the transaction costs of collaboration (Feiock 2004). Separate suburban governments generate distinct parochial interests, which inhibits broader collaboration. Weak administrative structures and frequent turnover of elected officials undermine the ability of local governments to collaborate and build trust over time. The 24:1 initiative faces all of these challenges: the name comes from the twenty-four municipalities that touch on the Normandy School District footprint. Many of these governments are small (average population 1,834 in 2010) and lack professionalism.[19]

What the Normandy area does have is Beyond Housing, a high-capacity regional nonprofit with a staff of over a hundred that has worked on place-based initiatives in the Normandy area for over fifteen years. In 2010 Beyond Housing extended its place-based work to the entire Normandy School District footprint under the banner of 24:1. After convening fifty-two community meetings with over four hundred attendees and a planning committee involving over a hundred participants, Beyond Housing announced a comprehensive revitalization plan with forty specific strategies in eleven focus areas.[20] 24:1 is a cutting-edge example of comprehensive community revitalization of the type the Obama administration would like to clone around the country. Indeed, 24:1 was recognized by the White House in its report on the Neighborhood Revitalization Initiative (Office of Urban Affairs 2011, 6).

In its short, three-year existence, Beyond Housing has seen over $50 million invested, enabling the following accomplishments:[21]

- It built the first full-service grocery store in the area in decades (work on this began well before 24:1 started).
- In an area awash in payday lenders, it opened a full-service bank branch located in a new senior housing complex.
- It provides every kindergartner in the Normandy School District with a free $500 college savings account ($288,000 invested) and 173 students are enrolled in savings accounts that provide $3 for every dollar saved.
- Beyond Housing has successfully funneled over $2.9 million in home repairs and $18 million in new home development.
- As part of 24:1 Beyond Housing staffed the Municipal Government Partnership, enabling city governments to improve services and coordinate economic development, through programs such as creating a Police Co-op across municipalities to do community policing and pooling CDBG funds to demolish roughly fifty dangerous and blighted homes.

Transit-Oriented Development as an Antipoverty Program

One of the priorities of the Obama administration has been to promote workforce housing as part of transit-oriented development (TOD) around transit stations. The light rail system in St. Louis runs through the Normandy area. The experience of 24:1 in working to do TOD in a weak market suburban setting highlights the promise and pitfalls of comprehensive community development.

As part of the process to create the 24:1 plan, residents complained that there must be some better use other than parking for the sea of asphalt that surrounded the Rock Road Transit Station. Hearing the desire of residents to reimagine the space, Beyond Housing began investigating the possibility of TOD at the Rock Road Station. It soon became clear that TOD had the potential to address the unemployment problem in the area. The Rock Road Station is located in Pagedale, which had a 17 percent unemployment rate in 2012. By developing workforce housing within a mixed-use TOD, Beyond Housing will enable residents to access almost 142,000 jobs within a half mile of stations on the light rail system in St. Louis City and County, including over 46,155 mid-level jobs that residents of the area, with limited education, would qualify for.[22] If some households in the TOD were able to give up a car or go from two cars to one, they could save about $8,000 a year.[23] Improving access to decent-paying jobs and lowering living expenses are two ways comprehensive community initiatives can help pull families out of poverty.

Beyond Housing began by funding a predevelopment study that showed that there would be a demand for living near a transit station but substantial subsidies would be required to make it work.[24] Beyond Housing then initiated a civic engagement process that included 300 engagement touches (face-to-face meetings or discussions) and over 4,000 individual pieces of feedback (some as the result of an interactive installation by a local artist). The first reaction of many local residents

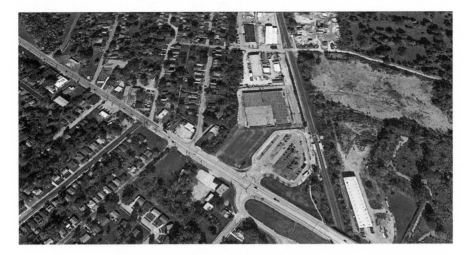

Figure 12.1. The Rock Road Station is now surrounded by a parking lot and vacant, underutilized land. Photograph: Google Images.

to the proposed TOD was "who would want to live near a transit station?" If housing was to be built there, 51 percent of those attending the first meeting preferred single-family housing. Higher-density housing was viewed negatively as too much like "the projects."

Initially, planners were taken aback by community opposition to higher-density housing but they presented information to residents on how higher density would support walkability and retail—as well as make the project more financially feasible. An evaluation of the civic engagement process found that 69 percent of the participants viewed multifamily housing under four stories more favorably as a result of the process. Participants' opinions also became more favorable toward retail and restaurants, as well as biking and pedestrian trails. Planners also changed their minds after hearing from the community. The Normandy area is not New York or Chicago. TOD needs to be adapted to the scale of inner-ring suburbs. Hearing the community's preferences for less dense development, Beyond Housing altered the plan to include single-family homes and duplexes. They developed a two-phase plan that gradually incorporates more density and as a result of the community input they included a community center, public bathrooms, more shade trees, places to eat, and other amenities not included in the original plan.

The final plan for the Rock Road TOD is a creative compromise synthesizing the preference of local residents, market imperatives, and planning principles. Implementing the plan will be challenging but Beyond Housing has made considerable progress. It has secured funding from an anonymous donor to purchase the land, and the local city government has agreed to pass an overlay zoning ordinance to permit the mixed-use development once the land is purchased. Beyond Housing is considering ten different subsidies and funding sources. Given new developments nearby and Beyond Housing's track record, there is good reason to believe the Rock Road TOD will become a reality. But the organizational and civic capacity required to pull off the project is truly extraordinary—especially in the face of a recent designation of the area as being in a flood plain.

The Limits of Comprehensive Community Revitalization: The Capacity Gap

The Obama administration's approach to urban policy is based on sound principles: severely distressed neighborhoods need to be treated holistically; federal agencies need to coordinate across policy silos; action needs to be based on a plan rooted in deep civic engagement; the plan needs to address social deficits and market realities; neighborhoods need to be linked to regional opportunity structures; and, finally, given the complexity of CCIs, enhancing the organizational and civic capacity of local actors should be a high priority of federal policy. The 24:1 case demonstrates that comprehensive community initiatives based on deep civic engagement can help distressed communities, even in challenging inner-ring suburbs.[25] The federal toolbox and Obama administration urban policies have been instrumental in the successes of 24:1. Clearly, the Obama administration is getting something right.

Having acknowledged the strengths of the Obama administration's approach, however, it must be said that there is something *radically incomplete* about Obama's urban policy. It is as almost if the federal government were saying to distressed neighborhoods—if you just became sufficiently comprehensive and collaborative in your approach, you could all lift yourselves up into healthy neighborhoods. But this is simply not true. First, the vast majority of distressed neighborhoods lack the extraordinary capacity necessary to devise and implement comprehensive revitalization plans. Even if they could develop that capacity, there would not be nearly enough federal, state, and local funds to implement their plans. Collaboration (no matter how comprehensive) is not enough.

Comprehensive community initiatives, like 24:1, are incredibly complex and demanding. Beyond Housing operates over thirty separate programs and coordinates over a hundred service providers that are active in the Normandy footprint. Civic engagement around the many different initiatives has involved hundreds of meetings and thousands of participants. Beyond Housing has become adept at using federal and state tools to fund its initiatives, including LIHTC to build affordable housing, CDBG to repair homes, Neighborhood Stabilization Program (NSP) funds to address foreclosures, and Federal Home Loan Bank funds for housing rehabilitation. Funds from the region's $4.8 million SCI grant were used to hire a Denver firm, with extensive experience in TOD, to do a preliminary land use plan for the Rock Road TOD.

Beyond Housing's success, however, begs the question of whether it can serve as a model for all distressed communities. Beyond Housing's success is rooted in its high organizational capacity, which is based, in turn, on its ability to hire energetic staff and outside consultants with expertise in key program areas, such as housing finance, civic engagement, and college savings accounts. Beyond Housing's organizational capacity building has been made possible by an anonymous investor who provided an initial $3 million grant to staff the 24:1 planning process and has continued to fund projects as needed, such as purchasing land for the Rock Road TOD. Clearly there are not enough funders in the St. Louis region to build this level of organizational capacity for every distressed neighborhood. And even if there were, not every organization could achieve the level of success that 24:1 achieved because the competition for public, private, and foundation community-development funding is zero-sum.

A recent anthology of best practices in comprehensive community development called for "routinizing the extraordinary" by identifying a community "quarter-back" that can coordinate all the functions that are necessary for comprehensive community collaboration (Erickson, Galloway, and Cytron 2012). The authors conclude that "any community can produce a quarterback." The authors are correct that we need capable quarterbacks, but I would submit that the number of distressed communities that are able to generate quarterbacks with sufficient capacity to devise and implement a comprehensive community revitalization plan is very small. A review of forty-eight major CCIs around the nation over a twenty-year period found that "many showed improvements in the well-being of individual residents who participated in programs in their target neighborhoods; but those programs did not produce population-level changes [such as reductions in poverty rates]" (Kubisch et al. 2010). Much of the reason why it is so difficult to turn around a distressed neighborhood with a CCI is that trends in the broader region can overwhelm local efforts.[26] Beside the limits of localism, however, the limits of capacity building in local communities present a huge challenge for CCIs.

Not only do we, as a nation, lack the capacity and political will to apply the comprehensive approach to all distressed neighborhoods, the effort to apply the approach in a context of limited resources creates its own disturbing inequalities. This 24:1 case highlights the challenge of uneven capacity. The Obama administration's model of urban revitalization relies on a partnership among public, private, and nonprofit actors, with much of the responsibility for coordinating complex place-based initiatives falling on local nonprofits, called lead agencies or quarterbacks. In effect, urban policy is "coproduced" with the assistance of local citizens and organizations. Elaine Sharp has observed that, under a coproduction model, public goods are distributed according to an "effort expended model," areas with the greatest capacity to contribute get the most government funding (Sharp 1990, 131).[27]

Capacity varies both within and among regions. With over one hundred staff, Beyond Housing is by far the highest-capacity nonprofit leading a comprehensive place-based initiative in the St. Louis metropolitan area. By contrast, more than 41 percent of all CDCs in the St. Louis region have two or fewer full-time employees

(Swanstrom and Guenther 2011, 16). No wonder Beyond Housing is able to capture a disproportionate share of the funding.

The capacity gap across metropolitan areas is just as large as the capacity gap within them. LISC has offices in thirty-one metropolitan areas around the country. If you happen to live in a disadvantaged community in one of those metropolitan areas, you are more likely to have a high-capacity CDC that can access federal and foundation grants. LISC prefers to work in metropolitan areas where local foundations commit significant resources to community development. (The same could be said of Enterprise, Living Cities, and other national intermediaries.) In short, metropolitan areas with large community foundations that invest in community development are more likely to attract national foundation funding.[28] In short, the comprehensive and collaborative approach to urban revitalization creates its cumulative inequalities based not on economic poverty but on organizational and civic poverty—though to be sure the two are highly correlated. Allocating resources based on local capacity does not meet minimal standards of fairness.

To its credit the Obama administration has recognized the capacity problem and is trying to address it with Choice Neighborhoods and Promise Neighborhoods planning grants and capacity-building programs, such as SC2. However, these efforts do not provide anywhere near the resources necessary to level the playing field. Few government programs provide the kind of flexible, long-term funding that the anonymous funder gave 24:1 to staff the initiative and do extensive civic engagement. Few city planning departments provide staff for civic engagement and neighborhood planning. As a result, most communities lack comprehensive community plans and end up pursuing, at best, isolated projects that help the community to cope with decline but not reverse it.

Critical Reflections: The Incompleteness of Comprehensive Collaboration

The Obama administration's emphasis on comprehensive approaches to revitalizing distressed neighborhoods, and especially its focus on capacity building, is sensible. We need comprehensive and collaborative initiatives to stop the downward spiral of distressed neighborhoods. The problem comes when this "moment" or part of effective community-development policy is mistaken for the whole.[29] Political forces are driving this narrow focus. Fear of suburban backlash to regional government causes political actors to fall back on neighborhood solutions. And in an age of partisan gridlock and deep distrust of government, policymakers are tempted to lift up collaboration and ignore conflict and the legitimate exercise of governmental authority.

More fundamental than the question of why disadvantaged communities do or do not have the capacity to devise and implement comprehensive revitalization plans is the question of why disadvantaged communities need such elaborate and expensive interventions in the first place. This question becomes even more acute when we acknowledge that the most disadvantaged communities need the most complex and comprehensive interventions. Severely disadvantaged neighborhoods, like the 24:1 area, require public, private, and nonprofit actors to coordinate interventions across the policy silos, simultaneously addressing crime, housing, education, jobs, health, municipal services, and transportation.

Most neighborhoods achieve healthy functioning without elaborate cross-silo interventions. Why is it that distressed neighborhoods require Herculean efforts at comprehensive policy collaboration to achieve healthy functioning? Disadvantaged neighborhoods need comprehensive interventions to stabilize themselves but *it was not a lack of comprehensive collaboration that caused them to decline in the first place.* Powerful federal, state, and local policies have tilted the playing field against older urban and minority neighborhoods, causing them to become areas of concentrated poverty and disinvestment. The policies and practices that have tilted the playing field include transportation policies that favor automobiles over public transit, walking, and biking; tax deductions that favor new homes over older homes and rental housing; exclusionary zoning laws that outlaw affordable housing in many suburban municipalities; and unequal funding of local public services and schools that disadvantage low-income and minority populations.[30] Comprehensive community collaborations are "swimming against the tide," in Alice O'Connor's resonant phrase, of "stealth" urban policies (O'Connor 1999).

The St. Louis metropolitan area is a case in point. Subsidized by a broad range of public policies, for many decades the region has built more new housing units on the suburban periphery than there were new households in the region (Bier and Post 2006). The inevitable effect has been population decline and housing abandonment in the older parts of the region, such as Normandy.[31] In the recent foreclosure epidemic, communities like the Normandy area were hit particularly hard. These neighborhoods suffered from high foreclosure rates not because they lacked comprehensive community plans but because a hole in the federal regulatory net enabled mortgage lenders to take advantage of vulnerable homeowners. Instead of enjoying a housing market with supply and demand in equilibrium, neighborhoods suddenly had a glut of housing on the market that drove down prices until a tipping point was reached in which disinvestment set in motion a vicious cycle of abandonment and decay. This, in turn, drove up crime and undermined the local tax base (Figure 12.2).[32] Research has shown that poverty rates above 20 percent in neighborhoods can generate negative contextual effects that are difficult to reverse.[33]

Once neighborhoods are beset by powerful feedback loops that create reinforcing cycles of decline, comprehensive interventions are necessary. Obama urban policy has this part right. However, insofar as Obama urban policy emphasizes comprehensive collaborations and ignores the public policies that create the necessity for those interventions in the first place, it is doing a disservice to disadvantaged neighborhoods. It is as if the administration gave highest priority to intensive care units for severely distressed neighborhoods while underinvesting in public health policies designed to prevent neighborhoods from falling into distress in the first

Figure 12.2. Foreclosures and reinforcing cycles of neighborhood decline.

place. It is much more cost-effective to prevent neighborhoods from falling into distress than it is to stabilize them once they are in decline. The Healthy Neighborhoods model recommends focusing on "middle" or transitional neighborhoods that are threatened by decline. Instead of comprehensive interventions, these communities may only need a housing rehab program that emphasizes visible repairs and marketing of the area to a mix of low- and middle-income households (see Boehlke 2012). Federal regulations, however, prevent many federal grant programs, such as CDBG and HOME, from being used in middle-market neighborhoods or for middle-income families to buy homes in poor areas. Many federal urban programs concentrate low-income housing in high-poverty, low-opportunity areas. And they do little to alter the broader regional dynamics that stress older urban and suburban neighborhoods.

In fairness to the Obama administration it must be said that it has pushed for policies that address some of the underlying dynamics of neighborhood decline. For example, Dodd-Frank and the creation of the Consumer Financial Protection Bureau have made the mortgage market safer for consumers and reduced the likelihood of another housing bubble and rash of foreclosures. The administration's urban policies, however, for the most part have not addressed the underlying dynamics of neighborhood decline in areas such as transportation policy, exclusionary zoning, and regional land use policies.[34] The administration could reasonably argue that progressive policies in these areas had no chance in the Republican-controlled House. At the very least, however, the administration missed an opportunity to educate the American public by introducing progressive legislation on these matters. Instead, the administration chose to focus its new initiatives on comprehensive community revitalization.

The emphasis on comprehensive community initiatives is also incomplete in its elevation of collaboration, or social capital, as a mechanism of change to the exclusion of conflict, or political processes and the exercise of sovereign power. The collaborative policy paradigm portrays public, private, and nonprofit actors as equal partners in comprehensive community-building initiatives. But government is not just another "stakeholder" or a kind of "super" foundation. Government laws determine the background conditions and establish the framework for community collaborations. In the absence of vertical relations of power, local collaborations will never be enough.[35]

Conflict is often necessary before collaborations can occur. A good example is the Community Reinvestment Act (CRA). Banks fought against its passage in 1977 and have tried to weaken it ever since. Only the political struggles of community-development groups and their allies have kept it alive and, indeed, have improved it over the years. According to one estimate, between 1977 and 2001 banks committed $1.97 trillion dollars as part of CRA bank lending agreements (NCRC 2001). According to another study, two-thirds of all corporations purchasing tax credits in 2007 were lending institutions motivated by CRA.[36] Banks across the country are collaborating with grassroots community-development organizations because they have been pushed by federal regulators. These collaborations have been made possible by the political struggles of advocates and the coercive power of the federal government.

In conclusion, we need comprehensive community revitalization initiatives to address our most disadvantaged communities. To fail to do so would be immoral. Realistically, however, we will never have sufficient capacity or resources to implement effective comprehensive revitalization initiatives in all distressed communities. We need policies to prevent neighborhoods from declining in the first place. A core purpose of government is to ensure that places, as well as people, are treated equally. This will require political struggle to dismantle the policies that presently tilt the playing field against disadvantaged neighborhoods.

Notes

1. Jacobs is quoting from the *1958 Annual Report of the Rockefeller Report* by Warren Weaver (1958).
2. My idea of capacity is similar to what Michael Rich and Robert Stoker term "good governance" in their insightful book, *Collaborative Governance for Urban Revitalization: Lessons from Empowerment Zones* (Rich and Stoker 2014).
3. For a history of the rise and fall of comprehensive approaches to national urban policy, see chapter 1 in Rich and Stoker (2014).
4. For a fascinating account of the origins of the War on Poverty in local foundation-funded community-development experiments, see Lemann (1991).
5. In theory, at least, policy tools like housing vouchers are self-implementing and have little in the way of capacity issues. In the real world of market failures and discrimination, however, vouchers are far from self-implementing.
6. For an analysis of the importance of local capacity in successful implementation of the EZ/EC program, see Rich and Stoker (2014).
7. Early national funders of CCIs included Annie E. Casey, Ford, Hewlett, MacArthur, Pew Charitable Trusts, Robert Wood Johnson, Rockefeller, Surdna, and W. K. Kellogg.
8. The three volumes of *Voices from the Field* document and critically evaluate foundation-inspired CCIs.

9. Of course, a significant proportion of foundation endowments is generated by the federal tax code, which permits the deduction of charitable contributions.

10. The nonprofits must qualify as Community Housing Development Organizations (CHDOs) with proof of capacity and representation by low-income persons in the community. For the regulations on CHDOs see 24 CFR 92 Subpart G, available at http://www.gpo.gov/fdsys/pkg/CFR-2003-title24-vol1/pdf/CFR-2003-title24-vol1-part92-subpartG.pdf.

11. For an early analysis of the role of networks in the community-development policy system, see Keyes et al. (1996).

12. For a preliminary evaluation of NCDI, see Walker and Weinheimer (1998).

13. Community foundations have played a key role in funding local community-development intermediaries and enhancing the capacity of CDCs. See Lowe (2006).

14. Federal outlays by HUD fell from $61.0 billion in 2009 to $56.6 billion in 2013 and the White House Office of Management and Budget (OMB) estimates HUD spending will fall to $39.5 billion by 2016. OMB Historical Tables, available at http://www.whitehouse.gov/omb/budget/historicals.

15. Castro is very supportive of comprehensive community revitalization. When he was mayor, San Antonio had the rare distinction of winning Choice Neighborhoods, Promise Neighborhoods, and Byrne Criminal Justice grants.

16. Congress did not fund SCI in FY 2012.

17. For an assessment of how successful the grants were at coordinating across policy silos, see Pendall et al. (2013).

18. 2010 census data as collected by the Public Policy Research Center at the University of Missouri, St. Louis, with the exception of the poverty rate, which is based on 2008–2012 American Community Survey data as reported at USA.com: http://www.usa.com/school-district-2922650-income-and-careers.htm#Poverty-Level.

19. For analysis of the 24:1 initiative and the importance of capacity building, see Swanstrom et al. (2013).

20. The 24:1 plan can viewed at http://www.beyondhousing.org/wordpress/wp-content/uploads/2012/08/24-1-Community-Plan-Final-7-18-11.pdf.

21. 24:1 accomplishments are reported in the 2013 report to the community (http://www.beyondhousing.org/wordpress/wp-content/uploads/2013/12/24–1-Annual-Report-to-the-Community-for-2013.pdf) and in the NSD Reformation Plan (http://www.beyondhousing.org/wordpress/wp-content/uploads/2014/02/NSD-Reformation-Plan.pdf).

22. Calculations by Public Policy Research Center, University of Missouri–St. Louis, based on U.S. Census Bureau, Longitudinal Employer-Household Dynamics (2009).

23. According to the American Automobile Association, the total annual cost of owning a "small sedan" driven 15,000 miles is $7,962; see https://exchange.aaa.com/wp-content/uploads/2013/04/Your-Driving-Costs-2013.pdf.

24. In the interest of full disclosure, my Des Lee professorship helped fund the predevelopment study and the civic engagement process for the Rock Road TOD. Information on the planning process for the Rock Road TOD is based on participant observation and *Beyond Housing 24:1 Initiative St. Charles Metrolink TOD Planning Process Final Evaluation Report,* Public Policy Research Center, University of Missouri–St. Louis (February 10, 2014), unpublished but available on request from author.

25. Beyond Housing, however, would be the first to acknowledge that it has not done nearly enough to turn the community around.

26. One study estimated that one-third of neighborhood change depends on regional trends (Weissbourd, Bodini, and He, 2009). David Rusk has stressed that without an "outside game" of supportive regional policies, it is very difficult to succeed with the inside game of community development (Rusk 1999).

27. Many scholars have documented that nonprofit capacity is unequally distributed across space in ways that can exacerbate inequalities. (See Allard 2009; Joassart-Marcelli and

Wolch 2003.) Lester Salamon argues that a main reason why government has partnered extensively with nonprofits is what he calls "philanthropic insufficiency": "the voluntary system often leaves serious gaps in geographic coverage, since the resources are frequently not available where the problems are most severe" (Salamon 1995, 45).

28. Lacking a large community foundation that has invested in the community-development system, St. Louis, for example, has not generally been successful at attracting national foundation funding.

29. Logically, mistaking the part for the whole is called the "fallacy of composition."

30. For a synthesis of the literature on how public policies have promoted suburban sprawl and inner suburban and urban decline, see chapter 4 in Dreier, Mollenkopf, and Swanstrom (2014).

31. In 1950 the "urbanized area" of the St. Louis region, as defined by the Census Bureau, had a population of 1.4 million. By 2010 the population in that same geography had fallen to 802,000, a stunning loss of almost 600,000 residents. Reported in Swanstrom and Webber (2014).

32. For an analysis of vicious cycles of urban decay caused by foreclosures, see Swanstrom (2012). Figure 12.2 is adapted from this article.

33. For a synthesis of the research on the negative effects of concentrated poverty, see chapter 3 in Dreier, Mollenkopf, and Swanstrom (2014).

34. Although these policies are generally controlled by state and local actors, there is much the federal government could do to promote more inclusionary regional development. See chapter 9 in Dreier, Mollenkopf, and Swanstrom (2014).

35. My argument draws from Weir, Rongerude, and Ansell (2009).

36. Moss (2008), as reported in Erickson (2009, 63).

References

Allard, Scott W. 2009. *Out of Reach: Place, Poverty, and the New American Welfare State.* New Haven, Conn.: Yale University Press.

Bier, Tom, and Charlie Post. 2006. "Vacating the City: An Analysis of New Homes vs. Household Growth." In *Redefining Urban and Suburban America: Evidence from Census 2000,* ed. Alan Berube, Bruce Katz, and Robert E. Lang, 167–90. James A. Johnson Metro Series. Washington, D.C.: Brookings Institution.

BNCP (Building Neighborhood Capacity Program). n.d. "About Us." http://www.buildingcommunitycapacity.org/about.

Boehlke, David. 2012. "Preserving Healthy Neighborhoods: Market-Based Strategies for Housing and Neighborhood Revitalization." In *Rebuilding America's Cities: New Directions for the Industrial Heartland,* ed. Alan Mallach, 143–62. New York: American Assembly.

Brophy, Paul and Rachel Godsil. 2009. *Retooling HUD for a Catalytic Federal Government: A Report to Secretary Shaun Donovan.* Philadelphia, Pa: Penn Institute for Urban Research.

Dreier, Peter, John Mollenkopf, and Todd Swanstrom. 2014. *Place Matters: Metropolitics for the Twenty-First Century.* 3rd ed. Lawrence: University Press of Kansas.

Erickson, David J. 2009. *The Housing Revolution: Networks and Neighborhoods.* Washington, D.C.: Urban Institute Press.

Erickson, David, Ian Galloway, and Naomi Cytron. 2012. "Routinizing the Extraordinary." In *Investing in What Works in America's Communities,* ed. Nancy O. Andrews and David J. Erickson, 377–406. San Francisco: San Francisco Federal Reserve.

Feiock, Richard C., ed. 2004. *Metropolitan Governance: Conflict, Competition and Cooperation.* American Governance and Public Policy Series. Washington, D.C.: Georgetown University Press.

Jacobs, Jane. 1961. *The Death and Life of Great American Cities.* New York: Random House.

Joassart-Marcelli, Pascale, and Jennifer Wolch. 2003. "The Intrametropolitan Geography of Poverty and the Nonprofit Sector in Southern California." *Nonprofit and Voluntary Sector Quarterly* 32 (1): 70–96.

Keyes, Langley, Alex Schwartz, Avid Vidal, and Rachel Bratt. 1996. "Networks and Nonprofits: Opportunities and Challenges in an Era of Federal Devolution." *Housing Policy Debate* 7 (2): 201–29.

Kneebone, Elizabeth, and Alan Berube. 2013. *Confronting Suburban Poverty in America.* Washington, D.C.: Brookings Institution.

Kubisch, Anne C. 2010. "Recent History of Community Change Efforts in the United States." In *Voices from the Field III: Lessons and Challenges from Two Decades of Community Change Efforts,* 8–14. Washington, D.C.: Aspen Institute.

Kubisch, Anne C., Patricia Auspos, Prudence Brown, and Tom Dewar, eds. 2010. *Voices from the Field III: Lessons and Challenges from Two Decades of Community Change Efforts.* Washington, D.C.: Aspen Institute.

Lemann, Nicholas. 1991. *The Promised Land: The Great Black Migration and How It Changed America.* New York: Alfred A. Knopf.

Lowe, Jeffrey S. 2006. *Rebuilding Communities the Public Trust Way: Community Foundation Assistance to CDCs, 1980–2000.* Lanham, Md.: Lexington Books.

MacGillis, Alec. 2007. "Obama Says He, Too, Is a Poverty Fighter." *Washington Post,* July 19.

Moss, Bob. 2008. "The LIHTC Correction for 2008 and How We Got Here," *Journal of Tax Credit Housing* 1 (5): 1–2.

NCCED (National Congress for Community Economic Development). 2005. *Reaching New Heights: Trends and Achievements of Community Development Corporations.* 5th National Community Development Census. Washington, D.C.: NCCED. http://community-wealth.org/sites/clone .community-wealth.org/files/downloads/report-ncced.pdf.

NCRC (National Community Reinvestment Coalition). 2001. "CRA Commitments." http://www .ncrc.org/images/stories/whatWeDo_promote/cra_commitments_07.pdf.

O'Connor, Alice. 1999. "Swimming against the Tide: A Brief History of Federal Policy in Poor Communities." In *Urban Problems and Community Development,* ed. Ronald F. Ferguson and William T. Dickens, 77–138. Washington, D.C.: Brookings Institution.

Office of Urban Affairs. 2011. "Building Neighborhoods of Opportunity: White House Neighborhood Revitalization Initiative Report." https://www.whitehouse.gov/sites/default/files /uploads/nri_report.pdf.

Orszag, Peter R., Melody Barnes, Adalfo Carrion, and Larry Summers. 2009. "Developing Effective Place-Based Policies for the FY 2011 Budget." August 11. Memorandum. http://www .whitehouse.gov/omb/assets/memoranda_fy2009/m09-28.pdf.

Pendall, Rolf, Sandra Rosenbloom, Diane Levy, Elizabeth Oo, Gerrit Knaap, Jason Sartori, and Arnab Chakraborty. 2013. *"Can Federal Efforts Advance Federal and Local De-Siloing? Lessons from the HUD-EPA-DOT Partnership for Sustainable Communities."* UI No. 08752-000-00. http://www.urban.org/sites/default/files/alfresco/publication-pdfs/412820-Can-Federal -Efforts-Advance-Federal-and-Local-De-Siloing-Full-Report.PDF.

Reckhow, Sarah, and Margaret Weir. 2012. "Building a Resilient Safety Net." In *Urban and Regional Policy and Its Effects: Building Resilient Regions,* ed. Margaret Weir, Nancy Pindus, Howard Wial, and Harold Wolman, 275–323. Washington, D.C.: Brookings Institution.

Rich, Michael, and Robert Stoker. 2014. *Collaborative Governance for Urban Revitalization: Lessons from Empowerment Zones.* Ithaca, N.Y.: Cornell University Press.

Rusk, David. 1999. *Inside Game/Outside Game: Winning Strategies for Urban America.* Washington, D.C.: Brookings Institution.

Salamon, Lester. 1995. *Partners in Public Service: Government-Nonprofit Relations in the Modern Welfare State.* Baltimore: Johns Hopkins University Press.

Sampson, Robert J. 2012. *Great American City: Chicago and the Enduring Neighborhood Effect.* Chicago: University of Chicago Press.

Sharp, Elaine. 1990. *Urban Politics and Administration: From Service Delivery to Economic Development.* New York: Longman.

Swanstrom, Todd. 2012. "Resilience in the Face of Foreclosures: How National Actors Shape Local Responses." In *Urban and Regional Policy and Its Effects: Building Resilient Regions*, ed. Margaret Weir, Nancy Pindus, Howard Wial, and Harold Wolman, 60–99. Washington, D.C.: Brookings Institution.

Swanstrom, Todd, and Karl Guenther. 2011. *Creating Whole Communities: Enhancing the Capacity of Community Development Nonprofits in the St. Louis Region.* Public Policy Research Center University of Missouri–St. Louis. https://pprc.umsl.edu/pprc.umsl.edu/data/Enhancing Capacity2011.pdf.

Swanstrom, Todd, and Hank Webber. 2014. "Rebound Neighborhoods in Older Industrial Cities: The Story of St. Louis." White paper. St. Louis, Mo.: Public Policy Research Center, UMSL and Center for System Dynamics, Washington University.

Swanstrom, Todd, Will Winter, Margaret Sherraden, and Jessica Lake. 2013. "Civic Capacity and School/Community Partnerships in a Fragmented Suburban Setting: The Case of 24:1." *Journal of Urban Affairs* 35 (1): 25–42.

Walker, Christopher, and Mark Weinheimer. 1998. *Community Development in the 1990s.* Washington, D.C.: Urban Institute. http://community-wealth.org/sites/clone.community-wealth.org/files/downloads/report-walker-weinheimer.pdf.

Weaver, Warren. 1958. "The Rockefeller Foundation Annual Report, 1958." The Rockefeller Foundation. https://www.rockefellerfoundation.org/app/uploads/Annual-Report-1958.pdf.

Weir, Margaret. 2011. "Creating Justice for the Poor in the New Metropolis." In *Justice and the American Metropolis*, ed. Clarissa Rile Hayward and Todd Swanstrom, 237–56. Minneapolis: University of Minnesota Press.

Weir, Margaret, Jane Rongerude, and Christopher K. Ansell. 2009. "Collaboration Is Not Enough: Virtuous Cycles of Reform in Transportation Policy." *Urban Affairs Review* 44 (4): 455–89.

Weissbourd, Robert, Riccardo Bodini, and Michael He. 2009. "Dynamic Neighborhoods: New Tools for Economic and Community Development." RW Ventures. http://www.rw-ventures.com/ftp/DNT%20Final%20Report.pdf.

13

THE OBAMA ADMINISTRATION'S
NEIGHBORHOOD STABILIZATION PROGRAM
From Foreclosure Crisis to What in Nashville's Chestnut Hill?

DEIRDRE OAKLEY AND JAMES FRASER

To help combat the devastating effects of rampant foreclosures resulting from the 2008 housing crisis, the Obama administration established the Neighborhood Stabilization Program (NSP). Using the case example of the "Chestnut Hill" NSP neighborhood in South Nashville, Tennessee, this chapter provides commentary on some of the preexisting NSP-targeted neighborhood investments, the programmatic challenges, and the mixed agendas that have emerged, as well as the outcomes to date. To put this case in context, we first provide a brief overview of federal urban policy initiatives that have sought to remedy the social problems of poor inner-city neighborhoods.

Federal programs focused on the revitalization and redevelopment of "distressed" urban communities are nothing new. The first major urban redevelopment initiative can be traced to the Housing Act of 1949, which targeted "blighted" inner-city neighborhoods until the program's demise in 1974 (Hays 1985). While improving housing conditions in poor inner-city neighborhoods was touted as the program's goal, according to Logan and Molotch (1987), "less than 20 percent of all urban renewal land went for housing; over 80 percent went for developing commercial, industrial, and infrastructure" (168). In fact, these authors state, "there seems to be little disagreement about the devastating effects of urban renewal on the poor and minorities" (168).

Under Lyndon Johnson's Great Society administration, the Model Cities program was created in 1966. Lasting less than a decade because it was subsequently terminated by Richard Nixon, Model Cities provided funds to localities for economic development in distressed neighborhoods (Olken 1971). The program was administered by the newly established U.S. Department of Housing and Urban Development (HUD) and required localities to submit an application spelling out their plan for use of Model Cities funding (von Hoffman 2011). Unlike urban renewal and slum clearance efforts of 1949 Housing Act Model Cities required community involvement, although this meant only citizen participation and not citizen control (Olken 1971).

The Community Development Block Grant (CDBG) program was initiated as part of the Housing and Community Act of 1974. The CDBG program turned forty years old in 2014 and is one of the longest continuous programs run by HUD (Rohe and Galster 2014). Using a need-based formula, the CDBG program provides annual funding to local and state governments for neighborhood and housing improvements. According to Rohe and Galster (2014), what has made this program unique is that it supplies localities with funds for a wide range of projects to improve the living environments in poor communities.

While the CDBG program is noted for its longevity, it suffered from funding cuts during the Reagan and Bush administrations in the 1980s as policies shifted toward market-based solutions. In fact, under Reagan, cities were essentially ignored in terms of federal subsidies. In addition, lack of oversight led to corruption scandals at HUD. According to Dreier (2004a), under Reagan, funding to local governments was cut 60 percent. As Dreier states, "The only 'urban' program that survived the cuts was federal aid for highways—which primarily benefited suburbs, not cities" (1).

Urban policy shifted to a more neoliberal approach under Clinton. The Empowerment Zone (EZ) and Enterprise Community (EC) Initiative (Public Law 103–66) was authorized by Congress in 1993 and funded in 1994. It offered targeted funding and tax incentives to distressed urban and rural communities. On December 21, 1994, President Clinton announced the urban areas designated by HUD, and the rural areas designated by the U.S. Department of Agriculture (Notice 1995). Of these designations, seventy-two were urban: six EZs, two Supplemental EZs, four Enhanced ECs, and sixty ECs. There were seventy-one urban areas designated in forty-one states and the District of Columbia.

This program was designed to (1) attract, concentrate, and coordinate a broad array of public and private resources to revitalize distressed neighborhoods; and (2) support community-based partnerships to expand employment opportunities and alleviate poverty for residents (Stegman 1995). It required the development of strategic plans in accordance with three key programmatic principles: (1) community-based partnerships, (2) economic opportunity, and (3) sustainable community development (Riposa 1996). These key programmatic principles were required to fit into a fourth, more general principle: an overall strategic vision for change. The program's approach to revitalization and community involvement was intended to set it apart from the "leave it to the free market" approach of the Reagan and Bush administrations, aligning it more fully with the goals of community economic development (Frisch and Servon 2004; Rubin and Stankiewicz 2001).

HOPE VI (Housing Opportunities for People Everywhere) was also initiated by the Clinton administration in 1993. This program sought to transform public housing by demolishing large, spatially concentrated—and in many cases deteriorating—developments and replacing them with mixed-income housing. This meant relocation for the majority of public housing residents to private market rental housing with the help of a voucher subsidy (Oakley, Ruel, and Reid 2013).

HOPE VI would remain funded during the George W. Bush administration. The EC designation expired in 2004, as did the federal funding for the EZ program. At that time Bush introduced the Renewal Community (RC) initiative, which provided tax breaks for redevelopment in distressed areas. In this respect, it was similar to the EZ/EC program but without any federal funding attached to it (Oakley and Tsao 2006). At the same time cities were faced with added expenditures in order to comply with federal homeland security and antiterrorism initiatives (Dreier 2004b). But the rapid increase in risky subprime lending meant that cities around the country were experiencing a housing boom, one that would subsequently burst and lead the country into one of its worst financial crises (Financial Crisis Inquiry Commission 2011).

The Neighborhood Stabilization Program

In response to the housing meltdown, Congress passed the Housing and Economic Recovery Act (HERA) in July 2008. This established the NSP program. Funding was allocated the following year through the American Recovery and Reinvestment Act (ARRA), as well as the 2010 Dodd-Frank Wall Street Reform and Consumer Protection Act. NSP's purpose has been to assist local governments in addressing foreclosure and abandonment at the neighborhood level through emergency funds for acquisition and rehabilitation. More specifically, the program provides funding that allows municipalities to purchase abandoned and/or foreclosed upon residential properties in neighborhoods hardest hit by the housing crisis, with the goal of property redevelopment or rehabilitation, and subsequent reselling. The program also allows for the acquisition and demolition of blighted properties and land-banking-purchased properties for future redevelopment. The underlying assumption is that such a strategy will "stabilize" the neighborhood in terms of mitigating declining property values of nearby homes.

There have subsequently been three rounds of NSP funding: $3.92 billion awarded to 309 local and state governments through NSP1; another $1.93 billion to fifty-six grantees through NSP2, and another $1 billion allocated through NSP3. Compared to the billions lost to foreclosures, the $7 billion allocated for all three NSP rounds pales in comparison. So the question is what impact this relatively small program has had in stabilizing foreclosed and distressed neighborhoods. In many regards, it may be too soon to know the program's efficacy at meeting its "stabilization" objectives because many NSP projects, particularly ones under NSP2, are not scheduled for completion until 2015. Funding for NSP2 is distributed through the CDBG program. There is also the question of what exactly stabilization means and for whom. Do the existing residents in the neighborhood fully benefit from the program or is this just another opportunity for developers to revitalize a neighborhood, eventually pricing longtime lower-income residents out?

While each round of NSP funding shares the same overall goal, the funding organization and eligibility criteria has changed. In addition, there have been some modifications to funding uses. For example, in 2010 HUD changed the definitions of "foreclosed" and "abandoned" to include properties where the mortgage was sixty days delinquent or tax payments ninety days or more overdue. This streamlined the acquisition process by allowing for short sales, a process whereby the net proceed fall short of any debts incurred against the property. In addition with NSP2 funds were set asides for technical assistance—$50 million for round two and about $20 million for round three.

However, what really separates NSP2 from the other rounds is that it was a competitive application process yielding far more applications that the other two rounds and the fewest number of awardees. Unlike the other two rounds, which were based on a formula allocation, it was open to local governments and nonprofits. In addition, collaborations between local government entities and private sector partners were encouraged, and the criteria for selection was based on census tract foreclose and vacancy scores calculated by HUD. Lastly, NSP2 funds were required to be spent within two years of the award date. Table 13.1 provides an overview of the three rounds of NSP, including program objectives and eligibility, and highlights the changes between the three rounds.

As of this writing, Abt Associates continues to conduct a national study of NSP sponsored by HUD to gain a deeper understanding of the program's effectiveness and the challenges localities have faced in implementing NSP. However, it is quite likely that some of the most important questions about the program may not be captured in this study.

According to Fraser and Oakley (2014), some questions that might not be captured include (1) how pre-NSP investment and/or disinvestment of targeted neighborhoods may impact the overall NSP strategies and outcomes on the local level; and (2) given that NSP was a relatively small investment in most places compared to the rates of foreclosures and vacant properties, what lasting effects will the program have on the neighborhoods that received investment, and what would we expect them to be? This second question is important because the Abt study's timeframe will not capture the longer-term impacts.

While these two questions may go largely unanswered due to the complexities of untangling the recent past, some existing studies have already concluded that the strategic small investments made by NSP projects in cities across the country will have multiplier effects and spur other private investments in the target areas (Reid 2011). Thus, NSP, though modest, may very well stimulate market demand. However, in terms of timing, speculative capital may be investing in NSP-targeted census tracts regardless of the program. Likely, both phenomena are operative. One known outcome is that many NSP awardees have purchased properties to "land bank" for future affordable housing development (Alexander 2009).

TABLE 13.1. NSP PROGRAM OVERVIEW

	NSP1	NSP2	NSP3
Year	Act passed in 2008 (Division B, Title III of the Housing and Economic Recovery Act [HERA] of 2008).	Announced and applications due in 2009 (Title XII of Division A of the American Recovery and Reinvestment Act of 2009, [the Recovery Act]). Awards announced 2010.	Passed July 2010 (Dodd-Frank Wall Street Reform and Consumer Protection Act).
Amount	$3.92 billion	$2 billion ($50 million set aside for technical assistance)	$1 billion (up to 2% set aside for technical assistance)
Methodology of Awards	HUD provided grants to all states and selected local governments on a formula basis.	Competitive application process open to local governments and nonprofits; collaborations were encouraged and could include private sector partners. Grantees were selected on the basis of foreclosure needs in their selected target areas, recent past experience, program design, and compliance with NSP2 rules.	Distributes funds by the formula allocation used for NSP1.
Eligible Uses	Establish financing mechanisms for purchase and redevelopment of foreclosed homes and residential properties.	Minimum purchase discount changed from 5% to 1% for individual properties, and from 15% to 5% average for the overall portfolio.	Funds available until expended.

(continued)

TABLE 13.1. NSP PROGRAM OVERVIEW (CONTINUED)

NSP1	NSP2	NSP3
Purchase and rehabilitate homes and residential properties abandoned or foreclosed.	In April, 2010, HUD changed the definitions of "foreclosed" and "abandoned" for the purposes of identifying eligible properties for NSP1 and NSP2 to include properties where the mortgage is 60 days delinquent or tax payments are at least 90 days delinquent. This allows for a property to be acquired through a short sale, and was intended to streamline the process of acquisition. Changes are retroactive to NSP1.	Grantees have 2 years from the date HUD signs their grant agreements to expend 50% of the funds and 3 years to expend 100%.
Establish land banks for foreclosed homes.		Establishes a minimum grant size of $1 million for cities and counties.
Demolish blighted structures.		Permits redevelopment or rehab of "vacant" properties to qualify for the 25% low-income set aside (previously only "abandoned or foreclosed" homes counted).

	Redevelop demolished or vacant properties.		
Applicants	N/A	482	N/A
Awards	309	56	270
Deadlines	Funds are to be obligated within 18 months of availability to recipient; and expended within 4 years.	Recipients must expend 50% of allocated funds within 2 years of the date funds are available to the recipient, and 100% of funds must be expended within 3 years.	Grantees have 2 years from the date HUD signs their grant agreements to expend 50% of the funds and 3 years to expend 100%.

Source: Table adopted from Neighborhood Works American, Stable Communities. Retrieved from http://www.stablecommunities.org/nsp-strategies, August 24, 2014.

Overview of NSP2 in Nashville

According to the Metropolitan Development Housing Agency (MDHA), Nashville's NSP2 program was comprised of a consortium of agencies, including MDHA, The Housing Fund, Inc., Urban Housing Solutions, Inc., and the Woodbine Community Organization (MDHA 2012). The consortium was awarded $30,470,000 in NSP2 funding during 2010. These funds targeted seventeen eligible census tracts in four city neighborhoods based on HUD's foreclosure and vacancy scores and included neighborhoods in North Nashville, East Nashville, South Nashville (Chestnut Hill), and Southeastern Nashville (MDHA 2011). According to MDHA (2012), each target neighborhood was severely affected by the 2008 housing crisis and had a unique set of housing market, credit, and employment needs.

HUD's foreclosure score is based on the estimated number and percentage of foreclosures, as well as a number of mortgages, change in housing prices, and change in unemployment. The vacancy score is based on the estimated foreclosure rate with vacancy rate. Both scores rank need from 1 to 20, with 20 being census tracts of greatest need (HUD 2009).

Among the variables included in the scores were (1) the estimated number of mortgages about to start the foreclosure process or be seriously delinquent in the past two years; (2) the estimated number of mortgages in a tract (the greater of census 2000 mortgages or total Home Mortgage Disclosure Act [HMDA] mortgages between 2004 and 2007); (3) the price change between peak value and December 2008 value in the metropolitan area (or nonmetropolitan balance); and (4) the change in average unemployment rate in the county between 2007 and 2008. Aside from the estimated foreclosure rate, the vacancy score includes the estimated percent of all addresses in a census tract vacant ninety days or longer (HUD 2014).

Applicants could choose targeted census tracts based on an average foreclosure score of 15 or higher or the average foreclosure and vacancy risk score of 18 or greater (HUD 2009). The targeted census tracts did not have to be continuous. Table 13.2 provides the scores by census tract for each of Nashville's NSP2 neighborhoods.

Interestingly, census tract 161 in South Nashville (Chestnut Hill) did not meet the HUD scoring criteria but was included anyway. The stabilization goals of the program in all four neighborhoods included (1) housing development and redevelopment for both renters and homebuyers, including former and/or foreclosed upon owners, within a mixed-income framework to balance potential gentrification; (2) leveraging development and redevelopment as a springboard for neighborhood revitalization; (3) using shared equity loans to sustain affordability and successful homeownership; and (4) incorporating green building technologies to promote financial and physical health and well-being (MDHA 2012). Aside from the scoring criteria, in selecting the seventeen census tracts for NSP2, the consortium of agencies also reviewed past and ongoing redevelopment and revitalization activities in those areas.

TABLE 13.2. NSP2 TARGETED GEOGRAPHY—NASHVILLE

Area	2000 Census Tract	Foreclosure Score	Vacancy Score
North Nashville	101.02	18	14
	127.01	17	14
	128.01	18	17
	136	16	18
	137	18	18
	138	18	16
	139	18	20
	143	17	19
South Nashville (Chestnut Hill)	160	16	20
	161	13	16
	156.11	18	11
	156.16	18	14
Southeastern Nashville	156.18	18	14
	156.20	19	14
	156.21	20	14
	113	17	19
	117	16	18
	118	16	19

Source: Adopted from Metropolitan Development and Housing (MDHA) Overall Stabilization Program Call for Public Comment, 2009.

The Case of Chestnut Hill

Nashville's Chestnut Hill is a small neighborhood a mere kilometer from the city's central business district. Like many "inner-city" neighborhoods, Chestnut Hill could be characterized as a place that was on a downward trajectory for much of the latter part of the twentieth century. The NSP2 consortium of agencies indicated that they had wanted to revitalize the area for decades. In addition, Chestnut Hill has been one of the only areas next to downtown providing affordable housing in the low-income private rental market. Once NSP2 funds were awarded, the consortium agency Urban Housing Solutions took on the bulk of the redevelopment and development efforts in the neighborhood.

Chestnut Hill comprises Nashville's census tracts 160 and 161. According to Bazuin and Fraser (2013), the neighborhood's boundaries include an interstate on the northwest, railroad tracks on the southwest, and a "flood-prone" creek on the east (296). Like many inner-city neighborhoods, prior to deindustrialization (1950s and before) it was a working-class neighborhood and racially diverse. Federal urban renewal programs of the 1950s and 1960s, as well as the availability of FHA mortgages beginning with the 1949 Housing Act, meant the building of the interstate surrounding the neighborhood, white flight to the suburbs, as well as increases in warehouse zoning. By the time of the 2008 housing crisis, that neighborhood had been depopulating since the 1960s and was composed primarily of working-class African American homeowners, working-class and poor mostly African American renters, and white "urban pioneers" (Bazuin and Fraser 2013).

Our case example is based on survey data that attempted to replicate the American Community Survey (ACS) with a random sample of 25 percent of the households (n = 89) in the neighborhood (Bazuin and Fraser 2013). In addition, interviews (n = 17) were conducted with all identifiable stakeholders, including developers, nonprofit staff, and neighborhood leaders. We also reviewed news media articles on Chestnut Hill and accessed available administrative data including the NSP application and information from the Nashville consortium that had been reported to HUD.

Prior to receiving the NSP award and before the housing crisis, Chestnut Hill had an increasing number of middle-class households moving into the area. This trend continued after the crisis, albeit at a much slower rate. Some small developers constructed new housing that far exceeded the housing values in the area, and the real estate industry in Nashville began marketing the area as the next place where vast returns on development investment could be made. On December 9, 2011, an article appeared in the *Nashville Ledger* reviewing the city's "emerging neighborhoods" or "Hot 'Hoods," and Chestnut Hill was prominently featured. The article was accompanied by "before and after" pictures of rundown houses that had been redeveloped.

Yet the write-up of Chestnut Hill in the *Nashville Ledger* article read like a real estate ad for a sure investment and clearly illustrated the complexities of untangling the impact of public and private investments. Note that the mention of federal stimulus money in the write-up is referring to NSP2 funds allocated to the neighborhood:

> Chestnut Hill, another neighborhood on the cusp of a major transformation. The emerging neighborhood has about 125 homes and some commercial and warehouse spaces on 1st, 2nd, 3rd and 4th Avenues South and is bordered by Greer Stadium, historic Nashville City Cemetery, Trevecca Nazarene University and the Tennessee State Fairgrounds. The area is active with construction and planned projects, funded by both public and private investors. Eight million dollars of federal stimulus money is jumpstarting several projects in the area—a mixed-use development with 10 residences and 2,000 square feet of retail space, the 1219 1st Avenue South project, a quadraplex designed by students from Tennessee State University, and a development of 11 affordable townhomes on 3rd Avenue South.
>
> Shawn Bailes, a private investor with a multi-million dollar investment in Chestnut Hill, is getting full list price for newly constructed townhomes at Southview on 2nd, an infill development of 11 cottage-style townhomes on 2nd Avenue South. The modern two- and three-bedroom urban condos, priced from $184,900 to $209,900, are attracting buyers in their 20s and 30s searching for affordable alternatives to hot areas such as The Gulch or upgrading from less expensive housing, Bailes says. Seven of 11 units on Southview and 2nd have sold or are under contract. "Chestnut Hill is the last downtown neighborhood that didn't get developed before the economic downturn," says Buck Snyder, affiliate broker at Worth Properties. "It's a neighborhood with good bones, and many of the properties make sense for rehab. The neighborhood still needs to hammer out an identity, but the numbers (for investors and homeowners) look pretty good. It's the "only place near downtown where you can get a two-bedroom condo for under $200,000." (*Nashville Ledger*, 2011)

And yet, ironically, when the NSP2 consortium initially went to a Chestnut Hill community meeting to present their plan for investing in the neighborhood during 2010, speculative developers cried foul, stating that the market would right itself. The overall sentiment among the developers was that they were having to compete with a government program for property acquisition. One developer even tried to derail an NSP-funded project by inviting neighborhood residents to speak out at a Board of Zoning hearing. This was indicative of the competition other studies have found between NSP awardees and speculative investors (Immergluck 2011). Regardless of this competition, however, both private developers and the NSP2 consortium initially agreed that a mixed-income housing strategy needed to be the template for Chestnut Hill's redevelopment.

Since there was predominantly low-income housing in the area, this meant building housing to attract higher-income people to the neighborhood. Much like the new private sector housing development going on in Chestnut Hill, the NSP2 consortium admitted that the new homes they were building for ownership were priced too high for existing neighborhood residents to be eligible. Stabilizing the neighborhood clearly meant bringing new people to the neighborhood. Simultaneously, the NSP2 consortium concentrated their efforts on purchasing abandoned and vacant single-home properties.

However, as the timeline for obligating NSP2 funds drew closer, the consortium switched their focus to buying up the vast majority of the multifamily housing stock in the area. Aside from the timeline, there were other factors driving this shift. When Urban Housing Solutions began purchasing multifamily dwellings, virtually all of the residents were displaced and had to find housing in other parts of Nashville. We learned through interviews with the organization's leader that he felt it was his job to use the NSP2 funding to root out people from the neighborhood who were suspected drug dealers and criminals stating, "There is a population of people that are hanging around and prostitutes."

Since some of the NSP2 consortium believed that "those people" typically lived in the multifamily apartment buildings, the NSP2 intervention appeared to be a logical choice. In this sense, NSP was used as a blunt instrument to move people out of Chestnut Hill for reasons that were not directly related to the stated mission of the program: addressing foreclosed and vacant properties. In this way the NSP served multiple purposes, and it is unclear whether any of the displaced residents have come back to the new rental properties.

Urban Housing Solutions' development and redevelopment efforts in Chestnut Hill were extensive. They purchased six apartment complexes, with new construction on vacant properties totaling 14 one- and two-bedroom apartments, as well as 1,500 square feet set aside for commercial use. They also acquired existing multifamily properties for rehabilitation, totaling ninety-one units (Urban Housing Solutions 2012). All of these projects were scheduled for completion in 2012 and met the deadline. However, the lion's share of the rehabbed units became one bedroom, which essentially meant that poor families could not move into these properties.

As of the first quarter of 2013, MDHA reported many of the Urban Housing Solutions' properties had leased up and were serving households between 70 percent and 120 percent of the area's median income range. However, the commercial space had yet to be leased, and no breakdown of leases by the area's median income range was provided. A 70 percent to 120 percent range clearly indicates that households living at or below the federal poverty line, which are typically at 50 percent of the area's median income, were not being served. This brings up broader questions about how affordability is defined and how the socioeconomic composition of Chestnut Hill may have been altered through NSP2 redevelopment. The 2007–11 ACS data really are not good indicators of potential neighborhood change because redevelopment was happening during this time period. There are also questions about the accuracy of this data since the error estimates go up for smaller census tracts (Bazuin and Fraser 2013).

Beyond inquiries about the amount of neighborhood change, there are also questions that cannot be answered without a targeted data collection effort of Chestnut Hill. For example, what was the process by which the implementing agencies made decisions about which properties to acquire, how to renovate or build on them, and how to set affordability? What were the specific investment and disinvestment activities that went on in Chestnut Hill prior to NSP2? Without answering these two questions it is difficult to gauge the net effect of NSP2 on the neighborhood. What we do know is that the redevelopment activities did not target very poor families.

Conclusion

Through this example of Chestnut Hill, which we have not put forth as representative of the NSP2 experience in other cities across the country, we highlight some of the challenges, as well as some of the elements of actual NSP implementation that could be interpreted as not meeting the program's objective to "stabilize" hard-hit neighborhoods. In addition, we have brought attention to how stabilization might mean different things to different stakeholders. To be sure, for the residents in Chestnut Hill who were forced to move in the wake of NSP2 implementation, "stabilization" meant displacement. Perhaps the take-home message is that local context and implementation strategies matter.

What does this mean for understanding the NSP program nationally? We suggest that any evaluation of the impact of NSP needs to take into consideration that places are constituted by multiple, ongoing projects of organizations—public, private, and nonprofit—that intersect with each other. Most salient is how the neighborhood was perceived by the real estate industry and local government entities prior to the crisis and what investments (or disinvestments) were happening at that time. This really matters in terms of truly understanding the impacts of NSP.

If we are to gain an understanding of the ways in which the NSP program has changed anything, in-depth, place-based studies will need to be conducted in urban neighborhoods that take into account the histories of the areas targeted by NSP initiatives, as well as acknowledging the ongoing efforts of multiple stakeholders that are transforming American cities.

References

Alexander, Frank S. 2009. "Neighborhood Stabilization and Land Banking." *Communities & Banking* (November): 3–5. http://www.communityprogress.net/filebin/pdf/nvpc_trnsfr/Alexander _stabilization_landbanking.pdf.

Bazuin, Joshua T., and James C. Fraser. 2013. "How the ACS Gets It Wrong: The Story of the American Community Survey and a Small, Inner City Neighborhood." *Applied Geography* 45: 292–302.

Dreier, Peter. 2004a. "Reagan's Legacy: Homelessness in America." *Shelterforce* 135 (May/June). http://www.nhi.org/online/issues/135/reagan.html.

———. 2004b. "Urban Neglect: Georgia W. Bush and the Cities: The Damage Done and the Struggle Ahead." *Shelterforce* 137 (September/October). http://www.shelterforce.com/online/issues/137/urbanneglect.html.

Financial Crisis Inquiry Commission. 2011. *The Financial Crisis Inquiry Report.* Washington, D.C.: FCIC.

Fraser, J., and D. Oakley. 2014. "The Neighborhood Stabilization Program: Stable for Whom?" *Journal of Urban Affairs* 37 (1): 38–41.

Frisch, M., and L. Servon. 2004. *Community Development since "Rebuilding Communities": A Review of the Literature, the Field, and the Environment.* Atlanta, Ga.: Association of Public Policy, Analysis and Management Conference.

Hays, R. Allen. 1985. *The Federal Government and Urban Housing: Ideology and Change in Public Policy.* Albany: State University of New York Press.

HUD (U.S. Department of Housing and Urban Development). 2009. "Notice of Fund Availability (NOFA) for the Neighborhood Stabilization Program 2 under the American Recovery and Reinvestment Act." Docket No. FR-5321-N-01.

———. 2014. "HUD Exchange: Neighborhood Stabilization Program." Accessed August 24, 2014. https://www.hudexchange.info/.

Immergluck, Dan. 2011. "The Local Wreckage of Global Capital: The Subprime Crisis, Federal Policy and High-Foreclosure Neighborhoods in the US." *International Journal of Urban and Regional Research* 35 (1): 130–46.

Logan, John R., and Harvey Molotch. 1987. *Urban Fortunes: The Political Economy of Place.* Berkeley: University of California Press.

MDHA (Metropolitan Development and Housing Agency). 2011. *Action Plan, Grant B-9-CN-TN-0024.* Nashville, Tenn.: MDHA.

———. 2012. *Performance Report, Grant B-9-CN-TN-0024.* http://www.comptroller.tn.gov/repository /CA/2012/1175-2012-MDHA-rpt-cpa656.pdf.

Nashville Ledger. 2011. "Hot 'Hoods: Homeowners, Developers Gamble on Nashville's Emerging Neighborhoods." December 9. Accessed December 12, 2011. http://www.nashvilleledger.com /editorial/ArticleEmail.aspx?id=56220&p.

Notice (Notice of Designation of Empowerment Zones and Enterprise Communities). 1995. Fed. Reg. 10018–10019 (Docket No. R-95–1702; FR-3580-N-06). (February 23)

Oakley, D., Ruel, E. and Reid, L. 2013. "Atlanta's Last Demolitions and Relocations: The Relationship between Neighborhood Characteristics and Resident Satisfaction." *Housing Studies* 28(2): 205–34.

Oakley, Deirdre, and Hui-Shien Tsao. 2006. "A New Way of Revitalizing Urban Communities? Assessing the Impact of the Federal Empowerment Zone Program." *Journal of Urban Affairs* 28 (5): 443–71.

Olken, Charles E. 1971. "Economic Development in the Model Cities Program." *Law and Contemporary Problems* 36 (2): 205–26.

Reid, Carolina. 2011. "The Neighborhood Stabilization Program: Strategically Targeting Public Investments." *Community Investments* 23 (1): 23–33.

Riposa, Gerry. 1996. "From Enterprise Zones to Empowerment Zones: The Community Context of Urban Economic Development." *American Behavioral Scientist* 39 (5): 536–52.

Rohe, William M., and George C. Galster. 2014. "The Community Development Block Grant Program Turns 40: Proposals for Program Expansion and Reform." *Housing Policy Debate* 24 (1): 3–13.

Rubin, Julia Sass, and Gregory M. Stankiewicz. 2001. "The Los Angeles Community Development Bank: The Possible Pitfalls of Public–Private Partnerships." *Journal of Urban Affairs* 23 (2): 133–53.

Stegman, Michael A. 1995. "Recent US Urban Change and Policy Initiatives." *Urban Studies* 32 (1): 1601–7.

Urban Housing Solutions. 2012. *Chestnut Hill Revitalization Efforts*. Nashville, Tenn.: UHS.

von Hoffman, Alexander. 2011. "Into the Wild Blue Yonder: The Urban Crisis, Rocket Science, and the Pursuit of Transformation Housing Policy in the Great Society, Part Two." Joint Center for Housing Studies, Harvard University. http://www.jchs.harvard.edu/research /publications/wild-blue-yonder-urban-crisis-rocket-science-and-pursuit-transformation.

14

SUSTAINABLE FAIR HOUSING?

Reconciling the Spatial Goals of Fair Housing and
Sustainable Development in the Obama Administration

EDWARD G. GOETZ

Enforcement of fair housing law has been resurgent in the Obama administration. Since 2008, federal agencies have expanded efforts to monitor and respond to housing discrimination and segregation, issued regulatory rules to formalize recognition of the so-called disparate impact standard and to enhance requirements made of local governments to further fair housing efforts. The extent to which these efforts are sustainable, however, is questionable. Though disparate impact survived review by the Supreme Court in *Texas DHCA v. Inclusive Communities Project, Inc*, the administration's fair housing spatial strategy exhibits internal contradictions, especially a possible conflict with the new urban sustainability initiatives the White House is pursuing.

The pursuit of fair housing goals in the Obama years has been characterized by wedding conventional fair housing issues of equal access to the growing use of an "opportunity" framework for housing programs at the federal level. The resulting effort is one of the most vigorous fair housing strategies since passage of the Fair Housing Act in 1968.

Fair Housing Enforcement

The Pendulum of Fair Housing

Wide swings from one presidential administration to the next in the enforcement of fair housing are not new. There are a number of dimensions on which fair housing enforcement varies, including the decision to pursue disparate impact cases (which require a finding of discriminatory effect rather than discriminatory intent), and the aggressiveness of HUD in initiating investigations and in pursuing claims brought to it. After Nixon's constrained use of the legal authority granted in the act, the Carter administration sought to significantly expand enforcement. The election of Ronald Reagan moved the federal government to a limited engagement with fair housing issues. Under Reagan, the Department of Justice (DOJ) insisted on pursuing only cases in which discriminatory intent could be shown, and federal litigation efforts were cut back dramatically. The Clinton years saw the pendulum swing back again, as the Department of Housing and Urban Development (HUD) moved to settle a number of desegregation lawsuits in which the agency itself was a defendant. Clinton also increased funding for local enforcement groups as well as expanded federal enforcement efforts (King and Smith 2011). The election of George W. Bush in 2000, in turn, saw a return to Reaganesque policies of budget cutbacks for enforcement and adoption of the discriminatory intent threshold for federal legal action in fair housing. These policy changes have led to a dismal assessment of fair housing enforcement by advocates.

One month after Barack Obama's election in 2008, the National Commission on Fair Housing and Equal Opportunity (NCFHEO), an independent group organized by fair housing advocates, issued a report expressing disappointment in the federal government's efforts to combat discrimination in housing (NCFHEO 2008). Specifically, the report stated that "fair housing enforcement at HUD is failing" and pointed to a number of deficiencies in the agency's efforts in the years prior to 2008 (13). Under the Fair Housing Act, HUD's Office of Fair Housing and Equal Opportunity (FHEO) receives and investigates claims of housing discrimination filed by individuals or local enforcement agencies. Where FHEO finds a "reasonable cause" for action, it charges the accused party and initiates an administrative law or judicial proceeding. Though estimates put the number of acts of housing discrimination in the nation at 3 to 4 million per year, HUD was issuing fewer than fifty charges per year from 2003 through 2007 (NCFHEO 2008). Staffing cutbacks at FHEO dragged out the review process and led to significant deficiencies in investigating and processing claims. The commission went so far as to recommend that fair housing enforcement be taken away from HUD and moved to a new agency. The federal government's disregard for effective enforcement of fair housing, according to the commission, extended as well to the DOJ, which under the law has the authority to initiate lawsuits against public and private actors engaging in "a pattern and practice of discrimination" in housing. The commission documented the small and declining number of housing discrimination cases filed by the DOJ through the first eight years of the new century.

In contrast, the Obama administration has made fair housing a central objective, which has resulted in a range of initiatives that fair housing advocates have applauded (see, for example, PRRAC 2013). The administration has strengthened the administrative basis for fair housing enforcement and expanded the number and type of discrimination cases pursued. To the National Alliance for Fair Housing, these changes and others have constituted a "sea change in the federal government's approach to fair housing" (National Fair Housing Alliance 2014).

Fair Housing under Obama

Fair housing enforcement is enjoying yet another renaissance under a Democratic presidential administration. In the Obama years, the federal government has stepped up enforcement of fair housing according to the common numerical indicators, the number of suits filed by the DOJ, the number of HUD-initiated complaints, and the number of cases resulting in a charge of wrong-doing (National Fair Housing Alliance 2014). In addition to more activity in these areas, enforcement under Obama has moved in new directions (e.g., prosecuting "reverse redlining") and involved important policy decisions related to disparate impact and guidelines for governmental actions at all levels of government that further fair housing goals.

Reverse Redlining

There is little debate over the fact that minority home-buyers were disproportionately targeted for higher-cost subprime and predatory loans in the years prior to the housing crash of 2007. This pattern of lending, called reverse redlining, constituted a new fair housing front facing the Obama administration as it took power in 2008. Having campaigned for greater federal efforts to deal with the lending practices that led to the housing crisis, Obama's DOJ moved quickly to file cases against some of the nation's largest lenders. In 2009 the DOJ took on Wells Fargo in a suit that led to a 2012 settlement in which the company agreed to pay $175 million. A year before, the federal government settled with Countrywide Financial, a subsidiary of Bank of America, for $335 million. HUD and the DOJ joined with forty-nine states in a single settlement with five mortgage companies that channeled $20 billion to borrowers and $5 billion to state agencies for loan-servicing practices that adversely affected borrowers.

In 2010 Congress established the Consumer Financial Protection Bureau (CFPB), and within it, an Office of Fair Lending and Equal Opportunity (OFHLEO), to examine how financial practices impact the protected classes of the Fair Housing Act. In 2012, Obama created a "Residential Mortgage-Backed Securities Working Group" to further investigate fraudulent lending practices (Squires and Hartman 2013).

Disparate Impact

The distinction between discriminatory intent and discriminatory effect, and the decision to pursue cases that hinge on disparate impact alone, has been an important point of variation in fair housing enforcement. Restricting judicial action to cases in which discriminatory intent can be shown significantly constrains fair housing enforcement, and this has been the choice for most Republican administrations over the years. Though appellate and district courts have repeatedly upheld the viability of discriminatory effects (or disparate impacts) claims, different administrations have decided for themselves whether to pursue such cases. For years the courts have acknowledged the validity of fair housing claims based on the discriminatory effects of practices in question as well as cases in which discriminatory intent can be shown. Aiming to standardize the interpretation of the disparate impact standard, the Obama administration issued regulations in 2013 that define the conditions under which disparate impact claims can be made.[1] The regulations had long been awaited by fair housing advocates, who hoped to formalize the government's recognition of a legal standard that would prohibit seemingly neutral policies and practices that have the effect of denying housing opportunities to members of the protected classes.

Despite overwhelming support for the notion of disparate impact in lower courts (nine U.S. appellate courts had confirmed disparate impact claims) until 2015 the Supreme Court had never considered the issue in the context of a housing discrimination case. In the summer of 2015, however, the court ruled in *Texas DCHA v. ICP et al.*, that such claims are allowable under the Fair Housing Act (*Texas DHCA v. ICP*, 571 U.S. 1, 2015).

Affirmatively Furthering Fair Housing

The Fair Housing Act of 1968 contains a provision requiring federal housing and community-development programs to be implemented in ways that "affirmatively further" the objectives of the act. The affirmatively furthering fair housing (AFFH) provision thus requires that in addition to regulating the actions of the private sector in housing, the federal government ensure that its own programs and actions further fair housing goals. The AFFH clause has been interpreted to directly apply to federal actions implementing housing programs (for example, governing the siting of federally subsidized housing to ensure that the placement of subsidized units does not maintain or enhance patterns of segregation) and more indirectly, to apply to the use of federal housing and community-development funds by state and local governments.

Fair housing advocates have long complained that the AFFH goals have typically been subordinated within HUD, taking a back seat to concerns about program implementation and housing production goals. In addition, activists have criticized the weak nature of federal oversight of local governments' compliance with AFFH obligations. As a result, the Obama administration issued a set of rules for AFFH in 2015. Specifically, the rules strengthen the requirements for local governments to assess local fair housing issues, and to incorporate fair housing goals into a plan of action. The administration signaled its intentions to strengthen monitoring of local governments by settling a high-profile lawsuit against Westchester County, New York, early in Obama's first term.

AFFH establishes the obligation on the part of the federal government to ensure that local governments spend federal housing and community-development funds in accordance with fair housing goals. Thus, local jurisdictions receiving federal

Community Development Block Grant (CDBG) or HOME funds, for example, must certify that they are affirmatively furthering fair housing in their use of these federal funds. The suit against Westchester County, one of the nation's wealthiest, claimed that the county had been spending federal grant funds in ways that reinforced patterns of racial segregation and, furthermore, had made false claims to the federal government about its programs.

As part of the settlement, Westchester County agreed to develop hundreds of subsidized units in predominantly white sections of the county and to prevent housing discrimination. As King and Smith note, the administration promised to apply the same "principles to the other twelve hundred jurisdictions around the country that received [community development] block grants" (King and Smith 2011, 137–38). Though the settlement has been plagued by the county's lack of progress in making good on its promises, the suit itself was a high-profile statement that the administration would take its responsibilities for fair housing very seriously.

The Obama administration has also elevated AFFH objectives in a number of additional ways. Central to the administration's efforts in this area are the continued support and expansion of mixed-income housing, the reduction of concentrations of assisted housing, and the increased access of HUD-assisted households to "opportunity neighborhoods" (generally defined by low levels of poverty). The HUD strategic plan emphasizes the need to reduce the concentration of HUD-subsidized families in less advantaged neighborhoods, and restates the agency's commitment to creating and maintaining mixed-income and racially diverse communities. Local grantees are now required to document plans for meeting fair housing goals, reducing racial segregation, and increasing the number of HUD-assisted households in low-poverty neighborhoods.

The agency has also embraced reforms of the Housing Choice Voucher (HCV) program to achieve fair housing outcomes. These include support for mobility programs in some major cities and the creation of small fair-market rents (FMR) areas designed to allow assisted housing in higher-rent areas. Efforts to disperse assisted households and create mixed-income communities are also reflected in the administration's Choice Neighborhoods Initiative and the Rental Assistance Demonstration program.

"Opportunity Neighborhoods" and Sustainability

While concerns for spatial equity, integration, and dispersal of assisted housing to opportunity neighborhoods have been prominent in Obama's HUD, a second set of policy initiatives pursued by the administration related to the pursuit of regional equity and sustainable urban development has the potential to conflict with the dispersal objectives of fair housing.

The concept of a "geography of opportunity" emerged in policy circles during the 1990s and is meant to describe the spatially differentiated pattern of life chances within metropolitan areas. The term was initially a response to increasing concerns about "neighborhood effects"—the hypothesized link between adverse neighborhood conditions and individual well-being in urban areas. In policy terms, the phrase "opportunity neighborhood" was used to denote locations that were desirable because of the range of private and public amenities they possess and for the advantages they confer upon residents, and typically contrasted with neighborhoods of concentrated poverty. On the assumption that residence in opportunity neighborhoods improves the quality of life of targeted populations, federal housing policy shifted during the 1990s to programs that were designed to move federally subsidized households toward opportunity neighborhoods. Opportunity neighborhoods have become the holy grail of U.S. housing policy since then with various local efforts across the country, both public and private, adopting the framework for a range of initiatives.

The opportunity neighborhood discourse originated outside of a narrow fair housing framework. In fact, for more than a decade it was carefully associated with the objective of poverty deconcentration rather than racial desegregation (Goering 2003). Early policy initiatives were aimed at moving people around in order to establish a better mix. Programs to enhance opportunity were predominantly displacement/relocation/redevelopment efforts. The Obama administration inherited these dispersal efforts and continued them.

Despite the rhetorical distance between racial desegregation on the one hand and opportunity neighborhoods on the other, the overlap between the two policy objectives are extensive. Concentrated poverty in the United States is heavily racialized—African Americans in poverty are many times more likely to live in concentrated poverty than their white counterparts, and the notion of the opportunity neighborhood has been embedded in various nonfederal racial desegregation initiatives, including programs that resulted from a number of desegregation lawsuits settled during the 1990s (Popkin et al. 2000). The Obama administration has to some extent attempted to merge these two agendas, thereby infusing many federal housing initiatives with fair housing objectives in ways not attempted by previous administrations. This has led the administration to continue place-based efforts such as HOPE VI, as well as introduce new ones such as the Choice Neighborhoods Initiative, that direct the breaking up of concentrations of minority poverty.[2]

That the opportunity agenda has merged with fair housing objectives is also seen in HUD's proposed AFFH rule, which requires analysis of "racially concentrated areas of poverty" and the promotion of initiatives to desegregate and deconcentrate those neighborhoods.

Reconciling Fair Housing and Transportation Investment

While the first wave of opportunity initiatives, federal and local, were focused primarily on housing policy and programs related to the location of assisted households (and assisted units), a second wave has increasingly involved a range of policy areas. Several advances in the notion of opportunity neighborhoods have simultaneously occurred. Most significant among these was the emergence of a more multidimensional definition of opportunity. Originally defined by poverty rates or by race, "opportunity neighborhoods" were initially identified by the characteristics of their residents. Over time analysts began to look less at the demographic makeup of neighborhoods and more at access to transportation and employment, the quality of educational opportunities, and exposure to environmental disamenities. PolicyLink, a national nonprofit organization, has worked to disseminate this model of analysis. It has sponsored four national "equity summits" to promote the "equity movement" and to advance "sustainable and equitable development" for communities and regions (PolicyLink 2011). Its framework has been adopted by a number of regions that have in the intervening years produced a range of equity maps and atlases. Thus, local initiatives across the country measured, for example, the quality of schools by neighborhood, access to employment opportunities, access to transportation, and the geographic patterns of crime and other safety issues (see Sadler et al. 2012; and Benner, Bridges, and Huang 2010).

A second advance, which followed from the first, was a more nuanced understanding of how opportunity arrays itself across an urban landscape, and how the several dimensions of opportunity are cross-cutting and in fact contradictory in some respects. Consequently, a third important development in the notion of "opportunity neighborhood" is the understanding that areas can be simultaneously high in some types of opportunity and low in others. Thus, the notion that some neighborhoods have opportunity while others do not should give way, and in some cases has given way, to the idea that areas differ in the types of opportunity that they provide or lack. Together, these developments in the concept of opportunity suggest a matrix of characteristics and places. Finally, current initiatives to operationalize and measure "opportunity neighborhoods" typically utilize geographic information system (GIS) technologies to map opportunity. GIS has allowed analysts to engage in opportunity mapping, sometimes called equity mapping, focusing on the distribution of multiple opportunity characteristics across a metropolitan landscape.

Transit investments have played a central role in propelling the idea of access to opportunity, as well as in helping to define the elements of opportunity. PolicyLink notes that transportation systems "can be a powerful vehicle for promoting regional equity" because of the ways in which they can facilitate or limit the access of lower-income households to the amenities within a region (PolicyLink 2002). While arguing for greater investment in transportation options of use to lower-income households, notably transit, as a way of increasing opportunities for disadvantaged populations, the document notes that "such investments can be a double-edged sword" (PolicyLink 2002, 10). Warning that transit investments can fuel gentrification, the organization argues for measures to mitigate such outcomes and protect community benefits for existing low-income residents.

Some of the recent efforts at measuring and mapping opportunity emerged from regional efforts to plan transit investments. These efforts have been aimed at maximizing the impact of transit on improving accessibility for lower-income, transit-dependent populations. Since the early 2000s, the federal government has attempted to align transportation and housing investments as a means of enhancing the access and mobility of subsidized households. The spike in gasoline prices and growing concerns about climate change have provided additional rationales for a more closely coordinated housing and transportation policy.

Location Efficiency

In 2003, HUD and the Federal Transit Administration (FTA) first initiated efforts to coordinate federal housing and transportation investments and to support "transit oriented development." Among other efforts, the FTA commissioned research on the demand for housing along existing transit lines which showed the potential for more than 8 million new units in transit corridors by 2030 (Center for Transit-Oriented Development 2004). In 2007 Congress signaled its interest in coordinating investment across federal agencies. The House Committee on Appropriations noted in that year that "the Committee strongly believes that transportation, housing, and energy can no longer be viewed as completely separate spheres with little or no coordination throughout the different levels of government."[3] As a result, Congress directed HUD and FTA to address the issue of the transit/housing nexus.

With these nascent efforts already in place, the Obama administration quickly initiated a number of efforts to connect subsidized housing to transportation infrastructure. The administration saw such coordination as an answer to rapidly rising energy costs and concerns about carbon-based emissions as a means of simultaneously facilitating greater transit use and reducing costs for households. The Obama administration is the first to promulgate and pursue a set of policy principles related to sustainable urban development and "livability." The largest first-term initiative in this area was the Sustainable Communities Initiative (SCI), a partnership effort between HUD, the Department of Transportation, and the Environmental Protection Agency. Grants to local and regional governments were made in 2010 and 2011 to support regional planning and development efforts that would coordinate housing, urban development, and transportation investments to reduce energy consumption, environmental deterioration, and greenhouse gas emissions in major metropolitan areas.

More than $167 million in grants were made to seventy-four regions to coordinate local planning aimed at achieving six livability principles for metropolitan areas.[4] The principles emphasize transit and housing equity, coordinated local investment strategies, and growth that supports existing infrastructure investments. At the center of SCI is the goal of coordinating housing and transportation policy.

HUD has taken an additional step in the direction of coordinating housing and transportation policy by developing a Location Affordability Index (LAI) as a new way of measuring housing affordability. The LAI measures the combined housing and transportation costs in a neighborhood, providing a more sophisticated understanding of the true cost of living in any given area. Whether it is used to determine how housing programs impact the transportation costs of assisted families, or where to place assisted housing in order to minimize transportation costs, the LAI highlights the advantages of locating affordable housing in core areas that are well-served by transit. When it is applied to a range of federal housing programs it turns out that residents of the Section 221(d)(4) HUD subsidized multifamily housing enjoy a 53 percent greater level of transit connectivity against a comparison population of low-income households. In fact, a number of subsidized housing programs fare well in connecting subsidized housing residents to transit, including the low-income housing tax credit program.

Finally, the Obama administration has provided support to local governments for transit-oriented development (TOD) as a way of maximizing both investments. TOD is seen by the administration as a more efficient form of land use in metropolitan areas, ensuring greater job accessibility for lower-income residents, and ensuring a greater ridership base for the transit systems the administration is supporting.

The Fair Housing Tightrope

The challenge within the administration, as yet unresolved, is to reconcile these two policy impulses that in their application have contradictory goals. The sustainability imperative for the administration is transit connectivity—the colocation of assisted housing and transit to reduce the transportation costs of assisted households—and more intensive use of existing infrastructure. Each of these strategies imply greater investment in affordable housing in core areas of metropolitan regions that are well-served by transit and other infrastructure. The fair housing imperative on the other hand, as operationalized by fair housing advocates and applied by the Obama administration, is to disperse and deconcentrate assisted households to opportunity neighborhoods, many of which are ill-served or entirely unserved by transit. While location-efficiency goals prioritize development in the core, the spatial objectives of fair housing emphasize the decentralization of low-income households of color.

The tension between the two is clearly recognized, at least by fair housing advocates. These groups have long complained, for example, that the Housing Choice Voucher program recipients are too clustered and do not disperse well enough into opportunity areas. These same advocates maintain that the low-income housing tax credit program and HUD-assisted rental housing are too concentrated geographically and that they perpetuate segregation. Most recently, fair housing advocates have voiced concerns about the potential adverse fair housing impact of location efficiency efforts. A leading national advocacy organization for fair housing, the Poverty and Race Research Action Council (PRRAC), for example, calls the LAI an "inappropriate tool for siting new low-income housing," and fair housing advocates have opposed TOD plans that call for affordable housing along transit ways because of fears that to do so would perpetuate segregation (Tegeler and Chouest 2011; Oak Park Regional Housing Center 2012).

In fact, fair housing activists worry that HUD and DOT are ignoring the multiple dimensions of opportunity by looking only at housing cost and transit access, and urge policymakers to "recognize the additional variables greatly impacting household costs and quality of life" (Oak Park Regional Housing Center 2012, 2). Yet, recent work in equity mapping suggests that opportunity comes in many forms and that neighborhoods vary by the type of opportunities they provide as much as by the quantity.

It is, however, hard to imagine that the administration, having created the interagency Partnership for Sustainable Communities, will back away from the livability principles that guide the partnership's action. Having taken more than a year to create the LAI, it is unlikely that the administration will actually refrain from using it to guide housing investment strategies, knowing that to do so would have implications for the cost of living of its assisted households. Strategies to colocate assisted housing and transit are already in place in several localities.

The spatial objectives of fair housing, chiefly the deconcentration and dispersal of assisted housing, are to an important extent in tension with the goals of sustainable urban development. These policy objectives, both embraced by the administration, will require a delicate balancing act, for the pursuit of one set of goals sacrifices the other. How or whether the Obama administration will move to reconcile these tensions is unclear.

Future of Fair Housing

The classic expression of the urban geography of opportunity has been to rely upon a pair of simple dichotomies. The first of these is the Manichaean notion of good and bad neighborhoods. Neighborhoods of high poverty (or racially segregated neighborhoods) are seen as possessing and producing socioeconomic processes that are without significant redeeming value; they are neighborhoods that disadvantaged people should leave, and in the case of social housing communities, areas that are deserving of total clearance and demolition. On the other hand, opportunity neighborhoods are seen as simplistically free of any problematic aspects for low-income households. The second dichotomy driving the early ideas about "opportunity neighborhoods" is a geographic one that juxtaposes central city and suburb, largely situating opportunity in suburban areas and its opposite in older, core areas of metropolitan areas (see, for example, Dreier, Mollenkopf, and Swanstrom 2001; Rusk 1999).

One of the most influential works in the second wave of opportunity policy was the framing paper "Promoting Regional Equity" (PRE) (PolicyLink 2002). PRE anticipated and shaped much of the opportunity mapping initiatives that followed in the next ten years by stressing the multidimensionality of opportunity. PRE is one of the first national efforts to define a set of policy areas central to the challenge of creating opportunity neighborhoods, and its call for cross-sector collaborations is echoed in virtually all subsequent equity mapping initiatives. But, most significant of all innovations embedded in PRE is what in shorthand might be called the *community-development* perspective that the document takes. While adopting the opportunity framework, PRE nevertheless calls for the preservation of housing affordability, community benefits, and greater amenities for lower-income households in core areas. PRE thus represents the first important national statement within the opportunity paradigm that acknowledges, in a centrally important way, a policy orientation other than mobility and relocation.

The innovative elements of PRE lie primarily in the discussion of seven key issue areas for regional equity. PRE specifically lists transportation, housing, economic opportunity, land use and infrastructure, education, environmental justice, and health as components of a healthy and equitable regional system. In doing so, PRE in effect presents an operational definition of opportunity neighborhood that contains seven dimensions. Virtually all opportunity-mapping exercises since PRE have utilized this approach by identifying a range of issues bearing on the concept of opportunity area. Many of the areas identified in PRE, furthermore, show up in all subsequent efforts. Certainly, transportation, housing, economic opportunity (sometimes labeled as "jobs" or "job accessibility"), and education are central to most opportunity-mapping efforts.

Second, PRE implicitly anticipates subsequent developments in the opportunity mapping movement by surfacing the cross-cutting nature of some dimensions of "opportunity." Perhaps the best example is what PRE says about transportation and transit. In a similar vein, PRE implicitly acknowledges that not all economic investments will produce greater opportunities for lower-income households of core neighborhoods, and thus that economic development efforts should explicitly link investment to community benefits through community benefits packages (now known as community benefits agreements, or CBAs). In the area of housing, PRE not only advocates for mixed-income housing and a greater distribution of affordable housing across regions (both of which are staples of the early opportunity neighborhood initiatives), but also for the preservation of existing affordable housing "so that low-income residents are not displaced" (PolicyLink 2002, 12) by other investments. Finally, in the area of health, PRE highlights the problem of food deserts and argues for strategies to improve the health of lower-income households *where they currently live.*

Each of these observations pointed the opportunity movement in a different direction than the dispersal imperative of previous opportunity-based initiatives.

Each of these envisions core neighborhoods as places in which lower-income households can remain, and therefore calls for programs to enhance conditions for those families in those neighborhoods. It is an acknowledgment of the role of community-development efforts within the framework of opportunity neighborhoods. It opens the door to an analysis of the benefits to low-income families of core neighborhoods, a possibility the opportunity movement had not previously entertained.

Fair housing advocacy and fair housing policy will have to reconcile, then, at least two sets of contradictory policy impulses. The first is the conflicting spatial strategies behind the desegregation impulse to disperse assisted housing on the one hand, and the sustainability impulse to connect assisted housing with areas of high transit connectivity. The second conflict is the pursuit of a more equitable geography of opportunity through dispersal and mobility of disadvantaged households versus the strategy of greater public investment in disadvantaged neighborhoods. The emergence of these dialectics during the Obama years leaves fair housing advocates, both inside and outside of government, a set of critical challenges for charting fair housing policy in the future.

Notes

1. 24 CFR Part 100 Implementation of the Fair Housing Act's Discriminatory Effects Standard; Final Rule. Federal Register Vol. 78 No. 32, February 15, 2013.
2. The degree to which these programs have actually resulted in the desegregation or deconcentration of the subsidized residents who are forcibly displaced is, however, quite limited. See Smith chapter in this collection.
3. Appropriations Committee. H. Rept. 110-238, "Departments of Transportation, and Housing and Urban Development, and Related Agencies Appropriations Bill, 2008. (2007). https://www.congress.gov/congressional-report/110/house-report/238.
4. The six principles are: (1) provide more transportation choices; (2) promote equitable, affordable housing; (3) enhance economic competitiveness; (4) support existing communities; (5) coordinate policies and leverage investment; and (6) value communities and neighborhoods.

References

Benner, Chris, Kendra Bridges, and Ganlin Huang. 2010. *Sacramento SCORECARD: Baseline Regional Report.* Davis: University of California–Davis Center for Regional Change. http://regionalchange.ucdavis.edu/ourwork/publications/other-projects/sacramento-scorecard-report-2010.

Center for Transit-Oriented Development. 2004. "Hidden in Plain Sight: Capturing the Demand for Housing Near Transit." *Reconnecting America.* http://www.reconnectingamerica.org/assets/Uploads/2004Ctodreport.pdf.

Dreier, Peter, John Mollenkopf, and Todd Swanstrom. 2001. *Place Matters: Metropolitics for the Twenty-First Century.* Lawrence: University Press of Kansas.

Goering, John. 2003. "Political Origins and Opposition." In *Choosing a Better Life? Evaluating the Moving to Opportunity Social Experiment,* ed. John Goering and Judith D. Feins, 37–58. Washington, D.C.: Urban Institute.

King, Desmond S., and Rogers M. Smith. 2011. *Still a House Divided: Race and Politics in Obama's America.* Princeton, N.J.: Princeton University Press.

National Fair Housing Alliance. 2014. *Fair Housing Trends: Expanding Opportunity: Systemic Approaches to Fair Housing.* http://www.nationalfairhousing.org/LinkClick.aspx?fileticket =MqO6AE6loGY%3D&tabid=3917&mid=5321.

NCFHEO (National Commission on Fair Housing and Equal Opportunity). 2008. *The Future of Fair Housing.*

Oak Park Regional Housing Center. 2012. "Affirmatively Furthering Fair Housing and the Center for Neighborhood Technology's H=T Affordability Index." Available from author.

PolicyLink. 2002. "Promoting Regional Equity." Paper presented at Promoting Regional Equity: A National Summit on Equitable Development, Social Justice, and Smart Growth, Los Angeles, Calif., November 17–19. http://community-wealth.org/sites/clone.community-wealth .org/files/downloads/report-robinson-et-al.pdf.

———. 2011. "Equity Summit 2011." Accessed June 1, 2013. http://www.equitysummit2011.org/.

Popkin, Susan J., George Galster, Kenneth Temkin, Carla Herbig, Diane K. Levy, and Elise Richer. 2000. *Baseline Assessment of Public Housing Desegregation Cases: Cross-Site Report*, Vol. 1. Washington, D.C.: U.S. Department of Housing and Urban Development.

PRRAC (Poverty and Race Research Action Council). 2013. "Affirmatively Furthering Fair Housing at HUD: A First Term Report Card." http://www.prrac.org/pdf/HUDFirstTermReport Card.pdfhttp://www.prrac.org/pdf/HUDFirstTermReportCard.pdf.

Rusk, David. 1999. *Inside Game/Outside Game: Winning Strategies for Saving Urban America.* Washington, D.C.: Brookings Institution.

Sadler, Bill, Elizabeth Wampler, Jeff Wood, Matt Barry, and Jordan Wirfs-Brock. 2012. *The Denver Regional Equity Atlas: Mapping Access to Opportunity at a Regional Scale.* Denver: Mile High Connects. http://www.reconnectingamerica.org/resource-center/books-and-reports /2012/the-denver-regional-equity-atlas-mapping-opportunity-at-the-regional-scale/.

Squires, Gregory D., and Chester Hartman. 2013. "Occupy Wall Street: A New Wave of Fair Housing Activism?" In *From Foreclosure to Fair Lending: Advocacy, Organizing, Occupy, and the Pursuit of Equitable Credit*, ed. Chester Hartman and Gregory D. Squires, 1–20. New York: New Village Press.

Tegeler, Philip, and Hanna Chouest. 2011. "'The 'Housing + Transportation Index' and Fair Housing." Poverty and Race Research Action Council, policy brief. http://www.prrac.org/pdf/fair _housing_and_the_H+T_Index.pdf.

15

REGIONAL POLICY IN THE AGE OF OBAMA

KAREN CHAPPLE

As concern about climate change and sustainability increases, regional planning has grown increasingly popular around the world. At the Rio+20 United Nations Conference on Sustainable Development in 2012, summit participants explicitly called for engaging regional in planning and implementing sustainable development (United Nations General Assembly 2012). But until President Barack Obama took office, the U.S. government had largely neglected regions; apart from the creation of the Tennessee Valley Authority in 1933 and of metropolitan planning organizations (MPOs) in the Federal-Aid Highway Act of 1962, little direct federal intervention had occurred. Yet, by 2011, HUD's Sustainable Communities Initiative-Regional Planning Grant (SCI-RPG) program had provided $165 million in competitive grants for collaborative regional planning efforts supporting more sustainable development patterns in seventy-four regions. It was the largest federal government investment ever in regional planning in the United States.

The new program arose due to a unique partnership between three cabinet-level federal agencies: the Department of Transportation (DOT), the Environmental Protection Agency (EPA), and the Department of Housing and Urban Development (HUD). Obama appointees at the three agencies brought a strong commitment to sustainability and the "three Es" (economy, environment, and equity), along with a passion for overcoming the fragmentation between agencies that hindered smart growth and livability goals (Pendall et al. 2013). Thus the federal Partnership for Sustainable Communities was born (Pendall et al. 2013).

Driving the new focus on the region as the appropriate scale for intervention was the recognition that issues of economy, environment, and equity crossed jurisdictional boundaries, and that regional fragmentation impeded effective decision-making. That the partnership, and HUD in particular, decided to work at the regional level was due mostly to the urging of Bruce Katz, leader of the Obama transition team.[1] A passionate and influential advocate for regionalism, Katz had founded the Metropolitan Policy Program at the Brookings Institution shortly after leaving his position as chief of staff at HUD under President Clinton.[2] In addition, two other factors supported the development of a regional sustainability planning program at the partnership: the growing maturity of blueprint planning and the economic downturn. Over time, federal and state reforms giving MPOs more carrots and sticks to link transportation investment to air quality goals have led to experimentation in blueprint planning processes around the country. Also, the Great Recession created new pressure on regions to enlist planning in the effort to revive economic growth and opportunity.

The agencies in the partnership quickly began to meet regularly, coordinate programs, integrate livability principles into decision-making, and revise their grant programs (Pendall et al. 2013). A new regional planning program, SCI, thus emerged at HUD's Office of Sustainable Housing and Communities, in order to (1) foster collaborations across the public, private, and nonprofit sectors and between different levels of government in a region; (2) create new or implement established regional blueprints; and (3) focus in particular on economic competitiveness and revitalization. At a minimum, the program restarted a century-old conversation about regions. Although it is too early to tell, it may also have created new capacity for regional planning that will lead to its resurgence.

This chapter begins by describing the emergence and growth of regional planning, and then discusses how regional planning came to address sustainable development as well. Based on a content analysis of applications for the SCI program, it then shows how U.S. regions defined themselves and proposed to address sustainability issues in response to the Obama program. A conclusion evaluates the prospects for regional planning and policy in the United States.

The Emergence of Regional Sustainability Planning

Origins and Definitions

Metropolitan and regional planning dates just to the nineteenth century, and there are no treatises on how to lay out regions: "Regional planning has become a necessity in most countries. But nobody seems to know quite what it is, and no nation seems to know how to do it" (Ross and Cohen 1973 quoted in Gore 1984, 1). There is also confusion about what constitutes a region. Regions are either an organic expression of life or an analytic area for designing and implementing policy solutions—or both. The organic region, then, is a subcontinental, subnational, or substate space with homogeneity of natural resources and/or culture, such as, for example, the California coast or the Andes (Markusen 1987). The homogeneity of this ecological region can mean that common problems arise, making it an appropriate scale for intervention as well.

But when we define regions for the purpose of making plans, we rarely can rely on the boundaries of the organic region. Typically, a plan defines the spatial entity that is most appropriate to meet its objectives: for example, transportation and land use linkages, infrastructure provision, or economic development. Thus, regional planning tends to take either a functional or an administrative form; that is, it is defined either by a function, such as the area within which commutes take place, or the governing entity (e.g., city, county, multiple counties, state) that administers the policies and plans to meet the objective.

In practice, then, most regional planning exercises today are based upon the metropolitan nodal region, that is, urbanization organized around a center or centers, which is the spatial entity that encompasses most functions and administration. Because most of the development needed to accommodate growth occurs within this urban system, this may be the most logical foundation for development policy. Over time, this city-based region may expand to incorporate multiple nodes or subcenters, but it remains a metropolitan region. In contrast to the ecological region, metropolises tend to be internally heterogeneous—complicating regional planning both technically and politically.

Regional Planning Institutionalized

The earliest efforts at regional planning emerged in mid-nineteenth century Europe in response to the industrial revolution, with the specific aim of exploiting natural resources and developing more productive industrial cities (Weaver 1984). This meant the coordination of infrastructure and housing development by the state, to create effective urban agglomerations of labor and capital. It also spurred an anarchistic reaction, with Proudhon, Kropotkin, and others advocating collectivist societies organized in decentralized producers' associations for local markets (Teitz 2012). Coordinating infrastructure and housing meant centralization and a metropolitan structure with a strong core and weak periphery. The vision of a collectivist society involved regional self-sufficiency, in some ways the earliest attempt at sustainability.

As railroad and streetcar suburbs grew into cities in their own right, questions of coordination across cities arose. At the industrial city's peak, most of the U.S. population was concentrated in the major central cities, but facilitated by transportation, decentralization was rapid. Progressive reforms in most states established home rule authority, protecting local government autonomy from state interference. Cities could raise their own taxes, issue bonds, and build large-scale infrastructure, which reinforced piecemeal development patterns. Cities also worked to expand their territories through annexation and consolidation, though progressive reforms made this challenging.

In the United States, the New Deal had kicked off a period of Keynesian stimulus with a set of programs that invested in and stabilized infrastructure and housing. Most of this investment was not explicitly regional, but it often reinforced the tendency for growth on the periphery of central cities. Where formal regionalism did not exist, jurisdictions developed their own mechanisms for coordination, in a de facto regionalism.

In the 1960s, another set of regional institutions arose to reshape transportation and land use and the growing uneven development across cities and suburbs.

In support of federal requirements mandating planning in transportation, services, and other areas, federal policy enabled the establishment of councils of government (COGs) in the 1960s, or voluntary organizations of local governments. Yet, with a one-city, one-vote structure of governance, and no real power to regulate and incentivize, this horizontal institutional form struggled to shape development. Land use regulation remained local, subject to home rule, and was rarely coordinated across levels or jurisdictions.

More promising was the creation of metropolitan planning organizations (MPOs), required by the Federal Aid Highway Act of 1962 for any urbanized area with a population greater than 50,000. In order to receive federal funds, MPOs were required to undergo a planning process. MPOs received a major boost in 1991 when Congress enacted the Intermodal Surface Transportation Efficiency Act (ISTEA), increasing their authority to program federal transportation dollars (Goldman and Deakin 2000). While allocating one-fifth of federal transportation funding to MPOs, ISTEA mandates the development of long-range (twenty years or more) regional transportation plans that conform to regional air quality plans while realistically taking into account fiscal constraints and other objectives. This then set the stage for regional sustainability planning.

But first, the neoliberal era added new fuel to the regionalism movement. The rise of new forms of governance, in which NGOs, the private sector, and other nonstate actors were given a more significant and active role in public decisions, policy-making, and planning, brought the potential for a more flexible form of governance—a potential way to overcome the roadblock in establishing regional government. At the same time, the rescaling of the state has often occurred without resources, leading places to seek the most effective way to facilitate an influx of capital (Deas and Ward 2000). Neil Brenner argues that these shifts have themselves led to intensified intercity competition for capital, greater administrative fragmentation, and uneven development (Brenner 2002).

In the late twentieth century, inequality among regions increased rapidly (Pastor et al. 2000). As urban agglomerations exacerbated differences between core and periphery, experiments around the United States emerged to address regional inequities and fragmentation. Among the most frequently cited were Minneapolis–St. Paul's experiment in tax-base sharing and the regional and state growth management in Portland, Oregon (Swanstrom 1996). But as these initiatives stalled, regional planning next began to converge with another movement, toward planning sustainably for the "three Es"—economy, environment, and equity.

The Rise of Regional Sustainability Planning

Sustainable development is "the need to ensure a better quality of life for all, now and into the future, in a just and equitable manner, while living within the limits of supporting ecosystems" (Agyeman, Bullard, and Evans 2003, 2). The region may be the most appropriate scale for understanding sustainability. Viewed from an environmental perspective, sustainability reflects the underlying ecosystem, so regional planning should integrate ecological systems, such as water, climate, and topography (McHarg 1969; Steiner 2011). The growth of population and economic activity impacts natural systems in specific places, through the destruction of habitat and the degradation of air and water quality. However, the impacts extend beyond localized areas: diminished air quality in one atmospheric system can spread to others.

Yet, in practice the movement for sustainability has largely emerged from cities rather than regions, and research has followed suit. City governments have taken action against climate change, by enacting energy efficiency and recycling programs that encourage individuals to take action, and by creating voluntary sustainability plans that set targets for the reduction of greenhouse gas emissions. The first generation of climate change plans had occurred in twenty-nine U.S. states by 2008 (Wheeler 2008). These plans typically featured targets for reducing greenhouse gas emissions based on the Kyoto goal (7 percent below 1990 emissions by 2008–12). But reducing automobile dependence is challenging, if not impossible, within city boundaries, since mode choice depends on destinations that are outside the city, and is thus shaped by regional labor and housing markets. Metropolitan fragmentation creates significant challenges for coordinating across cities. And with little discretionary funding of their own, cities struggle to effect changes in behavior.

Meanwhile, most global climate change policy-making occurs at the national and international level. At their best, international agreements and national legislation provide standards that reshape local policy-making and behavior. For example, the Kyoto Protocol sets emission reduction targets, asking developed countries to assume primary responsibility. The United Nations has taken the lead in advocating sustainable development globally, with a 2012 summit (building on the 1992 Earth Summit) that negotiated sustainable development goals. But in the end, such standards will not be effective if there is no funding to incentivize changes in behavior, and if they are enacted at an institutional level—state or city—that does not correspond to the scale of the problem being addressed. If the issue is transportation, or water quality, or housing, or economic development, or labor, that scale needs to be regional.

The current generation of regional sustainability plans emerges from the convergence of the sustainable development movement with blueprint planning. Blueprints—"collaborative planning processes that engage residents of a region in articulating a vision for the long term future of their region" (Booz Allen Hamilton et al. 2014, 109)—emerged in the 1990s as a civil society response to the costs of sprawl, the market and demographic pressures for smarter growth, and the frustration with the lack of planning and coordination across the policy arenas of transportation, the environment, the economy, and housing (Barbour and Teitz 2006). Enabled by the federal reforms that funded MPOs to take the lead in developing long-range regional transportation plans, planning processes appeared around the country; among the best documented are Portland, Sacramento, Salt Lake City, San Francisco, San Diego, Denver, Chicago, and Washington, D.C. (Calthorpe and Fulton 2001; Knaap and Lewis 2011). Thus, blueprint planning was soon linked to sustainability. As states also enacted greenhouse gas reduction targets, many MPOs began integrating them into regional transportation plans.

Thus, significant capacity existed in U.S. cities and regions to engage in a sustainability planning program. The Obama team added strong leadership and experience to the mix. The only piece lacking, perhaps, was broad-based political support.

About the HUD Program

HUD's 2010 notice of funding availability (NOFA) describes the purpose of the SCI program, which—in line with Katz's suggestion to work at the metropolitan scale to overcome issues of fragmentation—is to "support metropolitan and multijurisdictional planning efforts that integrate housing, land use, economic and workforce development, transportation, and infrastructure investments" (HUD 2010, 2). The goal of these planning efforts is to make improvements in the areas of "(1) economic competitiveness and revitalization; (2) social equity, inclusion, and access to opportunity; (3) energy use and climate change; and (4) public health and environmental impact" (HUD 2010, 3). Guiding the selection would be the joint livability principles of DOT, EPA and HUD, which support "a measure of integration of the housing, transportation, environmental, and employment amenities accessible to residents. A livable community is one with multiple modes of transportation, different types of housing, and destinations located close to home" (HUD 2011, 11–12). The NOFA also focused on social equity, specifying that grantee activities should further Title VI of the Civil Rights Act, Section 504 of the Rehabilitation Act of 1973, and the Fair Housing Act by incorporating inclusionary zoning, environmental justice, and the coordination of housing development and public transportation into their plans. It called for meaningful stakeholder engagement in planning processes, from the development of vision to its implementation, with particular attention to marginalized communities. The NOFA required applicants to organize a consortium of government entities and nonprofit partners, including the region's principal city or county, additional cities to represent no less than 50 percent of the region's population, the MPO or regional planning agency, and a nonprofit organization, foundation, or educational institution. Applicants defined the boundaries of their regions themselves, based on consortium membership.

The SCI-RPG awarded a total of $98 million in grants in 2010 and $70 million in 2011 to two types of regions—those interested in implementing existing sustainability plans, and those who had yet to complete any regional planning efforts. Grant amounts depended on the size of the region, with $25 million reserved for small- and medium-sized regions in 2010 and $17.5 million reserved in 2011 (HUD 2010, 4).[3] Applicants could use HUD-SCI funding to improve regional planning and decision-making processes, coordination among agencies, and data collection. Improving regional planning might involve creating integrated plans for inclusive housing, sustainable transportation, and economic development. Coordination among agencies could include conducting scenario planning or climate impact assessments (HUD 2010, 22–25).

Study Methodology

The research team collected data for this project by contacting individual lead applicants and requesting their application materials.[4] There were 354 applications submitted to the SCI-RPG in 2010 and 2011, from 289 different regions. The study sample included applications for half (144) of the regions that applied for a grant.[5]

When comparing applications, it is important to understand the political climate in which a given region is situated. We use states' presidential vote as a proxy for their political environment. Even if a region is somewhat more "blue" or "red" than its state as a whole, it still is impacted by state priorities. If the state voted for McCain for president in 2008, it was considered a red applicant; for Obama, a blue applicant; and if the margin of victory was less than 6 percentage points, it was a swing state applicant. Overall, the applicant sample was 51 percent blue, 28 percent red, and 20 percent swing state.

Approaches to Regionalism and Sustainability in the Age of Obama

Defining Regions and Regionalism

A metropolitan approach to regional planning dominated throughout the applications for the Obama sustainability program: of the applicants, over two-thirds defined their region around a metropolitan node. The remainder were mostly agglomerations of counties (e.g., the twenty-seven counties in Montana, Wyoming, and Idaho that form the Yellowstone Business Council), single rural counties (e.g., Kaua'i), or metropolitan subareas (e.g., Montgomery County). Almost all of the large regions (over 500,000 residents) defined themselves as metropolitan, along with half of the medium regions (population 200,000–499,999); however, just one-third of the small regions (less than 200,000 in population) centered on a metropolitan area. How regions defined themselves may also have been related to political affiliation: regions located in swing states were much more likely to define themselves around a metropolitan core compared to those in red or blue states.

Applicants assembled many different types of consortia, with most (78 percent) led by an MPO, COG, or joint MPO-COG, typically with joint involvement of cities, nonprofits, counties, and universities (Figure 15.1). Participation by private sector or foundations was much rarer, and only a few proposed consortia had federal or state agency involvement. In blue states, foundations, COGs, and counties were

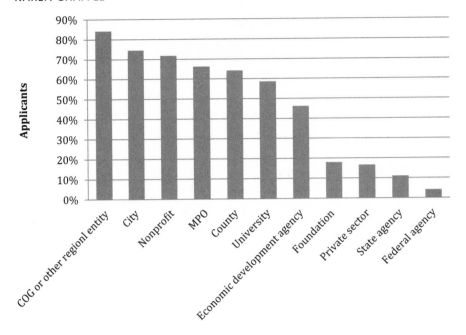

Figure 15.1. Organizations involved in consortia.

disproportionately likely to join the project as core partners, while in red states, economic development agencies and the private sector were more likely partners, and in swing states, universities.

Given the deep experience of many cities with sustainability planning, the regional agencies relied heavily on their participation: over 80 percent of the consortia included both a regional agency and a city or nonprofit. But it was largely the projects centered on a metropolitan area, rather than the region, that engaged in such a top-down/bottom-up collaboration: 90 percent of the metropolitan initiatives, compared to just two-thirds of the regional initiatives, involved collaboration between the regional and the local levels. Almost all consortia in blue and swing states involved a top-down/bottom-up collaboration, but just two-thirds of those in red states.

Defining Sustainability

How do regions approach sustainability today? The applications for the Obama administration program revealed that regions were quite confused about what they were supposed to be doing. HUD defines "sustainability" as activities that "actively promote sustainability through energy-efficient, environmentally friendly, healthy design, including elements of visitability and universal design" (HUD 2011b, 2). However, most of the applications offered no specific definition of sustainability but instead implied one of four different approaches to sustainability: (1) the 3 *Es,* or comprehensiveness, making reference to balancing social, economic, and environmental concerns (one-third of applicants); (2) *livability,* or the accessibility of transportation, housing, and work choices (one-fifth of applicants); (3) *location efficiency,* or minimizing the costs of sprawl while maximizing the efficient use of existing infrastructure (one-fifth of applicants); or (4) *environment,* a perspective that emphasized climate-change adaptation, ecological preservation, or environmental quality (one-fifth of applicants). These approaches then guided their proposed activities. For example, an applicant emphasizing comprehensiveness might propose green infrastructure as an economic development strategy for downtown businesses; a "livability" applicant might suggest pedestrian improvements near transit stations; a "location efficiency" applicant might put forth a proposal for developing new job centers near residential enclaves; and an applicant with an environmental focus might be planning a regional trail system. The use of one definition or another did not vary across regions by type (metro or region), with one exception: only one-tenth of the regions were interested in location efficiency (compared to over one-fifth of the metros). Similarly, red- or swing-state applicants showed relatively little interest in location efficiency, as well as comprehensive approaches that balance the tradeoff, instead emphasizing environmental and livability benefits.

Many regions have struggled to incorporate social equity issues into sustainability planning, in part because of the conflicts between values and need for tradeoffs (Campbell 1996). Because of the requirements of the HUD NOFA, almost all of the regions focused on incorporating more equitable and participatory processes in their regional plans; many emphasized social equity as an outcome as well. To analyze approaches to procedural equity, we examined the public participation mechanisms proposed. We sorted strategies into four modes, roughly based on Sherry Arnstein's 1969 ladder of citizen participation: from simply educating the public (often through Web sites, reports, or presentations), to interacting with a select group (e.g., via working groups, agency taskforces, or citizen advisory committees), to interacting with the public (typically in community meetings, workshops, or charrettes), to actually building local capacity (typically through intermediaries, leadership development, or training programs) (Arnstein 1969). Proposed participation strategy varies significantly by region type (Figure 15.2). Blue states score higher on the participation ladder, favoring strategies that engage the public. Red states tend to rely on public education strategies or work through committees. Although utilizing strategies higher on the participation ladder may empower communities, there is also an argument for the more top-down approach of educating the public: some regions might need to learn more about the potential benefits of sustainability strategies before embarking on their own community-based processes.

Winning Applications

HUD staff winnowed the pool of 354 applicants to 74 winners in a rigorous selection process that involved almost forty agencies and philanthropic foundations as

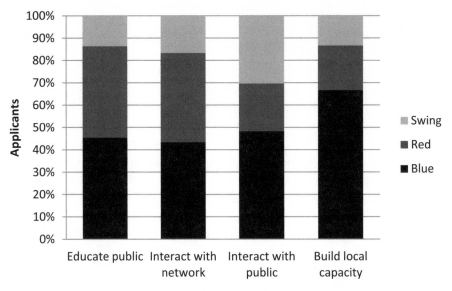

Figure 15.2. Participation strategy by 2008 state vote.

reviewers. Many of the foundation reviewers had worked for decades on antipoverty and community-development programs. Of course, HUD's program considerations guided selection, so application characteristics—such as match funding offered and whether the applicant applied in both years—played a significant role (according to regression analysis). How regions defined themselves and sustainability also seemed to matter. Metropolitan and strong market areas were more likely to be selected, controlling for all else, but so were regions located in red states (Chapple and Mattiuzzi 2013). HUD staff may have picked metros for their greater capacity, and red states because of an interest in developing a broad support base for sustainability policies. Of all the potential collaboration partners, including nonprofits, in the consortium helped ensure a win; HUD likely saw the nonprofit involvement as a way to maintain the focus on social equity. Finally, HUD was significantly more likely to select applications that offered a more comprehensive approach to sustainability, as well as an equity focus, testifying to its commitment to the 3 Es: focusing on environmental quality or the economy is not enough. Overall, the results suggest a deliberate strategy on the part of the Obama administration to advance social equity goals at the regional scale.

Regional Sustainability Planning Moving Forward

U.S. regions have long engaged in planning, increasingly with a sustainability focus. The lack of formal, empowered regional institutions has meant the rise of ad hoc regionalism, or cooperation agreements between cities and subregions with shifting membership depending on the issue. Not surprisingly, then, the initial wave of climate change plans came from cities acting alone. But with MPOs taking charge of regional transportation planning, and cities adding their capacity, regions have a structure in place for addressing sustainability issues.

Given the opportunity to engage in regional sustainability planning by the Obama administration, many different types of organizations and collaborations across the country expressed interest. HUD leadership seems to have uncovered a pent-up demand for planning. Those interested included large metropolitan regions, blue in politics, bringing together regional and local actors in collaborations. Others were at the table for the first time, often in red states. These efforts often connected agencies who had never worked together, using broad language of environmental quality to smooth over value conflicts, keeping the public at a careful distance (Pendall et al. 2013). The administration selected both types.

As of this writing, most of the regions are completing their work. All are concerned about the sustainability of their efforts.[6] Even the grantees who are able to influence transportation planning in their region express doubts that they will be able to continue the focus of the Obama administration program on livability and social equity. Although the administration was able to require an equity focus through federal legislation such as the Fair Housing Act, such mechanisms do not exist in many states. Ideally, transportation funding would be the carrot to push cities toward more equitable development, but federal and state transportation funders are not ready to incorporate criteria such as affordable housing, job creation, and community participation. The Obama administration undoubtedly planted the seed, but systemic change awaits a more unified epoch.

Notes

1. Personal communication, senior HUD official, February 13, 2015.
2. For more on the motivation behind the Brookings' program, see Bruce Katz's speech at the Brookings National Issues Forum, "Forging Metropolitan Solutions to Urban and Regional Problems" (1997).
3. A number of "runners up" in the 2010 round were granted "Preferred Sustainability Status" (PSS) and were give greater consideration in the 2011 round.
4. Although HUD was willing to cooperate with us for the study, they do not have an archive with all the applications or even all the winning applications, so it had to be developed from scratch.
5. We obtained 34 percent of the 2010 applications and 53 percent of the 2011. We obtained 81 percent of the winners, compared to just 37 percent of the losers. The sample slightly over-represents several regions, including the South Atlantic, Mid Atlantic, East North Central, West North Central, Mountain, and Pacific census regions, and slightly underrepresents East South Central and New England. Only in the West South Central division did underrepresentation pose a methodological concern, with just eleven of thirty-four nonduplicate applications (34 percent); response was particularly low in Arkansas and Louisiana.
6. Personal communication, senior HUD official, March 7, 2014.

References

Agyeman, Julian, Robert D. Bullard, and Bob Evans. 2003. *Just Sustainabilities: Development in an Unequal World.* Cambridge, Mass.: MIT Press.

Arnstein, Sherry R. 1969. "A Ladder of Citizen Participation." *Journal of the American Institute of Planners* 35 (4): 216–24.

Barbour, Elisa, and Michael B. Teitz. 2006. *Blueprint Planning in California: Forging Consensus on Metropolitan Growth and Development.* San Francisco: Public Policy Institute of California.

Booz Allen Hamilton, National Cooperative Highway Research Program, Transportation Research Board, and National Academies of Sciences, Engineering, and Medicine. 2014. *Strategic Issues Facing Transportation, Volume 4: Sustainability as an Organizing Principle for Transportation Agencies.* Washington, D.C.: National Academies Press.

Brenner, Neil. 2002. "Decoding the Newest 'Metropolitan Regionalism' in the USA: A Critical Overview." *Cities* 19 (1): 3–21.

Calthorpe, Peter, and William Fulton. 2001. *The Regional City.* Washington, D.C.: Island Press.

Campbell, Scott. 1996. "Green Cities, Growing Cities, Just Cities? Urban Planning and the Contradictions of Sustainable Development." *Journal of the American Planning Association* 62 (3): 296–312.

Chapple, Karen, and Elizabeth Mattiuzzi. 2013. *Planting the Seeds for a Sustainable Future: HUD's Sustainable Communities Initiative Regional Planning Grant Program.* Berkeley, Calif.: Center for Community Innovation. http://communityinnovation.berkeley.edu/SCIRPGFinal (080713).pdf.

Deas, Iain, and Kevin G. Ward. 2000. "From the 'New Localism' to the 'New Regionalism'? The Implications of Regional Development Agencies for City–Regional Relations." *Political Geography* 19 (3): 273–92.

Goldman, Todd, and Elizabeth Deakin. 2000. "Regionalism through Partnerships? Metropolitan Planning since ISTEA." *Berkeley Planning Journal* 14 (1): 46–75.

Gore, Charles. 1984. *Regions in Question: Space, Development Theory and Regional Policy.* London: Methuen.

HUD (U.S. Department of Housing and Urban Development). 2010. "Notice of Funding Availability (NOFA) for HUD's Fiscal Year 2010 Sustainable Communities Regional Planning Grant Program." http://portal.hud.gov/hudportal/documents/huddoc?id=DOC_35393.pdf.

———. 2011a. "FY 2011 Notice of Funding Availability (NOFA) Policy Requirements and General Section to HUD's FY 2011 NOFAs for Discretionary Programs." FR-5500-N-01. http://portal.hud.gov/hudportal/HUD?src=/program_offices/administration/grants/nofa11/2011 gensecanncmt.

———. 2011b. "Notice of Funding Availability (NOFA) for HUD's FY 2011 Sustainable Communities Regional Planning Grant Program." FR-5396-N-03. http://portal.hud.gov/hudportal/documents/huddoc?id=DOC_35393.pdf.

Katz, Bruce. 1997. "Forging Metropolitan Solutions to Urban and Regional Problems." Opening remarks at the Brookings National Issues Forum, May 28. http://www.brookings.edu/research/speeches/1997/05/28metropolitanpolicy-katz.

Knaap, Gerrit J., and Rebecca Lewis. 2011. "Regional Planning for Sustainability and Hegemony of Metropolitan Regionalism." In *Regional Planning in America: Practice and Prospect,* ed. Ethan Seltzer and Armando Carbonell, 176–221. Cambridge, Mass.: Lincoln Institute of Land Policy.

Markusen, Ann. 1987. *Regions: The Economics and Politics of Territory.* Totowa, N.J.: Rowan and Littlefield.

McHarg, Ian L. 1969. *Design with Nature.* New York: Natural History Press.

Pastor, Manuel Jr., Peter Dreier, J. Eugene Grigsby III, and Marta López-Garza. 2000. *Regions That Work: How Cities and Suburbs Can Grow Together.* Minneapolis: University of Minnesota Press.

Pendall, Rolf, Sandra Rosenbloom, Diane Levy, Elizabeth Oo, Gerrit Knaap, Jason Sartori, and Arnab Chakraborty. 2013. "Can Federal Efforts Advance Federal and Local De-Siloing? Lessons from the HUD-EPA-DOT Partnership for Sustainable Communities."

UI No. 08752-000-00. Washington, DC: Urban Institute. http://www.urban.org/sites /default/files/alfresco/publication-pdfs/412820-Can-Federal-Efforts-Advance-Federal-and -Local-De-Siloing-Full-Report.PDF.

Ross, George W., and Stephen S. Cohen. 1973. *The Politics of French Regional Planning.* Baltimore: Johns Hopkins University Center for Metropolitan Planning and Research.

Steiner, Frederick. 2011. "Plan with Nature: The Legacy of Ian McHarg." In *Regional Planning in America: Practice and Prospect,* ed. Ethan Seltzer and Armando Carbonell, 17–52, Cambridge, Mass.: Lincoln Institute of Land Policy.

Swanstrom, Todd. 1996. "Ideas Matter: Reflections on the New Regionalism," *Cityscape* 2 (2): 5–21.

Teitz, Michael B. 2012. "Regional Development Planning." In *Planning Ideas That Matter: Livability, Territoriality, Governance, and Reflective Practice,* ed. Bishwapriya Sanyal, Lawrence J. Vale, and Christina D. Rosan, 127–52. Cambridge, Mass.: MIT Press.

United Nations General Assembly. 2012. "The Future We Want." 66/19. Accessed January 10, 2014. http://www.un.org/ga/search/view_doc.asp?symbol=A/RES/66/288&Lang=E.

Weaver, Clyde. 1984. *Regional Development and the Local Community: Planning, Politics, and Social Context.* Chichester, U.K.: Wiley.

Wheeler, Stephen M. 2008. "State and Municipal Climate Change Plans: The First Generation." *Journal of the American Planning Association* 74 (4): 481–96.

16

MAKING POLICY IN THE STREETS

LORRAINE C. MINNITE AND FRANCES FOX PIVEN

Many commentators have a sense that we are living in a new movement era (see, for example, Sitrin and Azzellini 2014; Castells 2012; and Mason 2012). On any given day, people in many places in the world are engaged in collective action and protest of one kind or another. These actions typically occur in cities, though observers rarely valorize the urban context. In fact, most of the social science literature on social movements pays little attention to spatial scale or dynamics, and therefore, to theorizing the role of the urban in the generation, ideation, composition, shape, force, or power of urban-based social movements.[1] For example, one early and important text defines urban political movements as simply movements of urban minority groups (Fainstein and Fainstein 1974, xi). Likewise, many urbanists pay little attention to social movements, perhaps inheriting a blind eye from the old pluralists and their paradigm of power in the city, which once played such a dominant role in the study of American politics. Pluralists mostly ignored or even denigrated social movements as aberrant and dangerous to the orderly functioning of democracy.[2] Although there has been a revival of Marxist approaches to anticapitalist urban struggles (Harvey 2012), and a flowering of "critical urban theory" that privileges the role of contestation in shaping urban space (Brenner 2012), the study of urban social movements remains uneven, like the rise and fall of urban movements themselves (Castells 1983; Hamel, Lustiger-Thaler, and Mayer 2000; Pickvance 2003; Hackworth 2006).

Given the shaky intellectual foundation, what can contemporary theorizing tell us about the capacity of urban social movements to exercise power? We begin by connecting our discussion to Castells's influential work of some three decades ago, which sees urban social movements as distinctive and homogeneous phenomena that share three basic characteristics. First, Castells argues that urban movement participants must see themselves as "urban" or related to the city; second, urban movements are locally based and territorially defined; and third, they tend to adopt three types of major goals: "collective consumption, cultural identity, and political self-management" (Castells 1983, 328).[3] What Castells calls "social change" results only when all three characteristics come together in a movement's practice. Social

272

change, however, is not the same as social transformation. Castells argues that because of their localism and particularity, urban social movements have a limited capacity for achieving structural reform. Instead, they are "reactive Utopias": they represent what people can do when they have no other choice. Castells says that "when people find themselves unable to control the world, they simply shrink the world to the size of their community" (331). The value of urban social movements, for Castells, is their continuity with a history of resistance to capitalist exploitation, and their function as the proving grounds for tomorrow's larger social movements. But their power potential is limited.

More recently, Mayer argues that contemporary urban movements coalescing under the motto of a "right to the city" marks a new phase in the development of urban social movements, with a broader capacity for challenging neoliberal planning and policies, though achieving their potential is problematic (Mayer 2012; Harvey 2012). In the developed West, urban social movements have emerged and subsided in response to neoliberalism's changing goals as described by Jamie Peck and Adam Tickell (2002), *roll-back* neoliberalism in the 1980s, *roll-out* neoliberalism in the 1990s, and the crisis of neoliberalism after the dot-com crash of 2001. The movements struggle to stay alive across the fragmenting urban terrain. In the United States in particular, community-based and housing movements have fallen prey to professionalization.[4] Mayer distinguishes between so-called first- and third-world cities and their various "right to the city" movements. In the developing world, these efforts represent the actual self-organization of the urban poor: "in resisting dispossession, eviction, police violence, and repression . . . [these movements] . . . have . . . developed their own local protest cultures, and have achieved— through mass mobilization, occupations, and political protest—improvements in their living conditions" (2012, 79). Mayer agrees with Castells that in the metropoles of the first world, the possibilities for transformative, progressive change are ultimately limited. However, Mayer holds out the possibility that first-world right-to-the-city movements will have a larger impact if they can find ways to take on *global* capital by identifying commonalities and connections to the struggles of the urban poor in the developing world. What is needed is a networking of organizations across space, and solidarity in linking issues together against a common enemy.

Merrifield is less optimistic about right-to-the-city movements. Drawing on his critical encounter with the work of Lefebvre, Merrifield writes of "the complete urbanization of society," a world of "planetary urbanization" in which "urbanization is increasing its reach everywhere; the urban is shapeless, formless and apparently boundless, riven with new contradictions and tensions that make it hard to tell where borders reside and what's inside and what's outside" (2013b, 910). If the urban is everywhere, Merrifield hypothesizes, location, in fact, is not central to experience. Merrifield would replace notions of rights and reclamation with the concept of *centrality,* which, borrowing from particle physics, he describes as akin to kinetic energy, with poles of repulsion and attraction bringing people together and dispersing them across space in new ways. Following Lefebvre, Merrifield argues that the urban brings everything together and in so doing, transforms all that comes together; the urban concentrates and consolidates, and the more it does, the more a "politics of the encounter" punctuates the urban landscape (2013a). Thus, Merrifield enters a line of thinkers about cities and political resistance who see cities as providing ideal conditions for nurturing social movements (Nicholls 2008), even if he, like Lefebvre ([1970] 2003), rejects the idea of the city as a container or a category in favor of a more fluid and ethereal notion of *the urban* (Merrifield 2002, 2014). However, it is precisely the significance of the city as a container and how that container is sometimes breached that is our concern here.

Boundaries and Borders

From the standpoint of a theory of politics, we want to quarrel with notions of the urban such as Merrifield's and others' that theorize space by minimizing the significance of borders and boundaries that define or demarcate space. To be sure, Merrifield's "politics of the encounter" recognizes difference, which is to say, what happens at the intersection of boundaries. To talk about an urbanism that is everywhere and therefore nowhere, however, is to reduce what makes the encounter a crossing of differences—the border—of little analytical value. Of course, boundaries are not simply physical territorial delimiters, nor may the territorial character of a physical border define what is most significant about it. There are many kinds of borders—physical, imagined, lived—across vectors of hierarchy and networks of social relations. Ironically, amidst the ascendance and domination of a globalization discourse and ideology of deterritorialization and a borderless world, "the study of borders has undergone a renaissance" in recent years (Newman 2006, 144). For example, theorists of human geography write of mental maps (Gould and White 1986) and "geographical imaginaries," as the "taken for granted spatial ordering of the world" (Gregory 2009, 282) that links identity to territory. In terms of geopolitics, boundaries reflect history and conflict, and embed legal meanings. They are reified as conveyors of political power, manifesting and circumscribing formal governing authorities. Newman states that, "for all disciplines, borders determine the nature of group (in some cases defined territorially) belonging, affiliation and membership, and the way in which the processes of inclusion and exclusion are institutionalized" (2006).

Interdependent Power in the City

The city, like the state, is embedded in complex bounded horizontal and vertical institutional relationships that represent varying histories, contain the present (Harvey 2009, 10–11), and construct reality. It is a site concentrating a multitude of intersecting social cleavages of race, class, gender, sexual orientation, and so forth. But it is also a space demarcated by authority-conveying borders—physical, legal, jurisdictional, and political. The formation of group identities, when they are contained by and within the city as a particular place, can hamper the emergence of broader movements from below. When boundaries are crossed, as they are, for example, in the process of political coalition-building, people are connected "horizontally," which can be a source of strength (Sitrin 2006, 2012).

"Vertical" or hierarchically ordered social relations are defined by inequalities of status, class, or material resources and sustained by systems of cooperation. In these social relations, interdependencies can become a source of power for those at the bottom because they provide opportunities to disrupt normal institutional relations. The challenge for strategists of urban social movements is in reading the map of entanglements, identifying "horizontal" opportunities for organizing and movement building, locating vulnerabilities in the hierarchical interdependencies of power, and leveraging them through disruptive action.

To examine the challenges facing urban movements in the developed world today, we rely on a theory of movement power developed over several decades by Piven and Cloward (1979, 2000, 2005) and more recently by Piven (2008, 2014), which she labels "interdependent power," but which has not been elaborated in the context of the city as either space or scale (Sites 2007, 126). Piven argues that interdependent power is

> a kind of power based not on resources, things, or attributes, but rooted in the social and cooperative relations in which people are enmeshed by virtue of group life. . . . Social life is cooperative life, and in principle, all people who make contributions to these systems of cooperation have potential power over others who depend on them. This kind of interdependent power is not concentrated at the top but is potentially widespread. (2008, 5)

To strategize interdependent power, people acting together must first map the terrain to locate important boundaries and borders, and the lines of authority and institutional entanglements that oppress them; they must identify leverage points, the places and intersections where their cooperation is expected and required for things to go on as they are; and they must activate that leverage by defying expectations and rules. Their ultimate power is in withdrawing their cooperation (Piven and Cloward 2005).

For both the theory of interdependent power and Lefebvre's notion of a "right to the city" as a revolutionary project (Harvey 2012; Purcell 2014), the roots of the struggle for a new humanism are in the social world itself and in the complex of social relations that sustains it. However, the theory of interdependent power stands in contrast to Lefebvre's emphasis on cooperation and collective ownership by arguing for the necessity of disruption and withdrawal from cooperation as sources of power for those at the bottom. Lefebvre's ideas for effecting humanizing social change revolve around the creation of a program for reorienting analysis, awareness, and understanding among those who inhabit the city, as well as throughout the entire society, toward a praxis that reveals to people the power they have to democratically manage their own affairs. Similarly, Piven and Cloward argue that a transvaluation in worldview is critical to the rise of movements from below:

> For a protest movement to arise out of these traumas of daily life, people have to perceive the deprivation and disorganization they experience as both wrong, and subject to redress. The social arrangements that are ordinarily perceived as just and immutable must come to seem both unjust and mutable. (1979, 12)

For Lefebvre, the activity of appropriating or reappropriating urban space as shared space, and of people using it for their own needs deepens and enriches what it means to be a citizen among citizens not so much of a state, but of a transformed society. As they work together and encounter each other, people find new ways to meet their needs and the controlling institutions of the state and of the capitalist economy seem less necessary. Following Marx, Lefebvre says they wither away (2009, 147). The theory of interdependent power and the work of Piven and Cloward, in general, however, does not reach for societal transformation in the same way. Instead, its focus is on conflict and power. Its subject is strategy and an analysis of the conditions under which poor people can act as historical agents of societal change to force concessions from above in order to improve their standing and the material conditions of their lives. Piven and Cloward were pragmatic but also cautious about the prospects for social reform and the power of the poor to extract very much from the state.

Much of the story Piven and Cloward tell in their best-known work on "poor people's movements" concerns the great upheavals in the United States of what were arguably urban social movements among the lower classes in the 1930s and 1960s. These include the political mobilization of the working classes in the industrial cities of the North during the period of the Great Depression; defiance of southern apartheid mounted in the cities of the South; and the welfare rights protest of the black urban poor during the tumultuous period of the 1960s. Each of these movements scored victories by jumping over the institutional borders that ordinarily limit urban movements. In what follows, we provide an illustration of how this occurred in the 1960s-era welfare rights movement, and then compare the historical case to emerging urban social movements in the "age of Obama" to assess how race and political economy have changed movement opportunities since the 1960s. We conclude with a discussion of the potential of urban social movements to advance a progressive urban agenda in the United States today. But before proceeding to the case studies, we outline what urban social movements must do to achieve policy reform.

Two Problems for Urban Social Movements

To exercise power sufficient to influence policy, urban social movements have to solve two main problems. The first problem deals with the well-known fragmentation of local movements across physical space. We call this the problem of horizontal boundaries. Movements breach these boundaries by developing their capacities to communicate and coordinate with one another. This can involve recrafting issue demands to move them beyond the parochial local context in which urban social movements find themselves, or the development of new organizational structures, or the deployment of new communication tools to build and strengthen networks that allow movements to grow.

Second, movements achieve victories when they act strategically. To act strategically, they must think strategically about power and leverage points. Thinking strategically means analyzing the problem of *scales*, not simply *scale* as it relates to size, but rather how the local is mapped to the center of power that must be disrupted in order to produce the desired change. In other words, movements must analyze and understand the network of hierarchical political and economic institutional relationships in which they are embedded if they are to correctly identify their target. We call this the problem of vertical boundaries.

Once sources of power are located, the challenge becomes activating those sources by engaging in coordinated disruptive actions that will ricochet across the map of hierarchical relations to leverage power into reform. There are many meanings of "disruption," and we want to be clear that our use of the term with respect to urban social movements refers to actions that withdraw contributions to social cooperation within institutional arrangements. Melucci argues that a social movement pushes conflict "beyond the limits of compatibility with the system in question, i.e., it breaks the rules of the game, puts forward non-negotiable objectives, questions the legitimacy of power" (1981, 176). Depending on the institutional context, withdrawing cooperation can take the form of active resistance in the ways Melucci suggests, or through other forms of collective refusal to conform to expected behavior. Piven argues that the term "disruption" means something different than unconventional or radical or noisy action:

[It denotes] the leverage that results from the breakdown of institutionally regulated cooperation, as in strikes, whether workplace strikes where people withdraw their labor and shut down production or the provision of services, or student strikes where young people withdraw from the classroom and close down the university; or as in boycotts, whether by consumers who refuse to purchase goods and thus threaten profits, or by the women "hysterics" of the late nineteenth century who refused their role as sexual partners and service providers, or by farmers who refuse to bring their milk to market; or as in riots, where crowds break with the compact that usually governs civic life; or as in mass demands for relief or welfare, where people break with a pattern of cooperation based on norms of self-reliance and self-denial. (2006, 21)

In this sense, movement activities and actions do not so much "jump scale" in the way Smith conceived scale-jumping (Smith 1992); rather, the effects of their actions pulse like electricity through the nodes of networked relations, both horizontal and vertical, the energy reconfiguring those relations to shrink the spaces in between, and bend authority in a favorable direction.

The Challenge of Scale and Localism in Contemporary Urban Social Movements

Welfare Rights as an Urban Social Movement

The 1960s-era welfare rights movement was a successful case of "scale-jumping" by an urban social movement. It shows how urban social movements from below can sometimes surmount the tangle of institutional hierarchies and social processes that lock in place the deep inequalities of urban life. It engaged thousands of poor women who, over roughly a five-year period between 1967 and 1972, used disruptive tactics such as mass claims for benefits backed by sit-ins, rallies, and demonstrations to press for income supports that would allow them to feed and clothe and raise their children in a decent way. By empowering poor women to claim a new right to income by simple virtue of their status as mothers, the welfare rights movement was a kind of "right to the city" movement. Women exercised interdependent power primarily by withholding their cooperation from an often degrading system of poor relief that counted on their quiescence for its smooth running. Their disruptive actions resulted in policy change and state concessions that reduced poverty by expanding the welfare rolls by millions of new claimants, who then got the support to which they were entitled under law. In addition, for those already receiving aid, grant levels rose. The food stamp program was also restructured and expanded, and the school lunch program launched. Later, in 1972, Congress granted fiscal relief to states and localities by absorbing the "adult categories" of federal social assistance into a new relief program called Supplemental Security Income or SSI (Cazenave 2007, 178). SSI was one of the more important federal poverty policy innovations of the post–World War II period.

How did a movement of the urban poor, most of them women, and most of them black, compel these reforms in such a short period of time? Patterns of migration from the South and Puerto Rico after World War II created large concentrations of minorities in the northern industrial states who often faced recurrent periods of unemployment and severe poverty in the cities. Piven and Cloward write that "these states and their localities were also the most exposed to ghetto discontent"

(1979, 279). At the same time, they were critical to the national electoral fortunes of the Democratic Party, creating the circuit of interdependencies that made the subsequent hurdling of vertical boundaries possible.

What began in 1963 and 1964 as a series of local actions by poor black women against ill treatment at the hands of the welfare bureaucracy in a handful of major U.S. cities rapidly built up to a national movement for welfare rights, largely through the organizing efforts of George Wiley and others, who would go on to found the National Welfare Rights Organization (NWRO). The federal government's antipoverty and community action programs helped nourish these protests in major urban areas against the "inadequacy and inhumanity" of the welfare system by mandating "maximum feasible participation" of the poor in the programs (West 1981, 22). This meant federal grant monies were being used to organize people and politicize the issue of poverty and abusive treatment by the welfare bureaucracy.[5]

Welfare rights as a protest against low grant levels and a humiliating process for receiving aid, got its start as a series of unconnected and isolated local actions. In Watts, Johnnie Tillmon, a single mother of six, whose chronic arthritis left her unable to do the laundry work she relied on to care for her family, went on welfare. The experience was so demeaning and degrading, Tillmon was moved to organize other women like her to demand better treatment. In 1963, she founded one of the first welfare rights organizations, ANC (Aid to Needy Children) Mothers Anonymous, to engage in direct action and stage sit-ins in welfare offices. In other cities, agitation by women on welfare was supported by private charities, churches, and social welfare groups, whose involvement helped to coordinate efforts. An example is the Ohio Steering Committee for Adequate Welfare, which was formed in the wake of state legislative cuts to welfare benefits in 1965 and represented a coalition of women on welfare from cities and towns across the state. The forging of solidarities across shared experiences of mistreatment by the welfare system created new, local, lateral networks of support that began to breach the problem of horizontal boundaries.

Unusually, welfare rights also developed at least the beginning of a strategy to overcome vertical boundaries. In New York City, Mobilization for Youth (MFY), a multipronged social service agency on the Lower East Side that served as the model for Lyndon Johnson's War on Poverty, stimulated the formation of dozens of local welfare rights organizing groups across the city. Located at MFY, Piven and Cloward conducted studies that revealed that for every one person on welfare, another was entitled to aid but was not getting it. "A huge pool of families with incomes below the prevailing welfare grant schedules had built up in the cities as a result of migration and unemployment" (1979, 275–76). They developed a "strategy to end poverty" that called on activists to help enroll these eligible people in welfare (Cloward and Piven 1966). They argued that the large discrepancies between the numbers of people receiving aid and those eligible were the result not of bureaucratic inefficiency, but of a deliberate policy of discouragement motivated by both antipathy to the black poor and fiscal concerns at the state and local levels. Information regarding the availability of aid was routinely withheld. Rules, such as "man-in-the-home" prohibitions or arbitrary evaluations of "unsuitable home" conditions (e.g., the presence of out-of-wedlock children) and the like, were promulgated to make access to entitlements for public aid more restrictive. In a paper circulated among organizers and later published in *The Nation* in 1966, Cloward and Piven forcefully argued that

> widespread campaigns to register the eligible poor for welfare aid, and to help existing recipients obtain their full benefits, would produce bureaucratic disruption in welfare agencies and fiscal disruption in local and state government. These disruptions would generate severe political strains, and deepen existing divisions among elements in the big-city Democratic coalition: the remaining white middle class, the white working-class ethnic groups, and the growing minority poor. To avoid further weakening of that historic coalition, a national Democratic administration would be constrained to advance a federal solution to poverty that would override local welfare failures, local class and racial conflicts and local revenue dilemmas. By the internal disruption of bureaucratic practices, by the furor over public welfare poverty, and by the collapse of current financing arrangements, powerful forces can be generated for major economic reforms at the national level. (1966, 510)

Their article mapped the terrain of borders and boundaries and located the leverage points for disruptive activity by people who are believed to lack power—black urban poor women. They discussed in some detail how these actions could ramify up through the governmental system, since welfare policy-making and funding were shared at the state, local, and federal levels. Disrupting the welfare system by withdrawing cooperation in the administration of restrictive policies and practices that depended on the submission of the poor would create new political divisions, argued Cloward and Piven, and compel the national government to "federalize" welfare policy and thus override the age-old systems of local poor relief that denied people the aid they needed and were arguably entitled to by law. Denying poor people the aid to which they were entitled itself was a kind of lawlessness.

We present our analysis of the welfare rights movement to illustrate how the challenges of localism and scale can be overcome. But what about U.S. urban social movements in the "age of Obama?" Do they have a strategic analysis of the relationship between necessarily local protests and the national and international centers of power that are the targets of protest? How well are they overcoming the horizontal fragmentation that weakens them? Are they mobilizing the mass defiance that can ramify upward and disrupt centers of power? Or, contrary to many expectations, did the election of the first black president, a liberal Democrat, have a stifling effect on progressive urban movements?

We first turn to the Occupy Wall Street (OWS) movement, which captured international attention and changed the terms of the debate over growing inequality in the wake of the financial crisis of 2007–8. Then we turn to a discussion of the potential of the labor movement as an urban social movement and the "Black Lives Matter" movement as the best hope for a transformative politics from below.

Occupy Wall Street as an Urban Social Movement

OWS was a quintessentially urban social movement. It intentionally framed itself in a way that merged diverse social identities together as "the 99 percent," emphasizing a single societal cleavage between us and them. Notions of "the other" as a deviant class are flipped—it is the rich, not the poor who are immoral—and "the other" is the tiny minority of the wealthiest people who have benefited most by the ascendance of finance capital. Diversity within unity strikes an urban chord, and the sharp focus on inequality references the problems of the city.

Second, OWS claimed urban space with its encampment strategy. The victims of globalization would sit-in and sit-down under the noses of the captains of finance. Then, in Castellsian fashion, their encampments shrank the world to the size of their community and created "in miniature, the kind of society that they wanted to live in," a society that took care of all its members' needs for food, clothing, shelter (Writers for the 99% 2011, 8).

The creative and effective use of new communications technologies allowed OWS to begin to hurdle the problem of horizontal boundaries. The use of social media condensed time and space, "allowing highly organized movements to quickly mobilize massive numbers of people" (Writers for the 99% 2011, 8), a process repeated from Tunisia to Tahrir Square, from the encampments of the "indignados" of Spain to the State House in Madison, Wisconsin. The transformation in communications technology means that the need for the sorts of organizations created by NWRO that lifted the welfare rights movement out of the northern ghettos of the United States and into the halls of Congress was less urgent. At least from the standpoint of overcoming the horizontal borders that isolate and contain local movements, external coordinating structures, if their principle role is to provide hubs for relaying information, may be less important.

We are less certain about how well OWS, as a movement, met the challenge of hurdling vertical boundaries. On the one hand, in the beginning, many occupiers struggled with the call for demands. "What do you want? What do you stand for?" the media asked. They taunted movement participants as silly hippies without a cause. Within OWS, the commitment to redefining democratic participation and the diverse constituency meant that demands of the kind the media was insisting on would take time to distill.[6]

Also, some participants rejected the idea of demands. As an original member of the New York General Assembly, the name given to the collective decision-making body open to all occupiers present at Zuccotti Park, the site of the occupation, put it:

> Most of us believe that what is most important is to open space for conversations—for democracy—real, direct, and participatory democracy. Our only demand then would be to be left alone in our plazas, parks, schools, workplaces, and neighborhoods so as to meet one another, reflect together, and . . . decide what our alternatives are. (Sitrin 2011, 8)

Thus, much of OWS's first act remained on a discursive plane, never drawing a clear and detailed map of the murky terrain that would have to be navigated if vulnerabilities in institutional arrangements—the cracks in the system—are to be uncovered. The complexity of modern life, the distance and alienation from the centers of political and economic power veil the intersections and connections that lead from those at the bottom to those at the top. Where invisibility shields fail, police power is there to repress resistance. So, it is complicated. The capacity for institutional disruption is not obvious. Many who were drawn to OWS do not play critical roles in dominant institutions, so their opportunities to exercise interdependent power by withdrawing their cooperation are limited.

Moreover, OWS skated across the discursive plane of rhetorical resistance in part because there were many temptations to do so. Activists with OWS were good at it. They were talented communicators. Operating in the networked world of the Internet, they took to social media, Twitter and Facebook, and almost instantly words and pictures fueled the spread of the movement.

The Labor Movement as an Urban Social Movement

Arguably, as historian Colin Gordon says, organized labor has always been an urban institution (Gordon 2013), and it has created vehicles, such as city federations or central labor councils through which unions and community groups can come together (Ness 2001; Rathke and Rogers 2001). Today, some of labor's most promising campaigns—the fight back by teachers against a neoliberal urban school reform agenda, the struggle for a living wage and the fast food workers' revolt—are unfolding in cities and their inner-ring suburbs.

The same forces of globalization that have transformed the urban political economy have devastated the U.S. labor movement. Its revival depends upon its reinvention as an insurgent movement from below that fights for the needs not only of unionized workers but for the communities in which those workers live. This requires overcoming traditional divisions between the organized and unorganized, the native- and foreign-born, women and men, whites and people of color. It also requires breaching the "city trenches" that historically have separated the workplace from the community and patterned the development of the U.S. working class (Katznelson 1981). Labor needs once again to become an urban social movement (Turner and Cornfield 2007; Fletcher and Gapasin 2008; Harvey 2012, 27–66). We highlight here two developments that suggest the importance of a disruptive and unruly labor movement to progressive politics and policy in the city.

THE CHICAGO TEACHERS' UNION STRIKE

The 2012 Chicago teachers' strike galvanized not only tens of thousands of public school teachers but a broad swath of Chicago's working-class communities of color who stood with the teachers in their defiance of Chicago's political hierarchy. The strike was the culmination of the transformation of the Chicago Teachers Union (CTU) from a complacent organization that bargained with city officials primarily for better wages and working conditions, to a bottom-up, dynamic union that successfully bridged the traditional divides between teachers, parents, and students, and unions and communities (Brecher 2014, 361–68; Uetricht 2014; Young 2014). In other words, the strategic problem that the teachers' campaign addressed was mainly horizontal: to build a coalition that brought together the labor and community groups that could exert pressure on local power centers.

The story begins with an insurgent caucus within the union formed by dissidents in 2008, during a budget crisis that Mayor Richard M. Daley used to push a privatization plan on the school system. The Caucus of Rank and File Educators (CORE) took a "social unionism" approach to organizing (P. Johnston 1994) that included both teachers and the community (Bartlett 2013). As new members joined, they were encouraged to participate in committees on research, communications, advocacy, and especially outreach to teachers and the public at large. Another committee worked on planned interventions in the union's governing procedures. CORE sought out allies in the community and organized public panels and events where teachers talked about the problems they were experiencing, from overcrowded classrooms to school closures, and where community residents discussed how the schools crisis was part of their larger concerns about poverty, housing, employment, and violence. They created an organizing department to mobilize union members to work alongside community groups (Uetricht 2014).[7]

All of this work resulted in the surprise election in 2010 of CORE's leader, chemistry teacher Karen Lewis, as the new president of the CTU. Meanwhile, organizing continued within the union. Events came to a head two years later when contract negotiations stalled. The city wanted to limit collective bargaining to financial issues, impose a 20 percent longer school day with no increased pay, institute merit-only raises, and raise health insurance premiums. In contrast, the union focused its demands on issues of educational quality—for example, smaller classes, adequate resources, an enriched curriculum, and wrap-around services in low-income communities (Kaplan 2013). The two sides were at loggerheads by early 2012, and mediation failed to bring them together.

CORE and the CTU prepared for a strike[8] by setting up contract committees in every school, with one CTU member for every five or ten workers serving as a liaison to the union, and the network functioning to relay what members were thinking and their collective contract demands from school to school and to the leadership. Meanwhile, the union continued to reach out to the community by organizing public events and keeping open the lines of communication. A 2011 state law engineered by Mayor Rahm Emanuel before he was elected required the union to meet a threshold of 75 percent approval for any strike authorization (Sustar 2013). In June, when CTU members voted to give the House of Delegates the authority to call a strike at the beginning of the school year, the affirmative strike vote was 90 percent of the membership and 98 percent of those casting ballots.

The several years of building a democratic union and including the community of parents and residents in the effort to defend Chicago's schools from austerity budgets and privatization schemes paid off (Gutierrez 2013). Horizontal boundaries had been hurdled; community support for the strike was organized before the strike began and remained high. The labor outreach working group of Occupy Chicago facilitated the bringing together of parents, students, community residents, and other trade unionists who later walked with the teachers in mass marches and rallies and participated on picket lines set up at nearly 700 schools throughout the city (Brecher 2014, 361–68). Occupy Chicago used its social networking skills and capacities to blunt the mainstream media's antiunion coverage and carry the CTU's message to the public (Young 2014, 10).

After four days, a tentative agreement was hammered out between the school board and the union, with the union refusing to call off the strike while its membership reviewed, discussed, and ultimately approved the contract. (This took several more days, despite Emanuel's effort to get a court injunction to force the teachers back to work.) It was a surprising if limited victory for the union and for the schools (Kaplan 2013). Included in the contract agreement were demands from the community to hire 600 more teachers in art, music, physical education, and languages, and where new monies could be identified (and the union identified them), more school nurses, social workers, and counselors. Of course, not everything the union wanted was won; it did not get, for example, the lower caps on class size that it demanded. And the mayor, undaunted, continued his verbal assault on teachers, promoting charterization through expensive ad campaigns, and the closing of more schools.[9]

FAST FOOD WORKERS AND THE LIVING WAGE MOVEMENT

While we cannot do justice in the space allotted here to the complex insurgency among low-wage workers unfolding in urban settings, we highlight one development in particular that suggests the importance of movement disruption. As the effects of the financial crisis and Great Recession continued to roil the lives and communities of working-class Americans, low-wage workers at hundreds of the nation's fast food chains began staging one-day walkouts in late 2012, demanding a pay raise to $15 per hour and the right to unionize. On September 4, 2014, protesting workers staged sit-ins in front of fast food chain restaurants, and engaged in civil disobedience by blocking traffic to advance what organizers called, "the Fight for 15 [dollars an hour]." Arrests followed in dozens of cities, from New York and Chicago to places like Richmond, Virginia; Rockford, Illinois; Flint, Michigan; and Little Rock, Arkansas (Cancino 2014; Greenhouse 2014b). More than fifty people were arrested in Kansas City, Missouri, for sitting in the street in front of a McDonald's and blocking a highway entrance (Jargon 2014; Stafford 2014). "We're a movement now," LaToya Caldwell, a Wendy's worker, told *NBC News* as she was arrested. A thirty-one-year-old single mother trying to raise four children on $7.50 an hour, Caldwell had lived in a homeless shelter until earlier in the year. "We know this is going to be a long fight," she said, "but we're going to fight it 'til we win" (Wessler 2014). Also joining the thousands of fast food workers nationwide who walked off the job in the seventh one-day strike in two years were a five-term congresswoman from Milwaukee (who was also arrested) (Silverstein 2014) and low-wage home care workers who connected their own fight for better wages and working conditions to the fast food workers' struggle for a living wage. And fast food workers from Ferguson, Missouri, where the murder of an unarmed black teenager by a white police officer sparked weeks of rioting the previous summer, joined the protesters in New York to link the movement for a decent wage to the fight against the treatment of young black men at the hands of the police.[10]

The revolt of the fast food workers is part of a larger living wage movement that began in Baltimore in the early 1990s, when activists pushed the city government to adopt an ordinance that required firms contracting with the city to pay their workers a "living wage" (Martin 2001; Luce 2004; Atlas 2010). The movement has a successful track record and broad public support (Luce 2005). In 2014, more than 140 cities and counties had living wage ordinances on the books,[11] and where cities have the authority to set municipal wage levels, a number of them, including San Diego, Washington, D.C., and Seattle, extended the living wage concept to cover all workers within the city, not just those working for city contractors (NELP 2014).

Fast food workers rapidly won a few victories and like the Occupy movement, their campaign influenced the national discourse on the state of the economy and growing inequality in the United States. This time, however, the issues of the urban poor were prominent in the media coverage of the strikers, the vast majority of whom appeared to be young people of color. Their demands for a living wage got a significant boost when President Obama, in a 2014 Labor Day speech in Milwaukee, said, "All across the country right now there's a national movement going on made up of fast-food workers organizing to lift wages so they can provide for their families with pride and dignity." He added that if he worked in the low-wage service sector, and "wanted an honest day's pay for an honest day's work, I'd join a union" (Greenhouse 2014a). Obama supported raising the federal minimum wage, but with opposition from Republicans in the House steadfast, the appeals of the strikers fell on deaf ears. Instead, the pressure was directed to states and localities to revise and index their minimum wage laws. Seattle and San Francisco followed through, adopting a $15-an-hour minimum wage. San Diego raised its minimum to $11.50 an hour by 2017, and in the most significant victory to date, Los Angeles, the nation's second largest city, voted to raise the minimum wage from $9 an hour to $15 an hour by 2020 (Dreier 2014; Medina and Scheiber 2015). Meanwhile, Massachusetts passed legislation to raise the state's minimum to $11 an hour by 2017, the highest state minimum in the country (K. Johnston 2015).

Black Lives Matter

Many commentators were quick to pronounce the Occupy movement dead, a flash in the pan with no lasting impact. But even as the Occupy protests were unfolding, so was anger spilling over in the streets of the central cities at police harassment of black youth. The anger was a long time coming. It was a reaction to decades-old nationwide criminal justice policies that dealt with urban youth who were not much needed in the labor force with "stop and frisk" practices of daily harassment, incarceration of hundreds of thousands black men and women, and a string of police murders reminiscent of white supremacist strategies for maintaining order through fear of the lynch mob. The national kick-off of the "Black Lives Matter" movement was the murder of seventeen-year-old Trayvon Martin by a neighborhood vigilante in a Florida gated community, and the failure of the criminal justice system to hold the murderer accountable. What began as a Twitter hashtag created by three black queer women quickly grew into a slogan and program for racial justice following the police homicide of another unarmed teenager, Michael Brown in Ferguson, Missouri (noted above). With the killing of Brown, Ferguson exploded in riots and showdowns with the National Guard, and then in 2015, the brazen police murder of Freddie Gray while in police custody escalated the rioting, this time in Baltimore. The street riot is of course a classic form of urban protest and is usually characterized as wanton and blind disorder. But the nationwide protests under the slogans "Black Lives Matter" and "Hands Up Don't Shoot" were neither wanton nor blind. They were a challenge to a long-standing urban policy that dealt with poverty and hopelessness with racist brutality and imprisonment.

As we write this, the Black Lives Matter movement is showing promising signs of the capacity to overcome the problems of localism and scale that challenge urban social movements. Unlike many urban social movements, Black Lives Matter does have targets at hand—local policing. And it has also spread to overcome horizontal boundaries, not only defined by place, but by issue area in linking abusive policing to demands for jobs, the "Fight for 15," better housing, and community schools. The movement quickly spurred the organization of dozens of local chapters allied with many other grassroots groups, and staged hundreds of local protests in 2014 and 2015. It garnered significant support from a wide range of local and national civil rights, racial justice, women's, and labor organizations, large and small. While not explicitly religious, a radical and inclusive Christian-influenced spirituality informs the movement's actions. In January 2015, two to three dozen Christian, Muslim, and Jewish clergy cried out, "Black Lives Matter," inside the Longworth Building cafeteria on Capitol Hill, widely trafficked by congressional staff, and lay down on the floor in front of the cash registers to draw attention to killings of unarmed blacks. There have been "Freedom Ride" bus trips ferrying hundreds to Ferguson and meetings with President Obama.

The relationship to Obama is complicated: on the one hand, it may well be that the first black president that young minorities helped elect had the effect of raising expectations but also delaying the explosion of rage. On the other hand, although it is difficult to point to concrete policies that are responsive to the movement's demands, the fact that the president is black, and his acknowledgment of black suffering, helped give the movement courage, as when he said that if he had a son, "he'd look like Trayvon" (Thompson and Wilson 2012).

Conclusion

Today, urban social movements have an important role to play in staunching and reversing the slide toward plutocracy in the United States. We have argued here that to do so they must first solve two big problems. They must overcome their fragmentation in local places to build their movements to scale; and they must think and act strategically to untangle the web of institutional relationships that connect people at the bottom to people at the top in order to identify the leverage points for exercising interdependent power. In other words, they must overcome what we call the problem of vertical boundaries created by the network of hierarchical political and economic institutional relationships in which they are embedded. Urban social movements need a strategy that maps local action to the centers of power that must be disrupted in order to produce the desired change. The welfare rights movement of the 1960s did this by educating poor people about what they were entitled to, encouraging them to claim their rights, and staging the actions that first disrupted local welfare offices and ultimately disrupted the welfare system. Restrictions on welfare collapsed, grant levels rose, and more people got aid because local actions reverberated across the country and to the top of political hierarchies. The challenge for other urban movements is to figure out how to do the same.

Notes

1. We set aside, for the purpose of this essay, the very important question of how movements interact with electoral politics. Some of the most energetic organizing is in fact occurring in cities, and benefiting from the interplay of local movements with urban electoral politics. It is useful to remember the significance of this movement-electoral dynamic in forging the victories of the black freedom movement in the 1960s. (See Piven 2006; and Piven, Minnite, and Groarke 2009).

2. Susan Fainstein and Clifford Hirst point out that before the civil disturbances of the 1960s and 1970s, political scientists who studied city politics focused their attention on the decision-making process and ignored the role of social movements and, more broadly, of conflict as a motor of change (Fainstein and Hirst 1995).

3. This formulation contrasts with Marxist theories of revolutionary agency that largely were not concerned with cities until the urban crises of the 1960s.

4. For a thoughtful treatment of the consequences of the turn away from broader political goals for community organizing and community organizations in the neoliberal era, see DeFilippis, Fisher, and Shragge (2010).

5. Jackson and Johnson's detailed study of welfare protest in New York in the 1960s concludes, "The federal government's antipoverty programs were primarily responsible for launching New York City's welfare rights movement" (1974, 94).

6. A participant in the September 17, 2011, initial sit-in described one circle's efforts to come up with demands this way: "Our job, as a single congregation, was to decide what was most important to us. . . . I wrote down the following list of potential demands: to repeal the *Citizens United* Supreme Court decision (through a constitutional amendment); to remove the bull sculpture from Wall Street . . . some form of debt cancellation (either for everyone or just for students); pay-as-you-go military intervention (so that wars could not be waged without Congress agreeing to finance each step immediately); taxes on small financial transactions (one version of this is known as a Tobin tax); full employment; a social wage or guaranteed income . . . universal care centers (for children and the elderly); to reinstate the Glass-Steagall Act . . . paid sick leave for all working Americans; greater political transparency in general" (Schmitt, Taylor, and Greif 2011, 4–5).

7. Young notes, "This is far from standard operating procedure for a big union . . . It's a big leap from strict collective bargaining to incorporating the concerns of other social movements. For many unions, it's a leap just to acknowledge that labor is a movement among other movements" (Young 2014, 7).

8. Illinois is one of only eleven states where public sector workers have the right to strike.

9. Never one to back down from a good fight, CTU president Karen Lewis was recruited by teachers and supportive community members to consider a run for mayor against Rahm Emanuel as he faced reelection in 2015. Lewis was leading Emanuel in the polls in the fall of 2014, when, tragically, she was diagnosed with brain cancer and withdrew from the race.

10. Ferguson fast food workers were not the only labor constituency that made the connection between their low-wage, dead-end jobs, racism, and police brutality. In a powerful speech delivered on September 15, 2014, at the Missouri AFL-CIO's annual convention, the national federation's president, Richard L. Trumka said: "Now, I'm going to stray from my usual convention speech. I'm going to talk about something that may be difficult and uncomfortable but I believe what I'm going to say needs to be said. You see, the question of unity brings up a hard subject, a subject all of us know about but few want to acknowledge— race. I'm talking about race in America and what that means for our communities, our movement and our nation. Because the reality is that while a young man named Michael Brown died just a short distance from us in Ferguson, from gunshot wounds from a police officer, other young men of color have died and will die in similar circumstances, in communities all across this country. It happened here but it could have happened—and does happen—anywhere in America. Because the reality is we still have racism in America. Now, some people might ask me why our labor movement should be involved in all that has happened since the tragic death of Michael Brown in Ferguson. And I want to answer that question directly. How can we not be involved? Union members' lives have been profoundly damaged in ways that cannot be fixed. Lesley McSpadden, Michael Brown's mother who works in a grocery store, is our sister, an AFL-CIO union member and Darren Wilson, the officer who killed Michael Brown, is a union member too and he is our brother. Our brother killed our sister's son and we do not have to wait for the judgment of prosecutors or

courts to tell us how terrible this is. So I say again, how can we not be involved?" See http://www.aflcio.org/Press-Room/Speeches/At-the-2014-Missouri-AFL-CIO-Convention, for a transcript of the full speech.

11. But see Stephanie Luce (2012) for a discussion of implementation and enforcement problems.

References

Atlas, John. 2010. *Seeds of Change: The Story of ACORN, America's Most Controversial Antipoverty Community Organizing Group.* Nashville, Tenn.: Vanderbilt University Press.

Bartlett, Robert. 2013. "Creating a New Model of a Social Union: CORE and the Chicago Teachers Union." *Monthly Review* 65 (2): 12–23.

Brecher, Jeremy. 2014. *Strike! Revised, Expanded and Updated.* Oakland, Calif.: PM Press.

Brenner, Neil. 2012. "What Is Critical Urban Theory?" In *Cities for People, Not for Profit: Critical Urban Theory and the Right to the City,* ed. Neil Brenner, Peter Marcuse, and Margit Mayer, 11–23. New York: Routledge.

Cancino, Alejandro. 2014. "50 Arrested in Local Fast-Food Wage Protests." *Chicago Tribune,* September 4.

Castells, Manuel. 1983. *The City and the Grassroots: A Cross-Cultural Theory of Urban Social Movements.* California Series in Urban Development. Berkeley: University of California Press.

———. 2012. *Networks of Outrage and Hope: Social Movements in the Internet Age.* Cambridge: Polity Press.

Cazenave, Noel A. 2007. *Impossible Democracy: The Unlikely Success of the War on Poverty Community Action Programs.* Albany, N.Y.: State University of New York Press.

Cloward, Richard A., and Frances Fox Piven. 1966. "The Weight of the Poor: A Strategy to End Poverty." *The Nation,* May 2, 510–17.

DeFilippis, James, Robert Fisher, and Eric Shragge. 2010. *Contesting Community: The Limits and Potential of Local Organizing.* New Brunswick, N.J.: Rutgers University Press.

Dreier, Peter. 2014. "The War over Wages, City by City." *Huffpost Politics* (blog), October 1. Accessed November 22, 2014. http://www.huffingtonpost.com/peter-dreier/the-war-over -wages-city-b_b_5916154.html.

Fainstein, Norman I., and Susan S. Fainstein. 1974. *Urban Political Movements: The Search for Power by Minority Groups in American Cities.* Englewood Cliffs, N.J.: Prentice-Hall.

Fainstein, Susan S., and Clifford Hirst. 1995. "Urban Social Movements." In *Theories of Urban Politics,* ed. David Judge, Gerry Stoker, and Harold Wolman, 181–204. Thousand Oaks, Calif.: Sage.

Fletcher, Bill, and Fernando Gapasin. 2008. *Solidarity Divided: The Crisis in Organized Labor and a New Path toward Social Justice.* Berkeley: University of California Press.

Gordon, Colin. 2013. "The Lost City of Solidarity." *Dissent,* April 17. Accessed October 11, 2014. http://www.dissentmagazine.org/online_articles/the-lost-city-of-solidarity.

Gould, Peter, and Rodney White. 1986. *Mental Maps,* 2nd ed. London: Routledge.

Greenhouse, Steven. 2014a. "Fast Food Workers Seeking $15 Wage Are Planning Civil Disobedience." *New York Times,* September 1.

———. 2014b. "Hundreds of Fast-Food Workers Striking for Higher Wages Are Arrested." *New York Times,* September 4.

Gregory, Derek. 2009. "Geographical Imaginary." In *The Dictionary of Human Geography,* ed. Derek Gregory, Ron Johnston, Geraldine Pratt, Michael Watts, and Sarah Whatmore, 282. New York: Wiley-Blackwell.

Gutierrez, Rhoda Rae. 2013. "Beating the Neoliberal Blame Game: Teacher and Parent Solidarity and the 2012 Chicago Teachers' Strike." *Monthly Review* 65 (2): 24–32.

Hackworth, Jason. 2006. *The Neoliberal City: Governance, Ideology, and Development in American Urbanism.* Ithaca, N.Y.: Cornell University Press.

Hamel, Pierre, Henri Lustiger-Thaler, and Margit Mayer, eds. 2000. *Urban Movements in a Globalizing World.* New York: Routledge.

Harvey, David. 2009. *Social Justice and the City.* Rev. ed. Athens: University of Georgia Press.

———. 2012. *Rebel Cities: From the Right to the City to the Urban Revolution.* New York: Verso.

Jackson, Larry R., and William A. Johnson. 1974. *Protest by the Poor: The Welfare Rights Movement in New York City.* Lexington, Mass.: D.C. Heath.

Jargon, Julie. 2014. "U.S. Fast-Food Workers Protest for Higher Wages." *Wall Street Journal,* September 5.

Johnston, Katie. 2014. "Minimum Wage Increase Doesn't Add Up to a Living Wage." *Boston Globe,* June 16.

Johnston, Paul. 1994. *Success While Others Fail: Social Movement Unions and the Public Workplace.* Ithaca, N.Y.: Cornell University Press.

Kaplan, David. 2013. "The Chicago Teachers' Strike and Beyond: Strategic Considerations." *Monthly Review* 65 (2): 33–46.

Katznelson, Ira. 1981. *City Trenches: Urban Politics and the Patterning of Class in the United States.* Chicago: University of Chicago, 1981.

Lefebvre, Henri. (1970) 2003. *The Urban Revolution.* Translated by Robert Bononno. Minneapolis: University of Minnesota Press.

———. 2009. *State, Space, World: Selected Essays.* Edited by Neil Brenner and Stuart Elden. Translated by Gerald Moore, Neil Brenner, and Stuart Elden. Minneapolis: University of Minnesota Press.

Luce, Stephanie. 2004. *Fighting for a Living Wage.* Ithaca, N.Y.: Cornell University Press.

———. 2005. "Lessons from the Living Wage Campaign." *Work and Occupations* 32 (4): 423–40.

———. 2012. "Living Wage Policies and Campaigns: Lessons from the United States." *International Journal of Labour Research* 4 (1): 11–26.

Martin, Isaac. 2001. "Dawn of the Living Wage: The Diffusion of a Redistributive Municipal Policy." *Urban Affairs Review* 36 (4): 470–96.

Mason, Paul. 2012. *Why It's Kicking Off Everywhere: The New Global Revolutions.* New York: Verso.

Mayer, Margit. 2009. "The 'Right to the City' in Urban Social Movements." *City* 13 (2–3): 362–74.

———. 2012. "The 'Right to the City' in Urban Social Movements." In *Cities for People, Not for Profit,* ed. Neil Brenner, Peter Marcuse, and Margit Mayer, 63–85. New York: Routledge.

Medina, Jennifer, and Noam Scheiber. 2015. "Los Angeles Lifts Its Minimum Wage to $15 per Hour." *New York Times,* May 19.

Melucci, Alberto. 1981. "Ten Hypotheses in the Analysis of New Movements." In *Contemporary Italian Sociology: A Reader,* ed. Diana Pinto, 173–94. New York: Cambridge University Press.

Merrifield, Andy. 2002. *Metromarxism: A Marxist Tale of the City.* New York: Routledge.

———. 2013a. *The Politics of the Encounter: Urban Theory and Protest under Planetary Urbanization.* Geographies of Justice and Social Transformation Series. Athens: University of Georgia Press.

———. 2013b. "The Urban Question under Planetary Urbanization." *International Journal of Urban and Regional Research* 37 (3): 909–22.

———. 2014. *The New Urban Question.* London: Pluto Press.

NELP (National Employment Law Project). 2014. "Minimum Wage Laws and Proposals for U.S. Cities." *Raise the Minimum Wage.* Accessed October 15, 2014. http://www.raisetheminimum wage.com/pages/minimum-wage-laws-and-proposals-for-major-u.s.-cities.

Ness, Immanuel. 2001. "From Dormancy to Activism: New Voice and the Revival of Labor Councils." In *Central Labor Councils and the Revival of American Unionism: Organizing for Justice in Our Communities,* ed. Immanuel Ness and Stuart Eimer, 13–34. Armonk, N.Y.: M.E. Sharpe.

Newman, David. 2006. "The Lines That Continue to Separate Us: Borders in Our 'Borderless' World." *Progress in Human Geography* 30 (2): 143–61.

Nicholls, Walter J. 2008. "The Urban Question Revisited: The Importance of Cities for Social Movements." *International Journal of Urban and Regional Research* 32 (4): 841–59.

Peck, Jamie, and Adam Tickell. 2002. "Neoliberalizing Space," *Antipode* 34 (3): 380–404.

Pickvance, Chris. 2003. "From Urban Social Movements to Urban Movements: A Review and Introduction to a Symposium on Urban Movements." *International Journal of Urban and Regional Research* 27 (1): 102–9.

Piven, Frances Fox. 2006. *Challenging Authority: How Ordinary People Change America*. New York: Rowman and Littlefield.

———. 2008. "Can Power from Below Change the World?" *American Sociological Review* 73 (1): 1–14.

———. 2014. "Interdependent Power: Strategizing for the Occupy Movement." *Current Sociology* 62 (2): 223–31.

Piven, Frances Fox, and Richard A. Cloward. 1979. *Poor People's Movements: Why They Succeed, How They Fail*. New York: Vintage.

———. 2000. "Power Repertoires and Globalization." *Politics & Society* 28 (3): 413–30.

———. 2005. "Rule Making, Rule Breaking and Power." In *The Handbook of Political Sociology: State, Civil Societies, and Globalization*, ed. Thomas Janoski, Robert Alford, Alexander Hicks, and Mildred A. Schwartz, 33–53. New York: Cambridge University Press.

Piven, Frances Fox, Lorraine C. Minnite, and Margaret Groarke. 2009. *Keeping Down the Black Vote: Race and the Demobilization of American Voters*. New York: The New Press.

Purcell, Mark. 2014. "Possible Worlds: Henri Lefebvre and the Right to the City." *Journal of Urban Affairs* 36 (1): 141–54.

Rathke, Wade, and Joel Rogers. 2001. " 'Everything That Moves': Union Leverage and Critical Mass in Metropolitan Space." In *Central Labor Councils and the Revival of American Unionism: Organizing for Justice in Our Communities,* ed. Immanuel Ness and Stuart Eimer, 35–52. Armonk, N.Y.: M.E. Sharpe.

Schmitt, Eli, Astra Taylor, and Mark Greif. 2011. "Scenes from an Occupation." In *Occupied! Scenes from Occupied America*, ed. Carla Blumenkranz, Keith Gessen, Mark Greif, Sarah Leonard, and Sarah Resnick, 4–5. New York: Verso.

Silverstein, Jason. 2014. "Rep. Gwen Moore Arrested at Fast Food Wage Protest." *Milwaukee Journal Sentinel,* September 4.

Sites, William. 2007. "Contesting the Neoliberal City? Theories of Neoliberalism and Urban Strategies of Contention." In *Contesting Neoliberalism: Urban Frontiers,* ed. Helga Leitner, Jamie Peck, and Eric S. Sheppard, 116–38. New York: Guildford.

Sitrin, Marina A. 2006. *Horizontalism: Voices of Popular Power in Argentina*. Oakland, Calif.: AK Press.

———. 2011. "One No, Many Yeses." In *Occupy!: Scenes from Occupied America,* ed. Carla Blumenkranz, Keith Gessen, Mark Greif, Sarah Leonard, and Sarah Resnick, 7–11. New York: Verso.

———. 2012. *Everyday Revolutions: Horizontalism and Autonomy in Argentina*. London: Zed Books.

Sitrin, Marina A., and Dario Azzellini. 2014. *They Can't Represent Us! Reinventing Democracy from Greece to Occupy*. New York: Verso.

Smith, Neil. 1992. "Contours of a Spatialized Politics: Homeless Vehicles and the Production of Geographical Scale." *Social Text* 33: 54–81.

Stafford, Diane. 2014. "Arrests Made in Kansas City Fast-Food Worker Protests." *Kansas City Star,* September 4.

Sustar, Lee. 2013. "Striking Back in Chicago: How Teachers Took on City Hall." *Alternet,* September 10. Accessed October 16, 2014. http://www.alternet.org/labor/striking-back-chicago-how-teachers-took-city-hall.

Thompson, Krissah, and Scott Wilson. 2012. "Obama on Trayvon Martin: 'If I Had a Son, He'd Look Like Trayvon.' " *Washington Post,* March 23.

Turner, Lowell, and David B. Cornfield, eds. 2007. *Labor and the New Urban Battlegrounds: Local Solidarity in a Global Economy.* Frank W. Pierce Memorial Lectureship and Conference Series 12. Ithaca, N.Y.: Cornell University Press.

Uetricht, Micah. 2014. *Strike for America: Chicago Teachers against Austerity.* New York: Verso.

Wessler, Seth F. 2014. "'We're a Movement Now': Fast Food Workers Strike in 150 Cities." *NBC News,* September 4. Accessed October 11, 2014. http://www.nbcnews.com/feature/in-plain -sight/were-movement-now-fast-food-workers-strike-150-cities-n195256.

West, Guida. 1981. *The National Welfare Rights Movement: The Social Protest of Poor Women.* New York: Praeger.

Writers for the 99%. 2011. *Occupying Wall Street: The Inside Story of an Action that Changed America.* New York: O/R Books.

Young, Ethan. 2014. "Teachers on Strike: Lessons from Chicago on How to Fight Back." *Rosa Luxemburg Stifting.* Accessed August 2, 2014. http://www.rosalux-nyc.org/wp-content/files_mf /young_ctu.pdf.

Conclusion

WHY URBAN POLICY?
On Social Justice, Urbanization,
and Urban Policies

JAMES DEFILIPPIS

> The city and the urban environment represent man's most consistent and, on the
> whole, most successful attempt to remake the world he lives in more after his
> heart's desire. But, if the city is the world which man created, it is the world in
> which he is henceforth condemned to live. Thus, indirectly, and without any clear
> sense of the nature of his task, in making the city man has remade himself.
> —*Robert Park*
> On Social Control and Collective Behavior, *1967*

> I'll begin with the following hypothesis: society has been completely urbanized.
> —*Henri Lefebvre*
> The Urban Revolution, *1970*

I start this concluding chapter with these two quotes, from very different kinds of thinkers about cities and urbanization, because they crystallize a set of issues. Park is perhaps the single most significant figure in the history of American urban studies, and from his perch in the Sociology Department of the University of Chicago in the 1920s and 1930s he shaped generations of thinkers about cities. The argument from him here is a complex one, in which the cities we have made are expressions of who we collectively are: our social systems, political economy, values, goals, preferences, and so on. But those expressions or outcomes of who we are act, in turn, to shape who we are. For Park, a central problem (perhaps *the* central problem) in this collective endeavor was the creation of mechanisms of social control; for the city is a product of us as a collective, but we each come to it as atomized individuals, detached from the bonds of social control of rural communal life. Without those bonds, he is asking, from where does social control come? The question of social control is not one that I am centrally concerned with here, but Park's broader point—that as we make our cities, so too do we make ourselves—is essential. Cities are products of our collective work. They may be partitioned into a myriad of discrete spaces (via private ownership, informal community demarcations of who is in and who is out, zoning regulations that delimit certain spaces for only certain kinds of activities, etc.). But it is still *our* society. For it is in our cities that our civilization is made, remade, defined, and redefined. Our cities are us, for better and for worse.

Lefebvre was writing from a completely different geographic, intellectual, and, of course, political position. After witnessing, and participating in, the uprising in Paris in 1968, Lefebvre broke with more orthodox forms of Marxism to embrace an explicitly urbanized conception of society and social change. The urban, for him, became both the arena for struggles for social change (and a not at all passive arena, at that, but an arena that shapes the contours of struggle) and the prize over which such struggles are fought. Lefebvre rejected the category of "the city" as an object and spoke instead of the urban—in much the same way I describe in this book's introduction. The urban is a process, or more accurately, a set of processes that find their most easily identifiable expressions in what we commonly call cities. I am not willing to follow Lefebvre to the point of rejecting "the city" as a category, but we do our understandings of cities a great disservice when we focus on them as objects, rather than on the urbanization processes that produce them.

When the two observations are brought together, we are left with the reality that cities are where we, collectively as people in society, shape the world to our heart's desires, and, furthermore, cities have long since been subsumed into a larger part of society-wide urbanization. It is thus not cities that reflect our efforts to make the world after our hearts' desires, but the urban process itself. Simply put, if we want a more equitable and just society, we must begin by transforming the urban. The question becomes, therefore, what kinds of policies should we have, for what kinds of urbanization processes, in our efforts to make and remake what we call cities?

On the Importance of the State in Making Our Cities

Despite the centrality of the urban in society, urban policy remains a backwater in the public realm, and HUD is a backbench cabinet department. Americans do not tend to think in the terms I have been using here. We rarely talk about urban issues, and when we do we are wedded to conceptions of the urban that are, at most, descriptions of characteristics in particular cities. When urban policies come up in the public realm, it is usually just the most visible of place-based policies, and these are regularly seen as a series of failures of government. The War on Poverty, for instance, and the specific policies that constituted it—particularly its place-based ones—is not a period in American social policy that is well regarded in mainstream politics, and often dismissed with little short of contempt.[1]

But as this book has repeatedly argued, there is a vital role for urban policy in shaping and transforming our urbanization processes. These policies may be explicitly place-based, and may focus on particular issues, people, or spaces within cities. And the outgoing administration has certainly brought more energy and interest to place-based policies than we have had in the White House since at least the Carter administration. But there is a limit to how much of an impact such policies can have on their own. Absent larger changes in the processes that produce our cities, intervening at the level of any particular place, or set of places, is always going to be an uphill struggle—swimming against the tide—against these much larger forces. And it has long been the case that it is difficult to argue that the problems *in a city* are simply *the city's* problems.

This is not to say that place-based policies are pointless or futile. I do not want to contribute to the "shaming of the inside game" so prevalent in liberal urban policy circles (Imbroscio 2006). Certainly if place-based policies are pursued ambitiously enough, then the transformation of localized dynamics can certainly shape the larger scale processes involved in urbanization. The relationship between particular places and larger processes is not unidirectional; and actors who work in particular places are not powerless in the face of the forces of the globalized capitalist political economy. Place-based policies, instead, can feed back into the larger forces to shape and alter them. And even when such policies are not big or impactful enough to transform the processes of urbanization, they can still improve places, and the lives of those within them, in important and meaningful ways. They can also, in a version of Brandeis's famous "laboratories of democracy," create new models that expand the realm of what is considered possible.

Urban policies may also, however, be policies that alter the workings of the larger political economy. As the contributors to Part II of this book ably demonstrate, a whole host of policies that are not explicitly place-based shape how urbanization occurs. Policies that govern capital and financial markets shape how urban areas are physically built, and with what logics, because it is such markets that control the flow of investment into the built environment. Policies that govern labor relations are urban policies because urban areas are, first and foremost, agglomerations of labor-utilizing productive activities; how those productive activities are structured and how the surpluses generated from them are distributed fundamentally shape the lives of those concentrated in urban areas. Immigration policies are urban policies for many of the same reasons—migration being fundamentally about the movement of labor in the global economy—and how such migrations occur, who participates in them, and under what conditions clearly shape the size and composition of our urban areas. The argument can be made for education, health care, and more, and the contributors to this volume have already done so—there is no need to belabor the point. Instead, the questions become, given the myriad forms that urban policy can take, how has the outgoing administration done, and what does it say about urban policy more generally in the twenty-first century?

Once More on Obama's Urban Policy Regime

In an article in the journal *Housing Policy Debate*, Immergluck described the federal response to the foreclosure crisis as "too little, too late, and too timid" (Immergluck 2013, 199). It is certainly tempting to steal that line from him and use it to describe the overall thrust of Obama's urban policy regime. The administration has pushed little pilot projects with small pots of money, when bolder action was demanded by the challenges of our time. This was even true in the face of the uprisings in urban areas from Ferguson to Baltimore, uprisings that threw into sharp relief the limitations of federal urban policies. The ACA notwithstanding, the administration did not begin to push a progressive set of ideas until the last quarter of its tenure, when there was little chance of realizing any legislative victories (hence the administration's efforts to use executive action). And it was far too timid in its reluctance to utilize the mobilized electorate that carried it into office in 2008; the mobilization ended the day after the election in 2008, and that timidity severely damaged the prospects for a transformation in the urban policy regime.

Accordingly, Obama has also been decidedly *not* a harbinger of change to urban policy. Despite the talk of change that animated the 2008 election campaign and mobilized the millions who worked in support of Obama's candidacy, the largest theme of this book is the sense of continuity with past policies. Urban policies have demonstrated a striking degree of path dependency, even in the facing of changing political leaders, constituents, and, importantly, political economic conditions. To some extent this is to be expected, and is a built-in feature of both the American constitution and the political institutions and organizations that constitute the realm of formal policy making in this country. But given both the aftermath of the housing bubble crisis and the dramatic character of Obama's election, the extent of the continuities in policies (and the logics that inform and partially constitute them) is notable, and frankly, lamentable.

There are several ways in which this continuity is evident. First, and most important, is the reliance on the market to solve urban social problems. Whether it is a lack of public sector resources—itself surely a product of political decisions—or a genuine belief that (individualized) market logics are inherently superior to (more collectivized) state logics is not the point here. Instead, it is simply the case that the market is the framework through which urban policies are made, understood, and implemented. This is evident in Lipman's chapter on education policy reform, a reform policy agenda dominated by both a market-centered language and ideology of "choice," and implemented by private sector actors. It is also clear in Khare's chapter on the Choice Neighborhoods Initiative (CNI), which highlights how important private sector financiers and developers are in CNI projects. Similarly, Janet Smith documents the repeated efforts to functionally privatize public housing, first via PETRA and then with RAD. What is striking is how impervious the logic of private finance capital being *the solution* is to the demonstrable crises in private finance capital—particularly in housing finance—in the latter part of the last decade.

Second, and closely related, the market-centered policies have often been very favorable to the wealthy and owners of capital. Theodore's description of the damage done to labor by the failure to pass the Employee Free Choice Act (EFCA) is emblematic of this. EFCA may or may not have been a vehicle large enough to revitalize labor, but it is nearly impossible to imagine greater equity in our urban areas without renewed strength in the labor movement. In a very different context, Oakley and Fraser worry that as the Neighborhood Stabilization Program was implemented, the real winners were likely to be real estate capital—often at the expense of the communities in and around NSP neighborhoods. Bratt and Immergluck similarly document how little was done to assist struggling homeowners, while large financial institutions had their interests taken care of via a myriad of different mechanisms. Finally, in different but related ways, both Lake and Newman document how social services and community development have been gradually reoriented toward finance capital—with the terms being set by finance, and those terms being to its advantage. Thus not only is the market viewed as the solution to social problems, but social problems are redefined in ways that privilege the market and benefit capital. Of course the reliance on the market, and the shaping of policy goals to suit private capital creates a whole set of problems—most notably, that if the market were able to do what the policies seek to do, then there would be little need for the policies in the first place. This, of course, has long been known and not a new critique. But in this vital way, the Obama administration's urban policy regime is fundamentally a continuation of its predecessors'.

Third, the Obama administration has continued the larger policy framework of relying on (often community-based) nonprofit organizations for the implementing of urban policies. This, of course, is part of the larger contracting out of the welfare state that has been such a dominant feature of American social policy for the last thirty-five years (Allard 2009; Grønbjerg and Smith 1999). This is certainly evident in Newman's chapter on community development, where the continuing reliance on community-development nonprofits to implement policies is striking. Similarly, Choice Neighborhoods as a policy framework relies on "wrap around" services that are provided by nonprofit sector entities. It is also evident education policies, where the "charterization" of public schools is often done by nonprofits—and where the Harlem Children's Zone became the model for the administration's Promise Neighborhoods Initiative. Swanstrom's chapter, however, is the one that really foregrounds these issues, and demonstrates that the administration's signature place-based policies—the Neighborhood Revitalization Initiative (NRI) and the work that would come out of it, the Sustainable Communities Initiative (SCI) and the Strong Cities, Strong Communities (SC2) program—all rely heavily on local nonprofit partners to implement them. The problem, of course, with this reliance on nonprofits is that the capacities of such entities vary a great deal, and a welfare state that depends upon them will be necessarily patchwork and uneven.

Despite these important continuities, it would be too easy or glib to say that nothing changed during the Obama administration. There have been meaningful and substantial changes. Some of these have come through the actions of Executive Department agencies, rather than through legislative changes. The near requirement of a sixty-vote filibuster-proof majority in the Senate, the Democrats' loss of control of the House of Representatives in the 2010 midterm elections, and, finally, the Republican takeover of the Senate in 2014 have all meant that winning significant changes through legislation has been difficult for the administration.

Brenner's chapter on immigration policy points to the very important actions on immigration enforcement, with Deferred Action for Childhood Arrivals (DACA) in 2012 and Deferred Action for Parental Accountability (DAPA) in 2014. While the courts are still weighing in on these, if allowed to stand, these are very significant actions on immigration policy. In a very different context, Goetz's chapter on fair housing shows that there has been a clear difference in enforcement, with the administration taking enforcement seriously and acting accordingly, which is a significant departure from preceding administrations. More generally, there has also been a shift in place-based policies within the executive branch. There is far greater emphasis on cross-departmental collaboration than there had been. And the focus on making the existing place-based policy regime more efficient and productive has been a welcome change from the preceding administrations who evinced no such interest in those policies and their implementation. We see such efforts at collaboration in the SCI, SC2 efforts, as well as in the regional planning discussed by Chapple.

There have also been some legislative victories, and it would certainly be incomplete not to mention them here. The ARRA in 2009 was a significant legislative achievement with substantial resources going to urban issues, whatever else its shortcomings might be. The administration also managed to get continued and increased funding for homelessness prevention, and this seems to have paid off, since homelessness has declined significantly. Finally, it is certainly the case that the very large increase in the number of people with health insurance that has come as a result of the ACA is a major accomplishment with important implications for urban areas. On balance, this is not a bad record, but it is also not a transformational one. A more equitable urban policy regime is still yet to be constructed.

The Elusive Questions of Urban Social Justice

The logical questions therefore become, why has it proven so difficult to construct a more equitable and just urban policy regime in the United States? Or, leaving aside the goal of social justice for the moment (which is a much larger discussion about the relative weakness of the left in American life), the question can be asked about why is there this myopia in the American public imagination about the urban and urban policy? There are several different explanations that can be justifiably invoked to answer this question.

To some extent, this is probably rooted in the cultural-historic American hostility to cities, a hostility evident in both the cultural elite[2] and in mass culture. The Germans have long had a saying that, "urban air makes you free"; it is exceedingly difficult to imagine a comparable expression taking hold in American public life. This hostility to cities and the urban has certainly not been aided by the fact that American urban areas have long been populated by "others," those different, or perceived and constructed as different, from the dominant group. These "others" were Eastern or Southern European immigrants in the late nineteenth and early twentieth centuries; blacks that participated in the Great Migration from the South in the early to middle portions of the twentieth century; and Latino and Asian immigrants that have come since the Hart-Cellar Act of 1965. Thus the content of the urban "other" has shifted over time, but the distance has remained (or, more precisely, been reconstructed). Place-based policies, in particular, therefore immediately become suspect because they are going to aid "those people."

The antiurban bias that characterizes American public life might (partially) explain why urban policy does not factor into the larger debates, but it does address the question of why the urban policies we do have continue to be so inequitable. Of course, such inequities have winners as well as losers, and therein lies much of the explanation. The current political economy offers a set of fairly clear benefits to the wealthy and owners of capital, benefits in the narrow realm of electoral politics, and in the much broader realm of politics as the contest over the governance of a society and the distribution of the resources within it. Simply, and admittedly crudely, put, those that benefit from the status quo are in positions imbued with significant power. It would be an analytically and politically damaging folly to pretend otherwise. This power has only increased in the last thirty-five years and seems likely to continue. This is not just because of incredible growth in wealth and income inequality, although that is part of it. But it is also because we have constructed a governing framework in which private capital is implementing much of public policy, and this, in turn, has shaped and transformed the contents, values, and logics behind those policies. Capital's power is simply increased when we insist on relying on private capital. Greater equity, conversely, would require a redistribution of wealth and a transformation of decision-making and policy-implementing processes; both of these would therefore be actively taking that which is currently enjoyed by the wealthy and powerful.

This explanation too, is only a partial one, however. There is also the failure to articulate a coherent and compelling vision of what more just and equitable urbanization processes might look like. That is not to say there are not a very useful and productive set of policies that, should they be pursued, would most likely make our cities more equitable. Certainly there is no shortage of ideas and frameworks that academics and urbanists have articulated as to what a just city or more just urbanization processes might be. Many of these have been published since Obama began his time in office in 2009 (Fainstein 2010; Hayward and Swanstrom 2011; Marcuse et al. 2009; Soja 2010). But it is to say that we have not yet the imagination to pull those together into something more coherent and complete. Nor have we conceptualized a clear role for the state in creating more just cities. Furthermore, the visions that we have, whatever their merits and appeal, have demonstrably failed to capture the imagination of a constituency willing to mobilize around them. Given the scale, depth, and breadth of the problems in American urban areas, the last eight years should have seen significant urban social movement and community organizing efforts. Instead, the opposite is true, and the relative lack of a mobilized populous making demands on capital and the state is one of the defining features of our time. That is not to suggest that no mobilizing has occurred; it certainly has—as Minnite and Piven's chapter ably demonstrates—instead it is to say that given the magnitude of our problems, such social movement mobilizing has been far more modest than what is needed. Even after the uprising/riots in Baltimore in the spring of 2015, shouting their "language of the unheard," as Martin Luther King Jr. famously put it, the response from elite policy-makers has largely been to shrug and move on.

The problem is for us to solve. We need to (re?)discover an urban imaginary for the United States. We need to embrace the best of urbanism and city life, and we need to transform the processes of urbanization that make our cities so inequitable and unjust. We need to construct a different set of social forces and processes, processes that operate with different kinds of values and logics than what we currently have. The times demand such a vision. And while thus far our efforts, like Obama's, have been too little and too timid, unlike Obama—whose time in the White House is almost up—for us, it is certainly not too late.

Notes

1. The ridiculing of the Great Society's place-based programs, perhaps first started with Tom Wolfe's famous essay, "Mau-Mauing the Flak Catchers" ([1970] 2009).
2. For a useful discussion of these issues among America's cultural elite, see White and Lucia (1962).

References

Allard, Scott. 2009. *Out of Reach: Place, Poverty, and the New American Welfare State.* New Haven, Conn.: Yale University Press.

Fainstein, Susan. 2010. *The Just City.* Ithaca, N.Y.: Cornell University Press.

Grønbjerg, Kirsten A., and Steven Rathgeb Smith. 1999. "Nonprofit Organizations and Public Policies in the Delivery of Human Services." In *Philanthropy and the Nonprofit Sector in a Changing America,* ed. Charles T. Clotfelter and Thomas Ehrlich, 139–71. Bloomington: Indiana University Press.

Hayward, Clarissa, and Todd Swanstrom, eds. 2011. *Justice and the American Metropolis.* Minneapolis: University of Minnesota Press.

Imbroscio, David. 2006. "Shaming the Inside Game: A Critique of the Liberal Expansionist Approach to Addressing Urban Problems." *Urban Affairs Review* 42 (2): 224–48.

Immergluck, Dan. 2013. "Too Little, Too Late, and Too Timid: The Federal Response to the Foreclosure Crisis at the Five-Year Mark." *Housing Policy Debate* 23 (1): 199–232.

Lefebvre, Henri. (1970) 2003. *The Urban Revolution.* Translated by Robert Bononno. Minneapolis: University of Minnesota Press.

Marcuse, Peter, James Connolly, Johannes Novy, Ingrid Olivo, Cuz Potter, and Justin Steil, eds. 2009. *Searching for the Just City: Debates in Urban Theory and Practice.* Questioning Cities Series. New York: Routledge Press.

Mufson, Steven, and Juliet Eilperin. 2015. "Baltimore Riots Put Obama Strategy for U.S. Cities under Closer Scrutiny." *Washington Post,* May 4.

Park, Robert. 1967. "The City as a Social Laboratory." In *On Social Control and Collective Behavior.* Chicago: University of Chicago Press.

Soja, Edward. 2010. *Seeking Spatial Justice.* Minneapolis: University of Minnesota Press.

White, Morton G., and Lucia White. 1962. *The Intellectual Versus the City: From Thomas Jefferson to Frank Lloyd Wright.* Cambridge, Mass.: Harvard University Press.

Wolfe, Tom. (1970) 2009. "Mau-Mauing the Flak Catchers." *Radical Chic & Mau-Mauing the Flak Catchers.* New York: Picador.

Afterword

BALTIMORE, THE POLICING CRISIS, AND THE END OF THE OBAMA ERA

CEDRIC JOHNSON

> Herein lies the match that will continue to ignite the dynamite in the ghettos:
> the ineptness of decision makers, the anachronistic institutions, the inability
> to think boldly, and above all the unwillingness to innovate. The makeshift
> plans put together every summer by city administrations to avoid rebellions
> in the ghettos are merely buying time.
> —*Stokely Carmichael and Charles V. Hamilton*
> Black Power: The Politics of Liberation in America *(1967)*

Throughout the late 1960s, black ghettos in many American cities were engulfed in annual summer riots, often touched off by incidences of police harassment and abuse. Against this backdrop of seasonal rioting, Stokely Carmichael and Charles V. Hamilton penned their best-selling 1967 book, *Black Power: The Politics of Liberation in America.* "White America can continue to appropriate millions of dollars to take ghetto teenagers off the streets and onto nice, green farms during the hot summer months. They can continue to provide mobile swimming pools and hastily built play areas," Carmichael and Hamilton warned, "but there is a point beyond which the steaming ghettos will not be cooled off." The book was read and debated amid the 1967 Newark rebellion, which provoked President Lyndon B. Johnson to convene the National Advisory Commission on Civil Disorders to study the root causes and develop suggestions for preventing future unrest. The official report issued by the Kerner Commission, as it came to be named after its chair, Illinois governor Otto Kerner, famously concluded that "our nation is moving toward two societies, one black, one white—separate and unequal" (Kerner Commission 1968, 1).

Carmichael and Hamilton's writing reflected the deep skepticism many black power militants held toward the liberal policies undertaken by local and national leaders. Johnson's War on Poverty had not gone far enough, many argued, to address the deplorable housing conditions, chronic unemployment, and crowded and underfunded schools separating black inner-city life from white suburban prosperity. They charged, "It is ludicrous for the society to believe that these temporary measures can long contain the tempers of oppressed people" (Carmichael and Hamilton 1967, 161). Like many of their contemporaries, Carmichael and

Hamilton saw black urban life as being hemmed in by institutional racism, not merely overt forms of interpersonal prejudice and discrimination, but by more subtle and systemic practices like redlining, restrictive covenants, and predatory lending. Liberal strategies might placate the simmering discontent among black ghetto dwellers, but unless systemic changes were made, the alchemy of racism, underdevelopment, and desperation would inevitably give way to rebellion. "And when the dynamite does go off," Carmichael and Hamilton wrote, "pious pronouncements of patience should not go forth. Blame should not be placed on 'outside agitators' or on 'Communist influence' or on advocates of Black Power. That dynamite was placed there by white racism and it was ignited by white racist indifference and unwillingness to act justly" (161).

Carmichael and Hamilton's words echo across the decades, and for some they may appear as relevant to our own times, in the aftermath of the April 2015 Baltimore riots and mounting protests against police brutality, as they did during the late 1960s. In the face of routine police violence against unarmed black citizens, many activists embrace a similar view of the contemporary United States, not as the post-racial meritocracy touted by some on the Right, but as an endemically racist and highly unequal society. Like an acoustic echo however, that resounds into a void, we should be careful not to mistake Carmichael and Hamilton's interpretation of their own historical context as speaking directly to our own times. Ghettos, riots, and pervasive inequality defined the late 1960s and the contemporary moment, but during the intervening years that separate our respective epochs, the political and social terrain has shifted in critical ways.

Carmichael was the charismatic leader of the Student Non-Violent Coordinating Committee who announced the slogan "black power" to the world during the 1966 Meredith March Against Fear, which was taken over by prominent civil rights leaders after James Meredith was shot by a white vigilante and hospitalized. Hamilton was an Oklahoma native who participated in the 1955 Montgomery Bus Boycott, before earning a PhD in political science from the University of Chicago. Together they set out to operationalize the notion of black power, to move it from a pithy slogan to a practical approach for realizing black progress. At certain turns they draw on the language of internal colonialism to describe the conditions of black oppression, and then on other pages, the text drifts back toward a view of black political empowerment rooted in well-established notions of ethnic machine politics, which they saw as the *realpolitik* of American city life, and the most effective path for blacks to take as white suburban exodus gave way to majority black voting publics in many cities.[1] Black power militants called for revolution, aligning themselves with third-world liberation movements, and their sharp criticisms of American society and heady rhetoric of armed struggle incited fear in reactionary whites who equated black self-assertion with black domination. In practice, however, black power would increasingly come to mean black control of political and economic institutions, what started as an antidote to racial integration—the "thalidomide drug of integration" for Carmichael—became its elixir (Carmichael 1971, 47). More black representation in civic life, business, and popular culture has not abolished the conditions of structural unemployment, uneven development, and racial injustice that Carmichael and Hamilton confronted, but rather it has provided a means of more effectively managing these social contradictions under late capitalism.

In a pointed analysis of contemporary African American politics, Keeanga-Yamahtta Taylor contends that the "uprising in Baltimore has crystalized the deepening political and class divide in black America . . . a new development in the black freedom struggle that historically has been united across class lines to fight racism" (Taylor 2015). I agree with the spirit of her criticism, but question the assertion of novelty, the emergence of a discrete class politics within black life where it was less pronounced, if not nonexistent before. While it is true that by the mid-1950s a broad consensus had developed within the black population, North and South, around dismantling the legal edifice of Jim Crow segregation; the very use of the term, the "black freedom struggle," a neologism adopted by many contemporary academics, papers over the range of ideological positions and material interests animating black public life at every historical juncture.

Even the mid-century moment of broad support for desegregation was defined by the presence of strong criticisms of liberal integration and the strategy of non-violent resistance by black nationalists who favored political and economic independence, and by the arguments of a veteran cohort of black unionists and former Communists who insisted that black advancement and the fight for social democracy were inextricable (T. Reed 2015b; Smith 2012; Jones 2013). Throughout the Jim Crow era, different African American political tendencies and constituencies have disagreed over how to advance the race, and fight racism for that matter, cleavages that would sharpen after the passage of landmark civil rights legislation and the rise of black power militancy. Although there is a tendency within both academic treatments and popular reminisce of the black power movement to emphasize its most revolutionary aspirations, hindsight should encourage a more sobering account. Black power meant different things to different people, and in retrospect the period saw the defeat of black political radicalism—both ideologically and by force—and the triumph and consolidation of a mode of black political life amenable to liberal democracy.

The class contradictions that Taylor identifies were woven into the genesis of post-segregation black politics, its unique prerogatives, and institutional constraints, and are a function of how black elite commitments to their core electoral constituencies have been modified amid the shifting electoral calculus and ideological direction of the Democratic Party since the late 1980s. Urban population shifts within most American cities after World War II, historic civil rights reform, and Great Society liberal statecraft combined to produce a post-segregation black political elite. This turn to black ethnic politics reflected in the writings of Carmichael and Hamilton and many of their contemporaries was encouraged and shaped by Johnson era social policy, namely the Community Action Programs of the 1964 Economic Opportunity Act and later the Model Cities legislation, which extended technical expertise, political access, and resources to the most well-positioned and articulate segments of inner-city black populations (Germany 2007; A. Reed 1999, 88–89).

Writing during the dawn of the Nixon era, Bay Area–based writer and activist Robert Allen was especially perceptive in grasping the nascent political realignments occurring underneath the most militant overtures of black power organizations, and the role that a new black professional and managerial stratum would play in the emerging political-economic order. Allen concluded that "the white corporate elite has found an ally in the black bourgeoisie, the new, militant black middle class which became a significant social force following World War II. The members of this class consist of black professionals, technicians, executives, professors, government workers, etc. . . . Like the black masses, they denounced the old black elite of Tomming preachers, teachers, and businessmen-politicians" (Allen 1969, 18–19). "The new black elite seeks to overthrow and take the place of this old elite" and to accomplish this, Allen continued, "it has forged an informal alliance with the corporate forces which run white (and black) America" (Allen 1969, 19).[2] Limited but significant political integration has changed the face of public leadership in most American cities, with some having elected successive black-led governing regimes. The crucial development revealed in the rubble and smoke of Baltimore worth noting here is the ascendant power of a bloc of neoliberal black political elites. Unlike their predecessors who operated within the waning days of the New Deal Democratic coalition, this newest cohort of black politicos is more integrated institutionally and ideologically into a New Democratic universe, and is not beholden to the movement pressures that defined black political life during the 1960s and 1970s.

The election of Barack Obama to the presidency in 2008 represented both a Jackie Robinson–like political milestone and perhaps more consequentially, the triumph of a refined New Democratic politics, liberal in terms of multicultural representation and inclusiveness, but strongly committed to neoliberalism, the ideological rejection of social democracy and left egalitarian interventionism, in favor of the active promotion of forms of regulation that enhance capital flows and profit-making (Harvey 2005, 4; Hackworth 2007; Peck, Theodore, and Brenner 2009; Peck 2010). Carmichael and Hamilton thought that black political control would yield more effective empowerment, sweeping aside the half-hearted reforms of white liberals to deliver real change in the lives of black urban dwellers. Almost five decades after their clarion call, actually existing black power has come to serve as a means of legitimating and advancing urban neoliberalization, the rollback of public goods and services, and maintenance of a pro-market order that relegates the unemployed, the undereducated, and the undocumented to a life of subsistence in the low-wage economy and often in the informal sector. The role that black political elites play in promoting nonprofit, privatized solutions to unemployment, poverty, failing schools, and socioeconomic inequality more generally, and the effect that identitarian assumptions about political affinity have on public debate are the most formidable barriers to developing a popular movement capable of transforming the prison state and resolving the ongoing policing crisis.

In April 2015, the death of twenty-five-year-old Freddie Gray brought the policing crisis to a national stage, and into President Barack Obama's backyard, making Baltimore the latest epicenter of national protests over police brutality, vigilante violence against blacks, and the build-up of the carceral state. Discontent over antiblack violence had been growing with a number of well-publicized police and vigilante murders of unarmed blacks, and local protests began to congeal into a national phenomenon after the 2012 killing of seventeen-year-old, unarmed Trayvon Martin at the hands of a self-appointed neighborhood watchman, George Zimmerman. The initial nonarrest of Zimmerman and, ultimately, his acquittal enraged many who saw this as another instance of lethal racist targeting and further evidence of a broken legal system. The police killing of unarmed teen Michael Brown in Ferguson, Missouri, sparked multiple waves of street protests and rioting during the fall of 2014. The apparent inexperience of the Ferguson police force in handling large crowds of demonstrators and their repression of peaceful protestors escalated the conflict. The undeserved deaths of scores of other black citizens at the hands of police has united previously disparate forces, local campaigns against police violence, the families of victims, long-standing civil rights organizations, and newer formations like #BlackLivesMatter, the Dream Defenders, We the Protesters, and the Black Youth Project, among others, around reforms that might end police brutality and the prison state, and address broader problems of racial inequality. The often-cited figure by activists is that police or vigilantes kill a black person every twenty-eight hours. Reformers have called for demilitarization of police forces, reductions in spending on policing, and mandatory body cameras for patrolling officers, among other measures.

Gray suffered a severe spinal cord injury while being transported by Baltimore police and lay in a coma for seven days before succumbing to his injuries on April 19. A cellphone video taken during Gray's initial arrest records him wailing in agony. At least one bystander reported that Gray's body was bent "like a pretzel" by police who ignored his requests for medical assistance. In the amateur footage, at least one of his legs appears to have gone limp. The officers drag him for a short distance before standing Gray on his feet and then lifting him into the awaiting police van. A second cellphone video, taken by bystanders near the corner of Mount and Baker Streets, shows the arresting officers removing Gray from the van and placing leg shackles on him. When the wagon arrived at the western district police station, Gray was unresponsive and not breathing. As the news of his death spread, marches and peaceful demonstrations were met by heavier police presence, with skirmishes and full-scale riots spreading across the city's west side. Officials estimated some $9 million in property damages. There were 150 reported vehicle fires and 60 structures were burned. Of the 250 people arrested, about half were released without being charged.

In comparison to other urban rebellions in recent memory, such as those in the Mount Pleasant section of the District of Columbia in 1991, South Central Los Angeles in 1992, Cincinnati in 2001, and even Ferguson, the Baltimore conflict was rather small in scale and duration. The April 2015 events seem especially tame when compared to the 1968 Holy Week riots that rocked the city after the assassination of Martin Luther King Jr. In 1968, order was restored through the deployment of nearly 11,000 National Guard and federal troops, and in the end, six people lay dead, 700 injured, and 5,800 arrested (Levy 2011, 8). A thousand businesses reported property damages totaling $12 million in insured losses (Levy 2011, 4–7). The core underlying problem that defines the urban context that Carmichael and Hamilton confronted, and that of our own times, is the problem of relative surplus population, where a growing segment of the proletariat struggles to meet necessity due to structural unemployment. Unlike newly arriving southern black migrants who found stable work and the promise of a better life in the factories, steel mills, and ports of many American cities during and after World War II, from the 1960s onward subsequent generations have faced a context of industrial contraction, fiscal abandonment, and carceral discipline.

Freddie Gray's life was in many ways typical of many young, black working-class men struggling to survive in a context of violence, few jobs, and constant police surveillance. Gray lived in the Gilmor Homes, a public housing development in the Sandtown-Winchester neighborhood. During his early years, Gray's family lived in such squalid conditions that he and his sisters tested positive for elevated, toxic lead levels in their blood. Such poisoning from peeling paint was so common in their social world that many referred to the settlement payments Gray and others received as "lead checks" (Hermann and Cox 2015; Karimi, Berryman, and Ford 2015; Kasperkevic 2015). Gray and his siblings struggled with education and health issues. An asthmatic, Gray asked for an albuterol inhaler during his fateful arrest. Conservative media pundits emphasized Gray's multiple arrests—the twenty court cases against him, most of which were drug-related and nonviolent offenses—but neighbors recalled a gregarious personality who loved football, and possessed an infectious smile and playful sense of humor. The picture that emerges from the testimonies of those who knew him best is of a young man who loved his family and friends, and did his best to take care of them financially and emotionally despite the losing hand that American society dealt him.

Geographer and for much of his adult life a longtime Baltimore resident, David Harvey once remarked that the city was "for the most part, a mess. Not the kind of enchanting mess that makes cities such interesting places to explore, but an awful mess" (Harvey 2000, 133; Harvey 1992). Of course Baltimore was not always in such a dismal state, not even for its black residents. Like many American industrial cities, it has followed what is by now a familiar arch of development, from a Fordist city with a densely populated streetscape of ethnic enclaves through an age of suburban residential expansion and prosperity after World War II, and then into an epoch of shuttered factories and shifting investment to the financial, tourism, and media sectors (Levine 1988; Lichtenstein 2002; Cohen 2003; Sugrue 1996; Bluestone and Harrison 1982; Stein 2010; Cowie and Heathcott 2003). Industrial contraction in Baltimore has hit the city's black population hard, especially when so many black workers secured gainful employment at one time in the city's steel mills, shipyards, and docks. In 1970, Bethlehem Steel employed 30,000, but by the turn of the twenty-first century, fewer than 5,000 were needed to maintain the same levels of productivity (Harvey 2000, 148). In a similar manner, containerization and the increased use of automated loading have greatly reduced the need for living labor in the docks of Baltimore and other cities worldwide (Bonacich and Hardie 2006). The twentieth-century era of the mass worker has been replaced by an hourglass economy with promising careers, material comfort, security, entertainment, and leisure for the mostly white, educated professional classes on the uppermost end, a shrinking core of unionized, well-paid, and relatively secure wage labor in the center, and on the bottom, deteriorating infrastructure, failing schools, contingent, low-wage service-sector employment, or precarious informal work for the reserve army (Williams 1993; Berger 2007).

By the time Gray entered this world, Baltimore had become a showcase of post-Fordist urban redevelopment, having begun the process in the 1970s of renovating its derelict wharfs, warehouses, and port infrastructure in the city's waterfront into a picturesque and coveted ensemble of tourist attractions. By the early 1990s, the Inner Harbor featured an aquarium, science center, chartered boat rides, a festival plaza, multiple restaurants, shopping arcades, numerous hotels and condo buildings, and, within a short walk, Orioles Park at Camden Yards, the home field of the city's National Baseball League franchise. In the mid-1980s, Baltimore elites began the conversion of Baltimore Gas and Electric Company's defunct Pratt Street power plant into an entertainment destination, a process that has undergone revolving tenancy and numerous cycles of boom and bust, all heavily subsidized by the public coffers (Harvey 1992, 141–42). The Inner Harbor provided Baltimore with a popular face of success, but as in so many cities, beyond the boundaries of its refurbished downtown lay an altogether different reality.

The reorganization of Baltimore's economy, subsidization of downtown tourism and financial sectors, and national shift toward workfare and prisonfare have produced a landscape of spectacular wealth and leisure amenities for the urban bon vivant on one hand, and residential apartheid and precarity for the city's mostly black poor on the other. Beginning after World War II, the exodus of more affluent whites and later blacks from the central city to the suburbs of Baltimore County and beyond created new patterns of segregation. Loïc Wacquant has characterized these contemporary spatial configurations in terms of hyperghettoization as a way of distinguishing the racial ghetto of the twentieth century, with its internal class diversity, from the conditions we find in places like Sandtown-Winchester today, which are class-exclusive zones where the black poor are relegated and policed (Wacquant 2010). In 2012, the unemployment rate for Baltimore City was 13.9 percent, but in Gray's Sandtown-Winchester neighborhood the rate was 24.2 percent (Kasperkevic 2015). And when riots erupted after his death, the city's unemployment stood at 8.4 percent, even though the national rate was falling. His neighborhood was 97 percent black, and 35.4 percent of the households lived in poverty (Kasperkevic 2015). Lester Spence points out how the city's spending priorities, its preference for incentivizing pro-corporate growth over neighborhood development and public goods and services, contributed to the 2015 crisis. The city has heavily subsidized local corporations like Under Armour, supporting the construction of their downtown headquarters with $35 million in tax increment financing (Spence 2015). Spence notes that as funding for public parks and recreation in Baltimore has stagnated, spending on policing has surged. While the city spent around $165 million on policing in 1991, it now spends $445 million (cited in Spence 2015). These spending patterns and policy priorities are not unique to Baltimore, but are reflective of a general tendency that has come to define American political life over the past three decades. In the face of growing inequality rooted in technological obsolescence and the elimination of the need for large quantities of living labor, American political elites and publics have come to support the extensive use of policing and incarceration to manage relative surplus population, and abandoned public works and the use of progressive state intervention to ensure some modicum of material necessity and equality for all citizens.

In the ruins of West Baltimore, the contradictions of the Obama administration's neoliberal approach to contemporary inequality have been forced out into the open; at the same time, the way in which the conflict was effectively managed reveals the social power of black political integration. Even before his election, Obama engaged in a form of underclass mythmaking, one that gestured toward racism and economic structures, before emphasizing the behavioral roots of contemporary inequality and calling for greater parental responsibility, patriarchal authority, and bourgeois aspiration as curatives to urban inequality. The notion of the underclass is essentially the view that black poverty is distinct from white poverty and the result of peculiar cultural deficits: lack of a work ethic, the prevalence of female-headed households, the lack of delayed gratification, and so forth. This ideology has its origins in the Cold War liberalism of Daniel Patrick Moynihan, who served as assistant secretary of labor in the Johnson administration, but over the past few decades has been adopted by generations of conservative Republicans, black nationalists, liberal academics, New Urbanists, and New Democrats (T. Reed 2015a). Despite the perception by many of his legions of supporters and as many rightwing critics who perceive Obama as politically left—either a

New Deal Democrat or closeted socialist—on matters of contemporary racial and urban inequality, his public statements have been consistently conservative, emphasizing the dysfunctional behavior of the poor and proffering market-oriented solutions. In Obama's hands, underclass moralizing has achieved renewed hegemony. Obama's blackness, the optics of his patriarchal, heteronormative family life, and his skill at emoting with black audiences have allowed him to restore the legitimacy of conservative ideas that were threatened during the 2000s, as a growing chorus of forces publicly criticized the power of global capital, and the military adventurism and domestic disaster that defined the administration of George W. Bush.

At the 2004 Democratic National Convention, Obama offered a full-throated celebration of American exceptionalism. He acknowledged the difficulties faced by contemporary American workers, but overall his speech elided class as a significant determinant in American life. According to Obama, "in a generous America you don't have to be rich to achieve your potential" (*Washington Post* 2004). He diminished the role of the state as a guarantor of equality of opportunity, and instead elevated popular conservative themes of individual responsibility and self-governance in a manner that swept aside the historical and contemporary demands of working-class and popular struggles for protection from volatile market forces. "The people I meet in small towns and big cities, in diners and office parks," Obama claimed, "they don't expect government to solve all their problems. They know they have to work hard to get ahead and they want to. Go into the collar counties around Chicago, and people will tell you they don't want their tax money wasted by a welfare agency or the Pentagon" (*Washington Post* 2004). He then recited now familiar conservative talking points regarding contemporary racial achievement gaps in education, namely the view that anti-intellectual culture and the lack of parental involvement are to blame. "Go into any inner city neighborhood, and folks will tell you that government alone can't teach kids to learn. They know that parents have to parent," Obama continued, "that children can't achieve unless we raise their expectations and turn off the television sets and eradicate the slander that says a black youth with a book is acting white" (*Washington Post* 2004). Where his predecessors might have been dismissed for their social meanness—recall Reagan's welfare queen mythmaking—Obama has been able to convey the same ideas about the black poor as distinct and uniquely depraved, but with a sense of sincerity and persuasiveness that resonates with some black audiences, while comforting broader publics.

In his numerous Father's Day speeches, often delivered from the pulpits of black churches, he calls on black men to be more responsible parents and role models. His delivery has the appeal of a closed-door chat with his core racial constituency, "his people," but like the speeches of any other modern president, such words are circulated widely within the American public. Obama's uncanny ability to speak in multiple registers and to different audiences simultaneously was a crucial ingredient in his national electoral success, and has been critical in maintaining the hegemony of the underclass myth during uncertain economic times. Time and again, whenever the problems of chronic inner-city poverty and violence have confronted him, Obama has resorted to skillful and charismatic deployment of the underclass ideology.[3]

Obama's response to mass shooting incidents provides an insightful comparison to his unique approach to black urban violence. Obama has delivered more speeches in the aftermath of mass shootings than any other president. After the October 1, 2015, massacre at Umpqua College in Oregon, he delivered his most impassioned call for tighter regulation of gun sales, sounding angrier and more resolute than in his fourteen previous addresses in the wake of mass gun violence. He has treated mass shootings as matters of national concern, but sans political pressure, he has been less likely to address routinized urban gun violence, and more apt to frame the problem as one of a specific stratum of U.S. society. In the face of both forms of gun violence, he makes a plea for reform of gun laws—more stringent background checks for gun consumers—often pointing out the powerful role of the gun lobby and an obstinate Congress in maintaining the status quo, before calling for the latter's support in reforming the current system to improve public safety. A consistent theme in his speeches on gun violence is sickness. A key difference, however, is that in the case of mass shootings, he emphasizes the fragile mental state of the lone gunman and calls for parents, teachers, and community members to watch for early warning signs, and to find help for the depressed and those in need of mental health services. When he turns to address the problem of urban violence, however, his emphasis is on cultural sickness, the alleged pathologies of the black urban poor as a whole.

More than once during Obama's tenure, the problem of urban violence has hit close to home as his adopted hometown of Chicago has faced waves of street violence. In 2009, less than a year into Obama's first term, Derrion Albert, a sixteen-year-old honor student, was killed in a melee between two rival gangs near Fenger High School in Chicago's Roseland neighborhood. The incident was captured on cellphone video and the gruesome image of the innocent bystander being bludgeoned to death with a rail tie stood in stark contrast to news coverage of the Obamas traveling to Copenhagen to make a case for the city of Chicago's Olympic bid (Street 2010, 140–42). At the start of his second term, Obama was faced once again with another highly publicized murder of an innocent black teen. This time fifteen-year-old Hadiya Pendleton was gunned down while sitting with her friends in a park less than a mile from the Obamas' Hyde Park home. Pendleton had performed at the president's second inauguration a week earlier as a majorette in her high school marching band. First Lady Michelle Obama represented the White House at Pendleton's funeral, and delivered the eulogy. After the Black Youth Project circulated a petition urging the president to come to Chicago to give an address on gun violence, he conceded, delivering a speech at the Hyde Park Career Academy in February 2013.

His Hyde Park speech alluded to the role of economic conditions and called for a modest increase in the national minimum wage, before turning to his familiar combination of remedies: more effective parenting, school privatization, and behavior modification. In a fashion that one would have expected from Reagan Republicans a few decades prior, Obama diminished the potential impact of public intervention, and valorized the role of civil society and the market. "When a child opens fire on another child," he said, "there's a hole in that child's heart that government can't fill—only community and parents and teachers and clergy can fill that hole" (*The Root* 2013). "There's no more important ingredient for success," Obama continued, "nothing that would be more important for us reducing violence than strong, stable families—which means we should do more to promote marriage and encourage fatherhood" (*The Root* 2013). In the realm of education, he lauded his former chief of staff and Chicago mayor Rahm Emanuel's program for rewarding high-performance preschools, and without explicitly endorsing charterization, he celebrated the work of some Chicago high schools, and urged "redesigning" schools for success.

His public remarks in the wake of Freddie Gray's death and ensuing protests extended these same interpretations and policy themes, despite pressure from antipolice-brutality forces who wanted him to give a sterner rebuke. During a White House Rose Garden press conference with visiting Japanese Prime Minister Shinzo Abe, a reporter asked Obama whether the unfolding events in Baltimore constituted a national crisis. In an extended response, he praised the peaceful protestors, "the kind of organizing that needs to take place if we're going to tackle this problem" and condemned looters, calling for the restoration of order, and arrests and punishment for "the handful of criminals and thugs who tore up the place" (Obama and Abe 2015). Obama then lauded the work of his taskforce on policing, a grant program to assist local departments in purchasing body cameras, and other measures, but he emphasized the limits of his authority—"I can't federalize every police department in the country and force them to retrain." He also, as he has in the past, resorted to the "few bad apples" explanation of police brutality, arguing that this is the fault of a small minority of disturbed or poorly trained individuals, not a problem endemic to the institution of policing itself. He then concluded on the familiar ground of underclass ideology, describing the environment of substance abuse, absentee fathers, desperation, and joblessness, where we "send police in to do the dirty work of containing the problems that arise there." Acknowledging again the difficulty of securing support from Congress for the kinds of reforms he would like, in this case more investment in urban communities, Obama then pivoted toward the neoliberal model—"we can make a difference around school reform and around job training, and around some investments in infrastructure in these communities trying to attract new businesses in" (Obama and Abe 2015). Obama, of course, was not alone in these sentiments. His words authorized the dominant mode of thinking about poverty, a view that thrives at the grassroots as well.

Further evidence of the underclass hegemony could be found in the overnight rise of Toya Graham, from an unemployed single mother into a national cause célèbre during the Baltimore riots. Graham became a media sensation when she publicly slapped her son multiple times after finding him among a group of masked protestors outside Mondawmin Mall in West Baltimore. Numerous cable news and talk show appearances, a GoFundMe campaign to raise money for Graham and her children, and job offers from Black Entertainment Television, Under Armour, and other companies soon followed. Although her son said he was there because he and many of his friends had been mistreated by police, his political views were drowned out in celebrations of his mother's heavy-handed parenting. For some, Graham represented the kind of parent that was missing in the lives of too many young black men, the strong disciplinarian who is willing to embarrass her progeny in order to keep him out of harm's way. The focus on disciplinary parenting, and the charitable response of foundations and corporations are long-standing approaches to addressing inequality that have gained an outsized role within the context of neoliberal dismantling of public goods and services. And as Carmichael and Hamilton made clear when faced with similar efforts to placate rebellion, these strategies do not alter the economic practices and fundamental conditions that produce obsolescence and inequality.

In retrospect, the historical significance of the 2015 Baltimore riot lay not in its scale, nor the ways this conflict galvanized the national protests against police brutality, but in how well the Baltimore events were mobilized by conservative reformist political tendencies, perhaps best represented in the Obama administration's My Brother's Keeper Alliance, and the local One Baltimore initiative launched by the city's black governing regime.

Obama responded to the Baltimore crisis by christening his My Brother's Keeper Alliance, a nonprofit expansion of the initiative he had created the year before. The program would draw on $80 million in private investments from corporate donors, including Sam's Club, Pepsi Co., and Sprint among a long list of others, and focus on improving the lives of boys and young men of color by targeting literacy education, improving graduation rates, workforce preparation, and programs designed to keep young men out of the criminal justice system (Thrasher 2015). Obama named pop singer and school privatization advocate John Legend as the honorary chairman of the alliance. Obama unveiled the new project at Lehman College in the Bronx, and coopted the language of #BlackLivesMatter, repeatedly asserting "you matter" to the group of young men gathered for the press conference (Obama 2015). This is yet another manifestation of the approach that has been the hallmark of his administration: soft overtures to left social criticism combined with promarket solutions. Local responses in Baltimore mirrored those of the White House in neoliberal form and political effects.

Even before Maryland State's attorney Marilyn Mosby issued indictments against the six officers involved in Freddie Gray's arrest, a broad alliance of national and local elites, celebrity philanthropists, Baltimore Ravens football players, old guard race men, small business owners, corporate and foundation board members, civic boosters, and activists rallied around peaceful demonstrations and acts of volunteerism as the most legitimate means for addressing the poverty and violence in the city's toughest neighborhoods. In the days after Gray's death, as images of burning buildings and youth overturning cars flooded social media and televised coverage, the nonprofit organization Big Brothers Big Sisters saw a 3,000 percent increase in inquires by volunteer mentors (Cassie 2015). Baltimore officials also launched the One Baltimore initiative to coordinate charitable work. Ironically, this official campaign usurped the name of the One Baltimore coalition, a group of grassroots organizations, unions, and churches who had rallied a year prior to protest the efforts of Veolia North America, a water privatization corporation, to secure a consultant contract with the city (Sherman 2014; Wenger 2014). This latest One Baltimore initiative formed by elites amid the riots, however, was decidedly pro-privatization, formed as a means of coordinating nonprofit and philanthropic resources and relief efforts in the riot-torn city (Broadwater 2015). City officials also created the Baltimore Business Recovery fund, to connect local businesses and firms affected by the riots to various sources of local, state, and federal aid for reconstruction. If the experience of New Orleans after the 2005 Hurricane Katrina disaster provides any indication of trajectory, we should expect these initiatives to absorb elements of the potential opposition and further erode support for genuinely public solutions to poverty and urban violence. Even more than New Orleans, Baltimore has long been a hub of national black political activity, due to its large and long-standing black middle class and proximity to the nation's capital.

In New Orleans, city elites embarked on a property owner–centered reconstruction that drew heavily on an extensive network of NGOs to carry out renovation and new builds of single-family homes. Equally consequential, various nonprofit think tanks, education entrepreneurs, for-profit schools, and temporary staffing organizations like Teach for America (TFA) united to overhaul the city's school system into the nation's first all-charter school district (Dixson 2011; V. Adams 2013; Arena 2012; Buras 2015). The weakening of both public housing and public schools in the city over the course of decades and the lore of local corruption all provided traction to privatization efforts. Furthermore, the fact that the neoliberal model was able to produce tangible results for some constituencies, in a context of diminished public goods and services, helped to cement support from a broad, multiracial swath of the city's weary natives, disgruntled activists, newcomers, and enterprising investors around an agenda of educational experimentation, volunteerism, and entrepreneurship. What has emerged in the post-Katrina context is an integrated, pro-growth coalition where the numbers of black politicos is somewhat diminished due to the loss of black population in the city. As in other places, black political and business elites, however, continue to play a crucial role in legitimating the processes of neoliberalization, softening the potential opposition among black neighborhood and activist constituencies by their presence and sometimes through direct appeals to concerns about black advancement. An illustrative case in point is the fate of public housing in post-Katrina New Orleans.

With public housing residents displaced by the flooding, a diverse coalition of wealthy developers, architects, local politicians, housing officials, as well as some former residents, nonprofits, and grassroots organizations coalesced around the demolition of last remaining public housing complexes in the city, the Big Four (the St. Bernard Development, the Lafitte, the B.W. Cooper, and the C.J. Peete) and the Iberville, and their replacement with mixed-income developments (Arena 2012, 145–86). In the wake of these changes, New Orleans renters face an especially dire housing crisis where monthly rent costs have soared past the national median, and some 16,000 families remained on the waitlist for public housing units as the city marked the tenth anniversary of the disaster (French-Marcelin 2015). The fight to preserve public housing and neighborhood public schools are central axes of conflict operating on the ground in the city, battlefronts which do not fall neatly along black–white lines as many academics and pundits have incorrectly surmised. The political conflicts over these public goods, and the saturation of New Orleans with charitable and voluntarist activity also revealed the ways that the advance of nonprofit organizations has had the effect of transforming and conflating the meaning of left political activism in some corners.

Rather than policy-oriented activity aimed at contesting and altering state power, some have come to view nonprofit work that furthers privatization as compatible with left activism. Ferguson #BlackLivesMatter activist DeRay McKesson's intimate ties and political commitments to school privatization organizations like TFA and the New Teacher Project suggest that the same confusion reigns within the ranks of anti-police-brutality forces as well (T. Adams 2015). McKesson and Johnetta Elzie, copublishers of the newsletter *This Is the Movement* were listed among *Fortune* magazine's World's 50 Greatest Leaders. This coziness with both neoliberal and corporate power does not square with the expressed left militancy of many #BlackLivesMatter activists. Although the forces aligned against police brutality have framed the problem largely in terms of institutional racism, often using civil rights and black power texts as palimpsests of their analyses of contemporary American society, the power of the humanitarian-corporate complexes in New Orleans and now Baltimore require critical analyses of black political history and contemporary conditions, and political strategies reoriented toward progressive public intervention.

If there is an Achilles heel of the contemporary fight against police brutality, it is the insistence of many advocates that what we are witnessing is the resurgence of Jim Crow racism. Michelle Alexander's popular book, *The New Jim Crow,* characterized the contemporary prison buildup in these terms, emphasizing how the punitive policies of the War on Drugs adversely and disproportionately affected blacks (Alexander 2010). James Forman Jr. and Marie Gottschalk have offered persuasive critiques of Alexander's analysis, and illuminated the ways that the origins and motives of the contemporary carceral state cannot be reduced to a reincarnation of Jim Crow racial animus—a point that Alexander herself ultimately concedes (Gottschalk 2015, 3–7, 119–67; Forman 2012, 101–46). As I have described here, the conditions facing many working-class blacks in U.S. cities are not only dissimilar from those confronting more affluent segments, but their plight is due to discrete, historical conditions—technological obsolescence, hypersegregation, and zero-tolerance policing and prisonfare—as the dominant means of managing surplus population. Still, the Jim Crow analogy has proven to be a powerful and enduring trope for many activists, one that recalls the nation's undemocratic history and rattles popular claims that the country has reached a post-racial epoch where colorblind meritocracy prevails. The Baltimore uprising spawned an outpouring of civil rights and black power era allusions in the mainstream press and memes on social media that recalled the now common comparison of contemporary police violence to Southern lynch law, references to the 1965 Watts uprising, James Baldwin's epistolary *The Fire Next Time,* the iconic images of armed Black Panthers, and King's poetic description of a riot as "the language of the unheard." There are a number of problems with the Jim Crow analogy, but foremost is the way it obscures contemporary dynamics, namely the fact of black political integration and the role that different forces within the black population play in legitimating the current project of urban neoliberalization.

The Ferguson case lent itself to popular assertions of a resurrected Jim Crow. Like the case of the "Jena 6," which drew thousands of protesters to a small central Louisiana town to support the case of black high school students who were expelled after a conflict with white classmates, and the killing of Trayvon Martin, who was killed in the courtyard of a middle-class subdivision in Sanford, Florida, the town of Ferguson was reminiscent of the kind of southern backwater town that most Americans associate with the Jim Crow regime, one where black life is managed by superordinate whites who control the economy, city hall, the police force, and the courts. Ferguson was an especially stark case where blacks remained disempowered even though they comprised a numerical majority of residents. Baltimore and other metropolitan areas pose a problem for this type of nostalgic, identitarian thinking, and for any politics that might be predicated on achieving social justice through hiring programs, and culturally relevant training as a remedy to police violence and unethical conduct. In Baltimore, the force of popular protest was effectively corralled by local and national black elites through the rapid mobilization of the humanitarian-corporate complex, which works as a soft disciplinary power in tandem with the repressive state apparatus.

There is potential to build a broad-based movement capable of abolishing poverty, ending zero-tolerance as the normative mode of policing, and rolling back the prison state. The current neoblack power rhetoric is ill suited to achieve these ends. The work of #BlackLivesMatter and other organizations carries a certain moral force and inhabits a mode of liberal social criticism descendant from the civil rights movement that is familiar to many Americans. Antiblack racism, however, does not adequately explain the current crisis of police violence where blacks are over-represented, but not the sole victims. At the time of this writing, there were 878 people killed by police in the United States in 2015, and of that number 414 were white, 217 were black, 126 were Latino, 16 were Asian or Pacific Islander, 11 were Native American, and the race/ethnicity of the remaining 94 was unknown (*Guardian* 2015). Rather than prompting some version of "all lives matter" post-racialism, these facts should encourage greater discernment on the part of activists and citizens who wish to create a more humane and just state of affairs regarding policing. The new Jim Crow rhetoric posits universal black injury where, in fact, police brutality and the carceral state are experienced more broadly across the working class. In a social context where the unemployed, the homeless, those who work within the informal economy, or who live in areas of the city where that economy is dominant are more likely to be regularly surveilled, harassed, and arrested. Some black lives matter, and others do not. Some white lives matter, and others do not. Likewise, Obama's approach to urban violence and the elite response to the Baltimore riots all indicate interracial support for neoliberal policies, which are a root cause of worsening conditions for black and brown inner-city residents, and segments of the black middle class whose livelihoods have been negatively affected by the rollback of public employment. If the various localized campaigns against police brutality are to congeal into a viable movement, activists need to devise a new language, one capable of connecting the policing crisis to the underlying problem of structural unemployment, and of uniting people across different social layers in protracted campaigns with the capacity to make concrete policy reform. Otherwise, more mentoring programs, police-community basketball leagues, ribbon-cuttings for mixed-income housing developments, and urban entrepreneurship incubators will serve the same function as the "mobile swimming pools" and "hastily built playgrounds" of the late 1960s, "merely buying time" for those who benefit from the status quo and forestalling the advancement of a real progressive urban agenda, one capable of achieving social justice for the greatest number.

Notes

1. On this matter of black power as black ethnic political succession, Carmichael and Hamilton wrote: "Black people have seen the city planning commissions, the urban renewal commissions, the boards of education and the police departments fail to speak to their needs in a meaningful way. We must devise new structures, new institutions to replace those forms or to make them responsive. . . . The concept of Black Power rests on

a fundamental premise: Before a group can enter the open society, it must first close ranks. By this we mean that group solidarity is necessary before a group can operate effectively from a bargaining position of strength in a pluralistic society. Traditionally, each new ethnic group in this society has found the route to social and political viability through the organization of its own institutions with which to represent its needs within the larger society" (Carmichael and Hamilton 1967, 42–45).

2. The essays collected in Laura Warren Hill and Julia Rabig's *The Business of Black Power* provide insightful, locally grounded accounts of the interplay of black power sentiments and corporate leadership approaches to integration (Hill and Rabig 2012).

3. Not long after his national debut at the 2004 Democratic National Convention, Obama endorsed comedian Bill Cosby's controversial remarks about the black poor. Cosby's comments were made on the occasion of the fiftieth anniversary of the Supreme Court's landmark 1954 decision in *Brown v. the Board of Education, Topeka, Kansas* which overturned the "separate but equal" precedent that had served as the cornerstone of Jim Crown segregation. While celebrating the progress of the black middle class since *Brown*, Cosby lamented that "the lower economic people are not holding up their part in this deal," and then proceeded to riff on the alleged behavioral dysfunction of the black urban poor. In some of his strangest claims, Cosby questioned the wisdom of antipolice brutality protests insinuating that the bad behavior of the poor should be scrutinized more than the police: "These people are going around stealing Coca-Cola. People getting shot in the back of the head over a piece of pound cake and then we run out and we are outraged (saying) 'The cops shouldn't have shot him.' What the hell was he doing with the pound cake in his hand?" History has proven Cosby to be an utter hypocrite, as dozens of women have come forward with testimonies that he drugged and raped them. At the time of his 2004 "Pound Cake" speech, as it has come to be known, however, he remained a highly respected public figure who was for decades the seemingly unimpeachable portrait of the wealthy black patriarch. Through both his fictional family, the Huxtables on the long-running *Cosby Show* sitcom, and real-life family with his longtime wife Camille, Cosby projected the perfect model of black middle class aspiration for the Reagan-Bush years. It is not surprising that Obama found consonance in Cosby's words. He asserted in an interview with Oprah Winfrey, "Bill Cosby got into trouble when he said some of these things, and he has a right to say things in ways that I'm not going to because he's an older man. But I completely agree with his underlying premise: We have to change attitudes. There's a strain of anti-intellectualism running in our community that we have to eliminate" (*O, The Oprah Magazine* 2004).

References

Adams, Thomas Jessen. 2015. "How the Ruling Class Remade New Orleans." *Jacobin*, August 29. https://www.jacobinmag.com/2015/08/hurricane-katrina-ten-year-anniversary-charter-schools/.

Adams, Vincanne. 2013. *Markets of Sorrow, Labors of Faith: New Orleans in the Wake of Katrina*. Durham, N.C.: Duke University Press.

Alexander, Michelle. 2010. *The New Jim Crow: Mass Incarceration in the Age of Colorblindness*. New York: The New Press.

Allen, Robert. 1969. *Black Awakening in Capitalist America: An Analytic History*. New York: Anchor Books.

Arena, John. 2012. *Driven from New Orleans: How Nonprofits Betray Public Housing and Promote Privatization*. Minneapolis: University of Minnesota Press.

Berger, Jane. 2007. "'There Is Tragedy on Both Sides of the Layoffs': Privatization and the Urban Crisis in Baltimore." *International Labor and Working-Class History* 71 (Spring): 29–49.

Bluestone, Barry, and Bennett Harrison. 1982. *Deindustrialization of America: Plant Closings, Community Abandonment and the Dismantling of Basic Industry*. New York: Basic Books.

Bonacich, Edna, with Khaleelah Hardie. 2006. "Wal-Mart and the Logistics Revolution." In *Wal-Mart: The Face of Twenty-First Century Capitalism*, ed. Nelson Lichtenstein, 163–87. New York: The New Press.

Broadwater, Luke. 2015. "Rawlings-Blake Announces 'One Baltimore' Campaign." *Baltimore Sun*, May 7. http://www.baltimoresun.com/news/maryland/baltimore-city/bs-md-ci-one-balti more-20150507-story.html.

Buras, Kristen L. 2015. *Charter Schools, Race and Urban Space: Where the Market Meets Grassroots Resistance*. New York: Routledge.

Carmichael, Stokely. 1971. "Berkeley Speech." In *Stokely Speaks: Black Power Back to Pan-Africanism*, 45–60. New York: Vintage.

Carmichael, Stokely, and Charles V. Hamilton. 1967. *Black Power: The Politics of Liberation in America*. New York: Vintage Books.

Cassie, Ron. 2015. "Big Brothers Big Sisters Sees 3000 Percent Jump in Mentor Inquiries." *Baltimore*, May 7. Accessed May 10, 2015. http://www.baltimoremagazine.net/2015/5/7/after -protests-big-brothers-big-sisters-sees-3-000-percent-increase-in-mentor-inquires.

Cohen, Lizabeth. 2003. *A Consumers' Republic: The Politics of Mass Consumption in Postwar America*. New York: Vintage.

Cowie, Jefferson, and Joseph Heathcott, eds. 2003. *Beyond the Ruins: The Meanings of Deindustrialization*. Ithaca, N.Y.: Cornell University Press.

Dixson, Adrienne. 2011. "Whose Choice? A Critical Race Perspective on Charter Schools." In *The Neoliberal Deluge: Hurricane Katrina, Late Capitalism, and the Remaking of New Orleans*, ed. Cedric Johnson, 130–51. Minneapolis: University of Minnesota.

Forman, James Jr. 2012. "Racial Critiques of Mass Incarceration: Beyond the New Jim Crow." *New York University Law Review* 87 (February): 101–46

French-Marcelin, Megan. 2015. "Gentrification's Ground Zero." *Jacobin*, August 28. https://www .jacobinmag.com/2015/08/katrina-new-orleans-arne-duncan-charters/.

Germany, Kent B. 2007. *New Orleans after the Promises: Poverty, Citizenship and the Search for the Great Society*. Atlanta: University of Georgia Press.

Gottschalk, Marie. 2015. *Caught: The Prison State and the Lockdown of American Politics*. Princeton, N.J.: Princeton University Press.

Guardian. 2015. "The Counted: People Killed by Police in the U.S." (interactive database). Accessed September 29, 2015. http://www.theguardian.com/us-news/ng-interactive/2015/jun/01 /the-counted-police-killings-us-database.

Hackworth, Jason. 2007. *The Neoliberal City: Governance, Ideology and Development in American Urbanism*. Ithaca, N.Y.: Cornell University Press.

Harvey, David. 1992. "A View from Federal Hill." In *The Baltimore Book: New Views of Local History*, ed. Elizabeth Fee, Linda Shopes, and Linda Zeidman, 226–49. Philadelphia: Temple University Press.

———. 2000. *Spaces of Hope*. Berkeley: University of California Press.

———. 2005. *A Brief History of Neoliberalism*. Oxford: Oxford University Press.

Hermann, Peter, and John Woodrow Cox. 2015. "A Freddie Gray Primer: Who Was He, How Did He Die, and Why Is There So Much Anger?" *Washington Post*, April 28. Accessed July 20, 2015. https://www.washingtonpost.com/news/local/wp/2015/04/28/a-freddie-gray-primer-who -was-he-how-did-he-why-is-there-so-much-anger/.

Hill, Laura Warren, and Julia Rabig. 2012. *The Business of Black Power: Community Development, Capitalism and Corporate Responsibility in Postwar America*. Rochester, N.Y.: University of Rochester.

Jones, William P. 2013. *The March on Washington: Jobs, Freedom and the Forgotten History of the Civil Rights Movement*. New York: W. W. Norton.

Karimi, Faith, Kim Berryman, and Dana Ford. 2015. "Who was Freddie Gray, Whose Death Has Reignited Protests against Police?" *CNN.com*, May 2.

Kasperkevic, Jana. 2015. "In Freddie Gray's Neighborhood, More Than a Third of Households Are in Poverty." *Guardian*, April 28. Accessed July 2, 2015. http://www.theguardian.com /us-news/2015/apr/28/freddie-gray-neighborhood-baltimore-poverty-unemployment.

Kerner Commission (U.S. Riot Commission). 1968. *Report of the National Advisory Commission on Civil Disorders*. New York: Bantam.

Levine, Rhonda F. 1988. *Class Struggle and the New Deal: Industrial Labor, Industrial Capital and the State*. Lawrence: University Press of Kansas.

Levy, Peter. 2011. "Dream Deferred: The Assassination of Martin Luther King, Jr. and the Holy Week Uprising of 1968." In *Baltimore '68: Riots and Rebirth in an American City*, ed. Jessica Elfenbein, Thomas L. Hollowack, and Elizabeth M. Nix, 3–25. Philadelphia: Temple University Press.

Lichtenstein, Nelson. 2002. *State of the Union: A Century of American Labor*. Princeton, N.J.: Princeton University Press.

O, The Oprah Magazine. 2004. "The O Interview: Oprah Talks to Barack Obama." November, 248–51, 288–92.

Obama, Barack. 2015. "Remarks by the President at Launch of the My Brother's Keeper Alliance," May 4. White House, Office of the Press Secretary. Accessed September 24, 2015. https:// www.whitehouse.gov/the-press-office/2015/05/04/remarks-president-launch-my-brothers -keeper-alliance.

Obama, Barack, and Shinzō Abe. 2015. "Remarks by President Obama and Prime Minister Abe of Japan in Joint Press Conference," April 28. White House, Office of the Press Secretary. Accessed June 3, 2015. https://www.whitehouse.gov/the-press-office/2015/04/28/remarks -president-obama-and-prime-minister-abe-japan-joint-press-confere.

Peck, Jaimie. 2010. *Constructions of Neoliberal Reason*. Oxford: Oxford University Press.

Peck, Jaimie, Nik Theodore, and Neil Brenner. 2009. "Neoliberal Urbanism: Models, Moments, Mutations." *SAIS Review* 29 (Winter–Spring): 49–66.

Reed, Adolph Jr. 1999. "The Black Urban Regime: Structural Origins and Constraints." In *Stirrings in the Jug: Black Politics in the Post-Segregation Era*, edited by Adolph Reed Jr., 88–89. Minneapolis: University of Minnesota.

Reed, Touré F. 2015a. "Why Liberals Separate Race from Class." *Jacobin*, August 22. https://www .jacobinmag.com/2015/08/bernie-sanders-black-lives-matter-civil-rights-movement/.

———. 2015b. "Why Moynihan Was Not So Misunderstood at the Time: The Mythological Prescience of the Moynihan Report and the Problem of Institutional Structuralism." *Nonsite* 17, September 4. Accessed September 4, 2015. http://nonsite.org/article/why-moynihan-was-not-so-misunderstood-at-the-time.

Root, The. 2013. "Transcript of Obama's Remarks at Chicago Academy," February 15. Accessed August 25, 2015. http://www.theroot.com/articles/culture/2013/02/transcript_obamas _remarks_at_hyde_park_career_academy.html.

Sherman, Megan. 2014. "'One Baltimore' Rally Unites Groups against Privatization." *The Real News.com* video, 7:45. Posted October 30. Accessed September 24, 2015. http://therealnews. com/t2/index.php?option=com_content&task=view&id=31&Itemid=74&jumival=12589.

Smith, Preston. 2012. *Racial Democracy and the Black Metropolis: Housing Policy in Postwar Chicago*. Minneapolis: University of Minnesota.

Spence, Lester. 2015. "Corporate Welfare Is Draining Baltimore." *Boston Review*, May 14. http:// bostonreview.net/blog/lester-spence-freddie-gray-baltimore-under-armour-corporate -charity.

Stein, Judith. 2010. *Pivotal Decade: How the United States Traded Factories for Finance in the Seventies*. New Haven, Conn.: Yale University Press.

Street, Paul. 2010. *The Empire's New Clothes: Barack Obama and the Real World of Power*. New York: Paradigm Publishers.

Sugrue, Thomas J. 1996. *The Origins of the Urban Crisis: Race and Inequality in Postwar Detroit*. Princeton, N.J.: Princeton University Press.

Taylor, Keeanga-Yamahtta. 2015. "Black Faces in High Places." *Jacobin*, May 4. Accessed May 10, 2015. https://www.jacobinmag.com/2015/05/baltimore-uprising-protests-freddie-gray -black-politicians/.

Thrasher, Steven. 2015. "My Brother's Keeper Initiative to Ensure 'You Matter,' Obama Explains in Bronx." *Guardian*, May 4. http://www.theguardian.com/us-news/2015/may/04/barack -obama-my-brothers-keeper-alliance-bronx-lehman-college.

Wacquant, Loïc. 2010. "Class, Race and Hyperincarceration in Revanchist America." *Daedalus* (Summer): 74–90.

Washington Post. 2004. "Transcript: Illinois Senate Candidate Barack Obama." July 27. http://www .washingtonpost.com/wp-dyn/articles/A19751-2004Jul27.html.

Wenger, Yvonne. 2014. "Baltimore Officials Say There's No Plan to Privatize Water System." *Baltimore Sun*, October 24. http://www.baltimoresun.com/news/maryland/baltimore-city/bs -md-ci-water-protest-20141024-story.html.

Williams, Rhonda M. 1993. "Accumulation as Evisceration: Urban Rebellion and the New Growth Dynamics." In *Reading Rodney King, Reading Urban Uprising*, ed. Robert Gooding-Williams, 82–96. New York: Routledge.

CONTRIBUTORS

RACHEL G. BRATT is professor emerita in the Department of Urban and Environmental Policy and Planning at Tufts University. She is senior fellow at the Joint Center for Housing Studies at Harvard University. She has written extensively on the role of nonprofit organizations in supplying decent, affordable housing to low-income households, as well as on broader issues related to housing and community development. In addition to her academic activities, she has worked as a professional planner in the City of Worcester, Massachusetts, and has served on many local, state, and national boards and advisory committees.

CHRISTINE THURLOW BRENNER is associate professor and chair of the Department of Public Policy and Public Affairs at the University of Massachusetts, Boston. Brenner researches how public policies impact immigrant integration into the life of communities. She takes an interdisciplinary approach in examining institutional effects on immigrant integration. Brenner is coeditor of *Dígame! Policy and Politics on the Texas Border*. Her work also appears in public administration, social policy, and political science journals.

KAREN CHAPPLE is professor of city and regional planning at the University of California–Berkeley. She specializes in housing, community, and economic development, as well as regional planning. Her recent book is entitled *Planning Sustainable Cities and Regions: Towards More Equitable Development*.

JAMES DEFILIPPIS is associate professor in the Bloustein School of Planning and Public Policy at Rutgers University. He is the author or editor of six books and numerous articles and book chapters, as well as other published reports, articles, and commentaries. His first book, *Unmaking Goliath*, was named "Best Book in Urban Politics, 2004" by the American Political Science Association. He has been a policy analyst for the Community Service Society of New York and on staff in the office of Congressman Bernie Sanders.

JAMES FRASER is associate professor in the Department of Human and Organizational Development at Peabody College, and affiliated faculty in American Studies at the Institute for Energy and the Environment, and Women's and

Gender Studies, and a Curb Public Scholar at Vanderbilt University. His work focuses on urban restructuring and governance, housing and neighborhood redevelopment, human dimensions of environmental change, and social justice. His current book project is *A People's Guide to Nashville*.

EDWARD G. GOETZ is director of the Center for Urban and Regional Affairs, and professor of urban planning at the Humphrey School of Public Affairs at the University of Minnesota. He specializes in housing and local community development, and how issues of race and poverty affect housing policy, planning, and development. His most recent books are *New Deal Ruins: Race, Economic Justice, and Public Housing Policy* and *Clearing the Way: Deconcentrating the Poor in Urban America,* which won the Paul Davidoff Award from the Association of Collegiate Schools of Planning in 2005.

DAN IMMERGLUCK is professor in the School of City and Regional Planning at Georgia Tech. He conducts scholarly and applied research on housing markets and community development, foreclosures and vacant properties, neighborhood change, development finance, and related public policies. He has served as a visiting scholar at the Federal Reserve Bank of Atlanta and as senior fellow of the Center for Community Progress. He is the author of many articles in scholarly journals, numerous applied research and policy reports, and four books, most recently *Preventing the Next Mortgage Crisis: The Meltdown, the Federal Response, and the Future of Housing in America*.

CEDRIC JOHNSON is associate professor of African American studies and political science at the University of Illinois–Chicago. His teaching and research interests include African American political thought, neoliberal politics, and class analysis and race. His book, *Revolutionaries to Race Leaders: Black Power and the Making of African American Politics* (Minnesota, 2007) was named the 2008 W. E. B. Du Bois Outstanding Book of the Year by the National Conference of Black Political Scientists. He is the editor of *The Neoliberal Deluge: Hurricane Katrina, Late Capitalism, and the Remaking of New Orleans* (Minnesota, 2011). In 2008, he was named the Jon Garlock Labor Educator of the Year by the Rochester Central Labor Council, AFL-CIO.

AMY T. KHARE is a research consultant whose work aims to shape solutions to urban poverty and inequality, with a focus on affordable housing and community development. She serves as a research affiliate with the National Initiative on Mixed-Income Communities at the Mandel School of Applied Social Sciences at Case Western Reserve University and is also working with Chicago's Metropolitan Planning Council to address growing racial and economic segregation. She is an adjunct faculty member at University of Illinois–Chicago, College of Urban

Planning and Public Affairs. Most recently, Amy worked as a research associate at the Urban Institute on the national evaluation of HUD's Choice Neighborhoods Initiative. In 2015, she was honored by the Urban Affairs Association with the Emerging Scholar Award. Amy received her PhD from the University of Chicago, School of Social Service Administration in 2016. Amy's ten years of professional experience in the field of community change serves as the catalyst to her research.

ROBERT W. LAKE is professor in the Edward J. Bloustein School of Planning and Public Policy and a member of the graduate faculties in geography and urban planning at Rutgers University in New Brunswick, New Jersey. He is the author or editor of five books and numerous articles in academic and professional journals. His research has examined the intersections of race and housing, community development, and environmental conflict. His current work focuses on the politics of urban land markets, collaborative and community-based planning, the privatization of public policy, and pragmatist approaches to the politics of knowledge production.

PAULINE LIPMAN is professor of educational policy studies and director of the Collaborative for Equity and Justice in Education (CEJE) at the University of Illinois at Chicago. Her interdisciplinary research focuses on race and class inequality in the education, globalization, and political economy of urban education, particularly the relationship of education policy, urban restructuring, and the politics of race. She is the author of numerous journal articles, book chapters, and policy reports on these topics. Her books include *High Stakes Education: Inequality, Globalization, and Urban School Reform* and *The New Political Economy of Urban Education: Neoliberalism, Race, and the Right to the City.*

LORRAINE C. MINNITE is associate professor of public policy and director of the Urban Studies Program at Rutgers, State University of New Jersey, Camden. She is the author of *The Myth of Voter Fraud* and, with Frances Fox Piven and Margaret Groarke, coauthor of *Keeping Down the Black Vote.* Her work focuses on inequality and American politics, poverty, race, class, and community development.

KATHE NEWMAN is associate professor in the Urban Planning and Policy Development Program at the Edward J. Bloustein School of Planning and Public Policy and director of the Ralph W. Voorhees Center for Civic Engagement. Her research interests include urban political economy and political theory, community-based research, urban redevelopment, gentrification, foreclosure, and community economic development, on which she has published widely.

DEIRDRE OAKLEY is professor in the Georgia State University Sociology Department, as well as its director of undergraduate studies. She is also a managing editor of the *Journal of Urban Affairs*. Her research, which has been widely published in both academic and applied venues, focuses on how social disadvantages concerning education, housing, and homelessness, as well as redevelopment, are often compounded by geographic space and urban policies. She has provided congressional testimony concerning public housing preservation and the Choice Neighborhoods Initiative to the Financial Services Committee. She was a guest coeditor of a special *Cityscape* symposium concerning public housing transformation that was published in its July 2013 issue.

FRANCES FOX PIVEN is distinguished professor of political science and sociology at the Graduate School and University Center of the City University of New York. An internationally renowned social scientist, scholar, and activist for the poor and for working people, she is the author or coauthor of more than a dozen books and two hundred articles on the functions of social welfare and poor relief, the welfare state, social movements, and power from below.

HILARY SILVER is professor of sociology and urban studies and professor of public policy at Brown University. Her research focus is social exclusion, urban poverty, and inequality around the world. She has served two terms as editor of *City & Community* and has made two documentary films, *Southside: The Fall and Rise of an Inner City Neighborhood* (2009) and *Direction Home* (2015), which follows seven chronically homeless people over seven years.

JANET SMITH is associate professor of urban planning and codirector of the Nathalie P. Voorhees Center for Neighborhood and Community Improvement, a research center at the University of Illinois–Chicago. Her teaching, research, and community service focuses on community development and local housing planning and policy implementation. Along with Larry Bennett and Patricia Wright she coedited and wrote *Where Are Poor People to Live? Transforming Public Housing Communities*. She is president of the International Sociological Association Research Council 43 Housing and the Built Environment. She recently wrote, with John Betancur, *Claiming Neighborhoods*, about neighborhood change in relation to accumulation.

PRESTON H. SMITH II is professor of politics at Mount Holyoke College. He is the author of *Racial Democracy and the Black Metropolis: Housing Policy in Postwar Chicago* (Minnesota, 2012) and coauthor of *Renewing Black Intellectual History: Ideological and Material Foundations in Black American Thought*. His research interests include class and African American politics, black intellectual history, urban political economy, and housing policy in the United States and the Netherlands.

TODD SWANSTROM is Des Lee Professor of Community Collaboration and Public Policy Administration at the University of Missouri–Saint Louis. He is author of *The Crisis of Growth Politics: Cleveland, Kucinich, and the Challenge of Urban Populism*, which won the Best Book Award from the Urban Section and Policy of the American Political Science Association (APSA). His coauthored *Place Matters: Metropolitics for the Twenty-first Century* won the Michael Harrington Award from the New Politics Section of APSA. He is coeditor, with Clarissa Rile Hayward, of *Justice and the American Metropolis* (Minnesota, 2011).

NIK THEODORE is professor of urban planning and policy at the University of Illinois–Chicago. His research pursuits include urban informality, labor market change, and worker organizing. He is coauthor, with Jamie Peck, of *Fast Policy: Experimental Statecraft at the Thresholds of Neoliberalism* (Minnesota, 2015). He is editor in chief of *Antipode: A Radical Journal of Geography*.

J. PHILLIP THOMPSON is associate professor of urban planning and politics at MIT. He specializes in the politics of labor and community organizations, race and urban politics, and in the political economy of community development. He is the author of *Double Trouble: Black Mayors, Black Communities, and the Struggle for a Deep Democracy*.

INDEX

abandoned, 242; defined, 23

Abe, Shinzo, 312

ABLE. *See* Adolescent Behavioral Learning Experience

Abt Associates, 234

ACA. *See* Affordable Care Act

accountability, 132, 143, 189; academic, 133, 138, 139, 310; achievement, 95, 166; education, 133; gaps, 139, 310; police, 75

ACS. *See* American Community Survey

Adams, Thomas, 75

adjustable-rate mortgages (ARMs), 204

Administrative Procedures Act (APA), 127

Adolescent Behavioral Learning Experience (ABLE), 48, 49, 55, 56

affirmatively furthering fair housing (AFFH), 249, 250

Affordable Care Act (ACA), 22, 29, 112, 114–15, 153, 157, 177–78, 185, 194, 296, 298; achievements of, 166; CBA of, 169; Medicaid and, 170; national exchange and, 164–65; political mobilization and, 165–70; Section 2007 of, 167–68; urban areas and, 3–4

Affordable Housing Goals, 88

AFL-CIO. *See* American Federation of Labor-Congress of Industrial Organizations

AIG, 30

air quality, 260, 262, 263

Albert, Derrion, 311

Alexander, Michelle, 315–16

Alinsky, Saul, 150

Allen, Robert, 305

Altgeld Gardens, 21

alt-labor, 159, 160

American Automobile Association, 227n23

American Community Survey (ACS), 113, 227n18, 240, 248

American Federation of Labor-Congress of Industrial Organizations (AFL-CIO), 149, 159

American Federation of State, County and Municipal Employees (AFSCME), 158

American Federation of Teachers (AFT), 149

American Recovery and Reinvestment Act (ARRA) (2009), 7, 12, 26, 39, 81, 153, 233, 298; Building of America Bonds, issuing, 28–30; RTTT and, 134–35

Americas Society/Council of the Americas, 119

ANC (Aid to Needy Children) Mothers Anonymous, 279

Annie E. Casey, 226n7

antipoverty programs, 181, 182, 219–21, 268

antiunionism, 152–55, 158

Apple, 136, 138

Arendt, Hannah, 178n4

Arnold Foundation, 46

Arnstein, Sherry, 267

ARRA. *See* American Recovery and Reinvestment Act

Associated Builders and Contractors, 149

Atlanta Public Housing Authority, 73

Atlantic, The, 50

Axelrod, David, 21

Bailes, Shawn, 241

Baldwin, James, 316

Baltimore, 1, 9, 18, 22, 24, 38, 74, 286, 296, 300, 305, 307–8, 313, 314, 315, 316; industrial contraction in, 308; minimum wage and, 285; public schools in, 139; redevelopment in, 308; riots in, 40n9, 317; social order in, 75; unemployment in, 309

Baltimore Business Recovery, 314

Baltimore Gas and Electric Company, 308

Banfield, Edward, 17, 171, 175

Bank of America, 248

banking, 79, 88, 199, 203; regulating, 13, 29; shadow, 205–6

bankruptcy, "cram down" modification, 92–93, 94

Barnes, William: on urban policy, 20